ASPCA®

Complete Guide to

dogs

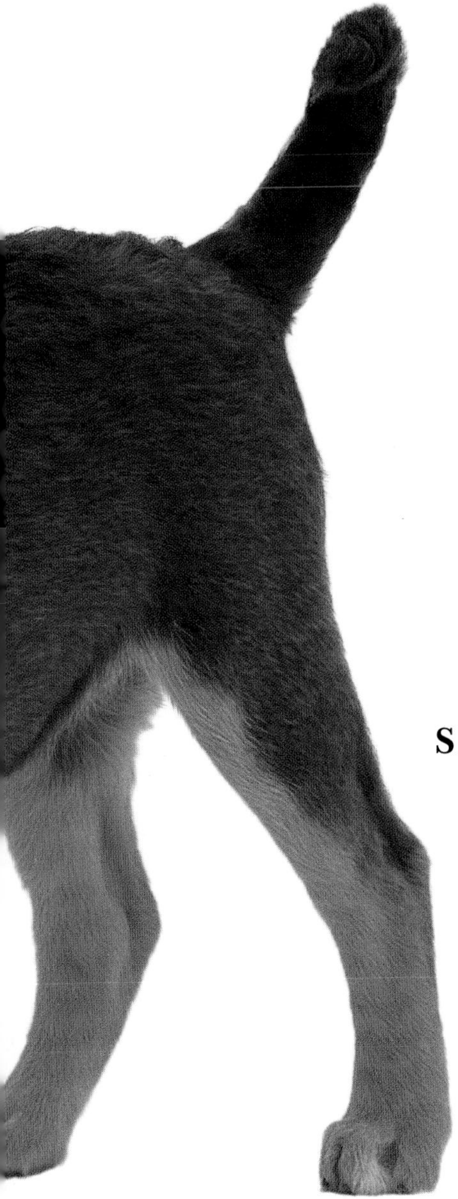

ASPCA®

Complete
Guide to
dogs

Sheldon L. Gerstenfeld, V.M.D.

with Jacque Lynn Schultz

CHRONICLE BOOKS

SAN FRANCISCO

First published in 1999 by Chronicle Books LLC.

One percent of the retail price of this book goes to the ASPCA for humane programs.

Prepared and produced by
Chanticleer Press, Inc., New York.

Color separations by
Bright Arts, Hong Kong.

Printed and bound in Singapore.

Library of Congress Cataloging-in-Publication Data

Gerstenfeld, Sheldon L., 1943–
  ASPCA complete guide to dogs / Sheldon L. Gerstenfeld.
    p.   cm.
  Includes index.
  ISBN 0-8118-1904-3
  1. Dogs. I. American Society for the Prevention of Cruelty to Animals. II. Title. III. Title: Complete guide to dogs.
SF427.G47   1999
636.8—dc21   99-10269
                                                         CIP

Distributed in Canada by Raincoast Books
9050 Shaughnessy Street
Vancouver, British Columbia V6P 6E5

10 9 8 7 6 5

Chronicle Books LLC
85 Second Street
San Francisco, California 94105

www.chroniclebooks.com

Contents

The Beginning and End of Life: Times for Special Care 479

Appendices 494

Foreword

People who work with animals generally agree that abandonment, neglect, and improper care often are not intentional acts but rather the unfortunate results of uninformed decisions. The decision to bring a dog into your life must be an informed one, and that is why the *ASPCA Complete Guide to Dogs* begins by telling you everything you need to know about how to determine whether a dog is the right pet for you and how to be sure that you are ready to take the plunge into dog ownership.

This volume provides all the practical information you'll ever need for selecting and caring for a canine companion. It helps you judge which breed or type of dog will make the best pet for you. It guides you through the process of finding and choosing your new dog; and it puts at your fingertips invaluable, easy-to-understand advice on the training, care, and enjoyment of your new dog, as well as information on common canine health problems, first aid, and times when your dog will require special care.

No one can guarantee that a dog will never bite, chew, or exhibit otherwise undesirable behavior. You are entering into a relationship that, like any other, will have wonderful "ups" and maybe also some vexing "downs."

Keep in mind that dogs are individuals. While purebred dogs do tend to have some reliable traits you can look for, personality and energy level vary greatly from dog to dog, purebred or mixed. Take into account your own character and lifestyle and be honest with yourself about how much grooming, exercise, and training you are really prepared to handle.

Throughout this guide you will be reminded that dogs are not idle or casual possessions but faithful friends and valuable members of your family. Your canine companion's health and happiness rest with you. Dogs need a great deal of care: the *ASPCA Complete Guide to Dogs* outlines your responsibilities and endeavors to help you meet them. With very few exceptions, dogs must be spayed or neutered. They need regular veterinary checkups and lifesaving periodic vaccinations. Their diets should be under your control and not hit or miss. They must receive the right kind and quantity of exercise, and they need to be given obedience training. In short, they need to be loved, cared for, and cared about by you.

Sharing your life with a dog is a wonderful thing. You will be taking on a friend for life. Make it a long, healthy, and happy life for your dog, and your own life is sure to improve in quality and perhaps in longevity as well.

Roger A. Caras, President Emeritus
American Society for the Prevention of Cruelty to Animals

How to
Use This Guide

The joys of owning a dog are many, but many, too, are the accompanying responsibilities. This book will prepare you for those joys and responsibilities by carefully detailing both your dog's long-term requirements and his everyday needs. The following pages will guide you through the entire process of owning a dog, from making the initial decision to bring a dog into your life to learning how to care for your pet in his old age. Dogs contribute an abundance of amusement and companionship to the lives of their owners. This book focuses on the contributions *owners* must make to ensure their dogs' health and happiness, from the first day to the last.

The *ASPCA Complete Guide to Dogs* is divided into four sections: How to Bring a Dog into Your Life, Reference Guide to Dog Breeds, What Makes a Dog a Dog?, and Taking Care of Your Dog. Together, they will tell you everything you need to know in order to have a successful and rewarding experience as a dog owner.

This volume begins with the questions any potential dog owner needs to ask and offers sensible answers for consideration. Key issues are broken down into segments guiding you through the process of deciding to get a pet, choosing the right dog for your home and family, preparing your home for your new pet, and knowing what to expect as a new pet owner.

Section II, the Reference Guide to Dog Breeds, will interest you whether you choose a purebred or a mixed-breed dog. A brief introduction explains breed standards and the basic terminology that is used to describe canine coat patterns and other physical features. A catalog of 166 entries follows, divided into eight groups that include common mixes. Each entry provides information about the breed's personality, appearance, grooming and exercise needs, origins, and health concerns.

Section III, What Makes a Dog a Dog?, begins with a brief history of the long relationship between dogs and humans. The section continues with How the Dog Works, a primer on the anatomy and senses of dogs that gives you inside-out information on what makes the dog such an incredible work of natural art. Understanding Your Dog explores why dogs behave the way they do and how they express themselves.

Section IV, Taking Care of Your Dog, is an essential guide to the daily care of your pet. The chapter Everyday Care covers feeding, grooming, training, exercising, and traveling with your pet, as well as preventing and solving behavior problems. Keeping Your Dog Healthy takes you through all the steps of home examinations and includes checklists and questions for visits to a veterinarian. Common Canine Health Problems outlines important ailments as well as possible treatments. Home Nursing follows with instructions for at-home health care. No pet owner ever wants to perform first aid on his dog, but knowing what to do in an emergency situation can vastly improve your dog's chances for recovery or even survival. The First Aid chapter walks you through the procedures every dog owner should know. Last is The Beginning and End of Life: Times for Special Care. The first part of this chapter gives an overview of canine mating, pregnancy, delivery, and postnatal care. The latter part of the chapter offers advice on caring for an elderly dog and dealing with a dog's death.

The appendices include six separate sections. The glossary defines dog-related terms used in this book. Important Telephone Numbers gives numbers for poison-control centers, veterinary help lines, and pet-loss hot lines. Breed Organizations and Kennel Clubs will help you find a breeder or register your dog with a breed organization. Organized Sports and Showing offers information on how to get involved in dog shows or dog sports such as agility trials and Flyball. Recommended Reading includes books on subjects beyond the scope of this guide. Finally, Resources lists Web sites and addresses of other organizations of interest to dog owners.

1

How to Bring a Dog into Your Life

Dogs enrich our lives in innumerable ways and are amazingly adaptable to family life. They are our companions and protectors. They amuse us with their antics and touch our hearts with their joyous zest for life. They are straightforward in their needs and love us unconditionally, giving generously of their affection and teaching us how to do the same. They awaken in us the ability to see the world from another perspective and, by luring us outdoors on a daily basis, they link us more closely to the miracles and mysteries of nature. Often they even improve our health by keeping us active and giving us comfort. They also represent a huge responsibility that we must take seriously every day. Dogs are cherished members of our families, requiring our constant attention and devotion. Not a day goes by that they do not need us to take them out for walks and playtime. We must constantly reinforce the socialization and training that begins in early puppyhood. When they are sick or old, we must give them the medical care and companionship that they deserve.

The dog–human relationship is one that too many people enter into lightly. Sadly, many dogs do not grow old in their first homes, and each year millions of dogs are left to roam the streets or are relinquished to shelters (and then often euthanized) because their

Companionship is one of the greatest benefits of having a dog.

owners find them to be too much trouble or inappropriate to their lifestyles. Countless other dogs are ignored, poorly trained, or left untrained, and so do not learn to fit comfortably into the family hierarchy and do not get to enjoy the many benefits of a comfortable home life.

The best thing you can do for your family and your future pet is to be as informed as possible before adopting an animal. This section of the *ASPCA Complete Guide to Dogs* is designed to help you ascertain whether you are ready to handle the responsibility of dog ownership, for it is not a relationship to enter into lightly. You will find advice on how to choose a dog that will fit into your living situation and how to welcome that dog into your home as smoothly as possible. It is also wise to read other sections of the book, such as Taking Care of Your Dog, before making your final decision, so you are prepared for what lies ahead. The information provided is meant to help you plant the seeds necessary to ensure a happy, healthy, and long-lasting relationship between you and your companion animal.

A pet dog's exuberant enjoyment of life is contagious.

First Things First:
Are You Ready for a Dog?

Dogs are dependent creatures. They need daily walks and feeding, training, veterinary care, and all the scratches and pats you can give. They leave hair on the furniture, they drool on the floor, and they knock things over with their tails. Before deciding to adopt a dog, take the time to consider seriously how a pet will affect your life. Begin by thinking about each of the following questions, which are meant to help you determine if you are prepared to bring a dog into your home. If you are bringing a dog into a family situation, include all members of the family in the decision-making process.

Is the timing right?

Before getting a dog, think about where your life is headed. As most dogs live ten to fifteen years, dog ownership is a long-term commitment (especially if you get a puppy). You will have to be ready to take into account the needs of an animal before making any life-changing decisions. If you have a job that requires you to travel often, or if you expect to get such a job in the near future, you need to think about who will take care of your dog while you are gone. If you think you might like to change environments, perhaps by moving from a house in the country to an apartment in the city, consider that some dogs will not adapt well. Keep in mind that many landlords do not welcome pets, especially dogs, thus limiting the choices you will have if you rent rather than own your home.

Bulldogs tend to snore. Carefully research any breed you are interested in adopting so that you are aware of any traits you might find disagreeable.

Dogs seek out human company.

How long are you away from home each day?

All dogs need to go out and eliminate several times a day. Regular physical exercise, mental stimulation, and social interaction are also essential. Puppies, of course, need almost constant supervision. Although many well-trained adult dogs can be left alone for up to twelve hours, it is not a good idea to leave a pet dog alone for such a long period of time on a regular basis. You may wish to hire a pet sitter or dog walker to care for the dog during the day (or even enroll your dog in "doggy daycare"), but you must be sure you can afford this expense on an ongoing basis. Keeping a dog outdoors, even in a fenced-in yard or run, when no one is at home is not recommended, as it can be dangerous and isolating.

Do you have children?

Most dogs love children, especially if they are introduced to them at an early age and are treated gently by them. Some dogs accept only the children in their own families, while others are uncomfortable around all children, especially those under about seven years old. Young children and dogs should never be left together without adult supervision, and any dog that

A dog and a young child can easily become close friends.

will be spending time around children must have proper obedience training. For specific information about finding a dog that can fit into a household with children and teaching children how to behave with dogs, read Dogs and Kids (page 28).

Dog Allergies

When people with canine allergies are around a dog their eyes itch and swell, they sneeze incessantly, their sinuses become congested, and they may cough and even become asthmatic. Allergy sufferers feel miserable, and while they are exposed to the allergen there is very little that can be done to make them feel much better. It is not a dog's hair that affects most allergy sufferers, but a protein in the dog's saliva. All dogs drool and lick themselves, so contact with the allergen is inevitable in a house with dogs. It can take weeks for enough allergens to build up in your home to affect certain people, so all allergies are not evident right away.

The safest way to predict a problem is to have everyone in the household spend time at the homes of people with different kinds of dogs, as well as at breeders, kennels, and shelters. It is essential that everyone also spend time with the dog you have chosen to adopt in his environment before you bring him home.

Some allergy sufferers seem to live tolerably well with dogs of certain breeds that don't shed or that shed minimally. Such breeds include poodles, bichons frises, and Kerry blue, cairn, and Norfolk terriers. Dalmatians and Chinese shar-peis are known to make some otherwise nonallergic people very itchy.

Is anyone in your household allergic to dogs?

Unfortunately, some people just can't live in a home with a dog. It's not fair to the person with allergies—or to the dog—to initiate a relationship that will ultimately be cut short. Before you decide to adopt a dog, you should make every effort to be sure that no one in your household is allergic. All members of your household should spend time handling the dog of your choice in the environment in which he has been living.

Are you an experienced dog owner?

If you have lived with dogs before and have gone through training with them, you'll probably be able to handle some of the more independent or stubborn breeds, such as briards, Bouviers des Flandres, rottweilers, or Akitas (or mixes descended from any of these breeds). However, you still need to ask yourself if you want to take on the full-time responsibility of caring for such a high-maintenance animal. If you are a first-time dog owner, don't overestimate your ability to establish dominance and maintain control over a canine. For most people it is a learned skill that requires work with a trainer and a lot of practice.

Dogs need to be walked several times a day—rain or shine. Dog-walking is especially pleasurable when shared with friends.

Do you have the time for a dog?

All dogs need training, exercise, and grooming, but the amount of time required for each of these activities varies depending on the size, coat type, and breed background. While German shepherds need vigorous daily exercise and intensive training, their grooming needs are moderate. Pomeranians have minimal exercise needs and are fairly easy dogs to train but require daily grooming. Dogs that are not trained and exercised sufficiently are likely to become destructive. They may chew the furniture or bark and whine, disturbing the neighbors. You should not get a dog if you will not be able to train and exercise him properly. (Under no circumstances should a dog be allowed to wander around outside unsupervised, nor should he be expected to exercise alone in a fenced-in yard.) Regardless of breed, most puppies are demanding day and night. You will have to be prepared to clean up accidents, take your puppy out in the middle of the night, and come home from work at midday to walk and feed him. You will also have to put in the many hours needed in order to obedience train and socialize your puppy so that he learns how to fit into your household.

Do you have other animals?

Talk to your veterinarian and/or a dog trainer about the type of dog you want to get, the kinds of animals you already have, and how all of them might adapt to life together. For example, if you have an intact (unneutered) territorial male and you plan to get another intact male, you may be witness to some serious dogfights. Observe your dog closely around other dogs to be sure she can get along with them. A terrier or terrier mix that hasn't been around cats or other small animals may chase them. For guidelines on introducing a dog and a cat, see page 79. Rabbits and guinea pigs will probably need to be exercised in a room closed off from the dog, unless the dog is socialized with them from a young age. Many dogs will not be able to resist chasing and perhaps attacking a bird flying outside of its cage. Tops of fish or reptile tanks should be closed securely when dogs are in residence.

Can you afford a dog?

No matter how much you pay to obtain a dog, owning a dog is expensive. You must be prepared to pay for food (which can cost hundreds of dollars a year), equipment (brushes, bed, crate), training, grooming, neutering, vaccinations, standard veterinary care, and perhaps boarding and a dog walker. You must also prepare for the unexpected, such as illnesses, accidents, or destructive behavior.

Do you live in a small apartment or in a city?

It is important to consider the size of your living space and the availability of outdoor space when deciding to get a dog. Many dogs live happily in cities as long as they are taken to a park or dog run for playtime each day. Toy and small dogs tend to do better than other dogs in city apartments, but some larger breeds, such as greyhounds and Great Danes, thrive in apartments because they are not particularly active between walks. High-energy dogs of all sizes need a lot of space, both indoors and outdoors. Dogs that bark a lot can be a problem if neighbors live in the same building or very close by.

The Cavalier King Charles spaniel adapts well to city living. Active city dogs need access to a park or dog run.

Are you prepared for the mess?

All dogs shed sometimes, but if you like to keep your house meticulously clean, it probably isn't a good idea to get a dog that sheds a lot, such as a collie, a German shepherd, a keeshond, an Alaskan malamute, or a dalmatian. Poodles, bichons frises, and certain terriers (cairn, Norfolk, and Kerry blue) shed minimally. Many dogs drool, especially large, loose-lipped dogs, such as bloodhounds, Newfoundlands, and Saint Bernards. Retrievers and other dogs with long, powerful tails tend to knock objects off shelves and low tables when wagging their tails. Breakable objects should be stored out of reach of all dogs.

If you get a puppy, you can expect an initial period of havoc and upheaval. Even with the most careful training and attention, a puppy is likely to do some damage when you're not looking, such as chew on the leg of an antique chair, scratch on a door, urinate on a rug, or tear up an important letter. If you are a renter, your landlord may charge you for damage to walls, doors, floors, and other parts of the home.

Do you receive a lot of visitors?

Some dogs, especially those that were developed as guardians, are naturally wary of outsiders. This doesn't mean that they can't be trained. It just means that you will need to devote a lot of time to acclimating your dog to new people and that you will need to supervise him especially carefully when children are around.

When long ears and beards like those on these bearded collies fall into food and water bowls, crumbs and slobber end up on rugs and furniture.

The Wrong Reasons
to Get a Dog

Because you are lonely
Dogs make wonderful companions, but if you want to be a responsible dog owner you must focus on your ability to meet a dog's long-term needs rather than a dog's ability to meet your short-term needs.

To teach a child how to be responsible
Although children can be given some responsibility for taking care of a dog, such as a morning feeding or an after-school walk, the dog's primary caretaker should be an adult. It is not fair to use a dog strictly as a teaching tool.

Because you feel sorry for a dog in a pet shop
Pity should not be the main motivating factor when you are considering getting a dog. Remember, this is a long-term commitment. In addition, pet stores usually are not reliable sources for dogs. See page 46 for more information on this subject.

Deciding to get a dog takes careful consideration.

Because you think your home needs protection
If the only reason you want to get a dog is to guard your home or property, you'll be better off getting an alarm system. Reliable protection dogs require extensive training and in some cases even more socialization and exercise than other dogs. They are often not appropriate family pets.

As a surprise gift
If you would like to buy someone a dog, you should involve that person in every aspect of choosing the animal. Make sure the recipient of your gift understands the responsibility of dog ownership and is prepared to take it on. Never buy a dog for someone as a surprise.

Matchmaking:
Which Dog Is Right for You?

Once you have decided that you are ready for a dog, you must consider such issues as whether you want a male or a female, an adult or a puppy, a large or a small dog, a mixed breed or a purebred. Take the time to find the right canine match. It is the best insurance you have for a long and happy life with your new best friend.

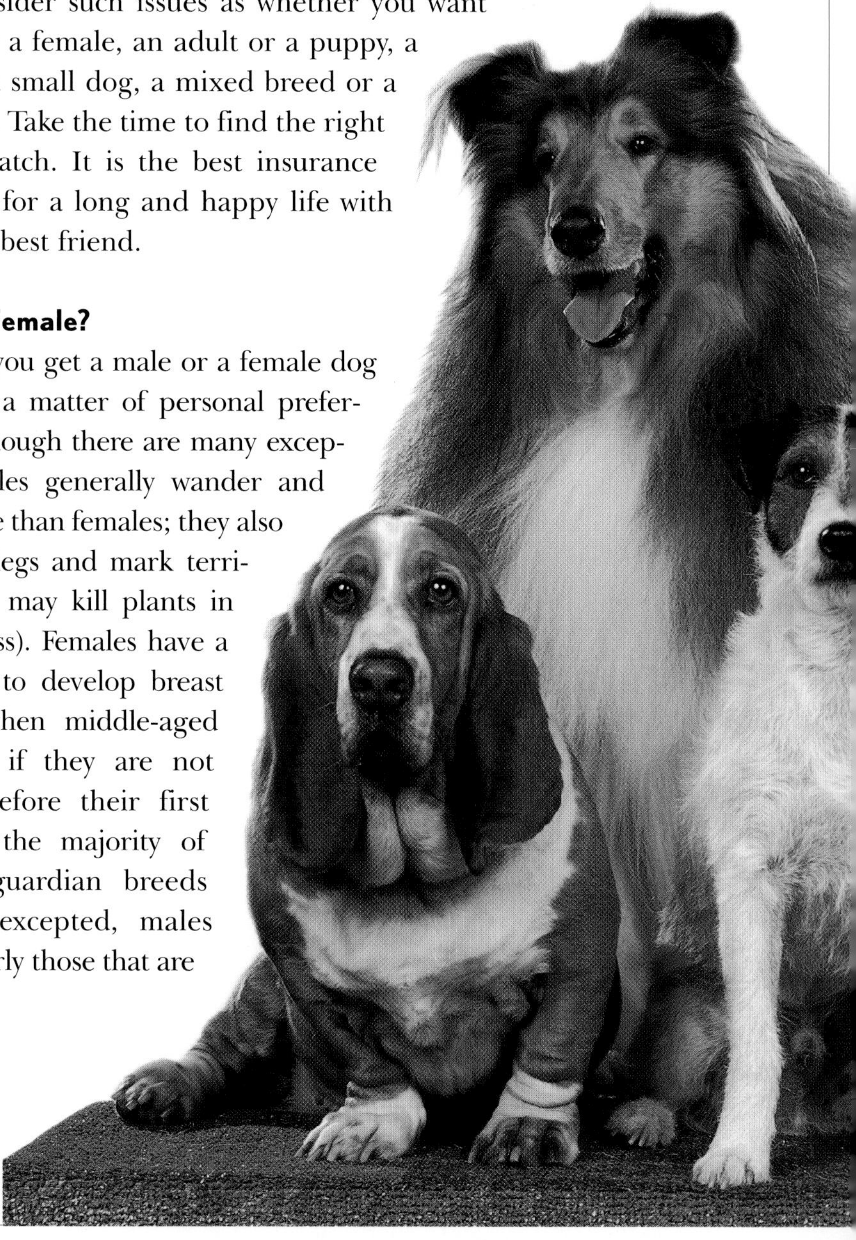

Male or Female?

Whether you get a male or a female dog is largely a matter of personal preference. Although there are many exceptions, males generally wander and fight more than females; they also lift their legs and mark territory (and may kill plants in the process). Females have a tendency to develop breast tumors when middle-aged or older if they are not spayed before their first heat. In the majority of breeds, guardian breeds possibly excepted, males (particularly those that are neutered) are more sociable and affectionate and almost seem to have a sense of humor. Females tend to take themselves more seriously.

Puppy or Adult?

Many people prefer to get a puppy because they feel as though they are starting with a clean slate and can shape the puppy's personality. Although this is true to a certain extent, puppies, like people, are born with distinct temperamental tendencies, and there is a limit to how much shaping you can do. A puppy needs a tremendous amount of care, which can take more time and energy than an owner wants or is able to give. Adult dogs usually require less work, although they may have some undesirable habits or behavioral idiosyncrasies that need to be addressed. Shelters, breeders, and rescue groups are all good sources for adult dogs that need homes.

Dogs come in all shapes and sizes (left to right): basset hound, collie, Jack Russell terrier, retriever mix, terrier mix, Labrador retriever, and cairn terrier.

Large or Small?

While both the pug and Great Dane are easy to groom and exercise, the costs for upkeep will differ tremendously.

In general, large dogs mean more of everything. They need more to eat. They produce more waste. They usually need more space and exercise. Boarding a large dog is more expensive than boarding a small dog. Traveling is more difficult with a large dog; many inns and hotels allow only small dogs, and many transit systems allow dogs only in carriers—an impossibility with a dog too big or heavy to carry. A large dog will also take up a substantial amount of room in your car. Medical expenses are higher for large dogs; they require larger doses of medication and hospitalization is more costly. In addition, large untrained dogs are harder on your back, knees, and neck. Smaller dogs usually need less food and space, are easier to travel with, and are often less costly to own. Some small dogs need just as much exercise and attention as some larger dogs. Many of the terriers, such as Jack Russells, have extremely high energy levels. Tiny dogs, like Pomeranians and toy Manchester terriers, are not a good choice if you have toddlers around because these dogs can be nippy.

Caring for a puppy, whether purebred like these boxers or mixed, is rewarding—and time-consuming.

Mixed Breed or Purebred?

Getting a mixed-breed dog can be more of a gamble than getting a purebred dog, especially if you can't see the environment in which the dog spent the beginning of his life or meet one or both of his parents. ("The apple doesn't fall far from the tree"—an adage that predates modern genetics—is typically true.) But there are thousands upon thousands of healthy, intelligent mixes just waiting to bestow upon their families years of love and affection. Mixed-breed dogs are generally less expensive to buy than purebreds. About 80 percent of shelter dogs are mixes, often available at a very low cost (an additional modest fee for sterilization, which is often mandatory, is sometimes charged); the shelter may also cover the cost of vaccinations.

The main advantage to getting a purebred dog is that you can see where and how the dog spent his puppyhood, what his parents were like, and what he's apt to look like when grown. The costs of food, veterinary care, boarding, grooming, equipment, and obedience classes are, of course, the same for mixes and purebreds. Before getting a purebred from a breeder, you may wish to visit a few shelters and think about saving one of the millions of unwanted dogs that are euthanized each year. Peruse the Reference Guide to Dog Breeds for information on the different breeds and on various mixed breeds.

The weimaraner is known for its seemingly boundless energy.

High or Low Energy?

A highly energetic dog will require more of your energy—robust runs and workouts and plenty of playtime day in and day out. High-energy dogs usually do best in the suburbs or the country, where they have spacious yards to run in, although some can live in the city if they have access to parks and dedicated, energetic human companions. Most puppies, no matter the breed, are energetic and inquisitive and require vast amounts of attention. In the Reference Guide to Dog Breeds, highly energetic breeds are indicated with the Special Exercise Needs icon or the High Energy Indoors icon .

Coat Type?

All dogs need grooming, but some require far more than others. Grooming can be time-consuming and expensive. Dogs with long, silky coats must be brushed every day, and some curly-coated dogs should be brought to a groomer every six weeks or so for trimming. Breeds with above-average grooming requirements are marked with the Special Grooming Needs icon ✄ in the Reference Guide to Dog Breeds. If you will be bothered by lots of dog hair on your clothing and furniture, bypass heavy or year-round shedders, but remember that almost all dogs shed. People with allergies sometimes suffer less with dogs that don't shed much, such as bichons frises, poodles, and cairn, Norfolk, and Kerry blue terriers (see Dog Allergies, page 17). If you plan to show your dog, coat color and type are important and you should research the breed standards before choosing a dog.

One Dog or More?

Experts advise against getting two dogs at the same time because the dogs may bond tightly to one another at the expense of the relationship with the humans in the family. The two dogs need their own time with humans and separate training, socialization, grooming, and playtime. Dogs that are raised together tend to become distressed if they have to be separated (for example, if one needs to be hospitalized), and may howl, try to escape, experience separation anxiety, or, in the worst cases, resort to self-mutilation. The best option is to wait until your first dog is trained and through adolescence before obtaining a second. Usually, neutered dogs of opposite sexes get along best.

This Chihuahua's smooth coat (left) is easy to care for, whereas the poodle's curly coat (right) requires extensive grooming.

Children and puppies, such as this Chinese shar-pei, need close supervision.

Dogs and Kids

When appropriately matched, dogs and children are a joyous sight. When there is a mismatch, however, the situation can become stressful and even dangerous—for both child and dog. Before bringing a dog into a home with children, carefully review the following important guidelines. For guidance in choosing a dog, look for breeds that are marked with the Good with Kids icon 🐕 in the Reference Guide to Dog Breeds.

Most dog experts advise against getting a puppy when your child is an infant. A new puppy and a baby both need undivided attention. It is better to wait until the child is at least five or six years old, and is mature enough to understand that a puppy needs special care and attention. Puppies can be exasperating, and an older child will be better able to handle the havoc.

Some dogs are uncomfortable around children under about seven years of age, who tend to be noisy, have unpredictable body movements, and may have difficulty understanding how to treat a dog gently. Children under seven are not usually developmentally suited for puppies under five months old or toy-size dogs (under fifteen pounds) of any age. If you already have a dog and are expecting a baby, see page 396.

Discuss getting a dog with the children in advance, rather than bringing a dog home as a surprise gift. This way the children have a chance to express their fears and desires, and it is clear from the beginning that the dog is a carefully chosen family member, not one person's possession. It is also important to discuss the responsibility that each member will take for the dog. Who will feed the dog? Walk the dog? Train the dog? Play with the dog? Ultimately, however, all care should be supervised by an adult, someone prepared to step in if the children don't uphold their responsibilities.

Teach your children how to handle dogs respectfully and gently and be honest in your appraisal of your children's ability to take on responsibilities. Everyone—the kids, the dog, and you—will be happier if the dog you choose is one that can thrive in your household.

Choosing a Dog with Your Kids
Make sure your children understand that there may be several trips to animal shelters or breeders before the new family pet is chosen. Expect both shelter personnel and breeders to request to see how the children behave around the chosen dog and vice versa before finalizing an adoption.

Whether you go to a breeder or a shelter, look for a dog that is friendly, attentive, and moderately energetic. Avoid hyperactive or excessively mouthy dogs (those that put their teeth on you frequently, although without necessarily biting). Be cautious of any pups that seem uncomfortable being touched or that run away from loud noises. If you have children under seven, you will want to avoid dogs that are sensitive to sound or touch. To test for sound sensitivity, drop a metal bowl on a hard floor in the same room as the dog. If the dog runs away and hides, she is not a good choice for a household with young children (don't worry if a dog is initially startled by a noise but then comes back to investigate). To test a puppy for touch sensitivity, pinch the skin between the toes. If the pup shows discomfort with a small amount of pressure, she is probably too touch-sensitive for a home with children. Do not try to test an adult dog's limits, as this can be dangerous; instead, discuss the subject with the dog's caretaker, such as the shelter worker or breeder.

Dogs often serve as playmates and close confidants for older children.

If you are going to a breeder for a puppy, ask if the pups were socialized with children. Ask for references of other families who have purchased puppies and call them to see how the dogs have gotten along with the children. Do not choose the boldest or shiest puppy of the litter; look for one that is mildly submissive or even-tempered. If you are getting a dog from a shelter, ask the staff to help you pick a dog that they believe will do well with children. Also ask them if they know where the dog came from and why he was given up.

Once you bring a dog into your household, you've got to do everything you can to instill harmony among all family members. A very young child may feel jealous of the attention the dog is getting (sibling rivalry!); talk to her before she starts taking out her angry feelings on the dog. If the dog is chewing a child's toys, respond by working out a training program to teach the dog to chew only appropriate items (you may have to start by banning the dog from the child's room). Involve the child in this training. Everyone must work together to make the dog a happy and loved family member.

How to Treat a Dog

It is crucial to teach your child or children how to behave around dogs. Begin by carefully reviewing the following dos and don'ts. This will help minimize the chances of your child being bitten, help lessen any fear he may have of dogs—or a false confidence that he may have in strange dogs—and help foster healthy, mutually satisfying relationships. These rules should, of course, be followed by adults as well.

- Never pet a dog that is not a member of your immediate family without permission from both the dog's owner and the dog herself. Once the owner gives you the go-ahead, begin speaking softly to the dog and simultaneously hold out a closed fist, palm side down. If the dog approaches in a friendly manner, begin petting gently. If the dog tenses up or withdraws when you extend your fist or begin petting, the dog has refused the request and should be left alone.

Children who treat animals gently and respectfully enjoy rewarding relationships with their dogs.

- Stroke a dog gently in the direction the fur grows. Most dogs do not like pats on the head or along the spinal column. Instead, after the dog has sniffed at the outstretched fist, stroke her down the side of her neck, scratch under her chin and around the ears, or pat her side.
- If a loose dog becomes excited and begins to bark, chase you, and jump up when you are playing, freeze and be silent until the dog walks away; then go to an adult for help. Some dogs are scared or can become overstimulated by certain types of play, such as running or screaming, or by repetitive movements, such as a bouncing ball or a swing moving back and forth.
- Do not stare into a dog's eyes. In canine body language, this is a challenge to fight.
- Do not tease a dog that is behind a fence, tethered on a leash, or confined in a crate. Teasing will incite the dog to act aggressively. If the dog gets loose, she may try to bite.
- Do not pester a dog that is eating, chewing on a toy, or napping. This is the dog's private time. By interfering, you may make the dog feel that she must protect her valuables.
- If you are chased or approached by a dog you do not know, stand very still until the dog loses interest. If the dog knocks you to the ground, curl up into a ball, bringing your knees up to your chest. When you are in this position, the dog sees that you are not a threat.
- Tell your parents if a dog ever growls, snaps at, or bites you. Try to remember what you were doing before the incident took place, and, if the dog is not your own, what the dog looks like and where it lives.

Choosing Your New Pet

You've evaluated your home situation and your commitment. You've talked it over with everyone in your household. You've decided that you want to get a dog. Congratulations! You are about to begin what will most likely be a wonderfully fulfilling adventure in canine love and responsibility. Now it's time to determine what kind of dog is right for your situation. First you must decide whether you want a mixed-breed or purebred dog, then you need to find just the right one. Don't be in a rush; you'll be spending years with this animal. To be fair to everyone involved, do some research following the guidelines presented here, visit with at least a few different dogs, and confer with your family. Carefully study the Reference Guide to Dog Breeds to find the mix or breed that will best fit in with your household.

Finding a Mixed-Breed Dog

Mixed-breed dogs are also called mongrels and mutts. Rather than the progeny of a long line of dogs of the same breed, mixed-breed dogs are a mélange of several or many breeds. Animal shelters are full of friendly, loving mixed-breed dogs—both puppies and adults—waiting to be adopted into caring households.

As captivating as a puppy can be, it is important not to adopt or buy one on a whim.

Adopting a Shelter Dog

The best sources for mixed-breed dogs are animal shelters. Good shelters are clean and well ventilated. The employees and volunteers are friendly, caring, knowledgeable, and helpful, and will both provide you with information on each dog—as much as is known about his history, health, and temperament—and screen you to make sure you are able to care for a dog. Often the dogs have been vaccinated, wormed, and neutered.

If you find a dog that you like, see if the shelter has a private room where you can interact more closely with him. Some dogs are very fearful when they are in a cage in a noisy shelter but will be very friendly if treated kindly in a separate, quiet room. Follow the guidelines on pages 49 and 50 to evaluate the health and temperament of the dog.

If you have another dog at home, before you even consider a visit to a shelter, take him to play with other dogs to make sure he gets along with them. At the shelter, ask the staff how the dog you are considering behaves around other dogs.

Animal shelters are a good source of mixed-breed dogs in need of loving homes.

A Mixed Breed's Ancestry

Often just by looking at a mixed-breed dog—assessing her physical form, energy level, and preferred activities—you can get a sense of her ancestry and, in the process, some hints about her disposition. If you are observing a dog at a shelter, you will certainly be able to evaluate her physical type. It may be more difficult to evaluate a shelter dog's energy level and preferred activities, es-

Determining ancestry is most difficult with young puppies because adult size and coat type are still a mystery.

pecially if she is a new arrival, as the dog may be distressed and therefore not feeling or acting like herself. When in doubt, assume a shelter dog is high energy.

Turn to page 82 of the Reference Guide to Dog Breeds for information on evaluating a mixed breed. Various types of mixes are pictured and described within the different breed groups (shepherd mixes, for example, are covered in the Herding Dogs group). More important than evaluating a dog's ancestry is assessing her physical condition and her temperament; see instructions on pages 49 and 50.

Mixed-Breed Show Dogs

Many canine organizations are devoted to purebred dogs, but there are plenty of opportunities for mixed breeds to join in the fun.

The American Mixed Breed Obedience Registry, an international registry for mixed-breed dogs, sponsors obedience competitions for its members, who are also eligible to compete in United Kennel Club obedience competitions. The American Kennel Club's Canine Good Citizen Program, open to both mixed breeds and purebreds, seeks to ensure that all dogs are trained and conditioned to display good manners in the home, in public places, and in the presence of other dogs. The ten-part test—which includes such skills as accepting a friendly stranger, sitting politely for petting, accepting being groomed by a stranger, and walking on a loose leash—is administered by kennel clubs, local specialty clubs, obedience clubs, private training schools, and other organizations, such as community colleges, 4-H clubs, and scouting organizations. See the appendix Breed Organizations and Kennel Clubs for addresses for both programs.

Finding a Purebred Dog

If you are looking for a purebred puppy, the most important part of the process is finding a reputable breeder—one that breeds for physical and mental soundness and refuses to breed any animal that exhibits a poor temperament or hereditary diseases. For example, a reputable breeder of golden retrievers or German shepherds will have her dogs screened for hereditary problems such as hip dysplasia and other bone and joint diseases (by the Orthopedic Foundation for Animals or by PennHip) and for hereditary eye diseases (by the Canine Eye Registry Foundation).

In some breeds, such as cocker spaniels and German shepherds, poor temperament is a serious problem that has been spread by breeders who are uneducated or care only about making a profit, not about helping to bring healthy dogs into the world. While a well-bred German shepherd can be a magnificent dog, a poorly bred one can be aggressive, extremely shy, or hyperactive and difficult to socialize. Reputable breeders take responsibility for all of their puppies. The price of a purebred will depend on her age and whether she is a show-quality dog, breeding stock, or a pet. The price can range from a few hundred dollars into the thousands.

A reputable breeder of German shepherds screens for hip dysplasia and other bone and joint diseases as well as for sound temperament.

As early as three weeks of age, pups like these English springer spaniels will be exposed by their breeder to a variety of textures and surfaces within their home environment.

Finding a Breeder

The first step toward getting a healthy purebred dog is finding a reputable breeder. The following tips should get you started.

An excellent place to meet breeders of many different types of dogs is at dog shows. Many of the people who participate in dog shows are serious about what they do and are intent on breeding for good physical and mental qualities. Unfortunately, some breeders strive for certain physical characteristics that they believe will win their dogs blue ribbons without regard for greater health issues. Thus it is important to evaluate carefully the breeders that you meet.

Try to attend a benched dog show. At a benched show, the dogs are on display when not being shown, and, most likely, the owners and handlers will be available to talk with you about their breed. Do some preliminary research so you have a basic knowledge of the breed. Don't pet any dogs without asking permission or interfere when the owners are getting ready to show their dogs. Buy a show catalog, which will have the names and addresses of breeders whom you can contact during or after the show.

Local veterinarians and obedience schools may be able to give you the names of reputable breeders and information on local clubs devoted to particular breeds. The dog magazines, such as *Dog World, Dog Fancy, AKC Gazette, Dogs USA,* and *Dogs in Canada,* run classified advertisements. Look for breeders in your area, but always ask for references. Any breeder—reputable or not—can take out an ad. Contact the American Kennel Club, the United Kennel Club, the Canadian Kennel Club, and local breed clubs. For addresses and other information, see the appendix Breed Organizations and Kennel Clubs.

Some breeders will allow you to pick a favorite from a litter of puppies; others will match you with the puppy they think will best fit your household. Above: Labrador retriever puppies.

Evaluating a Breeder

A reputable breeder puts health and safety before profit and produces dogs that are likely to be of sound mind and body. It isn't always easy to tell what kind of person you are dealing with, but there are often telltale signs. Read this section before you make your rounds so that you can be prepared.

Reputable breeders will check you out while you check them out. They will ask you about your lifestyle, your experience with dogs, and why you want one of their dogs. They may even ask you for personal references. If you have children, they will want to see them interact with the chosen animal before finalizing the adoption. (For more information about children and dogs, see page 28.) A reputable breeder will expect you to request a tour of the area where the dogs are kept (to make sure it is neat and clean) and to ask questions.

The following questions will help you evaluate each breeder you visit. If a breeder is evasive or doesn't answer questions willingly, you should assume he has something to hide. If you suspect that you have run across a breeder who is in it for the money rather than the health of the breed, do not support his business by buying one of his animals.

Can you tell me about the history of the breed? Good breeders are knowledgeable about their breed and will be enthusiastic about sharing their knowledge with you. They should tell you what the breed was developed for and what this history means in terms of the breed's behavioral and personality tendencies.

What are this breed's best and worst qualities? No breed is without its quirks, and a reputable breeder will not hesitate to admit this. In fact, a good

The history of a particular breed is a good place to begin your research. Above: French bulldog puppy.

breeder will want you to understand both the pros and cons of the breed so that you can prepare yourself for what lies ahead. Be sure to find out about the breed's trainability and grooming and exercise needs, and, if necessary, how it gets on with other pets or children.

Are you a member of national and local breed clubs? Often breed club members are required to sign a code of ethics, but club membership is no guarantee of reputability. Few clubs have readily accessible phone numbers, and most won't tell a caller about members who are not as responsible as they ought to be.

How long have you been breeding this particular type of dog? The most experienced breeders often have the best litters and will have a number of references at the ready. In some cases newer breeders are more careful and enthusiastic, although they do not yet have an established track record.

How often do you breed your dogs? For health reasons, a female dog should not be bred before her second or after her seventh birthday. Most females should not be bred more often than every other season (or period of heat), although healthy females that have easy deliveries can be bred two seasons in a row as long as they are given the third season off to rest and are retired earlier than females bred every other season. Male dogs used for breeding should be between two and ten years old. Breeders who breed their dogs more often are probably more interested in financial profit than they are in canine health.

Do you show your dogs? Breeders who show their dogs will be proud to show you awards their dogs have won. Remember that awards and certificates alone are not evidence of a breeder's seriousness. You will want to make sure that the

A reputable breeder will not mate a female dog before her second birthday. Right: female miniature pinscher.

breeder is concerned with not only the characteristics of a dog that will win blue ribbons but also the overall physical and mental health of the dog.

Are the puppy's parents or other relatives on the premises? Usually just the mother will be present along with the litter; the father is often brought in only for the mating. Ask about the father, and ask to see pictures and records. Observe whether the dogs living with the breeder are physically sound and friendly (not aggressive, nervous, or timid). The puppies—if they are socialized properly—will grow up to have physical and mental characteristics similar to those of their relatives.

Do you screen for hereditary diseases? Do your homework. Refer to the Reference Guide to Dog Breeds to find out which diseases your breed should be screened for, such as hip dysplasia and/or progressive retinal atrophy. The breeder should be knowledgeable about the breed's health issues and be willing and able to address your

At five weeks, these Pembroke Welsh corgi pups are too young for adoption.

concerns. Ask to see evidence that the dogs have been screened by such organizations as the Orthopedic Foundation for Animals, PennHip, or the Canine Eye Registry Foundation. Request other records if the breed is prone to certain problems.

Are your puppies examined and vaccinated by a veterinarian? Although many breeders vaccinate their litters themselves, the puppies should be seen by a veterinarian who can examine them for congenital problems, such as heart defects, loose kneecaps (patellar luxation), umbilical hernias, deafness, and eye problems (entropion and retinal defects). The puppies should receive their first vaccinations at six to eight weeks of age.

How do you socialize the puppies? From day one, breeders should begin to handle their puppies for brief periods, such as the time it takes to weigh them. When the puppies are about three weeks old, other people, such as the breeder's family or staff, should begin to handle them as well. When the pups are four to five weeks old, the breeder should invite outsiders, such as selected buyers, to meet the pups. From this time onward, the puppies should be exposed to a wide variety of sights and sounds.

How long will I have to wait for a puppy? Reputable breeders don't often have extra puppies on hand. Many breed only after they have commitments from pre-screened buyers. Reputable breeders sell their puppies at seven to twelve weeks of age. At six weeks and under, a puppy is too young to leave her mother. Dogs who stay with their littermates too long (over twelve weeks) may become dog-oriented and have little need for people. Such dogs are fine to bring in as a second dog—a pal for your resident dog—but seldom make satisfactory only pets.

May I have the names of several people who have purchased dogs from you? Confident breeders will not hesitate to give you references. Call at least two or three of the people whose names the breeders give you and inquire about their experiences with the breeders' puppies. Although breeders will not knowingly give you the names of dissatisfied customers, you may still be able to learn valuable information about the breeder and the breed from these people.

What kind of instructions will you provide when I take the puppy home? A concerned breeder will give you a lot of instructions, such as information about feeding (including the brand of food the puppy is accustomed to), house training, what the puppy's schedule has been, and tips about keeping the breed healthy and happy.

Some breeders may keep puppies until they are twelve to sixteen weeks of age to determine which ones will make the best show dogs.

Do you have "papers" for the dogs you are selling? You should receive pedigree documentation and health and vaccination records. The pedigree documentation (a diagram of the family tree) will list your dog's ancestors for three or more generations and include any championships and obedience titles they have won. Kennel club registrations indicate only that the dog is the product of a registered purebred sire and dam of the same breed; they say nothing about the quality of the dog you are buying. The breeder should provide you with an application to register the puppy or a certificate to transfer ownership of a named and registered dog to you.

Do you provide a contract? You should insist on a contract. The contract may require you to contact the breeder if at any time in the future you are unable to keep the dog (in which case the breeder may have the option of taking the dog back free of charge or finding another home for it). It may require you to have a male dog neutered or a female dog spayed. Some breeders issue co-ownership contracts so they can maintain some control over the future reproduction and showing of the dog. You may want to contact a lawyer if you are unfamiliar with this kind of arrangement. Unless you are interested in a show dog or breeding stock, avoid breeders who insist on complicated co-ownerships or contracts that go beyond neutering requirements and return policies.

Make sure all of the paperwork—contract, registration form, and health records—is in order before taking a dog from a breeder.

Do you provide a guarantee? A reputable breeder will offer you another puppy or a refund under some circumstances, such as the diagnosis of certain health or temperament problems within a specific period of time. The guarantee terms and period should be in the contract.

Other Sources for Purebred Dogs

You do not have to go to a breeder to get a purebred dog. Shelters, breed rescue groups, and service-dog organizations are all worth checking out. About 20 percent of the dogs in shelters are purebreds.

Breed Rescue Groups If you want a purebred dog and would like to save money on the purchase price, breed rescue groups—groups of volunteers devoted to caring for and finding homes for unwanted dogs—may be the way to go. These volunteer groups, many of which specialize in certain types of dogs, such as greyhounds, dalmatians, or Jack Russell terriers, may have their own shelters or may keep a list of dogs that are available from private homes or in foster care and shelters. They are usually familiar with each dog's physical condition and temperament. In most cases, the dogs have been checked by a veterinarian, vaccinated, and neutered. The price of the dog is usually very reasonable.

The largest breed rescue effort has been for greyhounds. This effort was mobilized in response to a startling statistic: more than 12,000 greyhounds that can't run fast enough to race competitively are euthanized each year in the United States. Greyhounds are sweet, gentle dogs that are usually good with children and mild-mannered by nature.

Retired racing greyhounds are available in large numbers from breed rescue groups and usually make wonderful pets.

To find a breed rescue group, send a self-addressed, stamped envelope to Project BREED (Breed Rescue Efforts and Education) for a directory of breed groups and their services. Call or write the National Greyhound Adoption Program, National Greyhound Adoption Network, or Greyhound Pets of America. (See the Resources appendix for contact information.) You may also wish to check with veterinarians, breeders, or shelters; search the Internet; call or write the American Kennel Club or the Canadian Kennel Club; or read the November issue of the *AKC Gazette,* which includes a list of the rescue coordinators for all AKC-recognized national breed clubs.

Service Dogs Organizations that breed dogs to work with the physically or mentally challenged, such as The Seeing Eye, Inc., and Dogs for the Deaf, sometimes make available for adoption animals that don't make the grade or that have served and retired (see the Resources appendix for contact information). These dogs are generally well socialized, intelligent, and healthy, and have great temperaments. For these reasons there are usually fairly long waiting lists for them. Contact service dog organizations in your area if you are interested in one of these dogs or if you would like to be a puppy raiser, which means that you foster the puppy for the first year or so of his life, before his specialized training begins.

When a service dog is wearing a harness, she is hard at work for her owner. Resist the urge to pet her.

Unreliable Sources for Dogs

Animal shelters, rescue groups, and reputable breeders are unquestionably the best sources for obtaining healthy, well-socialized dogs. People do get wonderful family pets from other sources, but most other sources are extremely risky. Some promote poor breeding practices, while others encourage the overpopulation that results in the killing of millions of animals yearly.

Pet shops often display exotic looking dogs, such as Chinese shar-peis, to tempt impulse buyers.

Pet Shops

While it is not impossible to get a healthy dog from a pet shop, in general it is a bad idea to support stores that sell animals (as opposed to stores that sell pet supplies—and sometimes offer cage space for animals from shelters or rescue groups). Many of the dogs sold in pet shops are the products of puppy mills, wholesale operations that breed dogs in large numbers purely for economic gain, often with very little concern for the behavioral or physical health or happiness of either the parents or the offspring.

Commercial Breeders

Large-scale commercial farms or kennels that breed so frequently they always have animals for sale cannot possibly provide each dog with the daily one-on-one attention that he needs and deserves. As a result, puppies that come from these sources often suffer from medical and behavioral deficiencies. Some of these breeders supply pet stores; others sell directly to the public.

Backyard Breeders

Although there are many reputable breeders who run their businesses out of their homes, it is not a good idea to obtain dogs from "backyard breeders," people who are not conscientious about their breeding programs and are more concerned with financial gain than with the health and well-being of their animals. A few red flags are breeders who are not knowledgeable about their breed, who do not check you out as well as you check them out, who are not active in their breed club or local canine organizations (such as the local humane society), who do not register their dogs, or who keep their dogs isolated in basements, garages, or other unpleasant spaces.

Stray Dogs

Rescuing a stray dog is always a gamble. Often strays have serious medical or behavioral problems that can require a lot of time and money to correct. You should call your local animal control agency if you encounter a stray that seems vicious or injured. If you find a stray and decide to keep him, take him to a veterinarian right away. You must be prepared to nurse him back to health, if necessary, or seek professional help to modify problem behaviors. If he is intact, have him neutered. If you do not want to keep him, turn him in to a shelter or to an animal control

If you decide to rescue a stray, take him to a vet right away to evaluate his health.

agency. If you can't keep him but want to take a more active role, file a report with animal control, run advertisements in local publications, put up "Found Dog" signs, and take the dog to a vet for a checkup. If no one claims the dog, start trying to find him a new home. It may take six to twelve months to find a home for an adult mixed breed.

Free to a Good Home

Finding a puppy through newspaper ads, signs, and posters may be slightly less of a gamble than rescuing a stray off the street, but it is still an unreliable means of obtaining a family pet. Often puppies advertised in this way are the result of an unplanned pregnancy (this is why it is so important for all dog owners to have their pets neutered). Sometimes the father is not even known, which makes it difficult to assess what the puppies' adult temperaments might be. In other cases the puppies are the result of a pregnancy initiated by people inexperienced and undereducated in responsible breeding practices. These puppies can carry genes for serious defects.

It is also risky to adopt an adult dog from a family, as the dog may have behavior problems. Most behavior problems can be remedied with careful, consistent training, but many such problems are best handled by a person experienced with dogs.

There are, of course, situations in which a family cannot keep a healthy, well-adjusted dog (for example, if someone in the home has become allergic to the animal), and will advertise his availability. If you are interested in adopting a family dog, speak with the owner, find out the dog's routine and habits, observe the dog in his home environment, and call the veterinarian who has been caring for the animal. If you like the dog and feel sure that you can handle him, consider going forward with the adoption.

Healthy dogs in need of new homes can make good pets. Above: a bearded collie mix (left) and a poodle mix (right).

A Labrador retriever should be energetic, even-tempered, and hardy.

Choosing a Healthy Dog

It is impossible to know everything about a dog before you take her home, but there are ways of making a general assessment about her temperament and health.

Judging Temperament

A dog's temperament—her tendency to be aggressive, timid, or easy-going—is thought to be inherited and then reinforced or diminished by early environmental influences. If you are looking at a purebred dog, become familiar with the characteristics of the breed before you visit so that you don't misconstrue her behavior. For example, some breeds, such as Akitas, are naturally aloof with strangers but warm up in time. For help in assessing a dog's temperament before making a final selection, you might even consider taking a trainer or behavior consultant with you to see the dog or litter of puppies.

When judging a dog's temperament, you must ask yourself a number of questions: If she is a young puppy, is she in a clean, homey environment with her littermates? Such an environment indicates that the pup is acclimated to normal household noises (important for good socialization) and that the pup has learned to keep clean, which will make housebreaking much easier than it would be with a puppy accustomed to lying in its own waste. Are the pup's parents friendly? If they are, chances are good that their offspring will be, too, having inherited good genes and having learned from good role models. Is the dog—whether a puppy or an adult—playful, calm, and trusting, and does she respond and wag her tail when you talk to her? These are all good signs. If she is frightened, tries to avoid you, or seems to mind being handled, she may turn out to be a shy and nervous dog. If the dog is a puppy, does she strongly resist being cradled on her back? Accepting cradling is a sign of submission and willingness to accept you as the leader of the "pack." A puppy that resists and does not settle down after ten to fifteen seconds might consider herself the leader and is probably not a good choice for an inexperienced dog owner. (Do not attempt to cradle an unknown adult dog.)

Judging Physical Condition

To get a sense of a dog's physical health, spend some time observing her. A healthy dog is not lethargic. Her coat should be glossy—with no hair loss or reddened, scabby areas—and free of fleas or ticks. There should not be any discharge from her eyes or nose. (Some dogs with "pushed-in" faces, like Pekingese, may have some clear discharge coming from the inner corner of the eyes.) The dog should not cough (a sign of a respiratory infection called kennel cough). Her gums should be pink. Her ears should not be inflamed and there should not be any black debris in the ear canal. Her bowel

Bright eyes, a clear nose, smooth skin, and a shiny coat are all signs of a healthy pup.

Most healthy puppies are playful, inquisitive, and trusting.

movements should be firm (if she has been weaned). To make sure the dog can hear (deafness can be a problem with older dogs and some purebred puppies, such as dalmatians), clap your hands or jingle car keys outside the dog's field of vision and see if you get a response.

If you do not think the dog you are looking at is in peak condition, discuss your concerns with the breeder or shelter staff and a veterinarian. Many conditions, such as kennel cough, can be treated. Request a written guarantee that allows you to return the dog if a veterinarian determines that she has a serious problem or one that would be costly to correct.

Preparing Your Home for Your New Dog

While picking up and bringing home a new puppy or adult dog is an exciting and happy event for people, it is a stressful time for the dog. Imagine being whisked away by a stranger, possibly even taken from the only environment you have known since birth. Fortunately, dogs adapt fairly quickly if treated kindly and gently.

Ideally, you should dog-proof your home and yard and obtain food, a collar and leash, and other essentials before bringing your dog home. In addition, choose a single area that you would like your dog to use for elimination and make sure that all family members are aware of it.

Dog-Proofing Your Home

The home is an exciting and potentially dangerous place for your new dog, especially a curious puppy. Dog-proofing in advance can go a long way toward preventing accidents. Dog-proof indoor living areas, as well as the garage and the yard.

Store out of your dog's reach anything that is toxic if swallowed, such as oven and drain cleaners, insect poison or traps, floor and furniture polishes, antifreeze, lawn chemicals, and old paint, sheet rock, and linoleum. (Refer to Household Poisons, page 476.)

Like toddlers, puppies are curious about everything and are unable to distinguish between safety and danger.

Make sure trash containers are securely covered to protect your puppy from ingesting unsafe contents.

Remove all electrical wires, string, tinsel, rubber bands, thread, needles, and ribbon from your dog's reach. Such material can be deadly if swallowed. Be especially alert during holiday times.

Keep all plants away from the dog. See page 475 for a list of plants that can be especially harmful.

Set up baby gates to keep the dog in safe areas.

If you have a fenced yard in which you intend to let the dog run off-leash, make sure the fencing is secure. It should be high enough to keep the dog—when he is an adult—from jumping over it, sunk deep enough to keep the dog from dig-

If you catch your puppy chewing on an inappropriate object, say "no" and replace the object with a chew toy.

ging a tunnel under it, and free of holes. Additional fencing should surround backyard pools, ponds, compost heaps, and prized gardens.

Make sure outdoor trash, compost bins, lawn chemicals, and toxic plants are out of the dog's reach, and that potted plants, gardening tools, or other outdoor paraphernalia are positioned so that they cannot be knocked over.

Setting Up an Outdoor Space

Some dog owners like to partition their yards so that their dogs have an exercise area but the owners still have an area for gardening, relaxing, and socializing. A fenced-in outdoor run is not a substitute for exercise and social interaction with your dog. The main part of your dog's life should be spent with the family.

Unleashed dogs are safe in a secured area, such as a fenced-in yard.

Outdoor Runs An outdoor run, in which your dog can run and play off-leash, must be fenced in. Experts recommend chain-link fencing that is high (six to eight feet) and sturdy enough to house the strongest and most athletic dog. The run should have an area protected from sun and rain, such as an overhang or a doghouse. Smooth stones (pea gravel) or cement make good flooring materials because they are easy to clean.

Doghouses A doghouse is important for a dog that spends a lot of time outdoors in hot or cold weather. The house should be just large enough for the dog to stand up and turn around in; if it is too large, it will not retain heat on cold days. It should be elevated off the ground so that it will not become saturated with water. It should be situated to offer protection from driving rain, wind, or snow, and it should have a canvas or plastic door flap to keep drafts out. The roof should be slanted so rain and snow can't accumulate. Inside the house, place a pad, blanket, straw, or hay. Clean the pad or blanket or change the straw or hay weekly. Doghouses can be built following the instructions in books available at libraries and pet or building supply stores, or they can be purchased ready-made.

Shopping List

You will need to embark on a shopping expedition before you bring your dog home. From day one, you'll need food and water bowls, food, a crate, bedding, a baby gate, a collar and leash, several chewies, and a form of identification. Ideally, you should obtain and arrange these items in your home before picking up the dog. You can purchase other items gradually, as the situation warrants them.

Very young puppies can share a food bowl, but once they are about eight weeks old they each need their own bowl. Otherwise, the dominant dog is likely to eat more than his fair share.

Food and Water Bowls
Tip-proof stainless steel or ceramic bowls are best because they are easiest to scrub clean. Plastic bowls sometimes cause irritation around the muzzle.

Food
Buy enough of the brand of food the dog has been eating to last a couple of weeks; an abrupt change in food can cause gastrointestinal upset. See page 356 for information on choosing a dog food for the long term and page 359 for advice on easing the transition from one food to another.

Crate

Although some people equate a dog crate with a cage and are resistant to using one, a dog perceives his crate as a secure den, a safe place to retreat to when tired or stressed. Placing a puppy in his crate to rest a few hours during the day and at night is an effective house-training method, as most puppies don't want to soil the area where they sleep. Crates are available in heavy molded plastic, fiberglass, and wire. Some wire crates can be folded and easily moved from the area of the house where the family congregates during the day to a bedroom at night. Crates can also be used in the car, and many molded plastic crates can be used for air travel. Choose a crate that will allow your dog—when he reaches full size—to stand up, turn around, and lie down comfortably.

Puppies, like people, appreciate a cozy spot for sleeping.

Bedding

If you are not using a crate, a molded plastic bed with light bedding or simply a double-sided imitation lambskin mattress will make your pup feel cozy and comfortable. You can also buy easy-to-wash puppy quilts at a pet supply store or use an old towel or blanket.

Baby Gate

Use a gate to keep your new puppy or adult dog in a designated safe area. Make sure the gate is sturdy and that the spacings are small so that your dog cannot get his head or jaws caught in them.

Automobile Restraint

Canine seat belts made out of nylon webbing can keep your dog from being propelled forward when a car stops suddenly. These restraints allow your dog to sit up and lie down. They install easily, and some can also be used as walking harnesses. Metal barriers or crates can also be used to limit your dog's movement in a car.

Everyday Collar

For everyday wear, choose a buckled nylon-web or leather collar to hold your dog's identification, license, and rabies tags. Rolled leather collars are best for dogs with long, thick fur, such as collies, because hair doesn't get caught in them. Flat or rolled collars are fine for dogs with shorter fur. Collars with quick-snap closures are also available, but many trainers find the buckled collars more reliable. To determine the correct fit, slide your finger under the collar when it is on

When you first put a collar on your new puppy, expect some resistance, such as pawing and rolling around.

your dog. You should be able to fit one or two fingers under the collar, but the collar should not be able to slip over the dog's head. In the beginning, leave a collar on your puppy only for short periods so that she can get used to it; remove the collar when she is left unsupervised. Once she is used to the collar (with tags), leave it on at all times in case she ever gets lost. As a puppy grows, you will need to replace the collar.

In order to be effective, training collars must be carefully fit and put on properly.

Training Collar

The slip collar, also called a choke collar, is a common type of training collar that tightens when you give the leash a quick pull to make a correction and loosens when you slack off. For best control and safety, the slip collar should be neither too tight nor too loose. To determine the correct size, measure your dog from under her chin to up around the widest part of her skull and add an inch or two. Puppies, small adult dogs, and cooperative larger dogs should not need a training collar; they should be able to learn with an everyday buckle collar. Put a training collar on your dog for training sessions or outdoor walks only. Always leave the everyday collar on your dog, even when also using a training collar. Never attach identification

tags to the slip collar—they can get caught in the collar and choke the dog. Remove the slip collar before allowing your dog to play with other dogs.

Harness

The harness is an ideal alternative to the collar for dogs that are prone to collapsed tracheas (narrowing of the windpipe), such as Yorkshire terriers and poodles, and for dogs with neck problems or kennel cough. The harness takes the pressure off the trachea so the dog can walk without coughing or injuring his neck. The harness goes around the chest and the leash is attached on top. It does not give the dog walker any extra control.

Harnesses are ideal for dogs recovering from kennel cough or neck injuries.

Head Halter

The head halter, an alternative to the slip collar, is useful for training shy dogs, dogs with high prey drives, scent hounds, and large dogs that are difficult to control. It is also useful for owners who lack physical strength, are pregnant, or have bad backs. The halter has two straps: one goes around the neck and buckles behind the ears, the other goes over the muzzle. The leash attaches to a ring under the chin. A halter controls the head of the dog, and the body follows.

Leash

A six-foot-long and half-inch-wide to three-quarter-inch-wide leather or cotton-web leash is suitable for both training and walking. Look for strong stitching or braiding on the handle and where the metal clasp attaches. Retractable

A six-foot leash gives a dog enough room to move around and to eliminate without infringing on the space of other pedestrians.

leashes, which allow the user to shorten or lengthen the leash with the touch of the button on the plastic handle, are a popular choice for walking a trained dog but are safe only in wide open spaces, not on city sidewalks.

Make sure your dog wears identification and rabies tags at all times. In some areas, a license tag might also be required.

Identification

All dogs need to wear or be marked with some sort of identification at all times. In many areas, a dog must be licensed (check with your local health department or ask your veterinarian about laws in your area), and will receive a license tag with some identification information printed on it. Most pet supply stores sell aluminum, plastic, or steel identification tags that can be clipped to a dog's collar. The tag should be engraved with the dog's name and your name, address, and telephone number, plus important medical information, such as a diabetes alert. Tattooing a number (such as your social security or kennel club registration number) on a dog's inner thigh is a permanent method of identification. The number is registered with an organization such as the National Dog Registry (800-NDR-DOGS). Another permanent identification option is a microchip containing an identification number. The chip is inserted under the skin between a dog's shoulder blades with a large needle. It is quick and almost painless. The microchip is read with a scanner passed over the dog. Check with your veterinarian or local animal shelter to find out if a scanning program has been implemented in your community.

Lost Dog If your dog gets lost, contact every place your dog has been registered, such as your local licensing bureau and the tattoo or microchip registry you have filed with. Check with local shelters, and continue to call them daily until the dog is found. Call outside at mealtimes, alert your neighbors, and place posters with the dog's photograph around your neighborhood.

Grooming Tools

Every dog needs a brush suitable for his coat type, a flea comb, a nail trimmer, and, for dental care, a small toothbrush (or gauze pads) and dog toothpaste. Talk to your veterinarian, breeder, or groomer about the specific brushes you need for your dog's coat type; see Bathing and Grooming, page 372, for advice and instruction.

Chewies

There are innumerable chew toys on the market, ranging from rubber items to animal products. Both nylon and rubber chew toys (especially those that can be filled with dog treats) can occupy some dogs for hours. Rawhide, which is dried cattle skin, and pig ears and cow hooves are enjoyed by many dogs but sometimes cause digestive upset. Watch to make sure your dog is not swallowing large, unchewed chunks. When purchasing rawhide, buy only American-made white rawhide. Foreign rawhide may contain harmful chemicals.

Toys

There are thousands of dog toys on the market, including squeaking toys, rope toys, flying disks, and balls. Some dogs can chew plastic, nylon, or plush toys to shreds in a few hours. Supervise your dog when he has a new toy until you are sure he won't destroy it and choke on the pieces. You may have to try a few types of toys until you find a sturdy one that your dog enjoys. Be sure all toys and balls that you give to your dog are too large to lodge in his throat.

If puppies are not given chew toys to gnaw on when they are teething, they will find other objects, such as furniture or shoes.

Welcoming Your New Family Member

The big day has arrived. Excitement is in the air, especially if there are children around. It's time to welcome your new family member into your home. Don't forget in your excitement that your new dog or puppy will find the day stressful. He may feel afraid when he first enters your home and will need some time to adjust to his new environment. Take the time to prepare your family and your home for the new arrival. Read through this section ahead of time so you know what to expect.

Preparation

Just before you pick up your dog, you need to make a few arrangements and set up the house for the new arrival. The ideal time to pick up your dog is at the beginning of a weekend or a longer vacation so that you will be able to focus completely on his needs. Make an appointment with your chosen veterinarian (see Finding a Veterinarian, page 418) to examine your new dog, preferably within twenty-four hours of the time you get him. Set up the dog's crate and bedding, and install baby gates, if needed. Choose a designated elimination area. If it is to be indoors, lay down newspapers.

Picking Up Your New Dog

It is important to act calmly when you arrive to pick up your dog. Greet him quietly and spend a few minutes petting and talking to him. Let him sniff you and other family members (first extend a closed fist, palm down), and be sure everyone stays quiet and calm. Do not try to lead the dog toward your car until he seems comfortable with you.

Left: Plan to pick up your new dog on a day when you don't have any other commitments.

Facing page: A gentle introduction to the new home and family will help the bonding process get under way.

Before you leave, ask the breeder or the shelter personnel for the following:

- A list of the types and dates of immunizations, dewormings, and any special tests that have been administered.
- The name and phone number of the veterinarian who has been caring for the dog.
- The dog's feeding schedule and the name of the food the dog has been eating.
- Pedigree and kennel club registration papers (if applicable) and the sales or adoption contract.

The Drive Home

Pick up your new dog with another family member or friend so that one person can do the driving and the other person can comfort the dog. A puppy or small dog can be allowed to sit beside or on the lap of the passenger, or he can be placed in a small plastic pet carrier. Large dogs should ride in the back seat, either on a leash and with the passenger or in a crate. Reassure the dog from time to time by talking quietly and petting him gently. Bring along a towel for him to lie on and paper towels to use if he gets carsick. If you do not have a car, arrange for taxi service in advance.

Cradle a puppy or small adult dog against your body.

How to Hold a Dog

Pick up a puppy or a small adult dog by putting one hand on the chest right behind the front legs and using the other hand to scoop up the rear end and legs so that you can cradle the puppy against your body (which will make him feel secure). Pick up a larger dog in the same way, except use your entire arm to support the dog's chest (not just your hand) from underneath. To pick up a dog that you think may bite, grab the collar at the back of the head with one hand and use the other hand to support the abdomen. Never pick up a dog by his front legs.

A New Puppy

Remember that your puppy will have to get used to her new home and family and adjust to living without her mother and littermates. She will need to learn where you want her to eliminate. If the spot you have chosen as the elimination area is outside, first carry the puppy there and give her the opportunity to eliminate. Praise her enthusiastically if she does so. Enter your home calmly and quietly, and allow your puppy to explore if she has eliminated outdoors; otherwise bring her directly to the indoor elimination area.

It's best to keep the atmosphere subdued for the puppy's first few days in her new home.

Your puppy may investigate new objects by "feeling" them with her mouth. Instead of scolding, substitute a chew toy for the inappropriate object. Although it is tempting to invite friends and neighbors over to see this cute little ball of fur, it is better to wait a few days and to introduce friends one at a time. Too many people or too much noise may frighten or overstimulate your puppy and make the bonding with your family more difficult. Remember to give the puppy plenty of time to sleep. To avoid accidents, take her to the designated elimination area frequently. (To work out a schedule based on the puppy's age, see the information in House Training, page 68.)

Introducing a Puppy to Other Pets

If you have other animals, such as cats, guinea pigs, rabbits, or ferrets, in the household, introduce them to the puppy in a calm setting. Keep the puppy on a leash so you can control her movements. Cats may not take to the new animal right away—they may hiss, strike out, or hide for a while—but they'll usually come around. If you have another dog, keep both animals on leashes for the introduction. Although most puppies can get along with all animals in their household if raised with them, some breeds, such as terriers, are genetically programmed to hunt small mammals, and even early introductions may not curb that desire.

A puppy's first night in a new home can be very stressful. Don't expect much sleep.

The First Night

The first night will probably be the most difficult for your puppy, and she may cry and whine. Do not scold her and do not expect that either of you will get a lot of sleep. To make the transition easier, try the following first-night strategies.

Keep your puppy near your bed in her crate or on her own blanket or bed on the floor so she doesn't feel isolated. Place a stuffed toy or a knotted large towel (which will feel like her littermates) on the puppy's bed or in the crate for comfort. Avoid the temptation to take her into your bed. Where the dog sleeps can be reevaluated when she is house trained and understands her place in the family pack.

Take your puppy to eliminate in the designated area every two to four hours. When she eliminates, praise her.

Placing a puppy in a crate to rest for short periods is often helpful for house training.

Introducing a Puppy to a Crate

It is important to make your puppy's first experience with his crate a pleasant one. The crate should be big enough for your dog to use when he is full grown. While he is a puppy, use a barrier to reduce the crate's size; you do not want him to be able to eliminate at one end and then relax comfortably at the other end. Your puppy will soil the crate if left in it for too many hours or if it is too large.

Do not add bedding, which can act like a diaper and wick waste away, until the puppy has succeeded at keeping the bare crate clean for at least a week. Then add a thin sheet or towel. If that stays clean, you may provide thicker bedding.

To introduce your puppy to his crate, place a toy and a treat or some dog food inside the crate, and leave the door open. Let the puppy enter the crate on his own; do not force him into it. When your puppy explores the crate, praise him enthusiastically. At feeding time, place his food at the back of the crate and close the door for a minute once he is inside. Praise him if he eats or is quiet and well behaved, and then open the door. Do not praise him when he comes out (you are trying to teach him that his crate is a nice place, so you don't want to reward him for leaving it); instead, say nothing. Repeat this process over the course of a few days' time.

As your puppy becomes more comfortable in the crate, increase the amount of time you keep the door closed, until he will stay quietly inside for two hours. Discourage whining and crying with a firm "no," or ignore it. If you ignore the whining and the dog receives nothing for his efforts, the behavior will extinguish itself. However, be prepared for the behavior to get worse before it gets better.

Do not keep your puppy in his crate for more than two to four hours. If you are going to be gone all day and no one can come over to let him out, leave the crate door open, set up baby gates to keep him in one room, and put newspapers down so that he can eliminate.

Do not use the crate to isolate the puppy. During the day, place the crate where the family congregates, such as in the kitchen or family room. At night, keep the crate next to your bed. If you don't have a crate that can be moved easily, consider purchasing two crates or borrowing one from a friend whose dog no longer needs it. Don't forget to listen for signs that the puppy needs to eliminate, such as whining or restlessness.

Introducing a Puppy to a Collar and Leash

Put a lightweight nylon collar on your puppy and let him wear it around the house for a day or two. The puppy may initially scratch at the collar or shake his head but will adapt to it quickly. Introduce a lightweight leash by attaching it to the collar and letting the puppy drag it around the house. As the puppy walks, pick up the leash and walk with him, holding the leash above his head so he can't chew on it. Speak to him in a friendly, encouraging voice. After your puppy is comfortable with the leash, try using it to guide actions by encouraging him to approach and walk with you while on-leash. Do not start using a slip collar, if you need to use one at all, until you take the dog to obedience class and learn how to use it properly.

House Training

House training is one of the first tasks for a dog owner and need not be overly difficult or stressful. Keep in mind that a puppy's bladder is still developing; a good rule of thumb is that a pup can hold her bladder for one hour for each month of age, up to ten hours. That means that a two-month-old puppy may need to go out every two hours (she will probably need to eliminate after waking, eating, or drinking, or after a play session); a five-month-old puppy may be able to wait five hours. At three and a half to four months, a dog can last for six to seven hours overnight without eliminating but probably won't be able to do that during the day. The more opportunities you give your puppy to go out and eliminate in an appropriate place, the more quickly she will learn.

Crate training is by far the fastest and most efficient way to house train a puppy. The puppy perceives the crate as her den, a safe, secure place of her own. She likes to spend time inside it and does not want to make a mess there.

House Training Tips Choose a single place for elimination and take your puppy to this spot all the time. The familiarity of the smells in this spot will encourage the puppy to eliminate. If you live in an apartment, you may choose to set up an elimination spot indoors until your puppy is old enough to make it outdoors without having an accident in the elevator or other common areas (see Paper Training, page 71). The following tips ought to help you and your puppy survive house training. There are bound to be a few accidents along the way, but in the end you will both succeed.

Some veterinarians, especially in large cities, recommend that puppies be kept inside until they have received all of their vaccinations. In these cases, paper training becomes a necessity.

•Watch for signals that your puppy has to eliminate, such as sniffing, circling, whining, and/or scratching on the floor. Take the puppy to the elimination spot immediately when you see these signals.

•Take your puppy to eliminate first thing in the morning, last thing at night, after eating, after playing, after naps, and at any other time that the puppy gives you a signal that she needs to go. Until your puppy reaches about four months of age, you will also need to take her to eliminate every two to four hours during the night.

•If you will be away from the house for more than a few hours, make arrangements for a trusted friend, neighbor, or pet sitter to come to the house to take the puppy to eliminate.

•When you take your puppy to her elimination spot, repeat a signal word or phrase, such as "Go potty" or "Hurry up," and then praise her when she eliminates. The puppy will make the connection and will learn to eliminate when prompted. This command is especially useful on cold winter mornings and when you are late for work.

•Praise your puppy whenever she goes on the paper or in the designated spot outside. Your puppy wants to please you and will respond to your praise.

•Some pups will sniff and sniff outside, then eliminate in the house within five minutes of the trip outside. Watch your puppy's signals carefully after returning to the house if she hasn't eliminated outside. After an unproductive trip, crate her for one to two hours, then return to the elimination area.

•Never punish your puppy if she has an accident. Clean messes as soon after they occur as possible with enzyme cleaners designed for this purpose. Don't use products with ammonia in them, as they will attract the puppy back to the same spot.

•Once the pup is successfully soiling outside, try to vary the surface so that she won't imprint on only one type, such as grass or asphalt. An unadaptable dog may make herself miserable if traveling with you away from home and unable to find the particular surface that she prefers.

•If you take your dog to eliminate in a public place, be sensitive to local laws and etiquette. Curb your dog whenever possible. Have male dogs mark on inanimate objects such as lamp posts and fire hydrants rather than bushes, trees, and garden plots.

•Always pick up feces if the dog eliminates off your property, and place waste in the appropriate receptacles. You may want to feed your puppy (and adult dog) premium dog food that is highly digestible and produces smaller, firmer stools than lower-quality foods.

Paper Training In some situations an owner may choose to paper train a puppy before she learns to eliminate outdoors. City dog owners may paper train a puppy if the vet has recommended keeping the puppy indoors until she has had her sixteen-week vaccinations and can go outdoors safely. Other owners choose paper training if they live in an elevator building and want to avoid accidents in public places.

Place several layers of newspaper on the floor of a chosen room, one in which the floor can be cleaned easily (such as a tiled kitchen or bathroom). Put the dog in the room and block the doorway so she cannot get out. For the first day, place a piece of paper with a small amount of your puppy's urine or feces already on it in the room; the scent will attract her to the paper. Once your dog has eliminated on the paper, remove the top, soiled layer; the paper underneath will retain the scent and remind your puppy to eliminate in the same place the next time. Take your puppy to the paper as you would to an outdoor elimination spot—on a leash and collar, at scheduled times, with a command, and with you next to her—so that when you make the switch to outdoors, the whole routine won't be foreign to the dog.

Paper train a puppy on a surface that is easy to clean, such as a tile floor.

Making a Puppy Part of Your Family

The first few weeks in your home are critical for your puppy, which needs time, love, gentleness, praise, socialization, mental stimulation, and consistent supervision, guidance, and training. Some people feel that a puppy's exposure to different people, places, and animals should be limited until after all of the puppy vaccinations have been administered, typically at fourteen to sixteen weeks of age. If you live in a large city, your veterinarian will most likely recommend this. However, the critical period for socialization in a puppy's development is seven to sixteen weeks of age. It is at this time that a puppy's attitude toward new stimuli—people, places, animals, noises, and other new experiences—is formed. Speak to your veterinarian about this dilemma. If your puppy is not one of the breeds that is particularly vulnerable to parvovirus (such as Dobermans and rottweilers), your veterinarian will probably encourage controlled social interactions. You may take your dog to see friends and to clean outdoor locations. Carry the puppy outdoors and let him see and hear the world from your lap or a picnic blanket. Allow him to play only with other animals that you know are vaccinated and healthy.

Dogs need plenty of love and attention in order to thrive.

Early Socialization The early socialization guidelines that follow will help you to "civilize" your puppy and guide him toward acceptable behavior so that he will grow into a dog with whom you, your family, and other people will want to spend time.

Make sure that at least one family member is at home with the puppy and has time to pet and play with him and take him to the designated elimination area every few hours. Puppies are programmed to be part of a pack (your family). If the pack is never around, the puppy may have difficulty learning how to interact and live with humans, which can lead to many different problems, including shyness, fearfulness, destructiveness, excessive independence, and disobedience.

Include your puppy in as many family activities as possible. A dog that feels extensively isolated from his "pack" will develop severe behavioral problems, although some social isolation helps the puppy learn to cope when left alone. When your puppy must be separated from the family, place him in his crate or in an area blocked off with baby gates. The puppy will find it less traumatic if he can at least see the family and if you give him a comfort item, such as a favorite toy.

Once he is used to his new home life, you can begin introducing your puppy to people, dogs, and other animals. Take him to friends' homes and to dog play groups (as long as all the dogs are healthy and vaccinated and your veterinarian approves). Let your puppy be held and touched by a lot of people. He will learn that other people can be kind, trustworthy, and fun. Some breeds, such as those that were originally bred for guarding livestock or property, can be cautious of outsiders, while others, such as golden retrievers, are usually trusting of everybody.

Playing a variety of games with your pup and providing him with a rotating array of toys will help him develop in a healthy way—and keep him out of trouble.

Exercises There are a number of socialization exercises and practices you can begin with a young puppy to prepare her for life in the world at large.

When your puppy is two to three months old, begin to include gentle dominance-down exercises in the daily routine to help her learn her place in the family "pack." Place her on her back cradled in your arms. Hold her firmly but gently with one hand on her chest. If she squirms or tries to nip, don't yell, just continue to hold her calmly. When she relaxes, pet her and say "Good dog," then let

Many puppies will sit when a toy is held over their heads. Lure-and-reward training can start at a very young age (see page 384).

her get up. Do not engage in this exercise with older puppies (over four months of age); instead, practice down-stay (see page 388).

Acclimate your puppy to a variety of different situations, such as car rides, traffic sounds, sudden noises, crowds, slippery floors, stairs, etc. The most adaptable adult dogs are those that have satisfying early introductions to new and varied situations.

Do exercises to instill trust and discourage the development of possessive and territorial behavior patterns. Take a toy out of your puppy's mouth, praise her, then return the toy or trade up to something better. While she is eating, take the food bowl away. Praise her, then give the food bowl back with something even better added to the bowl.

Provide your puppy with a rotating array of toys for physical and mental stimulation. If she starts chewing on an inappropriate object, say "Uh-uh" or "Phooey," and redirect her attention to a proper chew toy. Frequent targets can be spritzed with antichew sprays so they no longer taste appealing.

If your puppy is about to sit down, give the sit command and offer a lot of praise once she has done so. You'll be planting the seeds for early learning (see Guidelines for Early Training, page 383).

Use positive reinforcement to encourage your puppy to learn. Praise her when she does something correctly. Say "no" only when absolutely necessary. It will be more effective if you don't use it constantly. Never hit your puppy—or any dog.

Begin to prepare your pup for all sorts of handling. Open her mouth and pop in a treat. Hold a rawhide chewie in one hand, and as the pup chews on it, give her a few strokes with a brush. Touch her paws—follow up by tossing a toy. Give her a bear hug while whispering sweet nothings in her ears, then give her a treat before releasing her. Your veterinarian and groomer will appreciate the time you make for these exercises, and your puppy will feel more comfortable being handled at the doctor's office or grooming salon.

An Urgent Reminder: Have Your Dog Neutered

It is very important to have your dog neutered at the first safe opportunity, which may be as early as two months old, depending on the size of the animal. Not only will it cut down on the serious overpopulation that leads to the abandonment (and subsequent euthanization) of millions of dogs each year, but it will benefit your dog medically and behaviorally.

Neutering of a female dog (also called spaying) involves removing the ovaries and uterus before the first heat, which usually happens at around six to nine months, depending on the breed type and the individual dog. A neutered female is less likely to develop breast cancer and will be protected from pyometra (pus-filled uterus). Neutering (removing the testicles) of a male can prevent testicular cancer, prostate disease, and hernias. It will also lessen a dog's impulse to roam, mark territory, and mount human legs or furniture.

Neutering will not affect a dog's instinct to protect its family—although it may calm a dog down and eliminate some aggression problems—nor will it cause a dog to become lazy. Some dogs gain weight after being neutered, but this can be counteracted with proper feeding and exercise.

To locate a low-cost spaying and neutering facility in your area, contact your local shelter or humane society or call 800-248-SPAY.

A New Adult Dog

Bringing a new adult dog into your home is not as complicated as bringing home a puppy. Every adult dog has his own fully developed personality that has been formed by life experiences about which you may have no information. Some of these experiences may have been positive, others negative. Many adult dogs will adjust very quickly to a new home; for others, it will take more time and effort.

Easing the Transition

Prepare your home so that it is quiet and welcoming on arrival day. Do not invite friends to meet the dog right away, especially if he is shy or fearful. If you have other animals, keep them separated for at least the first few hours. Your new dog will smell other animals in the home, even if he can't see them. (See pages 78 and 79 for guidelines on introducing your new dog to other animals in residence.)

Give your new dog the opportunity to relieve himself in the designated area outside, then allow him to investigate the different rooms of your home. Supervise him and leave his leash on during this time so that he is dragging it and you can grab it if necessary. Show the dog where his food, water, toys, and bedding are located. After the initial investigation of the home, limit the dog to a smaller area. Give him some time to calm

It takes a few months to get to know a new dog.

down. Stroke him confidently and massage him gently if he is tense. Then sit and read or listen to restful music without really focusing on the dog. In this way you begin the bonding process. After a bedtime walk, take the dog to his sleep spot, offer a chew toy, and turn the lights out, ignoring any vocalizations he may make (unless neighbors start to complain). In the beginning it is often a good idea to crate, gate, or tether the dog to the foot of your bed at night; later on, once he proves responsible, he can be given more freedom.

Making a Dog Part of Your Family

Consider the first weeks, even months, a learning period for you and your new dog. From the beginning, set up a routine of feeding, walking, exercising, training, and leaving your dog alone on a consistent schedule. When you leave home without the dog, keep him in a dog-proofed space, such as in a crate or a gated area. Let him know the rules of the household but do not expect too much at first. Some dogs are on their best behavior for the first ten to fourteen days, too afraid to test the waters. These dogs may get much bolder after the "honeymoon" period. You may discover fears or phobias during the first thunderstorm or the first time a delivery person comes to the door. You may never learn why your dog responds the way he does, but take comfort in knowing that he can learn new positive associations with new experiences. You can almost always teach an old dog new tricks, although sometimes this requires the assistance of a professional trainer or behaviorist.

Start obedience training at home immediately (see page 383). A few weeks after acquiring the dog, it is also a good idea to begin formal classes, such as beginner obedience, Canine Good Citizen, or agility training. For high-drive dogs with strong working instincts, you may try herding trials or other types of activities. Classes will help you bond with your new canine partner, as well as establish your role as leader in the relationship. It is important to train the dog so that he knows the household rules and learns to behave. He will be happier if he knows his role and will have an easier time becoming a part of the family.

Dogs get to know each other by sniffing.

Introducing a New Dog to a Resident Dog

If you already have another dog, introduce the two on leashes in a neutral territory, such as a nearby park or playground. Ask a neutral person (not your resident dog's best pal) to handle the new dog. If the dogs seem to be getting along, return to the house. Ask the neutral person to handle the new dog on-leash, and allow the resident dog to wander freely, though dragging a leash so that you can grab her easily if necessary. If the dogs continue to get along, take their leashes off in thirty minutes to an hour; the neutral person can leave shortly thereafter, if all is proceeding nicely.

The first day feed the dogs in separate rooms. The next day feed them at opposite ends of the same room. Gradually bring them closer together during feeding time, watching carefully to make sure that neither dog is eating the other dog's rations. Whenever you offer toys and chewies, make sure you have enough for both dogs. If they fight over toys, chewies, or other belongings, offer these treats to them only when they are in separate rooms or crated.

When you leave your home during the first few weeks, you may want to keep the dogs in separate rooms, even if they are getting along.

If the dogs frequently fight during this get-acquainted period, they may not be compatible. Separate them as necessary and consult immediately with a behaviorist or trainer about how to handle the situation.

Introducing a New Dog to a Cat

To introduce your dog to a cat, put the dog on-leash and make sure the cat has an escape route out of the room or to a spot the dog can't reach, such as a shelf or under a bed. Set up a gate so that the cat can leave the room if he wants to and the dog cannot chase him. If the dog and cat seem calm together, let the dog walk around dragging the leash. If the dog starts to chase the cat, step on the leash to put an end to it quickly. Be particularly cautious with old or sick cats that will have a hard time running away from the dog.

If they are socialized together from a young age, a dog and a cat can become close friends.

If the dog has not been socialized around other small pets, such as birds or rabbits, do not leave her in the same room with them unsupervised. Over time, if the dog proves uninterested in hurting the animals, you can consider changing this rule.

Now What?

You've chosen a dog, prepared your home, and brought the dog home. You've begun house training (if you have a puppy) and socialization. Now what? Turn to What Makes a Dog a Dog? (beginning on page 307) to read about how a dog works from the inside out. Turn to Taking Care of Your Dog (beginning on page 353) to learn about the daily care that will keep your new companion happy and healthy for a long time to come.

Bringing home a dog is just the beginning of your adventures with your new canine companion.

Reference Guide to Dog Breeds

Once you have concluded that you are indeed ready to adopt a dog, the next step is to choose the kind of dog that is best suited to your living situation—city or country, apartment or house, family or individual. This section of the book will help you narrow your choices.

Presented in this reference guide are 166 breeds and breed mixes chosen from among the more than 500 breeds currently recognized by major kennel clubs and breed organizations. The dogs included here are those that are most widely available and that have proven over time to make the best pets. They are divided into eight groups: companion dogs, guardian dogs, herding dogs, northern breeds, scent hounds, sight hounds, sporting dogs, and terriers, with a sampling of mixes showcased at the end of each group. The dogs in each of the eight groups share, to varying degrees, a common ancestry and/or common geographic origins and were developed to do a certain job, such as hunt rabbits, herd sheep, or keep humans company. While every dog is an individual and in some ways defies categorization, knowing a dog's breed history does make it possible to predict some of its behavioral tendencies. For example, a briard will, by nature, herd and protect, and a Manchester terrier will chase rodents. With such information, you can develop appropriate and effective training methods for the dog of your choice. Determining the ancestry of a mixed-breed dog is, of course, a greater challenge than determining that of a purebred, though some information can be ascertained by examining the dog's physique, energy level, and preferred activities.

Evaluating a Mixed-Breed Dog

Mixed breeds—frequently referred to as "mongrels" or "mutts"—are the offspring of parents that are either mixed breeds or crossbreeds. (Crossbreeds are the offspring of purebred parents of different breeds, such as an Irish setter mother and a Labrador retriever father.) The mixed-breed entries presented here are intended to give you an overview of what, for example, you might expect of a terrier, shepherd, scent hound, or guardian mix in terms of appearance, behavior, temperament, and grooming and exercise requirements.

If you are looking at a mixed-breed dog and want to get a sense of her possible ancestry, first evaluate her physical type. Take note of the ear shape and placement, the shape and size of the skull, the type of feet, the depth of the chest, the length and shape of the tail, the texture and color pattern of the coat, and the overall body shape. Next evaluate her energy level and preferred activities. For example, observe whether the dog is extremely active, long on stamina, moderately active, low-key, or a couch potato. Does she seem to be a natural retriever, a happy herder, an ever-alert watchdog, or a cautious protector? Is she chasing everything that moves or keeping her nose glued to the ground in pursuit of scent? Keep in mind that the most common breeds in a particular area foster the most mixes. For example, a lot of pit bull and rottweiler mixes are found in urban areas, while herding and retriever mixes are more common in suburban and rural regions. Once you have completed this evaluation, read about the physical characteristics, temperament, and behavior in the introductions of the appropriate breed groups. The information these pages contain will provide clues about behavior patterns and temperament to watch for as you welcome a new mixed-breed dog into your home.

Above, left to right: An Airedale terrier mix, a bearded collie mix, and a golden retriever mix. Examining ear shape and placement, head shape, body type, coat, and tail can help you determine a mixed-breed dog's probable ancestry.

How to Use the Reference Guide to Dog Breeds

It is important to make a responsible decision when choosing a pet. Don't turn your selection into a beauty contest, picking one breed or mix solely on the basis of its appearance. Be honest with yourself about how much grooming, training, and exercise you really want to take on. If you are sedentary, don't choose a dog with strong working instincts and high energy, such as a Brittany spaniel. If you're looking for an easygoing pal for yourself and your kids, avoid a dog that constantly needs firm guidance, such as an Akita.

Before you look through the reference guide, review the guidelines presented beginning on page 15 of Section I, which will help you to narrow down your choices to those dogs best suited to your lifestyle. Then turn back to the reference guide and read carefully about the dogs you are considering. Learn about their behavior and personality, appearance and size, grooming and exercise needs, health, and ancestry.

When you are ready to search for your new canine companion, return to Section I (pages 32 to 79) once again for advice on finding reputable sources for dogs, assessing a dog's physical health and temperament, and preparing your home for a new dog's arrival.

If you provide a stable environment, sufficient exercise, and lots of affection, your dog can give you unbounded loyalty and companionship.

Breed Groups

Natural relationships among the many dog breeds are not always known, so any method of categorizing canines is to some degree artificial. Some organizations devoted to dog breeds include catch-all categories such as "nonsporting dogs." This reference guide organizes the breeds into more recognizable categories, mainly according to what they have been bred to do and following groups set by the United Kennel Club. The eight breed groups are introduced on the following pages.

Breed Group Introductions and Pictorial Charts

Each of the guide's eight breed groups begins with a brief introduction explaining what the dogs in that category have in common in terms of their ancestry, geographic origins, and physical and personality characteristics. Accompanying each introduction is a chart with pictorial symbols designating each dog's general size—small, medium, large, or giant—as well as symbols indicating breeds with unusually high energy levels indoors; breeds that have special exercise or grooming requirements; breeds that make particularly effective watchdogs; and breeds that are exceptionally good with children. All such extraordinary characteristics and potential problems are explained in the subsequent breed entries.

In centuries past, dalmatians were working dogs. These days they serve as family pets and are therefore grouped with other companion dogs.

Breed Entries

Each breed entry gives a brief overview of the breed, with a personality assessment, a physical description, grooming and exercise advice, a concise account of the breed's ancestry, and notes on problems with the breed or other considerations worth noting. Together, the photographs and text give a complete view of each breed's physical attributes, including overall body conformation, coat colors, and coat texture. For breeds that come in an array of colors and color combinations, a sampling is shown.

The entries outline the general tendencies of each breed. Individual dogs will inevitably display characteristics that differ from these standards. The personality of any individual dog depends not only on breed type but also on the personalities of his parents and how he was socialized as a puppy.

Each breed account is structured as follows:

Opening Paragraph
The first lines of each entry describe the general characteristics that are associated with a breed or mixture of breeds, how it responds to training, and how it gets along with people and other animals.

Appearance
A number of physical features distinguish each breed. The physical description will tell you about the breed's coat color, texture, and other features, and, when appropriate, body, ear, head, or tail shape.

Grooming and Exercise Needs
All dogs need regular grooming (one or two weekly brushings as well as periodic baths) and regular exercise (at least three walks per day). Particulars about a breed's grooming and exercise requirements, which may influence your decision on what breed of dog to choose, are noted.

Origins
Here you will find information about the breed's ancestry and the uses for which it was bred.

Special Alerts
A paragraph marked with the ☺ symbol provides information about any health concerns or potential problems associated with the breed. Many breeds are prone to a daunting number of hereditary ailments, but if you get your dog from a reputable breeder, he will have screened the parents carefully, before breeding, to avoid these illnesses. If applicable, the breed's suitability for inexperienced dog owners or for city life will also be noted here.

Margin Notes
In the colored strips along the edge of each breed entry you will find icons (pictorial symbols) that correspond to those on the breed group charts. The icons indicate only that there is a strong tendency for a particular characteristic within a breed and are not meant to be taken as absolute truths. You may find several symbols.

LARGE

At the top of the margin there is an icon representing the breed's general size, taking into account both average weight and overall dimension. Size categories (small, medium, large, and giant) are intended only as a general guide. More exact information about a breed's height and weight, as well as its average life span, is given at the bottom outer edge of the page.

HIGH ENERGY INDOORS This symbol designates a dog that is very energetic and that may be especially demanding of its owner's attention. These dogs, which are frequently small, are constantly on the move while indoors.

SPECIAL EXERCISE NEEDS Although all dogs need daily exercise—three walks a day is considered standard—some dogs have explosive energy levels and can develop behavioral problems if they are not allowed extraordinary amounts of exercise. Such dogs are frequently best suited for life in the country or suburbs.

SPECIAL GROOMING NEEDS Breeds assigned this icon have unusually exacting grooming needs, such as daily brushing by their owners and/or professional grooming every six to twelve weeks.

GOOD WATCHDOG This symbol appears for breeds that can be counted on to sound an alarm when an acquaintance or stranger—whether human or otherwise—approaches their territory.

GOOD WITH KIDS This icon is given to those breeds known to be particularly patient, gentle, and trustworthy with children. This is not to say that breeds missing this symbol are necessarily unsuitable

Breed Standards

Determining what constitutes a "good" specimen within a breed is, to some degree, a subjective process. Breed organizations may therefore differ in their standards. Each major kennel club—the American Kennel Club, the United Kennel Club, The Canadian Kennel Club, and The Kennel Club (Great Britain)—has its own roster of recognized breeds based on standards set by the national parent club of each breed. Some clubs, for instance, accept white German shepherds while others accept only black and tan ones, and the American Kennel Club only recently recognized the Jack Russell terrier, a very popular dog in North America, as a breed. Contact the club of your choice if you are interested in showing a dog and need to know the official standards.

From the smallest to the largest, every breed recognized by a kennel club or breed organization has a set of standards of appearance by which show dogs are judged.

companions for children or are unhappy around them. Nor should you assume that every individual in a breed famous for gentleness and patience is, in fact, gentle and patient. As always, parentage, socialization, and proper training are integral to any dog's temperament and behavior.

Size and Life Span
The breed's estimated height, weight, and life span are given at the bottom of the margin notes. The range of heights indicates the average size of a typical adult male, measured from the shoulder to the ground. A weight range is given indicating the average size of a typical adult male. Note that males tend to outweigh females by 10 to 20 percent. A range of the average number of years that you can expect a dog of each breed to live is also given here.

Mixed Breeds

Because of the enormous variety possible in mixed breeds, the mixed-breed accounts are not as specific as those for the purebreds. But some generalizations can be made for mixes within their groups. Each mixed-breed account includes a description of some of the likely physical, temperamental, and behavioral traits. A selection of photographs shows a variety of mixes within each group. Because mixed breeds vary so greatly, no size specifications or icons are assigned.

Coats and Clips for Showing

All show dogs—but especially those that have curly or long hair—are extensively groomed before being shown. Longhaired dogs, such as Afghan hounds, Yorkshire terriers, Shih Tzus, Malteses, and American cocker spaniels, are bathed and their coats are dried with hairdryers while being brushed. Their hair may be tied up until just before the show, so the coat will be clean and without tangles for the show ring. Some breeds, such as poodles, Bedlington terriers, and Portuguese water dogs, must be clipped according to certain standards before they can be shown. When these breeds are kept as family pets, they are usually groomed in a simpler pet clip, which is easier to maintain. Dogs less than one year old may be shown in what is known as a puppy clip.

In the breed's native Afghanistan, a long coat protected the Afghan hound from cold weather. In the show ring, the Afghan's luxuriant coat is all about style. It requires intensive grooming from a dedicated owner. Even if the dog is not being shown, the coat needs to be brushed every day.

Cropping and Docking

Some breeds have traditionally had their tails docked and/or their ears cropped for reasons of appearance while they are puppies, but this practice is becoming increasingly controversial. The ASPCA discourages unnecessary amputations of tails and ears. In most cases, there is no need to crop a dog's tail unless it has been damaged, in which case amputation may be necessary. The cropping of ears is also unnecessary; in fact, it is illegal in some countries.

Two pairs of Doberman pinschers, one set with cropped ears and one with natural, uncropped ears. Dogs' ears are cropped only for reasons of appearance.

Terminology

Dog fanciers have a specialized vocabulary to describe the physical characteristics of the different breeds, but in this book we have used general terms and photographs to describe the breed's basic body type; the texture and pattern of the coat; the formation of ear, foot, and tail; and the type of head. Learning to distinguish these physical characteristics can help you compare different breeds and discern clues to the ancestry of mixedbreed dogs. (For more information about ear shapes, see the caption on page 333; for head shapes, see page 324.)

This smooth fox terrier has a particolor coat, with distinct patches of two or more colors—in this case, black and white. The small spots are called ticking.

A red roan English cocker spaniel. Similar coats with a mixture of colored and white hairs are called "belton" in English setters.

Although the actual range of colors of dogs is not very extensive—dogs are generally black, white, cream, tan, red, brown, gray, or a combination of these colors—the variety of shades is enormous. Dog fanciers have developed a specialized vocabulary to describe the range of shades that are acceptable for each breed in competition. To add to the confusion, the same color can be known by different names. "Chocolate" and "liver" are both terms that are used to describe brown in different breeds; Labrador retrievers are "yellow," while golden retrievers are "golden."

Coat patterns also have their confusing terms. A fine mixture of colored hairs with white hairs is called "roan" in English springer spaniels, "belton" in English setters, and "grizzle" in Norwich terriers. "Pied" and "particolor" both mean coats with large patches of two or more colors. And "merle" and "dappled" both refer to mottled or variegated coat patterns, such as those sometimes seen in collies and Australian shepherds. "Brindle" means a combination of darker and lighter hairs that creates a tiger striping. Definitions for many unfamiliar terms are given in the glossary (page 494).

This blue merle smooth collie has a coat that is marbled or spotted with black and "blue" (gray) hairs, showing dark blotches against a lighter background. This coat pattern is frequently seen in Australian shepherds and Cardigan Welsh corgis.

This bullmastiff has a brindle coat consisting of dark hairs on a lighter background that form loose, dark striping. Brindle coats are also commonly seen on boxers, American Staffordshire terriers, and Boston terriers.

Companion Dogs

Although some companion breeds may have been bred for work, their primary role has long been lapdog and companion. Above: Yorkshire terrier.

Dogs in the companion group are intensely devoted to their human family and crave first and foremost their owner's attention; social isolation is the worst punishment they can endure. Most are diminutive, but a few are medium-size to large.

Certain early companion dogs were probably bred from species "dwarfs"—typically characterized by broad, rounded back skulls; thickened joints; long bodies; and squat legs. The Pekingese (one of the oldest breeds), Lhasa apso, Shih Tzu, Japanese Chin, and Tibetan spaniel retain such characteristics. Some breeds, on the other hand, are miniaturizations of larger breeds, with no evidence of dwarfism. Examples include the French bulldog and the toy poodle.

Among the most ancient companion breeds, bichons—including the Maltese, bichon frise, Havanese, Bolognese, and Coton de Tulear—were brought to the Mediterranean region 2,000 years ago by the Phoenicians. They all have a silhouette that is longer than it is tall, a tail that curls over the back, and a sweet social temperament—traits inherited from their common ancestors.

Toy-size terriers are represented in the category by silky, Boston, and Yorkshire terriers; Brussels griffons; miniature pinschers; and affenpinschers. Most of these pint-size watchdogs are quick to sound an alarm and quite willing to challenge larger dogs over territory. They are also playful, active, humorous dogs—and a training challenge because of their self-possessed stubbornness.

Brains and beauty can be found in a more manageable package in the English toy spaniel, King Charles spaniel, and papillon. These easygoing, cooperative dogs excel in obedience and agility—especially the papillon.

The country of origin for both the Chihuahua and Chinese crested may be in dispute, but their roles as bedwarmers and close confidants are not.

Several larger breeds fall into the companion-dog category: the Tibetan terrier (once used for herding), the firehouse dalmatian, and the water-retrieving standard poodle. These household companions have higher energy levels and are much more demanding than their smaller group mates.

Japanese Chin

Lhasa apso

Pekingese

Pug

Companion Dogs		HIGH ENERGY INDOORS	SPECIAL EXERCISE NEEDS	SPECIAL GROOMING NEEDS	GOOD WATCHDOG	GOOD WITH KIDS
JAPANESE CHIN *page 94*	SMALL					
LHASA APSO *page 95*	SMALL			●	●	
PEKINGESE *page 96*	SMALL			●	●	
PUG *page 97*	SMALL					●
SHIH TZU *page 98*	SMALL			●		●
TIBETAN SPANIEL *page 99*	SMALL				●	●
TIBETAN TERRIER *page 100*	MEDIUM			●	●	●

Shih Tzu

Tibetan spaniel

Tibetan terrier

Bichon frise

Bolognese

Coton de Tulear

Havanese

Maltese

Companion Dogs		HIGH ENERGY INDOORS	SPECIAL EXERCISE NEEDS	SPECIAL GROOMING NEEDS	GOOD WATCHDOG	GOOD WITH KIDS
BICHON FRISE *page 101*	SMALL			●		●
BOLOGNESE *page 102*	SMALL			●		●
COTON DE TULEAR *page 103*	SMALL			●		●
HAVANESE *page 104*	SMALL			●		
MALTESE *page 105*	SMALL	●		●	●	
CAVALIER KING CHARLES SPANIEL *page 106*	SMALL					●
ENGLISH TOY SPANIEL *page 107*	SMALL					
PAPILLON *page 108*	SMALL					●
AFFENPINSCHER *page 109*	SMALL				●	
BRUSSELS GRIFFON *page 110*	SMALL				●	

Cavalier King Charles spaniel

English toy spaniel

Papillon

Affenpinscher

Brussels griffon

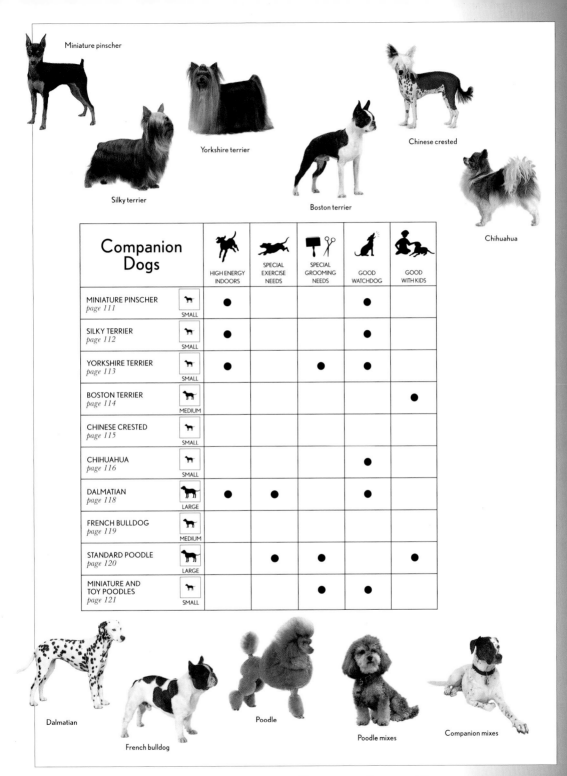

Miniature pinscher

Yorkshire terrier

Silky terrier

Boston terrier

Chinese crested

Chihuahua

Companion Dogs		HIGH ENERGY INDOORS	SPECIAL EXERCISE NEEDS	SPECIAL GROOMING NEEDS	GOOD WATCHDOG	GOOD WITH KIDS
MINIATURE PINSCHER *page 111*	SMALL	●			●	
SILKY TERRIER *page 112*	SMALL	●			●	
YORKSHIRE TERRIER *page 113*	SMALL	●		●	●	
BOSTON TERRIER *page 114*	MEDIUM					●
CHINESE CRESTED *page 115*	SMALL					
CHIHUAHUA *page 116*	SMALL				●	
DALMATIAN *page 118*	LARGE	●	●		●	
FRENCH BULLDOG *page 119*	MEDIUM					
STANDARD POODLE *page 120*	LARGE		●	●		●
MINIATURE AND TOY POODLES *page 121*	SMALL			●	●	

Dalmatian

French bulldog

Poodle

Poodle mixes

Companion mixes

SMALL

Japanese Chin
(or Japanese Spaniel)

Japanese Chins are intelligent, sociable, responsive dogs that need very little obedience training. They get along well with people and other animals and are fine with children over eight years old, provided the children are reasonably gentle. These dogs do well in the city, suburbs, or country. They have catlike tendencies in that they use their paws to scoop food and clean their faces, and will climb into cozy places for naps.

Appearance The Japanese Chin's profuse coat is long, soft, straight, and silky, with a thick mane, or ruff, on the neck and abundant "feathering" on the thighs and tail. Coat color is black and white or red and white. The head is round and broad with large, dark, wide-set eyes.

Red and white Japanese Chin

Grooming & Exercise Needs Surprisingly, the Japanese Chin needs to be brushed and combed just twice a week. This dog considers jumping up on people's laps a vigorous workout.

Origins The Japanese Chin is thought to have originated in China, where it was kept only by royalty. Likenesses have been found in Chinese temple paintings and on ancient pottery and embroidery. Introduced to Japan around A.D. 700, it became a favorite of Japanese royalty. In Japanese, the word *chin* means "royalty."

(!) Breed-related health concerns include undescended testicles.

HEIGHT 9"

WEIGHT 4–11 LBS.

LIFE SPAN 12–14 YRS.

Black and white Japanese Chin

Lhasa Apso

Most Lhasa apsos are even-tempered and friendly but not demonstrative. They are wary of strangers at first meeting but usually warm up before too long. Some Lhasas can be nippy with children. Early obedience training and socialization with children, adults, and other animals are important. When praised and treated gently, they do very well in obedience training.

SPECIAL GROOMING NEEDS

GOOD WATCHDOG

Appearance The coat is long, heavy, straight, hard, and dense (not woolly or silky). Coat color is sandy, honey, slate, smoke, dark grizzle, black, white, brown, or particolor.

Lhasa apso with a show coat

Grooming & Exercise Needs
Lhasas need to be brushed and combed daily to avoid matting. The coat can also be clipped shorter for easier grooming. They need two to three short walks daily.

Origins Small, shaggy dogs were known in Tibet as early as 800 B.C., and the dog we recognize today as the Lhasa apso has been known there since the 7th century A.D. The little "lion dogs" that barked at intruders became important watchdogs in Buddhist temples and monasteries.

(!) The Lhasa apso is unsuitable for inexperienced dog owners. Breed-related health concerns: entropion (page 434), progressive retinal atrophy (page 435), congenital kidney problems, atopy (page 437), intervertebral disc protrusion (page 456), patellar luxation (page 443).

Young particolor Lhasas with older friend

HEIGHT 10-11"

WEIGHT 14-15 LBS.

LIFE SPAN 12-14 YRS.

Pekingese

SMALL

SPECIAL GROOMING NEEDS

GOOD WATCHDOG

Some Pekes are stubborn and independent, making obedience training a challenge. They are cautious of strangers and are not fond of children under about ten years old. While they can be aloof or aggressive with other dogs, they are usually good with cats. They can be alarm barkers, alerting the household when visitors arrive. Pekingese are well suited for apartment life, especially with an adult household.

Appearance The outercoat is long, straight, and coarse, yet soft; the undercoat is thick. Feathering on the thighs, legs, tail, and toes is long and bushy, around the neck is a lion-like mane. The coat may be red, fawn, black, black and tan, sable, brindle, white, or parti-color. The Peke has a distinctive black mask and a short, broad, wrinkled muzzle.

Grooming & Exercise Needs The Peke needs to be brushed and combed daily. Rather than exercise, this short, bowlegged dog likes to lounge on laps.

Pekes are playful and very loyal.

Origins Known as the Lion Dog of China, the Pekingese is thought to be an ancient breed—for centuries a favorite of the Chinese Imperial Court. In 18th-century China, stealing a Peke was punishable by death.

⚠ Breed-related health concerns: umbilical hernias (page 441), eye problems, patellar luxation (page 443), undescended testicles, intervertebral disc protrusion (page 456), deformities of the nose and mouth that can interfere with breathing.

HEIGHT 8-9"

WEIGHT 8-14 LBS.

LIFE SPAN 13-15 YRS.

Pug

Pugs are playful, outgoing, loving, and very responsive to their families. They learn quickly and can do well in obedience classes. Most get along well with children and strangers and are friendly with other animals. Pugs are a good choice for city families with children.

Appearance The pug's coat is fine, smooth, soft, short, and glossy. Coat color is silver, apricot-fawn, or black with a black mask and small, velvety black ears. Large, dark eyes are promi-nent on the short, blunt, wrinkled muzzle. The body is square and stocky, the tail tightly curled and twisted.

Silver pug

Grooming & Exercise Needs Pugs need only a quick brushing once a week, though their head wrinkles need frequent cleaning with cotton balls moistened with water. A leisurely walk around the block suits pugs fine.

Apricot-fawn pug

Origins This delight-ful breed originated in ancient China, where it served as a loyal companion to royalty.

(!) It is especially important to obtain a pug from a reputable breeder. Breed-related health concerns: deformities of the nose and mouth that can interfere with breathing, Legg-Perthes disease (page 443), patellar luxation (page 443), Demodex mange (page 440), eye and eyelid problems, susceptibility to heatstroke, bladder stones (page 453), urethral obstruction (page 454).

HEIGHT 10–11"

WEIGHT 14–18 LBS.

LIFE SPAN 12–14 YRS.

Shih Tzu

SMALL

SPECIAL GROOMING NEEDS

GOOD WITH KIDS

Shih Tzus are outgoing, happy, and affectionate companions that respond well to gentle obedience training. They love children, and get along with other animals and strangers. These small lapdogs are well suited to apartment living.

Appearance The luxurious double coat is long, dense, and flowing, sometimes with a slight wave. Hair on top of the head is customarily tied up not only to enable the dog to see and to prevent eye infections, but also to be fashionable. All colors and markings are seen; the most common are black and white, gray and white, and tan and white. The heavily coated ears hang down, and the densely plumed tail curves well over the back.

Shih Tzu in show coat

Grooming & Exercise Needs This breed must be brushed and combed daily to avoid severe matting. Most Shih Tzus are satisfied with a daily walk around the block and an occasional romp.

Origins Over the centuries, depictions of this breed have appeared on Chinese carvings, embroideries, and other art objects. They were valued companions in Imperial China.

(!) It is especially important to obtain a Shih Tzu from a reputable breeder. Breed-related health concerns: congenital kidney problems, eye problems, hypertrophic pyloric gastropathy (a thickening of the junction of stomach and small intestine resulting in obstruction and vomiting), von Willebrand's disease (common disorder that causes excessive bleeding during or after surgery), atopy (page 437).

HEIGHT 8–11"

WEIGHT 9–16 LBS.

LIFE SPAN 12–14 YRS.

Three-month-old Shih Tzu puppies

Tibetan Spaniel

SMALL

Tibetan spaniels are friendly, low-maintenance dogs well suited to life in the city, suburbs, or country. Eager to please, they do well in obedience training. They love to play with gentle children and get along very well with other animals. They may be cautious with strangers and will sound the bark alarm when someone comes to the door.

Tibetan spaniels have a distinctive plumed tail.

GOOD WATCHDOG

GOOD WITH KIDS

Appearance The outer-coat is silky in texture; the undercoat is dense and soft. The neck is covered with a mane or "shawl" of longer hair. The coat color is fawn, cream, white, black, black and tan, or red. The tail is richly plumed and carried in a curl over the back.

An eager-to-please Tibetan spaniel

Grooming & Exercise Needs Tibetan spaniels need to be brushed every other day. They are content with a brisk daily walk around the block and some indoor playtime before curling up in their owners' laps.

Origins The Tibetan spaniel is not a spaniel—it is probably related to the Pekingese, pug, and Japanese Chin—but seems to have originated, perhaps as early as 200 B.C., in Tibet, where it sat on the outer walls of Buddhist monasteries barking out warnings when strangers approached.

(!) Breed-related health concerns include progressive retinal atrophy (page 435).

HEIGHT 9-11"

WEIGHT 9-15 LBS.

LIFE SPAN 12-15 YRS.

Tibetan Terrier

MEDIUM

SPECIAL GROOMING NEEDS

GOOD WATCHDOG

GOOD WITH KIDS

Tan and white Tibetan terrier

Tibetan terriers are good-natured, playful, curious companions suitable for city, suburban, or country living. Very responsive to obedience training, they enjoy the company of gentle children about eight years or older, and get along with most other animals. They may be wary of strangers and have the solid bark their ancestors used when guarding Tibetan monasteries.

Appearance The coat of the Tibetan terrier is fine and long, almost touching the ground. The outercoat is thick and fine, but never silky or woolly, and may be wavy or straight; the undercoat is soft and woolly. There is often a natural part over the neck and back. The well-furred tail falls forward over the back. There is abundant hair on the head. Coats can be any solid color or solid and white.

Grooming & Exercise Needs Tibetan terriers need to be brushed and combed daily. They need several brisk walks each day.

Origins The Tibetan terrier originated nearly 2,000 years ago in the rugged mountains of Tibet, where it was kept by Buddhist monks for companionship and luck. It was also given by the monks as a gift of good luck to visitors. The Tibetan terrier is not a terrier at all, but is believed to be a relative of the Lhasa apso.

Black and white Tibetan terrier

HEIGHT 14 –17"

WEIGHT 18–30 LBS.

LIFE SPAN 12–15 YRS.

(!) Breed-related health concerns: hypothyroidism (page 452), progressive retinal atrophy (page 435).

Bichon Frise

SMALL

SPECIAL GROOMING NEEDS

GOOD WITH KIDS

The bichon frise is gentle, playful, and affectionate and gets along with children and other animals. It loves to please and so is an outstanding obedience-class student, though sometimes it has difficulty with house training. This is an ideal dog for the city or suburbs, for the young or elderly.

Appearance The undercoat is soft and dense, the outercoat coarser and curlier. The combination of the two feels like plush or velvet and springs back when patted. Coat color is white, possibly with shades of buff, cream, or apricot on the ears.

White bichon frise

Grooming & Exercise Needs The bichon frise requires extensive daily brushing to avoid an unkempt, matted appearance. Professional grooming every eight to twelve weeks is recommended. The bichon frise requires only a few leisurely walks around the block and some playtime daily.

Origins The bichon frise originated in the Mediterranean area in the Middle Ages, but its ancestry is not known. A favorite of European royalty, it was bred to be an ideal companion.

(!) It is especially important to obtain a bichon frise from a reputable breeder. Breed-related health concerns: patellar luxation (page 443), epilepsy (page 455), dental problems.

Eight-week-old bichon frise puppy with cream ears

HEIGHT 9–12"

WEIGHT 10–14 LBS.

LIFE SPAN 12–15 YRS.

Bolognese

SMALL

SPECIAL GROOMING NEEDS

GOOD WITH KIDS

The Bolognese is a gentle, sensitive, affectionate dog that is ideal for the city or suburbs, the young or elderly. Eager to please and a quick study, it does very well in obedience classes. The Bolognese enjoys playing with gentle children and gets along well with other animals.

Appearance The long, cottony coat falls in tufts without lying flat against the body, giving a slightly clumpier appearance than the bichon frise. The tufts cover the entire head, body, tail, and limbs. Coat color is white.

Bolognese have long, cottony white coats.

Grooming & Exercise Needs The Bolognese requires daily brushing to avoid an unkempt, matted appearance. It also needs a few long walks and some playtime daily.

Origins The Bolognese traces its ancestry back to the 13th century. It was a favorite of the wealthy and elite of Renaissance Italy.

(!) The Bolognese does not take well to being left alone for long periods of time, and so is not suitable for households that spend the entire workday outside of the home.

Bolognese require daily brushing.

HEIGHT 10–12"

WEIGHT 5–9 LBS.

LIFE SPAN 14–15 YRS.

Coton de Tulear

The Coton de Tulear gets along with everybody, including children, strangers, and other animals. Gentle, affectionate, cheerful, and intelligent, this breed does well in obedience classes and can adapt to city, suburban, or rural living.

Appearance The fine, slightly wavy, fluffy coat is about three inches long and has a cottony texture. Coat color is white overall, white body with champagne head, or black and white.

Grooming & Exercise Needs The Coton de Tulear needs to be brushed and taken on long walks daily.

White Coton de Tulear with champagne head

Origins European merchants probably introduced bichon-type companion dogs to the island of Madagascar, in the Indian Ocean off the African coast, in the 16th century. The interbreeding of these dogs resulted in the Coton de Tulear. *Coton* is French for "cotton," and Tulear is the name of the Madagascan port where the Europeans landed. Only royalty and the Madagascan upper classes were allowed to own Cotons.

Coton de Tulears are known for their wavy, fluffy coats.

HEIGHT 10–12"

WEIGHT 12–15 LBS.

LIFE SPAN 12–14 YRS.

Havanese

SMALL

SPECIAL GROOMING NEEDS

A happy and sweet dog, the Havanese learns quickly and does very well in obedience classes. It enjoys playing with gentle children, is friendly with other animals, and is usually interested in strangers. This dog is a good choice for a family or an adult household in the city or suburbs.

Color diversity is a trait of the Havanese.

Appearance It may take two to four years for the Havanese's soft, thick double coat to reach its full length—six to seven inches—and thickness. The hair on the forehead may form a curtain in front of the eyes and so is often held away from the face with a rubber band. The tail is covered with long, silky hair that blends with the rest of the coat when the dog is at rest. All colors and combinations are seen. In fact, great color diversity is a distinguishing characteristic of this breed.

Grooming & Exercise Needs The Havanese needs to be brushed daily to prevent matting. It also requires slow-paced daily walks and playtime.

Origins The Havanese originated in the 18th century. More than likely its ancestors were such small companion dogs as the Bolognese or the Maltese, which developed in the Middle Ages around major port cities of the Spanish Empire. The most common bichon-type dog in Cuba, the Havanese is also called bichon Havanais, bichon Habañero, and Havana silk dog.

⚠ Breed-related health concerns: cataracts (page 434), patellar luxation (page 443).

HEIGHT 8–11"

WEIGHT 7–14 LBS.

LIFE SPAN 14–15 YRS.

Unlike Maltese, Havanese are shown in an untrimmed coat.

Maltese

SMALL

HIGH ENERGY INDOORS

SPECIAL GROOMING NEEDS

GOOD WATCHDOG

The Maltese is a gentle, playful, affectionate dog that loves to be the center of attention. It is very receptive to gentle training based on positive reinforcement. Early socialization with people outside the family and with other dogs helps counteract a tendency to be nippy with strangers and to take on larger dogs. The Maltese will tolerate gentle children over about eight years old and is friendly with cats. This is an ideal dog for city or apartment dwellers because of its diminutive size and minimal exercise needs.

The hair on a Maltese's head is frequently tied away from its eyes.

Appearance The Maltese's coat is long and silky. The hair on its head may be tied or left hanging. Coat color is pure white, sometimes with light tan or lemon on the ears.

The long, silky Maltese show coat

Grooming & Exercise Needs The Maltese needs to be brushed and combed daily. It is highly energetic indoors but requires only short daily walks outside.

Origins As its name suggests, this breed originated on the island of Malta. It was a favorite home companion of the upper classes of ancient Egypt, Greece, and Rome. More recently, in Victorian times, women matched the color of the satin ribbon they tied around the Maltese's topknot with their own wardrobe.

(!) Breed-related health concerns: hypoglycemia (page 452), patellar luxation (page 443), deafness (page 436), undescended testicles, dental disease.

HEIGHT 5-8"

WEIGHT 6-8 LBS.

LIFE SPAN 12-15 YRS.

Cavalier King Charles Spaniel

SMALL

GOOD WITH KIDS

Cavaliers are gentle, sweet, sporty spaniels that get along with everyone, including children, although they must be treated gently. They demand to be included in all family activities and show their appreciation with abundant kisses. Cavaliers do well in obedience classes and love praise.

Two Blenheim (chestnut and white) Cavalier King Charles spaniels

Appearance The Cavalier's coat is moderately long, slightly wavy, soft, and silky. Color may be rich chestnut on a pearly white background; jet-black on a pearly white background with tan markings; jet-black with tan markings; or solid red.

Grooming & Exercise Needs Cavaliers need to be combed and brushed weekly. Happy just sleeping on their owners' laps, they also enjoy activities reminiscent of their hunting days—walks in the woods to "point" birds or squirrels, or romps in the backyard with a ball.

Origins The Cavalier King Charles is descended from the English toy spaniel. The Cavalier King Charles, named for Charles II, was a popular 17th-century ladies' lap companion. It was also used for hunting rabbits and other small game.

(!) Breed-related health concerns: patellar luxation (page 443), heart problems, fly catching (a disorder of the nervous system that causes the dog to bite at the air—as if for flies), epilepsy (page 455).

HEIGHT 12-13"

WEIGHT 10-18 LBS.

LIFE SPAN 9-14 YRS.

Black and tan
Cavalier King Charles

English Toy Spaniel

The English toy spaniel is delightfully affectionate with everyone, including gentle children and other animals. Obedience training usually goes well as long as there is positive reinforcement and praise. Many toys can be yappy, mistrustful, and nippy, but not the English toy spaniel. It is an ideal dog for city living.

Blenheim (chestnut and white)
English toy spaniel

Appearance The long, silky coat can be straight or wavy. There are four varieties of the breed based on coat colors: the Blenheim (white with chestnut patches), the Prince Charles (white, tan, and black), the King Charles (rich, glossy black and bright mahogany), and the ruby (rich mahogany red). In all varieties the short, upturned nose is pink at birth but turns jet-black as the dog matures.

Grooming & Exercise Needs The English toy spaniel's coat needs to be brushed twice a week. This dog is content to take short walks. It also enjoys chasing and retrieving balls.

Origins A favorite lapdog of British royalty and aristocracy since the 17th century, this tiny dog was never developed as a hunting dog as so many spaniels were.

(!) Breed-related health concerns: patellar luxation (page 443), susceptibility to umbilical hernia (page 441), cataracts (page 434), heart defects.

Ruby English toy spaniel

HEIGHT 9–11"

WEIGHT 8–14 LBS.

LIFE SPAN 12–14 YRS.

Papillon

SMALL

GOOD WITH KIDS

Papillons are friendly and gentle. They do very well in obedience school and love other animals and children, provided they are socialized with them early. Papillons are ideal for apartment dwellers and for people with sedentary lives.

Appearance The papillon's abundant, flowing coat is long, fine, silky, and straight. It is predominantly white with patches of any other color, most commonly black, tan, or chestnut red. The distinctive butterfly-like ears—*papillon* is French for "butterfly"—are well fringed, the insides covered with silken hair of medium length.

Papillons have distinctive butterfly-shaped ears.

Grooming & Exercise Needs Papillons need to be brushed and combed two to three times a week and trimmed every three months. They do not require a lot of exercise, although they enjoy long, brisk walks.

Origins The papillon was developed in the 17th century as a companion dog for European royalty. Both Marie Antoinette and Madame de Pompadour owned papillons. These elegant little dogs appear in Italian frescoes and in paintings by Rubens, Rembrandt, Fragonard, and Titian.

(!) Breed-related health concerns: patellar luxation (page 443), deafness (page 436).

HEIGHT 8-11"

WEIGHT 8-10 LBS.

LIFE SPAN 12-15 YRS.

Papillons with dropped ears are called phalenes.

Affenpinscher

SMALL

GOOD WATCHDOG

Loyal family members, affenpinschers get along with children if treated gently, but can be difficult to train. They also do well with other animals if socialized with them early. Affenpinschers are determined and fearless. They are cautious of strangers—and sometimes snappy with them. They are often good watchdogs.

Black and tan affenpinscher

Appearance The affenpinscher's stiff, wiry coat is short and dense on the body; longer and shaggier on the face, legs, and chest. Its color is black, gray, red, silver, or black and tan.

Grooming & Exercise Needs The affenpinscher is a low-maintenance breed. It requires only a few daily walks around the block, a quick brushing every week, and, every few months, a little trimming.

Origins The affenpinscher appeared in 17th-century Europe as a hunter of rodents. Its origins are not known, but its name—which translates as "monkey terrier"—suggests a German connection. It resembles and is probably related to the Brussels griffon, which also has a no-nonsense personality.

! Breed-related health concerns: patent ductus arteriosus (page 449), Legg-Perthes disease (page 443).

Black affenpinscher

HEIGHT 9-11½"

WEIGHT 7-10 LBS.

LIFE SPAN 14-16 YRS.

Brussels Griffon

SMALL

GOOD WATCHDOG

The Brussels griffon is outgoing, intelligent, affectionate, and spunky. It can be a challenge to train and so should be enrolled in obedience classes at an early age, especially since some Brussels bark excessively. Some of these little dogs are friendly with strangers; others are timid. Early contact with humans and other animals is encouraged for proper socialization.

Rough-coated Brussels griffons

Appearance The coat of the Brussels griffon may be rough or smooth. The rough coat is wiry and dense; the smooth coat is straight, short, tight, and glossy. Coat color can be reddish brown with a little black at the whiskers and the chin, black mixed with reddish brown, black and tan, black with reddish brown markings, solid reddish brown, or solid black.

Grooming & Exercise Needs The Brussels griffon should be combed and brushed a few times a week and trimmed about four times a year. While this dog enjoys a good romp, vigorous daily exercise is not mandatory for its health and happiness. It is satisfied with leisurely walks and the chance to lie by its owner's side.

Origins This breed, which originated in Brussels in the 19th century, is probably the descendant of the back-alley "rat dog" of the time, which provided help with rodent infestation problems. The Brussels griffon of today resulted from crossings with other breeds, such as the pug, affenpinscher, and ruby spaniel.

HEIGHT 8-10"

WEIGHT 8-12 LBS.

LIFE SPAN 12-14 YRS.

Smooth-coated
Brussels griffon

Miniature Pinscher

The miniature pinscher, or "minpin," is a spirited, sometimes stubborn dog that needs an experienced owner-handler. It does well in obedience training if started early, especially important because of its tendency to bark excessively. Some minpins get along with children, but others can be nasty. They can also be suspicious of strangers and aggressive with other dogs.

Appearance The minpin's coat is smooth, short, straight, and lustrous. Coat color is red, stag red, black with sharply defined rust-red markings, or chocolate with red-rust markings. The minpin has a distinctive gait—a high-stepping, forward-reaching, free and easy prance.

HIGH ENERGY INDOORS

GOOD WATCHDOG

Black and tan miniature pinscher with cropped ears

Grooming & Exercise Needs Miniature pinschers need only a quick weekly brushing. They have a great deal of energy and need several short vigorous walks a day to relax them.

Origins The miniature pinscher originated in 18th-century Germany, where it was used to control rats. Today this bold little dog, reminiscent of a miniature Doberman, is kept strictly as a companion.

(!) The miniature pinscher is not suitable for inexperienced dog owners. Breed-related health concerns: Legg-Perthes disease (page 443), skin problems, progressive retinal atrophy (page 435).

Red miniature pinschers with natural (uncropped) ears

HEIGHT 10-12"

WEIGHT 8-10 LBS.

LIFE SPAN 13-14 YRS.

Silky Terrier

Silkies are intelligent, energetic, curious, and perpetually in motion. They do well in obedience training as long as their owners are able to maintain dominance. Some silkies are friendly with strangers, others are reserved. They may be nippy with other dogs and with people who handle their possessions. Because they like to chase cats and other small animals, silkies should be allowed to run off-leash only in secured areas. Their bark serves as a good alarm but can become a nuisance if not kept under control.

Silky terriers have long, glossy coats.

Appearance The silky's straight, glossy coat is five to six inches long, and is parted from the head to the base of the tail. Coat color is blue and tan with a prominent topknot that may be silver or fawn.

Grooming & Exercise Needs The silky needs to be brushed and combed two to three times a week and trimmed every three months. A few brisk walks each day as well as a play period are necessary to satisfy this dog.

Origins The silky terrier originated in the 19th century in Australia, the result of a cross between the Australian terrier and the Yorkshire terrier.

ⓘ Breed-related health concerns: storage disease (a fatal nervous system disorder), yeast dermatitis (a skin infection), elbow dysplasia (page 442), tracheal collapse (page 448), patellar luxation (page 443), Legg-Perthes disease (page 443).

HEIGHT 9-10"

WEIGHT 8-10 LBS.

Silky with a silver topknot

LIFE SPAN 14-16 YRS.

Yorkshire Terrier

SMALL

HIGH ENERGY INDOORS

SPECIAL GROOMING NEEDS

GOOD WATCHDOG

Yorkshire terriers are energetic, assertive, demanding toy dogs with large-dog attitudes. They are responsive obedience students but want to rule at home, and even larger dogs will defer to them. In general, they get along with other animals. They are fine with gentle children over about eight years old, especially if socialized with them at an early age. Yorkies bark to announce the arrival of strangers but are usually friendly.

A Yorkshire terrier with a show coat

Appearance The coat is glossy, fine, silky, straight, and long. The long hair on the head is either parted or tied up with bows. The hair on the muzzle is very long. Coat color is steel blue and golden; puppies are born black and tan.

Grooming & Exercise Needs Yorkies need to be brushed and combed every day. Because they burn up lots of energy dashing around the house, a walk around the block a few times a day is sufficient.

Origins The Yorkshire terrier originated in 19th-century England where it was used for ratting.

! It is especially important to obtain a Yorkshire terrier from a reputable breeder. Breed-related health concerns: hypoglycemia (page 452), patellar luxation (page 443), Legg-Perthes disease (page 443), portocaval shunt (a congenital condition resulting in liver failure, seizures, and possibly death), dental problems, hair loss.

Eight-week-old Yorkie puppies

HEIGHT 7–9"

WEIGHT 3–7 LBS.

LIFE SPAN 12–14 YRS.

Boston Terrier

MEDIUM

GOOD WITH KIDS

The Boston terrier is known as the "Little American gentleman" because of its classic tuxedo attire and its sweet, lovable, happy, and outgoing personality. These dogs are easy to train and love everybody, including children and other animals. Often happy to simply lie by its owner's side with a chew toy, the Boston can adapt to city, suburban, or country life.

Appearance The Boston terrier's coat is short, smooth, bright, and fine. Coat color is brindle, seal, or black, all with white markings on the muzzle between the eyes and on the forechest.

Brindle Boston terrier

Grooming & Exercise Needs
The Boston terrier sheds minimally and requires only occasional brushing and bathing. This dog's exercise needs are minimal; short walks will suffice.

Origins Developed in the 19th century by crossing an English bulldog with a white English terrier, the Boston terrier was the first American-bred dog.

(!) It is especially important to get a Boston terrier from a reputable breeder. Breed-related health concerns: deafness (page 436), heart defects, cataracts (page 434), patellar luxation (page 443), Demodex mange (page 440), breathing problems, susceptibility to heatstroke, Cushing's syndrome (page 451).

HEIGHT 15-17"

WEIGHT 10-25 LBS.

Litter of five-week-old
Boston terrier puppies

LIFE SPAN 12-15 YRS.

Chinese Crested

SMALL

This elegant, graceful dog is friendly to everyone—especially if socialized early with people and other animals—and does well in obedience training. The Chinese crested is more comfortable with gentle children over five years old than with younger children. This is a fine dog for first-time dog owners and for city and apartment dwellers.

Hairless and powder puff Chinese cresteds

Appearance The hairless variety has hair on the head (crest), tail (called a plume), and on the feet from the toes to the "wrists" on the front legs and up to the "ankles" on the hindlegs (called socks). The coat texture is soft and silky. The powder puff variety is completely covered with a double coat, which consists of a soft undercoat and coarser guard hairs. The Chinese crested is seen in all colors. The powder puffs are often particolor (white with patches of gray, tan, or black). The hairless usually have gray skin with pink patches; the fringe can be a variety of colors.

Grooming & Exercise Needs The hairless Chinese crested needs only some minor combing on the crest, plume, and socks. The powder puff should be combed and brushed a few times a week. This breed appreciates a few leisurely walks daily and expects to play with its owner indoors.

Origins The Chinese crested, which probably dates back about 3,000 years, may not have originated in China but may have been brought to Asia by traders from Africa.

Hairless Chinese crested

(!) Breed-related health concerns: sunburn (the hairless) and dental problems (page 444).

HEIGHT 11–13"

WEIGHT 5–10 LBS.

LIFE SPAN 12–15 YRS.

Chihuahua

SMALL

GOOD WATCHDOG

Longhaired Chihuahuas in three different colors

HEIGHT 6-9"   Longhaired Chihuahua

WEIGHT 2-6 LBS.

LIFE SPAN 12-15 YRS.

The Chihuahua is the smallest of all dog breeds. Because of their tiny size and sensitive nature, Chihuahuas are usually not a good choice for households with small children. They are, on the other hand, ideal companions for apartment dwellers and elderly people. As long as Chihuahuas are obedience-trained and socialized early with adults, children, and other animals, they make playful, confident companions.

Smooth-coated Chihuahua

Appearance The Chihuahua's coat may be smooth with soft, close-lying hair or long and soft with fringe on the ears and feathering on the tail. All coat colors are seen. The most common are red, fawn, and black and tan. The "apple-domed" head and large ears are this breed's most recognizable features.

Grooming & Exercise Needs The Chihuahua requires only occasional brushing and is satisfied with short walks.

Origins The Chihuahua may have developed in the 9th century from the Techichi, a toy breed of the Toltec Indians of Central America. Or it may have been brought to Central America by the Chinese or Spanish.

(!) Breed-related health concerns: patellar luxation (page 443), heart problems.

Smooth-coated Chihuahua puppies

Dalmatian

LARGE

HIGH ENERGY INDOORS

SPECIAL EXERCISE NEEDS

GOOD WATCHDOG

Dalmatians are loving with their families, but because they can be very stubborn, they must be socialized and begin obedience classes early. Most dalmatians are aloof and wary of and/or territorial with strangers. They get along with other dogs and most other small animals, though birds and squirrels may look like dinner to them, so they must always be walked on a leash and exercised in a secured area. Dalmatians have a lot of energy and do best in the suburbs or country, where they have room to run around.

Black and white dalmatian

Appearance The dalmatian's coat is short, dense, fine, sleek, glossy, and close-lying. Coat color is pure white with black or liver spots.

Grooming & Exercise Needs Dalmatians shed constantly and so should be brushed daily. They need vigorous exercise and extensive training to avoid serious behavior problems.

Origins Brought to England during the Crusades from the Arabic coastal area of Dalmatia, the dalmatian is thought to have a hunting pointer in its background, but British sportsmen discovered it was better at guarding its owner's horses, carriages, and coach inhabitants than hunting. It is best known for its work as a firehouse dog.

(!) It is especially important to obtain a dalmatian from a reputable breeder as many are poorly bred individuals. Dalmatians are not suitable for inexperienced owners. Breed-related health concerns: deafness (page 436), bladder stones (page 453), allergies.

HEIGHT 19-24"

WEIGHT 45-65 LBS.

LIFE SPAN 10-12 YRS.

Black and white dalmatian puppy

French Bulldog

MEDIUM

French bulldogs are very intelligent and eager to please, although some can be stubborn. Still, most do well in obedience training. They are ideal for apartment dwellers and elderly people. These sweet-tempered dogs will tolerate most strangers, enjoy the company of gentle children, and like other animals. But actually they prefer the company of a single person—one who showers them with attention and love.

Brindle French bulldog

Appearance The French bulldog's short, smooth coat may be brindle, brindle and white, fawn, cream, or solid white. The skin is soft and loose, forming wrinkles at the head and shoulders. The body is compact and muscular, and the batlike ears sit high on the large, square head. The nose is extremely short and heavily wrinkled.

Brindle pied French bulldog

Grooming & Exercise Needs The French bulldog needs only a quick weekly brushing and combing. The ears and the skin between the facial wrinkles need to be cleaned two to three times a week. A walk around the block is considered a big workout for the French bulldog.

Origins The French bulldog was developed in the 19th century when the French crossed the miniature English bulldog with several French breeds, possibly terriers.

⚠ Breed-related health concerns: breathing problems, atopy (page 437), susceptibility to heatstroke, cancer (page 430).

HEIGHT 10–12"

WEIGHT 18–28 LBS.

LIFE SPAN 10–12 YRS.

Poodle

SPECIAL EXERCISE NEEDS

SPECIAL GROOMING NEEDS

GOOD WITH KIDS

White standard poodle in an agility trial

Well-bred poodles are among the brightest and most responsive breeds. There are three sizes: standard, miniature, and toy. All sizes are playful, affectionate, eager to please, and energetic. They enjoy working and get along well with other animals. Miniature and toy poodles may be more reserved with strangers and less tolerant of children than standard poodles unless socialized with them at an early age. They are also more prone to biting than standards. Poodles shine in obedience classes, which should begin early, as should socialization. They enjoy a good bark when someone comes to the door but are not aggressive. Poodles do well in cities as long as they get enough exercise and social interaction. Beware of "teacup"-size poodles (which are tinier than toys); they seem to have a lot of temperament and health problems.

Appearance The coat is abundant and dense and can be curly or corded. Coat color is solid gray, silver, apricot, black, white, blue-gray, brown, or cream.

Grooming & Exercise Needs Poodles do not shed but still need to be combed and brushed a few times a week and clipped, scissored, and shaped every four to six weeks. Poodles need several long, brisk walks and romps in a secured area daily. Standards need more exercise than miniatures and toys.

HEIGHT 22-27"

WEIGHT 45-70 LBS.

LIFE SPAN 10-14 YRS.

Gray miniature poodle with English Saddle clip

Apricot miniature poodle with English Saddle clip

MINIATURE

SMALL

SPECIAL GROOMING NEEDS

GOOD WATCHDOG

Origins The standard poodle originated in Germany during the Middle Ages and was used as a water retriever. Even then the coat was clipped (as it is today) to reduce water resistance and to enhance buoyancy. In 19th-century France the standard poodle was used often as a water retriever and circus dog. Miniature and toy poodles were developed in England in the 18th century (during the reign of Queen Anne) and served as truffle hunters, performers, and companions. "Poodle" comes from the German *pudelin*, which means "to splash in the water." Poodles of all sizes are sometimes erroneously referred to as French poodles.

ⓘ It is especially important to obtain a poodle from a reputable breeder. Breed-related health concerns for the standard poodle: hip dysplasia (page 442), eye problems including progressive retinal atrophy (page 435), epilepsy (page 455), bloat (page 445), sebaceous adenitis (a skin disease resulting in scabs, hair loss, and predisposition to bacterial infections), kidney disease.

Brown standard poodle with a sporting clip

For miniature and toy poodles: atopy (page 437), eye problems, deafness (page 436), patellar luxation (page 443), heart and blood disorders, epilepsy (page 455), Cushing's syndrome (page 451).

HEIGHT
TOY TO 10"
MINIATURE 11–15"

WEIGHT
TOY 5–7 LBS.
MINIATURE 14–16 LBS.

LIFE SPAN 10–14 YRS.

Poodle Mixes

Poodle mixes are usually bouncy, perky, affectionate dogs with lots of energy indoors and out. These dogs are so outgoing, playful, and smart that they are easy to train. Poodle mixes are usually rather small. Because they are sensitive to pain, they are not suitable for households with children under seven years of age.

This poodle mix's coat was recently cut down to ease grooming.

Appearance Poodle mixes have wavy to curly coats that often need to be professionally groomed or trimmed. Most mixes are small, but those originating from standard poodles can be medium to large. Purebred poodles are always solid colors, but poodle mixes inherit coat patterns from different breeds and can have various markings and ears of a contrasting color.

Grooming & Exercise Needs The coat needs several brushings a week and professional trimming or grooming about four to six times a year. Poodle mixes usually need several long, brisk walks a day.

A poodle mix shows the diminutive size and alert expression common to miniature and toy poodles.

Poodle mixes can be quick studies in obedience classes.

The two-tone coat on this poodle mix shows the varied coat patterns of mixed breeds. Purebred poodles have solid coats.

A toy poodle-Yorkie mix. Mixed breeds like this can be very active and quite vocal.

Companion Mixes

Companion-breed mixes, such as Shih Tzu mixes or Pekingese mixes, desire close companionship with their owners. They love to be petted and need lots of attention. They look forward to outings, and most are portable enough to be carried. Many of these dogs are high-strung but reasonably easy to train; some terrier mixes can be stubborn. Small companion dogs are not suitable for households

A Lhasa mix with a cut-down coat for easy grooming

with children under seven years of age. Some of the toy mixes can be nippy with children.

Appearance The facial features of companion mixes range from long-muzzled to snub-nosed. They tend to have small builds, although some mixes have longer legs than others. Coat color, length, and texture varies widely and depends on the breed mix.

Grooming & Exercise Needs Long coats require frequent brushing (as much as once a day, depending on the breed background); short coats need only weekly brushing. Long-legged mixes, such as those with dalmatian blood, require more exercise than the short-legged, long-bodied varieties.

This Chihuahua mix puppy shows the distinctive apple-domed skull and delicate features of the pure breed, although this puppy will grow to be a larger dog.

A dalmatian mix, usually an energetic dog, in a rare quiet moment. This dog has the protective nature of its purebred brethren.

A Lhasa-Shih Tzu mix with a well-feathered tail arching over its back

Snow-white Maltese mix with a curlier coat than the breed standard

Guardian Dogs

Rottweilers are naturally powerful and protective.

Many dogs are naturally protective of their family and their home territory, but none are more so than the guardian breeds, which can be divided into four categories: flock protectors, bull breeds, mastiffs, and other guard breeds.

Flock protectors were among the first canine workers. They probably originated thousands of years ago in the mountainous areas around what is now known as Iran and Iraq, and then in different regions developed into the distinct breeds now known as the Bernese mountain dog, Greater Swiss mountain dog, Great Pyrenees, komondor, and Kuvasz. Their imposing size and formidable strength made them effective protectors, while their thick coats shielded them from the elements and from attack by animals seeking to prey on their flocks. To this day, flock protectors are known for their quiet, intense loyalty. But they are also independent workers that don't readily take direction.

Mastiffs are descended from ancient dogs known as Molossians, which probably originated in Asia and were spread throughout Europe by Alexander the Great (356–323 B.C.). Back then, such dogs were used as bodyguards and war dogs, jobs for which their massive bulk, powerful jaws, and thick skin served them well. Like the flock protectors, mastiffs were interbred with local dogs in different regions. Temperaments among today's mastiff breeds range from laid-back to sharply aggressive. Breeds considered unsuitable as pets are not covered in this book. The mastiff breeds described in the following pages are the bullmastiff, Dogo Argentino, Dogue de Bordeaux, mastiff, Neapolitan mastiff, and Tibetan mastiff. All bear the mastiff physique: a massive, blocky skull and tremendous jaw, a thick and powerful neck, and an immense and muscular body that is slightly longer than it is tall. Mastiffs can be stubborn and need intensive obedience training early on, since they are invariably stronger than their owners.

The bull breeds may have originated as early as the 1200s. These breeds were created by crossing mastiffs with terriers, and were used for bullbaiting, a sport in which dogs were set upon a chained or confined bull. Bulldogs were therefore bred to be strong, tenacious, and impervious to pain. After bullbaiting was outlawed in England in 1835, bulldog breeders began to breed out the aggressive traits. The bull breeds of today—the American bull-dog, English bulldog, and boxer—all make enjoyable family companions. They remain somewhat protective but are much easier to handle than their mastiff brethren.

Other breeds classified here as guardians are the Doberman pinscher, Great Dane, Newfoundland, rottweiler, and Saint Bernard. These dogs share many traits with the mastiff breeds. They are intensely loyal to their families and generally range from aloof to wary with strangers, except for the New-foundland and the Saint Bernard, which have outgoing dispositions.

Guardian Dogs		HIGH ENERGY INDOORS	SPECIAL EXERCISE NEEDS	SPECIAL GROOMING NEEDS	GOOD WATCHDOG	GOOD WITH KIDS
BERNESE MOUNTAIN DOG *page 130*	LARGE				●	●
GREATER SWISS MOUNTAIN DOG *page 131*	GIANT				●	
GREAT PYRENEES *page 132*	GIANT		●	●	●	

Bernese mountain dog   Greater Swiss mountain dog   Great Pyrenees

Komondor

Kuvasz

American bulldog

English bulldog

Guardian Dogs		HIGH ENERGY INDOORS	SPECIAL EXERCISE NEEDS	SPECIAL GROOMING NEEDS	GOOD WATCHDOG	GOOD WITH KIDS
KOMONDOR page 133	LARGE	●	●	●	●	
KUVASZ page 134	LARGE		●		●	
AMERICAN BULLDOG page 135	LARGE		●		●	
ENGLISH BULLDOG page 136	MEDIUM					●
BOXER page 137	LARGE		●		●	●
BULLMASTIFF page 138	GIANT				●	
DOGO ARGENTINO page 139	LARGE		●			
DOGUE DE BORDEAUX page 140	LARGE				●	

Bullmastiff

Dogue de Bordeaux

Boxer

Dogo Argentino

Mastiff

Neapolitan mastiff

Tibetan mastiff

Doberman pinscher

Guardian Dogs		HIGH ENERGY INDOORS	SPECIAL EXERCISE NEEDS	SPECIAL GROOMING NEEDS	GOOD WATCHDOG	GOOD WITH KIDS
MASTIFF *page 141*	GIANT				●	●
NEAPOLITAN MASTIFF *page 142*	GIANT				●	
TIBETAN MASTIFF *page 143*	GIANT			●	●	
DOBERMAN PINSCHER *page 144*	LARGE		●		●	
GREAT DANE *page 146*	GIANT				●	
NEWFOUNDLAND *page 147*	GIANT					●
ROTTWEILER *page 148*	LARGE		●		●	
SAINT BERNARD *page 149*	GIANT				●	

Newfoundland

Saint Bernard

Great Dane

Rottweiler

Guardian mixes

Bernese Mountain Dog

LARGE

GOOD WATCHDOG

GOOD WITH KIDS

The Bernese mountain dog is sweet, gentle, and family-oriented. It does well in obedience training. It is friendly to people it knows—including children—and other animals, but may be aloof with strangers. The Bernese is a good watchdog.

Appearance The Bernese's coat is soft, silky, shiny, long, and slightly wavy. Its color is jet-black with rich rust and pure white markings. Rust appears over each eye, on the cheeks, on each side of the chest, on all four legs, and under the tail. There is a white blaze and muzzle band. A white marking on the chest typically forms an inverted cross. The tip of the tail is white.

Adult Bernese mountain dog

Grooming and Exercise Needs The Bernese needs weekly brushings and a few long walks daily.

Origins The Bernese mountain dog is descended from the huge mastiff fighting dogs that accompanied the Romans into northern Europe 2,000 years ago. Until the early 20th century, it was used for cowherding.

(!) Breed-related health concerns: hip and elbow dysplasia (page 442), osteochondritis dissecans (page 442), malignant histiocytosis (a malignant form of cancer characterized by infiltration of the spleen and liver with malignant cells).

HEIGHT 23-27½"

WEIGHT 80-90 LBS.

LIFE SPAN 10-12 YRS.

Six-week-old Bernese puppy

Greater Swiss Mountain Dog

Greater Swiss mountain dogs are bold, alert, and vigilant. They are good family dogs and are protective of their property and families, patient with children, and get along with other animals, although they can be troublesome with other dogs.

Adult male and female
Greater Swiss mountain dogs

Appearance The outercoat is dense and one to two inches long; the undercoat may be thick and shows through on the neck, belly, and underside of the tail. Color is jet-black with rich rust-and-white markings on the face, neck, chest, and legs, and rust markings over each eye.

Grooming & Exercise Needs The Greater Swiss mountain dog only needs to be brushed once a week. It needs a lot of room and exercise so is best suited to the suburbs or country.

Origins Greater Swiss mountain dogs are descended from Roman mastiffs and have been used in the steep mountain villages of Switzerland as herding and guard dogs since the Middle Ages.

! The Greater Swiss mountain dog is not suitable for inexperienced owners. Breed-related health concerns: hip dysplasia (page 442), bloat (page 445), panosteitis (page 442), mega-esophagus (dilation of the esophagus causing vomiting, weight loss, growth impairment, and/or pneumomia; can be fatal in some cases).

Greater Swiss mountain dogs have rust and white markings over a jet-black coat.

HEIGHT 23¹/₂–28¹/₂"

WEIGHT 130–135 LBS.

LIFE SPAN 11–13 YRS.

Great Pyrenees
(or Pyrenean Mountain Dog)

GIANT

SPECIAL EXERCISE NEEDS

SPECIAL GROOMING NEEDS

GOOD WATCHDOG

Great Pyrenees are calm, gentle, patient dogs. They are also independent and need early obedience training. They are loyal, territorial, and protective, and may be wary of strangers and unknown dogs.

Great Pyrenees guarding a flock of sheep

Appearance The Great Pyrenees has a weather-resistant double coat: the outercoat is long, thick, and straight or slightly wavy; the undercoat is dense, fine, and woolly. Its color is all white or mainly white with badger, gray, or tan markings.

Grooming & Exercise Needs The Great Pyrenees must be brushed daily to prevent matting. Frequent baths are recommended since the coat can get quite smelly. The Great Pyrenees needs vigorous daily exercise and is best suited to suburbs and country.

Origins For centuries this dog protected sheep, goats, and cattle from wolves and bears in the Pyrenees Mountains of France and Spain.

(!) This breed is not suitable for inexperienced dog owners. Breed-related health concerns: hip dysplasia (page 442), patellar luxation (page 443), entropion (page 434), bloat (page 445).

White Great Pyrenees with tan markings

HEIGHT 25-32"

WEIGHT 90-125 LBS.

LIFE SPAN 11-15 YRS.

Komondor

LARGE

HIGH ENERGY INDOORS

SPECIAL EXERCISE NEEDS

SPECIAL GROOMING NEEDS

GOOD WATCHDOG

Early socialization and obedience classes are mandatory for these independent, stubborn, and powerful dogs. Although komondorok (plural) are playful and completely devoted to their families, people with young children or small animals should be wary. Owners must be firm and assert dominance early (under the guidance of a dog trainer) or these dogs will become disobedient and possibly aggressive.

Komondor with a show coat

Appearance The undercoat is dense, soft, and woolly. The coarser hairs of the outercoat intertwine with the softer undercoat, forming the breed's distinctive tassel-like cords; this occurs at one to two years of age. The coat is white; the skin is usually gray.

Grooming & Exercise Needs The komondor needs to be shampooed and thoroughly rinsed monthly, because the cords absorb moisture and the dog can become quite smelly. Drying takes several days. Brushing and combing are not necessary, but the cords need to be separated weekly, a task that takes one to two hours. Trimming the cords one to two times a year is also helpful. Komondorok need space and several long, brisk daily walks.

Origins The komondor has protected livestock since the 16th century in Hungary. It probably arrived there with the Magyars over a thousand years ago.

⊘ Komondorok are not suitable for inexperienced dog owners or for city living, nor do they do well with children. Breed-related health concerns: hip dysplasia (page 442), bloat (page 445), skin infections and allergies (page 437), cysts.

Komondorok have distinctive tassel-like cords.

HEIGHT 25½-30"

WEIGHT 70-120 LBS.

LIFE SPAN 10-12 YRS.

Kuvasz

LARGE

SPECIAL EXERCISE NEEDS

GOOD WATCHDOG

Kuvaszok (plural) are aggressive and independent. They have an extremely strong instinct to protect the children in their families and are wary of strangers. Likewise, they are good with other animals in their households, but not necessarily friendly with outsiders. Early and ongoing socialization and obedience classes and a firm, consistent owner are mandatory.

Kuvaszok can have wavy or straight coats.

Appearance The double coat can range from quite wavy to straight. The outercoat is medium coarse; the undercoat is fine. The color is white and the skin is heavily pigmented, often slate gray or black.

Grooming & Exercise Needs Kuvaszok should be brushed twice a week to prevent tangling and matting. Bathing will decrease the odor of the highly absorbent coat. This aggressive breed needs a lot of exercise, including vigorous leashed walks as well as opportunities to run.

Origins The Kuvasz's ancestors originated in Tibet in the 13th century. The breed was further developed by the Hungarian aristocracy from the 15th through 19th centuries for guarding, hunting, and herding. The name comes from the Turkish *kawasz*, which means "armed guard."

⚠ The Kuvasz is not suitable for inexperienced dog owners, or for city or apartment life. Breed-related health concerns: hip dysplasia (page 442), deafness (page 436), bloat (page 445).

HEIGHT 26–30"

WEIGHT 70–115 LBS.

LIFE SPAN 10–12 YRS.

Kuvaszok have white coats and gray- or black-pigmented skin.

American Bulldog

LARGE

SPECIAL EXERCISE NEEDS

GOOD WATCHDOG

Red and white particolor American bulldog

The self-assured American bulldog is alert, outgoing, and friendly with family members and others accepted by the family, but is wary of strangers and may be aggressive toward other dogs. It gets along with children and other animals, including cats, if socialized with them at an early age. Obedience training should also begin early, as American bulldogs can be very stubborn.

Appearance The coat is short and stiff to the touch. Coat color is white, white with brindle or red, or brindle or red with white.

Grooming & Exercise Needs The American bulldog requires only a quick brushing weekly. If not used as a working dog, it needs brisk daily walks.

Origins Derived from English bulldog stock, the American bulldog originated in the United States in the 18th century. Traditionally, this breed has been used for working cattle and hogs and as a watchdog.

! The American bulldog is not a good choice for inexperienced dog owners and is unsuited to city or apartment life unless well trained and sufficiently exercised. Breed-related health concerns: hip dysplasia (page 442), Demodex mange (page 440), atopy (page 437).

White with brindle American bulldog

HEIGHT 21-27"

WEIGHT 60-120 LBS.

LIFE SPAN 11-12 YRS.

English Bulldog

MEDIUM

GOOD WITH KIDS

Bulldogs are calm and gentle dogs that get along with everyone. They are patient and loving with children—although they won't frolic with them for hours—and usually get along with other dogs and with cats. They are observers and sleepers, not property protectors. Early training is recommended.

Fawn and white English bulldog

Appearance The bulldog's coat is short and soft. It comes in all colors and mixtures except black; the most common colors are red brindle, brindle, white, and fawn.

Grooming & Exercise Needs Bulldogs need a quick brushing once a week. The facial and nasal folds and the area around the muzzle need to be cleaned frequently. Bulldogs are sedentary; a daily walk around the block is often enough exercise for them.

Origins The original bulldogs of early 19th-century England were bred for bullbaiting and dogfighting and were ferocious and tenacious, but beginning in the 1830s—by which time these inhumane sports were illegal—bulldogs were bred to be gentle.

(!) It is important to obtain a bulldog from a reputable breeder who breeds for calm temperament and good health. Breed-related health concerns: difficult births, hip and elbow dysplasia (page 442), eye problems, heart problems, hypothyroidism (page 452), lymphoma (page 432), skin problems, structural deformities of the nose, mouth, and throat that can interfere with normal breathing.

HEIGHT 12–16"

WEIGHT 40–55 LBS.

LIFE SPAN 8–10 YRS.

Ten-week-old brindle and white English bulldog puppy

Boxer

LARGE

The well-bred boxer is energetic, gentle, and fun loving with adults and children, although it is wary of strangers. Boxers generally get along with other dogs, but some females may be aggressive and some males inclined to fight for dominance. Early obedience training is therefore very important. With a consistent, determined owner, the boxer does well in obedience classes.

SPECIAL EXERCISE NEEDS

Appearance The boxer's coat is short, straight, and shiny and lies smooth and close to the body. Coat color is fawn (ranging from light tan to mahogany) or brindle (with heavy to light black striping). There are white markings on the muzzle, chest, and legs.

GOOD WATCHDOG

GOOD WITH KIDS

Fawn boxer with natural (uncropped) ears

Grooming & Exercise Needs The boxer needs only occasional brushing and bathing. It needs considerable daily exercise, including several brisk walks and playtime. Because boxers are good jumpers, high fences are a good idea.

Origins The boxer was probably developed in the 19th century for bullbaiting and dogfighting. Today it is often used for police and guard work.

(!) It is especially important to obtain a boxer from a reputable breeder. Breed-related health concerns: tumors, hypothyroidism (page 452), cardiomyopathy (page 450), colitis (inflammatory disorder of the colon), atopy (page 437), corneal ulcers (slow-healing wounds on the cornea often requiring surgery), deafness (page 436), bloat (page 445).

Boxer with cropped ears

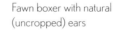

HEIGHT 21-25"

WEIGHT 55-75 LBS.

LIFE SPAN 8-10 YRS.

Bullmastiff

GIANT

GOOD WATCHDOG

Bullmastiffs are fearless and confident, yet docile. They are reliable, intelligent, and have a natural instinct to guard their families. Early obedience training is essential for these powerful, active, and stubborn dogs. Games like tug-of-war and wrestling are not recommended. If socialized, bullmastiffs accept strangers and are affectionate and patient with children and other animals in their family. They will not, however, tolerate trespassers. Some are heavy droolers.

Appearance The coat is short and dense. Coat color is red, fawn, or brindle. The muzzle is black, fading toward the eyes. The ears are darker than the body.

Fawn bullmastiff with a black mask

Grooming & Exercise Needs
Bullmastiffs need to be brushed weekly. They need several brisk walks and a run in a secured area daily.

Origins The bullmastiff—40 percent bulldog, 60 percent mastiff—was developed in England in the 19th century to pin down, but not maul, poachers on large estates. Its original dark brindle color—lighter today—was perfect nighttime camouflage.

(!) Bullmastiffs are not recommended for inexperienced dog owners. Breed-related health concerns: skin problems, hip and elbow dysplasia (page 442), bloat (page 445), entropion (page 434), progressive retinal atrophy (page 435), cancer (page 430).

HEIGHT 24-27"

WEIGHT 100-130 LBS.

LIFE SPAN 8-10 YRS.

Brindle bullmastiff

Dogo Argentino
(or Argentine Dogo)

LARGE

SPECIAL EXERCISE NEEDS

Dogos are loving companions, loyal protectors, and fierce hunters. They require early socialization with humans and other animals and early obedience training. They get along with children and other animals if raised with them but can be wary of and aggressive toward strangers.

Appearance The completely white coat is short, thick, smooth, and glossy.

Grooming & Exercise Needs The Dogo's short coat, which sheds minimally, needs to be brushed weekly. This breed needs vigorous exercise daily.

The Dogo Argentino has a smooth, completely white coat.

Origins The Dogo Argentino was Argentina's first native purebred dog. It was created in the 1920s to be a silent, fearless hunter of jaguar and puma and to be agile, brave, and strong. It is a descendant of Spanish fighting dogs with bull terrier, mastiff, boxer, American bulldog, and harlequin Great Dane mixed in.

(!) The Dogo Argentino is not suitable for inexperienced dog owners, or for city or apartment life. Breed-related health concerns: hip dysplasia (page 442), deafness (page 436).

Dogo Argentino with cropped ears

HEIGHT 24½–27"

WEIGHT 80–100 LBS.

LIFE SPAN 10–12 YRS.

LARGE

GOOD WATCHDOG

Dogue de Bordeaux

The Dogue de Bordeaux is a vigilant guard.

The Dogue de Bordeaux boasts a very deep, intimidating bark. It guards its property with vigilance and great courage but usually without aggression. This breed becomes very attached to its owner and is affectionate with children but can be aggressive with unfamiliar dogs. Early socialization and obedience classes will help to control any tendencies toward dominance or aggression and can make it possible for this breed to live with other animals, including cats. Some are heavy droolers.

Appearance The fine-haired, short coat is soft to the touch. Coat color is solid mahogany (reddish brown) or various shades of golden fawn—the more common color in the United States. The Dogue de Bordeaux has a massive head lined with symmetrical wrinkles and a broad, powerful jaw.

Grooming & Exercise Needs The Dogue de Bordeaux's short coat needs only occasional brushing. As with most large, heavy breeds, exercise needs are moderate.

Origins The Dogue de Bordeaux, or Bordeaux mastiff, originated in France and was trained in ancient times to attack bulls, bears, and other dogs. Today it is a companion and guard dog. Although intimidating in appearance, this dog has a calm temperament.

(!) The Dogue de Bordeaux requires an experienced owner. Breed-related health concerns: hip dysplasia (page 442), bloat (page 445).

Golden fawn Dogue de Bordeaux

HEIGHT 23–27"

WEIGHT 80–100 LBS.

LIFE SPAN 10–12 YRS.

Mastiff

GIANT

GOOD WATCHDOG

GOOD WITH KIDS

Properly bred, socialized, and trained mastiffs are gentle, good-natured, and easygoing. They love children and usually get along with other animals. They can be stubborn when being obedience trained but will come around if handled with patience and gentleness. They are usually friendly with strangers—in their own reserved way—but may be territorial and are therefore good watchdogs. Their power and massive size can be formidable, so it is important that any signs of dominance or aggression be addressed immediately with a trainer. Mastiffs thrive on companionship and should be included in family activities. They can be heavy droolers.

Fawn mastiff

Appearance The outercoat is straight, coarse, and moderately short; the undercoat is dense, short, and close. Coat color is fawn, apricot, or brindle. The muzzle, ears, and nose are darker than the body. A small patch of white may appear on the chest. The head is massive.

Grooming & Exercise Needs Mastiffs need only quick weekly brushings. They need long daily walks and occasional opportunities to run and play in a secured area.

Origins Mastiffs have inhabited Europe and Asia for thousands of years, but their origins are unclear. Historically, they have been hunters, guards, and fighters.

(!) It is especially important to purchase a mastiff from a reputable breeder. Breed-related health concerns: hip and elbow dysplasia (page 442), ectropion (page 434), bloat (page 445).

Apricot mastiff

HEIGHT 27½-33"

WEIGHT 175-190 LBS.

LIFE SPAN 8-10 YRS.

Neapolitan Mastiff

GIANT

GOOD WATCHDOG

Neapolitan mastiffs are massive and powerful. If bred for gentle temperament and socialized early, they are good with children. They are accepting of strangers as long as they are not threatened, generally get along with other animals, and are dependable watchdogs. Early obedience training is a must. Some are heavy droolers.

Appearance The coat is short, dense, and smooth. Coat color is solid gray, black, mahogany, tawny, or tawny stag; each may be brindled, and there may be small white patches on the chest and the tips of the toes. The

Neapolitan mastiff with cropped ears

skin all over the body is loose, with wrinkles and folds covering the head and pendulous lips forming an ample dewlap.

Grooming & Exercise Needs The dewlap area needs cleaning daily. A walk around the block is an intense workout for this breed.

Origins The Neapolitan mastiff, probably a descendant of ancient mastiffs, originated about a thousand years ago.

(!) This breed is not suitable for inexperienced dog owners. It is especially important to obtain a Neapolitan mastiff from a reputable breeder. Breed-related health concerns: bloat (page 445), hip and elbow dysplasia (page 442), cardiomyopathy (page 450), anterior cruciate rupture (page 442), Demodex mange (page 440), pyoderma (bacterial skin infection).

HEIGHT 24–31"

WEIGHT 110–180 LBS.

LIFE SPAN 8–10 YRS.

Neapolitan mastiff with natural (uncropped) ears

Tibetan Mastiff

GIANT

SPECIAL GROOMING NEEDS

GOOD WATCHDOG

Gold Tibetan mastiff

Protective and territorial, Tibetan mastiffs treat strangers with extreme suspicion and can be aggressive with other dogs. With their families they are loving, but not needy, and are good with children if socialized with them at an early age. Early obedience training and skilled handling are a must. Tibetan mastiffs do best in large, open spaces.

Appearance The outercoat is hard, straight, fairly long, thick, and fluffed out by the undercoat, which is heavy and woolly in cold weather, sparse in warmer months. The neck and shoulders are heavily coated, giving a mane-like appearance. The tail is bushy and curls over the back. Coat color is rich black, black and tan, brown, various shades of gold or gray, or gray with gold markings. A white star on the breast and white markings on the feet may appear. Tan and gold markings appear above the eyes, on the lower part of the leg, and on the tip of the tail.

Grooming & Exercise Needs Tibetan mastiffs should be brushed daily. These large dogs are low energy but need a few brisk, long walks daily to keep them from gaining too much weight and developing joint problems.

Origins The Tibetan mastiff was bred more than a thousand years ago to guard livestock and property in the rugged Himalayas.

Brown Tibetan mastiff

HEIGHT 24–28"

(!) The Tibetan mastiff is not suitable for inexperienced dog owners or for city or apartment life. Breed-related health concerns: hip dysplasia (page 442), bloat (page 445), hypothyroidism (page 452).

WEIGHT 140–200 LBS.

LIFE SPAN 10–12 YRS.

Doberman Pinscher

LARGE

SPECIAL EXERCISE NEEDS

GOOD WATCHDOG

Dobermans are highly energetic, sensitive dogs that respond well to love and praise but not to heavy-handed discipline. Well-socialized Dobermans get along with children and other animals if raised with them and if treated with respect, but they can be aggressive with other dogs. Do not play aggressive games, such as tug-of-war, with Dobermans. While they are natural guard dogs, some Dobermans are so sweet and submissive they will let strangers take anything from their homes in exchange for petting and playtime. Basic obedience training is mandatory to socialize young Dobermans and enhance bonding with their owners.

Black Doberman pinscher with cropped ears

Appearance The coat is smooth, short, hard, thick, and close-lying. Coat color is black, red, blue, or fawn. Sharply defined rust markings appear above each eye and on the muzzle, throat, forechest, all four legs and feet, and below the tail. There may be a gray undercoat on the neck.

Grooming & Exercise Needs The Doberman sheds very little and needs only a quick brushing with a rubber brush once a week. This highly energetic athlete needs a secure space to run off-leash in rapid bursts of speed. Walking or jogging is usually not enough.

HEIGHT 24–28"

WEIGHT 66–88 LBS.

LIFE SPAN 10–12 YRS.

Black Doberman with natural (uncropped) ears

Red Doberman pinscher with natural ears

Origins The Doberman was originally bred in the late 19th century by Louis Dobermann of Apolda, Germany. Herr Dobermann was the town's dogcatcher and also a policeman at night. He wanted to develop a guard dog to accompany him on his nightly rounds and probably crossed German pinschers, rottweilers, black and tan terriers, and greyhounds to produce the elegant Doberman.

(!) It is especially important to obtain a Doberman pinscher from a reputable breeder, as poorly bred Dobermans may suffer from severe health or aggression problems. The Doberman is not suitable for inexperienced dog owners. Breed-related health concerns: cardiomyopathy (page 450), cervical vertebral instability (malformation of the neck vertebrae resulting in a wobbling gait), hypothyroidism (page 452), von Willebrand's disease (a common disorder that causes excessive bleeding during or after surgery), osteosarcoma (page 431), parvovirus (page 426), acral lick dermatitis (page 438).

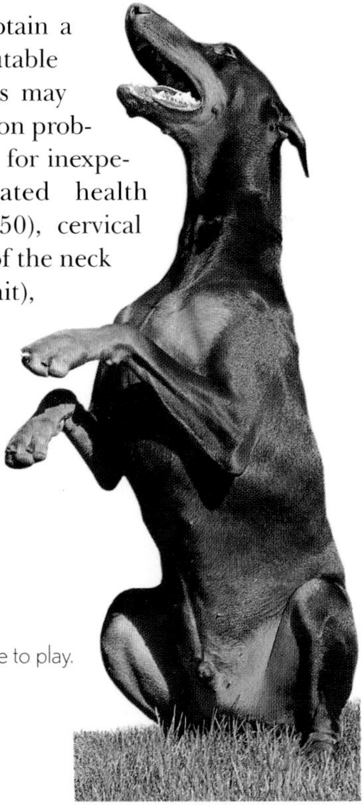

Doberman pinschers love to play.

Great Dane

Eager-to-please Great Danes are friendly, easygoing, and gentle with children in the family as long as they are treated with kindness. They will bark deeply when someone comes to the door but aren't usually aggressive. They may be shy around strangers. Introducing them at an early age to a variety of people and situations will help them become flexible and adaptable. Obedience training is very important for such large, powerful dogs. Training should be firm, calm, and gentle. Tug-of-war or other aggressive games should not be played. Some are heavy droolers.

Appearance The coat is short, dense, smooth, and glossy in brindle, fawn, steel blue, black, or harlequin.

Grooming & Exercise Needs Great Danes should be brushed weekly. They can live comfortably in the city, suburbs, or country as long as they get enough exercise every day. A brisk walk or a romp in the park is recommended.

Fawn Great Dane

Origins The Great Danes of today are far removed temperamentally and physically from their mastiff-like ancestors, which were bred in Germany in the Middle Ages to hunt wild boar.

(!) Breed-related health concerns: bloat (page 445), hip dysplasia (page 442), osteosarcoma (page 431), hypertrophic osteodystrophy (a developmental disorder causing painful swelling of bones), cervical vertebral instability (a malformation of neck vertebrae causing a wobbling gait).

HEIGHT 28-32"

WEIGHT 100-130 LBS.

LIFE SPAN 6-8 YRS.

Harlequin Great Dane

Newfoundland

GIANT

Brown Newfoundland

While Newfoundlands are sweet-tempered, devoted companions, particularly for children, their size and deep bark make them good guard dogs as well. If left alone too often Newfies will develop behavioral problems, notably home destruction. These dogs can be heavy droolers.

GOOD WITH KIDS

Appearance The double coat is flat and water resistant. The outercoat is coarse, moderately long, and thick, either straight or with a wave; the undercoat, thinner in summer, is soft and dense. Coat color is black, black and white, brown, or gray.

Grooming & Exercise Needs Newfoundlands need brushing and combing weekly, more often when shedding, to avoid matting. They need long walks and occasional swims.

Origins The Newfoundland was developed on its namesake island in the 18th century to haul fishing nets and pull carts. They were also used to save people who were shipwrecked.

(!) It is especially important to obtain a Newfoundland from a reputable breeder and from stock whose hips have been certified by the Orthopedic Foundation for Animals or PennHip. Breed-related health concerns: hip and elbow dysplasia (page 442), bloat (page 445), ectropion/entropion (page 434), allergic dermatitis (page 437), hypothyroidism (page 452), pemphigus foliaceous (an autoimmune skin disease causing ulcers and scabs to develop on the skin all over the body), subaortic stenosis (page 449).

Black Newfoundland pulling a cart

HEIGHT 26–28"

WEIGHT 100–150 LBS.

LIFE SPAN 8–10 YRS.

Rottweiler

LARGE

SPECIAL EXERCISE NEEDS

GOOD WATCHDOG

Rottweilers are robust, courageous, protective, and powerful. With proper and early obedience training and socialization, they are generally calm and confident as well. Proper training is especially important for rottweilers that will be around young children and other animals—many cannot be trusted around small dogs or cats. Rough play and aggressive games, such as tug-of-war, should be avoided.

Appearance The coat is short, straight, coarse, and dense. Coat color is black with rust to mahogany markings above each eye and on the cheeks, muzzle, chest, legs, and feet.

Rottweilers have black coats with rust markings.

Grooming & Exercise Needs Rottweilers should be brushed once a week. They need considerable exercise—long walks and romps daily—and do best in the suburbs or country.

Origins This ancient breed was used by Roman cattle drovers to herd cattle to market and then protect the master's profits on the way home. The breed takes its name from "Rottweil," the German town at the "end of the line" for those early cattle drives.

ⓘ It is especially important to obtain a rottweiler from a reputable breeder. This breed requires experienced and authoritative owners. Breed-related health concerns: hip and elbow dysplasia (page 442), deafness (page 436), parvovirus (page 426), neurological disorders, kidney failure (page 453), bloat (page 445).

HEIGHT 22-27"

WEIGHT 90-130 LBS.

LIFE SPAN 9-11 YRS.

Rottweilers need a lot of exercise and do well in the country.

Saint Bernard

GIANT

GOOD WATCHDOG

Well-bred, trained Saint Bernards are gentle and affectionate, but unruly or disobedient ones can be dangerous. They must be socialized and enrolled in obedience classes early. They are good with children if introduced to them early and usually get along with other animals, although males may try to dominate. Their great size and ominous bark deter intruders. Avoid aggressive games. Some Saint Bernards are heavy droolers.

Appearance The shorthaired Saint Bernard has a short, dense coat; the longhaired is longer and slightly wavy. Coat color is red and white and brindle with white markings. Dark shadings on the face and ears are common.

Grooming & Exercise Needs Both varieties need brushing once a week. Getting them to exercise is sometimes difficult.

Longhaired Saint Bernard

Origins This breed is probably descended from Roman Molossians of the 2nd century A.D. In the 17th century, monks of the Hospice of Saint Bernard in the Swiss Alps kept Saint Bernards as guards and mountain guides and to find lost travelers. These dogs also showed an uncanny ability to detect approaching avalanches.

(!) It is especially important to obtain a Saint Bernard from a reputable breeder. This breed is not suitable for inexperienced dog owners. Breed-related health concerns: hip and elbow dysplasia (page 442), lymphoma (page 432), osteochondritis dissecans (page 442), osteosarcoma (page 431), bloat (page 445), epilepsy (page 455), hemophilia (a bleeding disorder), cardiomyopathy (page 450), eye problems.

Shorthaired Saint Bernards

HEIGHT 25-30"

WEIGHT 110-200 LBS.

LIFE SPAN 8-10 YRS.

Guardian Mixes

Guardian mixes are watchful, protective dogs that often have dominant personalities. Their energy level is medium to high, depending on their mix. Some Doberman mixes can be quite high-energy, and mixes with both guardian-breed and sporting-dog blood can be very active. Some guardian mixes can be dominant and aggressive, especially with women and children, if not properly trained. These dogs are recommended only for experienced dog owners.

This boxer-mastiff mix shows the strong chest and blocky skull typical of guardian mixes.

Appearance Dogs with guardian-breed blood may have a massive and/or muscular build, brindle or black and tan coloring (especially points, as in rottweilers and Dobermans), and a short, easy-to-care-for coat.

Grooming & Exercise Needs Grooming will depend on which breed your guardian mix most resembles. Many of the guardian mixes need intensive aerobic exercise daily.

This Doberman mix has the fine bone structure and attentive gaze of the purebred.

A rottweiler mix guarding his trucker-owner's rig; rottweilers are known to be steadfastly protective dogs.

A three-year-old rottweiler-Labrador mix has the strong, broad chest of a rottweiler and the glistening coat of a Labrador. Dogs like these can be extremely loyal to their families but wary of strangers.

The broad chest and attentive look common to guardian dogs is apparent in this black and white mix, keeping watch on his owner's porch. His short coat is easy to care for.

Herding Dogs

Border collies were developed in Great Britain and Ireland to herd sheep.

When humans began to raise sheep and cattle, they needed help keeping their herds together and driving them to market. Herding dogs were bred and trained to perform both these tasks. Some breeds were developed to herd sheep, others specifically to work cattle, while others herded both or herded other animals. These strong, active, medium-to-large dogs played a crucial role in community economies, rounding up strays and keeping loss of stock to a minimum. The breeds known as cattle drovers move large animals by nipping at the backs of their legs and heels, while other breeds herd by staring down their charges and barking.

Having a herding dog as a pet demands ingenuity and a commitment to aerobic-level exercise, lest the dog become destructive. The owner must understand that the dog's instinct to herd may extend to humans. However, because these dogs are genetically programmed to work closely with human shepherds, most of the breeds take to training quickly. They shine in agility contests, herding trials, Flyball, and obedience competition. Just keep in mind that raising a herding dog is like raising a gifted child: you must always keep one step ahead of her.

The oldest known cattle-herding breeds still active today are the long, low-slung Cardigan and Pembroke Welsh corgis. These foxy-faced canines have been driving cattle for more than a thousand years. Other cattle herders include the giant schnauzer and the Bouvier des Flandres, now often used as guard dogs, and the Australian kelpie and Australian cattle dog, which herded both cattle and sheep. Among the breeds developed to herd sheep are the Belgian sheepdog, briard, puli, Polish Owczarek Nizinny, bearded collie, Border collie, Canaan dog, Old English sheepdog, Shetland sheepdog, rough- and smooth-coated collies, German shepherd, and the American-bred Australian shepherd.

Australian cattle dog

Australian kelpie

Bouvier des Flandres

Giant schnauzer

Herding Dogs		HIGH ENERGY INDOORS	SPECIAL EXERCISE NEEDS	SPECIAL GROOMING NEEDS	GOOD WATCHDOG	GOOD WITH KIDS
AUSTRALIAN CATTLE DOG *page 156*	MEDIUM		●			
AUSTRALIAN KELPIE *page 157*	MEDIUM		●			
BOUVIER DES FLANDRES *page 158*	LARGE		●			
GIANT SCHNAUZER *page 159*	LARGE	●				

Cardigan Welsh corgi

Pembroke Welsh corgi

Australian shepherd

Herding Dogs		HIGH ENERGY INDOORS	SPECIAL EXERCISE NEEDS	SPECIAL GROOMING NEEDS	GOOD WATCHDOG	GOOD WITH KIDS
CARDIGAN WELSH CORGI *page 160*	MEDIUM				●	
PEMBROKE WELSH CORGI *page 161*	MEDIUM					
AUSTRALIAN SHEPHERD *page 162*	LARGE		●			
BEARDED COLLIE *page 163*	MEDIUM		●			●
BELGIAN SHEEPDOG *page 164*	LARGE		●	●	●	
BORDER COLLIE *page 166*	MEDIUM	●	●			
CANAAN DOG *page 168*	MEDIUM				●	

Bearded collie

Belgian sheepdog

Border collie

Canaan dog

Briard

Collie

German shepherd

Shepherd mixes

Herding Dogs		HIGH ENERGY INDOORS	SPECIAL EXERCISE NEEDS	SPECIAL GROOMING NEEDS	GOOD WATCHDOG	GOOD WITH KIDS
BRIARD *page 169*	LARGE	●	●	●	●	
COLLIE *page 170*	LARGE			●	●	●
GERMAN SHEPHERD *page 172*	LARGE		●	●	●	
OLD ENGLISH SHEEPDOG *page 176*	LARGE		●	●		
POLISH OWCZAREK NIZINNY *page 177*	MEDIUM		●	●		
PULI *page 178*	MEDIUM		●	●	●	
SHETLAND SHEEPDOG *page 179*	SMALL			●	●	

Old English sheepdog

Polish Owczarek Nizinny

Puli

Shetland sheepdog

Herding mixes

MEDIUM

Australian Cattle Dog

SPECIAL EXERCISE NEEDS

The Australian cattle dog is a strong, healthy breed that herds cattle by nipping at their heels but without the nonstop barking common to many other herders. Wary by nature, the Australian cattle dog needs early obedience training and social contact with both people and other animals. Without such training it will try to dominate the family "pack." Small children playing and squealing will trigger its herding instinct unless this dog is exposed to such behavior at an early age.

Blue-mottled Australian cattle dog puppy, about twelve weeks old

Appearance The Australian cattle dog has a moderately short and straight outercoat and a short, dense undercoat. Coat color is blue, blue mottled, or red speckled.

Grooming & Exercise Needs The Australian cattle dog, which sheds heavily in the spring, requires daily brushing during shedding season. This dog needs a lot of exercise, such as daily vigorous romps and/or fast-paced walks.

Origins The Australian cattle dog was bred in the late 19th century to herd cattle in rough terrain and extreme heat. It counts collies, dingoes, and dalmatians among its ancestors.

(!) This breed is not suitable for inexperienced dog owners and is not recommended for city or apartment living.

HEIGHT 17–20"

WEIGHT 33–55 LBS.

LIFE SPAN 10–13 YRS.

Blue Australian cattle dog

Australian Kelpie

MEDIUM

SPECIAL EXERCISE NEEDS

Kelpies are intense and independent. They need a strong, experienced trainer and early socialization and obedience training. Otherwise they tend to herd everything, including young children and other animals. The kelpie likes hard exercise and wandering and is not very happy living in the city or with an owner who favors an armchair over hiking.

Australian kelpie at a sheepdog trial

Appearance The Australian kelpie is a solid, medium-size dog with a foxlike head. The weather-resistant outercoat is harsh and glossy; the undercoat is thick and soft. The color is usually black but can be black and tan, red, red and tan, fawn, chocolate, or smoke blue.

Grooming & Exercise Needs The Australian kelpie needs to be brushed and combed weekly. These dogs need an athlete's training schedule—exercise, exercise, exercise—or they may develop severe behavioral problems.

Origins The Australian kelpie originated in the 1870s from the breeding of a Border collie and a black and tan random-bred female named Kelpie.

(!) The Australian kelpie is not suitable for inexperienced dog owners and does not adapt well to city or apartment life.

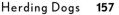

Chocolate Australian kelpie

HEIGHT 17-23"

WEIGHT 25-45 LBS.

LIFE SPAN 12-14 YRS.

Bouvier des Flandres

LARGE

SPECIAL EXERCISE NEEDS

Bouviers des Flandres have a strong guarding instinct.

The Bouvier des Flandres loves life in the country or the suburbs. Because it has strong guarding instincts and is naturally territorial, this dog needs early obedience training and socialization. If the Bouvier is going to be around children, they should be part of his world from puppyhood. The Bouvier likes to dominate but will respond well to a strong leader.

Appearance The Bouvier's rough, tousled, thick outercoat and its soft, dense undercoat withstand even the most inclement weather. The coat can be any color from fawn to black (but never white or chocolate brown) and sometimes has white markings on the chest. This breed's distinguishing characteristics are a thick mustache and beard.

Grooming & Exercise Needs The Bouvier's coat doesn't shed much but needs to be combed and brushed or it will become matted. This dog needs a lot of exercise, such as a few long, brisk walks and a romp daily, or it may develop behavioral problems.

The Bouvier is a well-muscled working dog.

Origins The Bouvier originated in Belgium in the 17th century. It aggressively protected cattle from packs of feral dogs and its owners' homes and families from thieves.

⚠ The Bouvier des Flandres is not suitable for inexperienced dog owners. Breed-related health concerns: hypothyroidism (page 452), lymphoma (page 432), bloat (page 445).

HEIGHT 23½–27½"

WEIGHT 65–100 LBS.

LIFE SPAN 11–12 YRS.

Giant Schnauzer

LARGE

HIGH ENERGY INDOORS

Giant schnauzers make excellent police and guard dogs. They're large, powerful, and want to dominate, so the private owner will need to have experience with the schnauzer and make sure extensive obedience training begins early. Some giant schnauzers get along well with other dogs and cats, but some are very aggressive. They will socialize with strangers, children, and other dogs and animals, but must be introduced to them from puppyhood.

Appearance The giant schnauzer's weather-resistant outercoat is hard, wiry, and very dense; its undercoat is soft. Coat color is either solid black or salt-and-pepper. Facial features include bushy eyebrows and a long, coarse beard.

Grooming & Exercise Needs Giant schnauzers should be brushed and combed twice a week and trimmed every three months. They need several long walks daily.

Solid black giant schnauzer

Origins The giant schnauzer—developed in Germany in the Middle Ages for herding cattle—may be the result of a cross between the standard schnauzer, the Bouvier des Flandres, and the black Great Dane.

! The giant schnauzer can be very aggressive. Choose a reputable breeder concerned with temperament as well as health. The giant schnauzer is not a good choice for inexperienced dog owners or for anyone who is not interested in intensive training and strong leadership. Breed-related health concerns include hip dysplasia (page 442).

HEIGHT 23¹/₂–27¹/₂"

WEIGHT 70–95 LBS.

LIFE SPAN 11–13 YRS.

Giant schnauzer with a shaved pet coat

Cardigan Welsh Corgi

MEDIUM

GOOD WATCHDOG

Cardigan Welsh corgis are loyal and affectionate family dogs, intelligent, and easy to train. This dog has a tradition to uphold—guarding its property, checking on strangers, and nipping the heels of running humans. Early training and socialization are important. The Cardigan Welsh corgi is a first-rate watchdog, barking when strangers are at the door but relaxing when they enter. They are not usually aggressive, but will confidently hold their own with larger dogs; two male corgis in a single household will fight for dominance. Cardigans accommodate small animals, such as cats, if socialized with them at an early age. They adapt well to city and apartment life.

Appearance The corgi's medium-length outercoat is harsh, dense, and weather-resistant; its undercoat is short, soft, thick, and insulating. Color is red, sable, brindle, black, or blue

Blue merle Cardigan Welsh corgi

merle, sometimes with white markings on the neck, chest, legs, face, feet, and tip of the tail. The tail is long and the ears round-tipped.

Grooming & Exercise Needs Cardigan Welsh corgis need to be brushed once a week. They adapt to the exercise schedule of their family and enjoy daily brisk walks.

Origins The Cardigan Welsh corgi is an ancient breed probably introduced to Wales by the Celts more than 3,000 years ago. Its long, low-to-the-ground body and short legs reflect its dachshund ancestors. In the 19th century this tough, fearless dog was a "heeler," directing livestock by nipping at its heels.

(!) Breed-related health concerns: progressive retinal atrophy (page 435), glaucoma (page 434), intervertebral disc protrusion (page 456), bladder stones (page 453).

Brindle Cardigan Welsh corgi adult and puppy

HEIGHT 10½-12½"

WEIGHT 25-38 LBS.

LIFE SPAN 12-15 YRS.

Pembroke Welsh Corgi

MEDIUM

Pembroke Welsh corgis are very bright and easy to train. They make good family dogs, especially if they get early training and are frequently exposed to children, whom they may otherwise try to herd by nipping at their heels. Pembrokes—usually reserved with strangers—make good guard dogs. They are friendly toward other dogs, although two male corgis in the same household are bound to fight for dominance. They get along with small animals, such as cats, especially if socialized with them at an early age.

Black and tan Pembroke Welsh corgi with white markings

Appearance The weather-resistant undercoat of the Pembroke Welsh corgi is short and thick; the outercoat is longer and coarser. Coat color is red, sable, fawn, or black and tan, with or without white on the legs, chest, neck, muzzle, underparts, and in a narrow blaze on the head. The ear tips are pointed and the tail is short.

Grooming & Exercise Needs
Pembrokes need to be brushed once a week. They need a couple of brisk walks around the block every day for exercise.

Red Pembroke Welsh corgi

Origins The Pembroke Welsh corgi was reportedly brought to the British Isles in 1100 by Flemish weavers who settled in Wales and used the Pembroke—known for its stamina and enthusiasm—to drive cattle.

(!) Breed-related health concerns: intervertebral disc protrusion (page 456), eye disorders including progressive retinal atrophy (page 435), hip dysplasia (page 442), bladder stones (page 453), epilepsy (page 455).

HEIGHT 10–12"

WEIGHT 25–30 LBS.

LIFE SPAN 12–15 YRS.

Australian Shepherd

Australian shepherd herding goats

Australian shepherds, although reserved with strangers, are loyal, affectionate, and playful dogs that are good with children if socialized with them early. Australian shepherds excel in herding, obedience, and agility trials.

Appearance The Australian shepherd's outercoat is moderately coarse; the undercoat is soft and thick. Coat color is blue merle, red merle, black, or red, with or without white markings or tan (copper) points. The male has a more pronounced mane than the female.

Grooming & Exercise Needs Weekly brushing and combing are required, especially during spring shedding. The Australian shepherd must be kept busy with sheepdog trials, agility sports, and/or long runs.

Origins Australian shepherds—bred for herding and guarding livestock—arrived in the United States by way of Australia in the 19th century, although they may have originated in Spain.

⚠ Avoid breed lines of Australian shepherds that show shyness or sharpness. Breed-related health concerns: hip dysplasia (page 442), cataracts (page 434), progressive retinal atrophy (page 435), collie eye anomaly (a congenital eye defect that occasionally causes blindness), deafness (page 436), nasal solar dermatitis (a rare disorder in which the nonpigmented areas of the nose become inflamed and sometimes ulcerated).

HEIGHT 18-23"

WEIGHT 35-75 LBS.

LIFE SPAN 12-14 YRS.

Black Australian shepherd with white markings and copper points

Bearded Collie

MEDIUM

Bearded collies are loving, affectionate, eager to please, and do well in obedience classes. They enjoy being around people, including children (whom they may try to herd) and other animals. They may bark when visitors arrive but are not known for protecting property. Beardies can live happily in rural, urban, and suburban settings as long as they get enough exercise, playtime, and mental stimulation.

Brown bearded collie

SPECIAL EXERCISE NEEDS

GOOD WITH KIDS

Appearance The bearded collie's outercoat is medium-length, straight, and harsh in texture; the undercoat is soft. Coat color is black, blue, brown, or fawn with white markings.

Grooming & Exercise Needs The bearded collie needs to be brushed and combed at least once a week to avoid matting. This playful, energetic dog needs long, vigorous walks and daily playtime.

Black and white bearded collie puppies

Origins The bearded collie probably originated in Scotland and northern England in the 16th century. Originally used for herding sheep, it has become increasingly popular as a family pet. The Old English sheepdog and the Border collie are both descendants of the bearded collie.

HEIGHT 20–22"

WEIGHT 40–60 LBS.

(!) Breed-related health concerns include pemphigus foliaceous (an autoimmune skin disease causing ulcers and scabs to develop on the skin all over the body).

LIFE SPAN 12–15 YRS.

Belgian Sheepdog

LARGE

SPECIAL EXERCISE NEEDS

SPECIAL GROOMING NEEDS

GOOD WATCHDOG

Belgian sheepdogs are extremely affectionate and friendly and want the constant attention of those they know well. They are very territorial and may not welcome animals or strangers on their property unless obedience trained and well socialized at an early age. They are comfortable with children when they are raised with them. When choosing a Belgian sheepdog from a litter, avoid any that exhibit shyness.

Laekenois Belgian sheepdog

Appearance The Belgian sheepdog is a square, medium-boned dog. Its lean head is set off by medium-size prick ears. Its four breed varieties have distinct coat colors and textures: the Groenendael has a long, straight, full, black coat; the Tervuren sports a long, dense coat, which ranges in color from rich fawn to russet mahogany with a black overlay; the Laekenois has a wiry coat in hues of reddish fawn with black shadings on the muzzle and tail; and the Malinois sports a short, hard, weather-resistant outercoat, which can be any color from fawn to mahogany, sometimes with black tipping, and has a black muzzle and ears.

Grooming & Exercise Needs
All varieties of Belgian sheepdogs shed and should be brushed on a regular schedule. The heavier-coated Groenendael and Tervuren need to be brushed several times a week, while one weekly brushing is adequate for the others. During

HEIGHT 21–26"

WEIGHT 55–65 LBS.

LIFE SPAN 10–14 YRS.

Tervuren Belgian sheepdog

Malinois Belgian sheepdog

shedding season, all these varieties need daily brushing. Belgian sheepdogs require an active outdoor life, and excel in herding, agility, and obedience programs.

Origins In 1891, a commission of canine experts was formed to determine whether there was one distinct "dog type" that could bear the title of Belgian sheepdog. By examining the dogs of the provinces, the commission determined that the Belgian sheepdog had a specific size, shape, and ear set, but that it had four varieties of coat color and hair texture. In any of its coats, the Belgian sheepdog proved to be an exceptional flock herder and guard as well as an intensely loyal protector.

(!) The Belgian sheepdog is not suitable for first-time or inexperienced dog owners.

Groenendael Belgian sheepdog

Border Collie

MEDIUM

HIGH ENERGY INDOORS

SPECIAL EXERCISE NEEDS

Border collie working a flock of sheep

The Border collie's reputation as the world's best sheepherding dog comes from its supreme intelligence, herding instinct, and demonstrated superiority in obedience and agility trials. These dogs must have constant stimulation or they may develop behavioral problems, such as household destruction or biting. Border collies are outgoing and friendly and get along with children and other animals.

HEIGHT 17–24"

WEIGHT 30–45 LBS.

LIFE SPAN 12–14 YRS.

Black and white Border collie

Appearance The Border collie's coat can be short and smooth, or medium-long and rough. Most commonly, its marking is black with traditional white blaze, collar, stockings, and tail tip, and occasionally tan points, although a variety of colors and markings is possible.

Grooming & Exercise Needs Border collies need to be brushed weekly. They also need to be kept busy to avoid behavioral problems. Sign this dog up for obedience, tracking, agility, or Flyball activities—or all of them!

Black and white rough-coated Border collie

Origins The Border collie has been used for sheepherding throughout Great Britain and Ireland for over 200 years.

ⓘ The Border collie is unsuitable for apartment living and needs an experienced owner. Breed-related health concerns: osteochondritis dissecans (page 442), progressive retinal atrophy (page 435).

Black and white smooth-coated Border collie

Canaan Dog

MEDIUM

GOOD WATCHDOG

The Canaan dog is territorial, devoted, and docile with its family, reserved and aloof with strangers. Early socialization with people and animals and early obedience classes may help the Canaan to overcome some of its natural wariness.

Appearance The Canaan dog's distinctive bushy tail curves over its back when the dog is alert. It has a wedge-shaped head; a coarse, medium-long outercoat; and a short undercoat that varies in thickness depending on the climate. This breed is predominantly white with colored mark-

Canaan dog with red markings

ings, or solid black, brown, sandy to reddish, or liver-color. Shadings of brown, tan, or rust on a black dog, or black on a brown or tan dog, or white on a black or brown dog are sometimes seen.

Canaan dog with black markings

Grooming & Exercise Needs Canaan dogs need to be combed and brushed once a week. Daily walks, participation in family activities, and some outdoor playtime will minimize barking, whining, and digging.

Origins Canaan dogs probably originated about four thousand years ago in what is now Israel, where they have been used as watchdogs, in shepherding, and, in modern times, by the military for search-and-rescue work and for landmine detection.

ⓘ The Canaan is not suitable for inexperienced dog owners. Breed-related health concerns include epilepsy (page 455).

HEIGHT 19–24"

WEIGHT 35–55 LBS.

LIFE SPAN 12–13 YRS.

Briard

LARGE

The briard has many of the qualities of a superb herding dog, and is protective of its herd/family and suspicious of strangers. It has an independent spirit and needs consistent obedience training from an early age (it's a slow learner). The briard is good with children and other animals if raised with them and well trained. The briard is not a wanderer; this dog prefers to stay home and guard the "flock."

Briard with natural (uncropped) ears

HIGH ENERGY INDOORS

SPECIAL EXERCISE NEEDS

SPECIAL GROOMING NEEDS

GOOD WATCHDOG

Appearance The briard's outercoat is generally six inches or longer and is hard, dry, and wavy; the undercoat is fine, dense, and tight. The coat color is fawn, black, gray, or tawny. The tail has a hook or crook at the end.

Grooming & Exercise Needs The briard needs to be brushed and combed every other day so its coat won't become matted. It has the energy level of a working dog—long walks or runs will thwart destructive behavior.

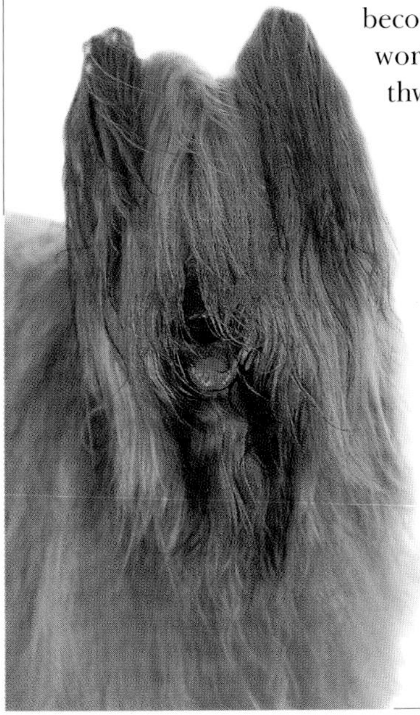

Origins The briard is the most popular sheepdog in France and has been used there as a livestock guardian and sheepherder since the Middle Ages. Probably named for the French province of Brie, the briard is vigorous, alert, strong, agile, and powerful.

(!) The briard is not recommended for inexperienced dog owners. Breed-related health concerns: hip dysplasia (page 442), bloat (page 445), hypothyroidism (page 452).

Briard with cropped ears

HEIGHT 22-27"

WEIGHT 70-90 LBS.

LIFE SPAN 10-12 YRS.

Collie

Smooth-coated collie pup

The collie's temperament makes it one of the finest family pets. These are highly responsive dogs that want to please their owners. They excel in obedience training when handled gently and with positive reinforcement, as long as the sessions are varied (repetitive activities bore these intelligent dogs) and interspersed with retrieving and jumping. Collies are affectionate with children, family members, and other familiar adults, and are generally friendly with other animals. Collies can be reserved with strangers without behaving aggressively, although they may bark when they feel they are needed as watchdogs or when they want attention.

Appearance The collie's coat can be rough or smooth. The coat of the rough variety is abundant except on the head and legs. The outercoat is straight and harsh to the touch; the undercoat is soft, furry, and so dense that it is difficult to see the skin. The smooth variety has a less abundant, hard, dense, and smooth coat. The collie is bred in four colors: sable and white, tricolor, blue merle, and white. While collies do not change color from birth, it may take several years for their coats to reach maximum pigmentation. The head shape is a lean, blunt wedge.

Blue merle smooth-coated collie

HEIGHT 22–25"

WEIGHT 50–75 LBS.

LIFE SPAN 12–14 YRS.

Grooming & Exercise Needs The rough collie's coat requires a considerable time commitment: it needs to be brushed every day when shedding and several times a week at other times or it will become

Sable and white rough-coated collie

severely matted and will need to be clipped. The collie typically sheds once a year in the spring, when a shedding rake is needed to remove the dense undercoat. The smooth collie requires only an occasional brushing. Collies don't need vigorous exercise, even though they are a herding breed. A few daily brisk walks around the block and ten to fifteen minutes of play are sufficient.

Origins Collies became popular in the 1860s, when Queen Victoria became infatuated with them after seeing them herd sheep during a visit to her estates in Balmoral, Scotland, and brought several back to Windsor Castle. The collie had been used as a herding dog in the border counties of northern England and Scotland. Its earliest ancestors may have been the herding dogs that accompanied the Romans across what is now Britain around 500 B.C.

(!) Breed-related health concerns: collie eye anomaly (a congenital defect that occasionally causes blindness), progressive retinal atrophy (page 435).

Sable smooth-coated collie in a herding trial

German Shepherd

LARGE

SPECIAL EXERCISE NEEDS

SPECIAL GROOMING NEEDS

GOOD WATCHDOG

Black and tan German shepherds

Well-bred and properly trained German shepherds are friendly, easy-going, playful, and eager to please. Because of their intelligence, responsiveness, and ability to focus, they are a joy to train. German shepherds are adaptable to city, apartment, suburban, and country living—as long as they are exercised and properly socialized when young. They are protective and will not retreat if their families or property are threatened. A well-bred and socialized shepherd can easily become a child's best friend, playing for hours and also protecting him. German shepherds may be wary of strangers. Obedience training must begin early.

Appearance The German shepherd has a double coat of medium length. The outercoat is dense, harsh, and straight, and lies close to the body; the undercoat is woolly and dense. Coat color is usually black and tan or solid black. White dogs exist but some breed registries do not admit them; others allow them as long as the skin pigment on the nose, eye rims, and lip folds is black. The hair on the tail is profuse. The erect, high-set ears give the impression of alertness. The chest is deep,

HEIGHT 22-26"

WEIGHT 65-95 LBS.

LIFE SPAN 11-13 YRS.

Black and tan German shepherd

the thighs are muscular and the rear legs are usually flexed. The tail is carried low when the dog is relaxed.

Grooming & Exercise Needs The German shepherd sheds year-round and should be brushed daily. A rake and comb are handy during the heavy shedding season. The German shepherd needs long walks and playtime every day to avoid boredom and prevent behavioral and medical problems.

German shepherd puppies

Origins The German shepherd originated in the 19th century as a sheepherding dog. Today this breed is better known for its skills in search-and-rescue, police, military, bomb-detection, tracking, and protection work. These highly trainable animals are also outstanding family dogs. Because of their popularity, however, they have been indiscriminately bred, and many undesirable traits have entered the shepherd gene pool. It is a great pleasure to own a good shepherd. The key is finding a reliable breeder who actively breeds for temperament and health.

ⓘ It is especially important to obtain a German shepherd from a reputable breeder; aggressive behavior can be a problem with poorly bred animals. Breed-related health problems include: hip and elbow dysplasia (page 442), intractable diarrhea (page 444), bloat (page 445), panosteitis (page 442), pannus (an inflammation of the cornea that may interfere with vision if untreated), von Willebrand's disease (a common disorder that causes excessive bleeding during or after surgery).

German shepherds are frequently trained to be seeing-eye dogs.

Shepherd Mixes

Shepherd mixes are generally outgoing dogs that take well to training. Most are fairly stable and some can even be submissive, but they can display a wide personality range, so it is important to assess temperament when choosing a shepherd mix. Some may be inclined to dominance, depending on their parentage and protection or guarding instincts. Such dogs can be aggressive with women and children; these need an experienced owner who can give them intensive training and maintain control.

Appearance Shepherd mixes usually have long, wolfish muzzles, with ears that are pricked, semi-pricked (bent over at the tips), or flopped down at the sides. Coats can be either short or long, thick, and wavy; colors range from black to tan, with markings of either color. Most shepherd mixes are medium-size to large dogs weighing between thirty-five and sixty-five pounds.

Shepherd mixes can be bright, people-oriented, energetic dogs.

Shepherd and other herding dog mix: compact, muscular, and ready to work

Grooming & Exercise Needs
Shepherd mixes are year-round shedders and need to be brushed at least twice a week. They have moderate to high exercise requirements. Most will need at least one hour of daily aerobic exercise beyond the usual three walks, and some may require even more physical activity.

A shepherd-husky mix with partly pricked ears is alert and always aware of what is going on in her environment. Her long, thick coat comes from her husky genes.

A patient shepherd-Doberman mother with a large litter that shows an even greater variety of coat colors and patterns than commonly seen in shepherds or Dobermans.

This shepherd mix appears to have inherited the dwarf gene that is sometimes visible in shepherds and shepherd mixes. It results in a dog with short, thick legs and a normal-size torso and head.

LARGE

SPECIAL EXERCISE NEEDS

SPECIAL GROOMING NEEDS

Old English Sheepdog

Old English sheepdog at work

Old English sheepdogs are generally good natured and fun loving, but lifetime training and socialization must begin from early puppyhood. Without that attitude and commitment from his owner, the sheepdog can become stubborn and unmanageable.

Appearance The Old English sheepdog's outercoat is shaggy, profuse, and hard in texture; its undercoat is a dense, waterproof pile. Coat color is shades of gray, grizzle, blue, or blue merle, sometimes with white markings.

Grooming & Exercise Needs Old English sheepdogs require an enormous amount of grooming—about an hour a day of brushing and combing to avoid serious matting. They need a lot of daily exercise.

Origins The Old English sheepdog was developed in England in the 19th century to drive sheep.

Old English sheepdog with a show coat

! It is especially important to obtain an Old English sheepdog from a reputable breeder. Old English sheepdogs must have experienced owners who can devote much time to their care and who live where the dog's exercise requirements can be met. Breed-related health concerns: hip dysplasia (page 442), juvenile cataracts (page 434), progressive retinal atrophy (page 435), cervical vertebral instability (a malformation of the neck vertebrae causing a wobbly gait), bloat (page 445), deafness (page 436).

HEIGHT 21-25"

WEIGHT 65-80 LBS.

LIFE SPAN 12-13 YRS.

Polish Owczarek Nizinny
(or Polish Lowland Sheepdog)

MEDIUM

SPECIAL EXERCISE NEEDS

SPECIAL GROOMING NEEDS

Their compact size and merry disposition make Polish Owczarek Nizinnys (PONs) a good choice for apartment dwellers. They are extremely loyal and devoted to their flocks/families, but they are sometimes aloof and suspicious with strangers. They do well with children if raised with them and treated gently and with respect. They may fight with strange dogs but can get along with other animals, such as cats.

The Polish Owczarek Nizinny has long hair on forehead, cheeks, and chin.

In obedience training, they require firm and confident handling.

Appearance The outercoat of the PON is long, dense, and shaggy and covers the eyes; the undercoat is soft and dense. All coat colors are seen; the most common colors are cream, black and white, and wheaten.

Grooming & Exercise Needs The PON needs to be brushed and combed daily to avoid matting. This dog needs several brisk walks and romps daily.

Origins The PON, a herding dog, originated in the 13th century in Poland.

(!) The PON is not suitable for inexperienced owners. Breed-related health concerns include patent ductus arteriosus (page 449).

Unlike the Old English sheepdog, the PON is shown in a natural coat.

HEIGHT 16–20"

WEIGHT 30–35 LBS.

LIFE SPAN 12–14 YRS.

Puli

MEDIUM

SPECIAL EXERCISE NEEDS

SPECIAL GROOMING NEEDS

GOOD WATCHDOG

Pulik (plural) are loyal, bright dogs that need early obedience training. Vigorous, active, and alert, the puli is a good home guardian and companion dog but usually does not make a good pet for children. They get along with other animals if raised with them but will probably attempt to herd them. Pulik may bark at strangers. They can live in the city as long as they get enough exercise.

The puli's corded coat requires a lot of care.

Appearance The dense, profuse, corded coat of the puli is weather-resistant. The long outercoat is wiry and wavy or curly; the undercoat is soft, woolly, and dense. The outer, wiry hairs connect with the woolly undercoat hairs to form long cords. Coat color is rusty black, black, all shades of gray, or white.

Grooming & Exercise Needs Pulik require an enormous amount of care. If trimmed short, they must be brushed every other day or severe matting will occur. If left long, cords must be separated by hand occasionally and rinsed well when shampooed. Pulik require a lot of exercise or they may develop behavior problems.

Origins The puli was developed in Hungary over a thousand years ago for sheepherding.

(!) The puli is not suitable for inexperienced owners. Breed-related health concerns include hip dysplasia (page 442).

HEIGHT 15-18"

WEIGHT 30-35 LBS.

LIFE SPAN 14-16 YRS.

Puli with a rusty black corded coat

Shetland Sheepdog

SMALL

SPECIAL GROOMING NEEDS

GOOD WATCHDOG

Shelties are bright, eager to please, and do well in obedience training. They're affectionate with familiar, quiet children but may try to herd small children. Shelties should be socialized early to avoid being overly shy as adults.

Sable Shetland sheepdog puppies

Appearance The sheltie's outer-coat is long, straight, and harsh; the undercoat is short, furry, and dense. Coat color is black, sable (ranging from golden to mahogany), or blue merle, all with varying amounts of white and/or tan trim. The hair on the face, feet, and ear tips is smooth. The mane and frill are abundant and impressive. Hair on the tail is profuse. The ears are small and three-fourths erect.

Grooming & Exercise Needs The sheltie needs to be brushed and combed daily or its coat will become severely matted. Some trimming is required every three months. A few brisk walks and romps daily will keep the sheltie happy.

Tricolor Shetland sheepdog

Origins The Shetland sheep-dog traces its ancestry to the Border collie. In the 18th century, the Border collie was crossed with small, intelligent, long-haired breeds in the Shetland Islands to produce the miniatur-ized sheltie of today.

⚠ Be sure to purchase a sheltie from a reputable breeder. Many shelties are not suitable for life in the city because of their sensitivity to noise. Breed-related health concerns: eye disorders including progressive retinal atrophy (page 435), bleeding disorders, deafness (page 436), autoimmune skin diseases (rare, occasionally fatal disorders causing tissue to destroy itself), hypothyroidism (page 452).

HEIGHT 13–16"

WEIGHT 14–18 LBS.

LIFE SPAN 12–14 YRS.

Herding Mixes

Herding mixes are bright, alert, and very responsive to training. They need lots of stimulation to focus their enormous physical energy and sharp intelligence. If these dogs aren't challenged in this way, they can develop behavior problems, such as household destruction or nipping. Herding mixes are usually of some sheepherding parentage, although in regions where the cattle industry is strong, mixes of cattle-herding breeds are more common.

Appearance These dogs are medium-size to large, with a thick coat in a variety of colors and lengths. The black and white, tricolor, merle, and speckled patterns seen in purebred herding dogs are also replicated in herding mixes.

A traditional black and white Border collie mix is always watchful and ready to go.

Another Border collie mix has different colored eyes—one blue, one brown—which shows her collie heritage.

This herding mix has the "china eye," the blue eye that puts intensity in the dog's stare and helps him do his work.

Grooming & Exercise Needs Most of these dogs need brushing twice a week, although some can need more frequent grooming. Because of their high energy and tremendous stamina, these dogs need three walks daily as well as frequent daily off-leash play and running time in a secured area.

A bearded collie mix climbs atop some farm equipment to get a better look at the world around him.

A three-month-old Border collie mix, pooped after a hard day.

Northern Breeds

Husky dog sled teams at work on a frozen lake in Greenland

No group has a more wolfish appearance than the northern or spitz-type breeds: prick ears, sharp muzzle, broad chest, thick double coat, strong, well-muscled body, and bushy tail curled over the back. These confident, vigorous dogs come alive in cool, crisp weather; taking part in winter sports with their families is what they live for.

Most of the northern breeds were developed in cold, Arctic regions hundreds of years ago and since then have served most often as draft or sled dogs. Alaskan malamutes pulled heavy supply sledges, while lighter Siberian huskies transported people at a swifter pace. Samoyeds, seen today in recreational sled racing, originally herded reindeer. The massive fore-assembly that makes these breeds function so admirably as sled dogs can also make them a challenge to walk on-leash without proper training.

Some northern breeds were used in hunting. The Finnish spitz and Shiba Inu went after small game, while the Norwegian elkhound ran down lynx, wolves, and elk. A number of northern hunters, including the Finnish spitz and the elkhound, used their voices to alert the hunter to the presence of game. This vocalism was passed on to smaller northern breeds, such as the American Eskimo dog, keeshond, Pomeranian, and schipperke, that were developed primarily as watchdogs.

The larger Asiatic northern breeds include the Akita, developed as a fighting dog and later used to hunt large game; the chow chow, once a source of food and fur as well as a carting and guard dog; and the Chinese shar-pei, first used in the dogfighting ring and then in hunting and herding. Their fighting and guarding backgrounds make these Asian breeds more reserved and at times more aggressive with strangers than other breeds in the northern group.

Finnish spitz

Norwegian elkhound

Samoyed

Northern Breeds		HIGH ENERGY INDOORS	SPECIAL EXERCISE NEEDS	SPECIAL GROOMING NEEDS	GOOD WATCHDOG	GOOD WITH KIDS
FINNISH SPITZ *page 185*	MEDIUM		●		●	●
NORWEGIAN ELKHOUND *page 186*	MEDIUM		●		●	
SAMOYED *page 187*	LARGE	●	●		●	●
SHIBA INU *page 188*	MEDIUM					
ALASKAN MALAMUTE *page 189*	LARGE		●			
SIBERIAN HUSKY *page 190*	LARGE	●	●			●

Shiba Inu

Alaskan malamute

Siberian husky

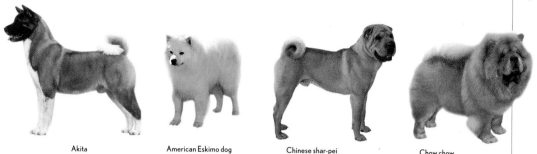

Akita American Eskimo dog Chinese shar-pei Chow chow

Northern Breeds		HIGH ENERGY INDOORS	SPECIAL EXERCISE NEEDS	SPECIAL GROOMING NEEDS	GOOD WATCHDOG	GOOD WITH KIDS
AKITA *page 191*	LARGE				●	
AMERICAN ESKIMO DOG *page 192*	SMALL MEDIUM					
CHINESE SHAR-PEI *page 193*	MEDIUM					
CHOW CHOW *page 194*	MEDIUM			●		
KEESHOND *page 195*	MEDIUM			●	●	●
POMERANIAN *page 196*	SMALL	●		●	●	
SCHIPPERKE *page 197*	SMALL	●	●		●	

Keeshond

Pomeranian

Schipperke

Northern mixes

Finnish Spitz

MEDIUM

Finnish spitzes are friendly, active, and lively companions. Eager to please, they do well in obedience classes. These dogs love children and usually get along with other dogs. They will bark when someone is at the door—their bark is part of their hunting persona—but warm up to most people quickly. If this dog is separated from family life—left alone in the backyard for long periods, for example—it will begin to bark or yap excessively.

Auburn-coated
Finnish spitz

SPECIAL EXERCISE NEEDS

GOOD WATCHDOG

GOOD WITH KIDS

Appearance The undercoat is short, soft, and dense, and sheds in warm weather; the straight, harsh guard hairs measure one to two inches. Coat color ranges from pale honey to deep auburn. The head is almost twice as long as the widest part of the skull. The bushy tail curves up in a tight, vigorous curve.

Adult Finnish spitz with puppy

Grooming & Exercise Needs The Finnish spitz needs to be brushed a few times a week and requires several brisk walks and some playtime daily.

Origins The Finnish spitz, which originated in the 19th century, is the national dog of Finland, where it is still used as a hunting dog.

ⓘ Finnish spitzes are not suitable for city or apartment life because of their extremely vocal nature. Breed-related health concerns: epilepsy (page 455), pemphigus foliaceous (an autoimmune skin disease causing ulcers and scabs to develop on the skin all over the body).

HEIGHT 15–20"

WEIGHT 25–35 LBS.

LIFE SPAN 12–14 YRS.

Norwegian Elkhound

MEDIUM

SPECIAL EXERCISE NEEDS

GOOD WATCHDOG

This affectionate, energetic, strong, and courageous dog makes a devoted family pet. A firm, patient owner and early socialization and obedience training are crucial. The elkhound is noisy and therefore a good watchdog, but it is not aggressive toward people. Although this dog can live in the city, it is better suited for the suburbs or country.

Norwegian elkhounds have a black, tapered muzzle.

Appearance The Norwegian elkhound's outercoat is thick, coarse, and straight; the undercoat is soft, dense, and woolly. Coat color is gray with black tips. The muzzle, ears, and tail tip are black; the legs, stomach, buttocks, and underside of the tail are silver.

Grooming & Exercise Needs The Norwegian elkhound's coat needs to be brushed and combed one to two times a week. This energetic dog needs several long, brisk walks and runs as well as playtime in a secure area daily.

Origins The Norwegian elkhound, a favorite of the Vikings, originated in Norway thousands of years ago and was used primarily for hunting.

(!) Breed-related health concerns: congenital kidney problems, progressive retinal atrophy (page 435), cataracts (page 434), glaucoma (page 434).

HEIGHT 19½–20½"

WEIGHT 44–55 LBS.

LIFE SPAN 13–14 YRS.

The underside of the Norwegian elkhound's curled tail is silver.

Samoyed

LARGE

Samoyeds are charming, intelligent family companions that are very good with children and other animals and respectful of strangers. Like most spitz-type dogs, they can be stubborn and independent and, as a result, difficult to obedience train; starting early makes the job easier. Samoyeds must be included in family activities or they will become destructive. These dogs are barkers; that's how they like to communicate when they are feeling happy, sad, nervous, or isolated.

HIGH ENERGY INDOORS

SPECIAL EXERCISE NEEDS

A Samoyed pair sport racing

Appearance The Samoyed's outercoat is long, straight, and harsh and stands out from the body; the undercoat is soft, short, thick, close, and woolly. There is a ruff around the neck and shoulders. Coat color is pure white, white and biscuit, cream, or biscuit. The tail is profusely covered with long hair and curls over the back.

GOOD WATCHDOG

GOOD WITH KIDS

Grooming & Exercise Needs Samoyeds need to be brushed two to three times a week, daily when shedding. They require vigorous daily exercise, such as long, fast-paced walks.

Origins The hardy, gentle, friendly Samoyed is an ancient breed. It was named for the Samoyed tribe of Siberia, where it herded reindeer, guarded the huts of the nomadic people, and was used as a sled dog.

(!) Breed-related health concerns: hip dysplasia (page 442), retinal problems.

Pure white Samoyed

HEIGHT 19-23½"

WEIGHT 50-75 LBS.

LIFE SPAN 10-15 YRS.

MEDIUM

Shiba Inu

Red Shiba Inu with white markings

Shiba Inus are bright, independent, clean and tidy dogs. They can be aloof and reserved with strangers as well as their families, but will accept children and other dogs and cats if raised with them. Like basenjis, they seldom bark but make their own distinctive sound reminiscent of a shriek. Shiba Inus need early and ongoing training to counteract their attempts to dominate.

Appearance The Shiba Inu's outercoat is strong and straight; the undercoat soft and dense. The hair on the ruff, rear, and tail is slightly longer. The ruff may form a crest encircling the neck. Coat color is red, red sesame, black, or black and tan, all with white markings. Its spitz heritage is revealed in its dense coat, small ears (to reduce heat loss and frostbite), wedge-shaped muzzle, thick fur between the toes, and bushy tail that curls forward over the back.

Grooming & Exercise Needs Shiba Inus need to be brushed and combed two to three times a week. They enjoy a couple of daily brisk walks or romps in a safe, secure area.

Origins The Shiba Inu is an ancient Japanese hunting dog that was used for hunting birds and small game for more than 2,000 years. The breed is a result of the interbreeding of three ancient breeds: the Sanin, the Mino, and the Shinshu. It is the most popular dog in Japan.

(!) Shiba Inus are not suitable for inexperienced dog owners. Breed-related health concerns include patellar luxation (page 443).

HEIGHT 13½–16½"

WEIGHT 15–25 LBS.

LIFE SPAN 12–15 YRS.

Red Shiba Inu in a show pose

Alaskan Malamute

LARGE

The Alaskan malamute is fiercely loyal to its "pack," loves the children of its own family, and gets along with other animals if socialized with them early on. It must have early obedience classes from an experienced trainer. Leave an untrained malamute alone and he will HOWL!

SPECIAL EXERCISE NEEDS

Five-week-old malamute puppy

Appearance The outercoat is long, thick, and coarse; the undercoat is dense, oily, and woolly, and can be two inches deep. Coat color is light gray and white, black and white, or all white.

Grooming & Exercise Needs The malamute requires weekly or twice-weekly brushing. Its undercoat sheds profusely once or twice a year, at which time it needs to be brushed daily. Without physical and mental stimulation, this dog becomes destructive both indoors and out. Jogging, hiking, or backpacking (the dog carrying its own pack) are perfect daily activities. During hot weather, stick to early-morning and late-evening workouts for this Arctic breed.

Origins This hardy dog was used by the Inuits 1,000 years ago for pulling sleds and for traveling long distances in sub-zero temperatures.

(!) The Alaskan malamute is not suitable for inexperienced dog owners or for apartment life. Breed-related health concerns: hip dysplasia (page 442), dwarfism, hemolytic anemia (a disorder of the red blood cells), congenital kidney problems.

Gray and white Alaskan malamute

HEIGHT 23-25"

WEIGHT 75-85 LBS.

LIFE SPAN 10-12 YRS.

LARGE

HIGH ENERGY INDOORS

SPECIAL EXERCISE NEEDS

GOOD WITH KIDS

Siberian Husky

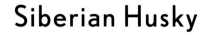

Siberian huskies are very gentle, friendly, alert, and playful, and they love human companionship. They're not easy to train, however (begin obedience classes early and never stop), and do best with experienced dog owners who live in the country. Huskies adore children and other dogs, but may chase cats. They also like to roam. Without proper care, they will howl and/or be destructive.

Gray and white Siberian husky

Appearance The Siberian husky has a double coat of medium length: straight and smooth-lying above, soft and dense underneath. Common colors are gray and white and chestnut and white. Eyes may be brown, blue, one of each, or blue and brown in the same eye. The tail is well furred.

Grooming & Exercise Needs Siberian huskies need to be brushed a few times a week, daily when shedding. They love long hikes, walks, and backpacking trips—and need to run off-leash in secure areas.

Origins The Siberian husky, bred more than 3,000 years ago by nomadic Siberian tribes to be a sled dog, was brought to North America by fur traders around the turn of the 20th century.

A racing-bred team of Siberian huskies

⚠ Obtain a Siberian husky only from a reputable breeder. This dog is not suitable for inexperienced owners. Breed-related health concerns: progressive retinal atrophy (page 435), corneal dystrophy (degenerative condition causing cloudiness of the cornea or even blindness), glaucoma (page 434), discoid lupus (an autoimmune disease causing ulcers on the nose), susceptibility to zinc deficiency.

HEIGHT 20–23"

WEIGHT 35–60 LBS.

LIFE SPAN 12–14 YRS.

Akita

LARGE

GOOD WATCHDOG

A litter of Akitas shows the breed's various colors and markings.

Akitas look like warm, cuddly dogs but they are aloof with outsiders. Obedience training is a must, and exposure to a lot of people at an early age is recommended. Some get along well with children, especially if introduced at an early age, but others do not. They bark when they perceive a threat.

Appearance Akitas come in all colors and can be solid or have patches of two or more colors, such as white and brindle. The medium-length outercoat is stiff; the undercoat is soft, fine, and dense. The Akita has a strong, broad muzzle and a bearlike expression. The tail is held high and curls forward.

Grooming & Exercise Needs The Akita's coat is easily cared for with weekly brushings. Akitas need a moderate amount of exercise, such as a few long walks and some playtime daily.

Origins The Akita descends from a spitz-like dog that existed about 5,000 years ago. It was named for the province of Akita on Japan's Honshu Island, where it was used by noblemen to hunt large game.

(!) The Akita is not suitable for inexperienced dog owners. It can be especially aggressive with other dogs. Breed-related health concerns: hyperthyroidism (overproduction of thyroid hormones), hypothyrodism (page 452) pemphigus foliaceous (an autoimmune skin disease causing ulcers and scabs to develop on the skin), hip and elbow dysplasia (page 442), sebaceous adenitis (skin disease resulting in scabs, hair loss, and predisposition to bacterial skin infections).

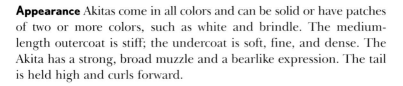

Akita in a show pose

HEIGHT 24–28"

WEIGHT 75–110 LBS.

LIFE SPAN 10–12 YRS.

American Eskimo Dog

Pure white toy American Eskimo dog

Eskies like to be with their families but may appear aloof or uncomfortable with strangers. They prefer adults but will tolerate children and usually get along with dogs and other animals. Early socialization and obedience training are necessary. Eskies are easy to train and like to perform and learn new tricks.

Appearance There are three different sizes of Eskies: toy, miniature, and standard. The outercoat is medium in length and thick; the undercoat is denser and softer. Coat color is pure white or white with biscuit.

Grooming & Exercise Needs The Eskie sheds heavily and requires weekly brushing and combing. They need regular exercise, including at least one vigorous walk and a play session daily.

Origins The American Eskimo dog probably never saw an Eskimo. In fact, the breed, which originated between 500 and 1,000 years ago, owes its physical and behavioral characteristics to the Nordic or spitz dogs of Europe with some Pomeranian and keeshond mixed in.

HEIGHT
TOY 9–12"
MINIATURE 12–15"
STANDARD 15–19"

WEIGHT
TOY 6–10 LBS.
MINIATURE 10–20 LBS.
STANDARD 18–35 LBS.

LIFE SPAN 13–15 YRS.

Eskies have always been popular stage and circus performers.

Chinese Shar-Pei

MEDIUM

The independent and sometimes stubborn shar-pei is devoted to its family, protective of its territory, and wary of human and animal strangers. Socialization and obedience classes at an early age are a must. The shar-pei does best with respectful children at least five years old. Confrontations with other animals can be a problem.

Three-month-old black Chinese shar-pei puppies

Appearance The coat may be one of three lengths: horse (under ½ inch long), brush (½ to one inch long), or bear (over one inch long). The coat is usually cream, fawn, red, or black, and the tongue either bluish-black or lavender (in light-coated dogs). The loose skin, small ears, thick rounded muzzle, and curled high-set tail are also distinctive.

Red shar-pei

Grooming & Exercise Needs Brush weekly to prevent skin infections, and examine skin folds and between digits regularly. The shar-pei needs daily brisk walks on a leash or a run in a secured area.

Origins The shar-pei originated in China over 2,000 years ago and was bred for hunting and dogfighting. Its thick, loose skin made it virtually impervious to an attacker's sharp teeth and claws, allowing the shar-pei to turn and bite even while being bitten.

(!) The Chinese shar-pei is not suitable for inexperienced dog owners. Breed-related health concerns: entropion (page 434), skin and ear infections, atopy (page 437), patellar luxation (page 443), hip and elbow dysplasia (page 442), hypothyroidism (page 452).

HEIGHT 18-10"

WEIGHT 35-55 LBS.

LIFE SPAN 8-12 YRS.

Chow Chow

MEDIUM

SPECIAL GROOMING NEEDS

The quiet, independent chow chow is a one-person dog. It is not very demonstrative and can be aggressive, stubborn, and difficult to train. Chows are reserved with strangers and have a tendency to bite; deep-set eyes give these dogs poor peripheral vision, making them more likely to bite if surprised from behind. Early obedience classes and socialization with adults, children, and other animals are very important. The chow will tolerate children when raised with them but will not be playful.

Rough-coated chow chow, showing its black tongue

Appearance The chow chow's coat may be smooth or rough. The abundant outercoat is straight; the undercoat is soft, thick, and woolly. Color is red, black, blue, cinnamon, or cream. Tongue is blue-black; feet are small; ears are thick and rounded. The tail curls over the back.

Grooming & Exercise Needs The rough-coated chow needs to be brushed daily; the smooth-coated variety needs to be brushed a few times a week, daily when shedding. The chow is content with short walks for exercise.

Origins Developed in northern China over 2,000 years ago, the chow chow was used for hunting, herding, pulling, protection of the home, and as a source of food and fur.

Rough- and smooth-coated chow chows

HEIGHT 17–20"

WEIGHT 45–70 LBS.

LIFE SPAN 10–12 YRS.

(!) Chows require experienced owners prepared for a significant time commitment. Find a breeder who breeds for temperament because chows can be aggressive. Breed-related health concerns: hip dysplasia (page 442), entropion (page 434), hypothyroidism (page 452), epilepsy (page 455), bloat (page 445).

Keeshond

MEDIUM

SPECIAL GROOMING NEEDS

GOOD WATCHDOG

GOOD WITH KIDS

Eight-week-old keeshond puppy

Lovable, gentle, affectionate, and adaptable, keeshonden (plural) are ideal family dogs. They are alert and do very well in obedience classes as long as they are kept focused with firm but gentle handling. They get along with other animals and enjoy the company of children. Keeshonden are friendly to strangers but will bark to let the household know that a visitor has arrived.

Appearance The keeshond's outercoat is abundant, long, straight, and harsh, and stands out from a thick, downy undercoat. The hair on the legs is smooth and short, except for feathering on the front legs and "trousers" on the back legs. Coat color is a mixture of black-tipped gray, black, and cream, with a very pale gray or cream undercoat. The plume of the tail is very light in color when curled on the back. The underside of the tail is cream colored, and the tip of the tail is black. "Spectacles" appear around the eyes.

Grooming & Exercise Needs To avoid severe matting, the keeshond needs be brushed and combed daily. This dog does not need a lot of exercise—a short, brisk walk or a lazy, long walk and some playtime will suffice.

Origins The national dog of Holland, the keeshond was used as a watchdog on river barges in the 16th century.

(!) Breed related health concerns: hip dysplasia (page 442), heart disease, epilepsy (page 455), hypothyroidism (page 452).

Keeshond, showing spectacles around eyes

HEIGHT 16–19"

WEIGHT 35–40 LBS.

LIFE SPAN 12–15 YRS.

Pomeranian

Pomeranians are eager to please, like training, and do very well in obedience classes. These spunky dogs may try to dominate other dogs, though they can get along with other animals. They may not be friendly with strangers, or even all family members, and may guard toys and food bowls and bark excessively if not socialized and trained at an early age. Pomeranians adapt well to apartment life and are a good choice for adult households.

Black Pomeranian puppy

Appearance The Pomeranian's outercoat is profuse, coarse, and straight, with a large neck ruff; the undercoat is soft and thick. Coat color is red, orange, cream, sable, black, brown, blue, particolor (white with colored patches), or sable or black with tan markings. The fox-like ears are small and erect, the tail curls forward.

Grooming & Exercise Needs Pomeranians need to be brushed two to three times a week and trimmed every three months. They need very little exercise.

Origins The Pomeranian is probably descended from a large German spitz dog of the 16th century. Bred to its current size in the 19th century, the Pomeranian still thinks of itself as a big dog.

(!) It is especially important to obtain a Pomeranian from a reputable breeder. Breed-related health concerns: undescended testicles, patellar luxation (page 443), tracheal collapse (page 448), patent ductus arteriosus (page 449), progressive retinal atrophy (page 435), tooth and gum disease (page 444).

HEIGHT 8-11"

WEIGHT 3-7 LBS.

LIFE SPAN 12-16 YRS.

Orange Pomeranian

Schipperke

SMALL

HIGH ENERGY INDOORS

SPECIAL EXERCISE NEEDS

GOOD WATCHDOG

The schipperke is constantly in motion, curious about everything and everyone—in short, a delightful, furry busybody. Smart and stubborn, this dog does well in obedience training only if its mulishness is pacified gently but firmly. Some schipperkes can be difficult to housebreak; others may be possessive of toys and food bowls. While most schipperkes enjoy children if socialized at an early age, some can be nippy with children who don't treat them gently. Schipperkes get along with other animals, yet strangers are treated warily. With adequate exercise, they do well in city, country, or suburb.

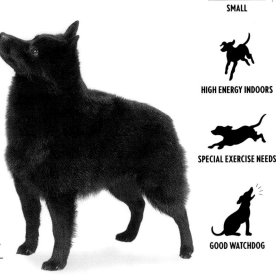

Schipperkes have abundant outercoats.

Appearance The outercoat is abundant, straight, and slightly coarse; the undercoat is softer, thick, and very dense around the neck. The hair is shorter on the face, ears, and legs. The hair on the rear forms a culotte that is as long as the ruff. Coat color is black. The face is foxlike, the ears small, triangular, and very erect.

The schipperke has a foxlike face.

Grooming & Exercise Needs Schipperkes should be brushed once a week. They need vigorous daily exercise, such as two or three fast-paced long walks.

Origins The schipperke originated in 16th-century Belgium, where it kept canal barges free of rats and watched for intruders. *Schipperke* is Flemish for "little captain."

(!) Breed-related health concerns: Legg-Perthes disease (page 443), hypothyroidism (page 452).

HEIGHT 10–13"

WEIGHT 12–18 LBS.

LIFE SPAN 12–15 YRS.

Northern Breed Mixes

A husky-retriever mix

While spitz-type northern-breed mixes show some continuity in appearance, the northern breeds have a great diversity of personalities. Siberian husky mixes may be friendly and outgoing but difficult to train. Akita mixes, reflecting their fighting-dog roots, may be dominant or aggressive, especially with women and children, if not trained. Chow and shar-pei mixes may be somewhat aloof. Energy levels also vary depending on the breed mix. Husky and other robust sled dogs have moderate to high energy levels, as do Samoyeds.

Appearance Spitz-type northern mixes have thick coats and thick bushy tails that usually curl over their backs. Their muzzles are foxy and wolfish looking. Their powerful builds are distinguished by strong shoulders and chests ideally suited for pulling (which can be an issue when walking these dogs on-leash). American Eskimo dog, Finnish spitz, and Shiba Inu mixes can be quite small. Coat colors vary widely among northern mixes, depending on the breed mix. Sometimes one or both eyes is blue (known as "china").

Grooming & Exercise Needs Northern mixes are heavy shedders, especially during spring and fall shedding seasons, and are more active in wintry, cold climates than in hot humid climates.

A chow-husky mix shows the thick double coat and prick ears of a husky and chowlike black markings on its tongue.

This husky-shepherd mix has a thick, bushy tail, which can keep its face warm when the dog curls up in cold weather.

Chow-mix dogs in red and black tones found in the purebred dogs. Their chow ancestry is apparent in the black markings on their tongues and their almond-shaped eyes.

Sled dog-mix puppies. Many sled dogs are bred more for their ability to pull sleds in teams than for pure-breed standards. Regions that have a dog sled tradition are likely to have a large population of sled dog mixes.

Scent Hounds

A bloodhound at work tracking a scent through a forest

Scent hounds are gentle if not terribly obedient dogs that are driven by their noses. Their long earflaps and pendulous lips work to gather in scent, making these dogs very effective trackers. With its nose to the ground, a scent hound catches and then follows the odor of its prey, howling out an alert to its handler. Unlike terriers, scent hounds rarely kill prey, but rather hold the prey at bay for the handler. Exceptional tracking ability can get these dogs into trouble, as it leads them into garbage or off to chase wildlife if they are not on a leash or confined to a well-secured area. Scent hounds were developed to hunt in braces (twos) or packs, so they are generally friendly with other dogs.

Long-bodied, slow-moving, dwarf scent hound breeds (basset hound, petit basset griffon Vendeen) were developed for tracking rabbits and hares. Unlike other scent hounds, the long, low dachshund boasts a feisty, terrier-like personality and can dive down a hole to chase out prey or catch and kill it underground. The small, well-proportioned beagle, one of the oldest scent hounds (dating to the fourteenth century), used its nose and speed to circle a rabbit back toward a hunter. Slightly predating the beagle, the swift, sturdy harrier is used to hunt both hare and fox. The leggier English and American foxhounds were developed to hunt fox in large packs.

The otter hound and the bloodhound are the largest of the trailing hounds. They are similar in build, but the otter hound has webbed feet and a rough, water-resistant coat ideal for hunting otter in the water, while the bloodhound trails animals and humans on land. The black-and-tan coonhound, a distant relative of both, was developed for its ability to hunt raccoon and opossum.

Scent Hounds		HIGH ENERGY INDOORS	SPECIAL EXERCISE NEEDS	SPECIAL GROOMING NEEDS	GOOD WATCHDOG	GOOD WITH KIDS
BLACK-AND-TAN COONHOUND *page 203*	LARGE		●			●
BASSET HOUND *page 204*	MEDIUM					●
PETIT BASSET GRIFFON VENDEEN *page 205*	MEDIUM		●			●
DACHSHUND *page 206*	SMALL MEDIUM				●	
AMERICAN FOXHOUND *page 208*	LARGE	●	●			●

Basset hound

Dachshund

Black-and-tan coonhound

Petit basset griffon Vendeen

American foxhound

Beagle

English foxhound

Harrier

Scent Hounds		HIGH ENERGY INDOORS	SPECIAL EXERCISE NEEDS	SPECIAL GROOMING NEEDS	GOOD WATCHDOG	GOOD WITH KIDS
BEAGLE *page 209*	MEDIUM	●				●
ENGLISH FOXHOUND *page 210*	LARGE	●	●			●
HARRIER *page 211*	MEDIUM	●	●		●	●
BLOODHOUND *page 212*	LARGE		●			●
OTTER HOUND *page 213*	LARGE		●	●		

Bloodhound

Otter hound

Scent hound mixes

Black-and-Tan Coonhound

LARGE

SPECIAL EXERCISE NEEDS

GOOD WITH KIDS

The black-and-tan coonhound is a gentle, affectionate, playful dog that gets along with everybody, including children and other animals. While never at the top of obedience class, coonhounds excel in tracking and are happiest when hot on the trail of a raccoon or opossum.

Black-and-tan coonhounds have a short, dense coat.

Appearance Because the coonhound's coat is short and dense, it is able to withstand rough terrain. The color is black, with rich tan markings above the eyes and on the sides of the muzzle, as well as on the chest, legs, and breeching, with black pencil markings on the toes.

Grooming & Exercise Needs The black-and-tan coonhound requires minimal grooming. Comb with a rubber brush once a week, especially when shedding is heaviest. This dog needs a lot of exercise—several vigorous walks and runs in a secured area daily.

Origins The black-and-tan coonhound is descended from the English Talbot hound, the bloodhound, and the foxhound (the Virginia foxhound of the 18th century, in particular).

(!) The coonhound's strong scenting instinct makes it ill suited to city or apartment life. Breed-related health concerns: hip dysplasia (page 442), ectropion (page 434), hemophilia (a bleeding disorder).

The coonhound's long, pendulous ears trap scent and direct it to the nose.

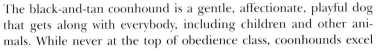

HEIGHT 23–27"

WEIGHT 50–75 LBS.

LIFE SPAN 10–12 YRS.

Basset Hound

MEDIUM

GOOD WITH KIDS

The sweet and gentle basset hound loves everybody, including children, and is usually well behaved with other animals. While bassets can be quite stubborn and difficult to house train, this can be corrected with early obedience training. Basset hounds slobber and drink water sloppily, so they are not a good choice for people who keep an immaculate household.

Appearance The basset hound is a short-legged, heavy-boned dog. It has a hard, dense coat over loose, elastic skin. All true hound colors—white, tan, and black in various combinations—are seen.

The basset has the true hound colors—white, tan, and black.

Grooming & Exercise Needs The basset hound sheds moderately and needs to be brushed and have its pendulous ears cleaned once a week to prevent infections. Its ears, chest, and belly can get quite dirty and may require frequent bathing. The basset needs a few long, brisk walks and playtime in a fenced area daily. It should be walked on a leash as it may wander off tracking a scent.

Origins The basset hound, a descendant of French scent hounds, was developed in the 16th century for hunting rabbits and hares.

(!) Basset hounds are more prone to illness and require more veterinary care than most dogs. Breed-related health concerns: osteochondritis dissecans (page 442), patellar luxation (page 443), elbow dysplasia (page 442), ectropion/entropion (page 434), glaucoma (page 434), otitis externa (page 435), cervical vertebral instability (a malformation of the neck vertebrae resulting in a wobbling gait), bleeding disorders, lymphoma (page 432), epilepsy (page 455), bloat (page 445).

HEIGHT 14"

WEIGHT 40–60 LBS.

LIFE SPAN 10–12 YRS.

Tan and white basset hound

Petit Basset Griffon Vendeen

MEDIUM

SPECIAL EXERCISE NEEDS

GOOD WITH KIDS

The happy, extroverted petit basset griffon Vendeen makes a loyal, affectionate companion. It does well in obedience classes, which should be started early. PBGVs get along very well with children if treated gently and introduced to them at an early age. They also enjoy the company of other animals, although they can be possessive of toys and food bowls and have a tendency to bark excessively if not corrected early. Well suited for country life, they can also live in the city or suburbs as long as they get enough exercise, playtime, and social interaction.

Lemon petit basset griffon Vendeen

Appearance With its long eyebrows, beard, mustache, and rough coat, the PBGV has an unkempt appearance. The outercoat is long and harsh to the touch; the undercoat is thicker and shorter. Coat color is white with any combination of lemon, orange, black, tricolor, or grizzle markings. The PBGV carries its strong, tapered tail like a saber.

Grooming & Exercise Needs PBGVs need to be brushed and combed once a week. They require a lot of play and brisk daily walks.

Origins PBGVs originated about 400 years ago in the Vendée region of western France, where they ran in packs to hunt hare. Its stamina and drive made it well suited for this rugged coastal area.

① Breed-related health concerns: hypothyroidism (page 452), allergies, epilepsy (page 455), ear infections.

Tricolor petit basset griffon Vendeen

HEIGHT 12½–15½"

WEIGHT 30–42 LBS.

LIFE SPAN 11–13 YRS.

Dachshund

MINIATURE

SMALL

STANDARD

MEDIUM

GOOD WATCHDOG

Dachshunds are clever, lively, playful, and love to be involved in all family activities. The breed's stubbornness can usually be counteracted through training. Dachshunds get bored with repetitious lessons but learn quickly if properly motivated. Ideal for city and apartment living, they can be cautious with strangers but get along with other animals. Poorly bred dachshunds can have serious medical and behavioral problems, such as biting, destructiveness, and digging. House training can sometimes be a problem.

Wirehaired miniature dachshund

Appearance The dachshund's body is straight, long, and muscular, with short, strong legs. Its narrow head tapers smoothly toward the small nose. The dachshund comes in two sizes, standard and miniature, and there are three types of coats: smooth, wirehaired, and longhaired. The smooth coat is short, thick, and shiny. The wirehaired coat is tight, short, and coarse; its undercoat should have softer, shorter hairs between the coarse hairs. (The wirehaired also has bushy eyebrows and a beard.) The longhaired coat is soft, sleek, and slightly wavy, longer under the neck and on the forechest. Coat color for all three types is black, red, brindle, gray, chocolate, or fawn, sometimes with tan markings. The dachshund can also be dappled (a dark base color with lighter highlights).

Smooth-coated miniature dachshund

HEIGHT
MINIATURE 5–9"
STANDARD 9–10"

WEIGHT
MINIATURE 9–11 LBS.
STANDARD 16–32 LBS.

LIFE SPAN 10–12 YRS.

Longhaired standard dachshund

Grooming & Exercise Needs Smooth dachshunds need to be brushed weekly, while longhaireds need to be brushed every other day (every day when shedding). Wirehaireds need to be brushed and combed one to two times a week. Dachshunds enjoy long walks, but if time is short, indoor ball chasing will suffice.

Origins The modern dachshund is related to a thirty-five-pound dynamo that was used to hunt badgers in medieval Europe. It was bred to be smaller about a hundred years ago in Germany to hunt rabbits and foxes. (*Dach* is the German word for badger; *hund* means dog.) The scrappy, short-legged dachshund worked aggressively without being intimidated by the fox or badger.

ⓘ It is especially important to obtain a dachshund from a reputable breeder. Breed-related health concerns: intervertebral disc protrusion (page 456), hypothyroidism (page 452), Cushing's syndrome (page 451), undescended testicles, kidney disease, polyuria (excessive urination caused by kidney disease).

Longhaired standard dachshund

LARGE

HIGH ENERGY INDOORS

SPECIAL EXERCISE NEEDS

GOOD WITH KIDS

American Foxhound

Pack of American foxhounds on the scent

American foxhounds are recommended only for very active people who like to exercise outdoors. These dogs are not happy lying around inside, though they are very sociable with adults and children. They get along with most other dogs but may chase unfamiliar cats.

Appearance The coat is close, hard, and medium length. The foxhound is seen in all colors, but the most common are tan and white, gold and white, and black and white.

Grooming & Exercise Needs A weekly brushing will keep the coat in good shape. This dog needs long daily walks and frequent romps in a large, fenced-in area.

Origins The American foxhound was derived from English stock in the 18th century.

(!) The American foxhound is not suitable for apartment life. If it is not called upon to use its remarkable nose in vigorous activity, behavior problems, such as howling, barking, or house-soiling, will result. Breed-related health concerns: thrombocytopathy (a bleeding disorder resulting from abnormal platelets).

Tan and white American foxhound

HEIGHT 21-25"

WEIGHT 65-70 LBS.

LIFE SPAN 12-13 YRS.

Beagle

MEDIUM

HIGH ENERGY INDOORS

Mother beagle with six-week-old puppy

GOOD WITH KIDS

The beagle is one of the most popular breeds because it is friendly with people and other animals, loves children, does well with moderate exercise, and can adapt to life in the city, suburbs, or country. Socialization and obedience training at an early age are necessary to avoid behavioral problems, such as digging holes in the yard or constant barking and/or howling. The beagle has a tendency to roam while following a scent.

Beagle in a show pose

Appearance The beagle, which is meant to resemble a miniature foxhound, has a close, hard, medium-length coat. All true hound colors—white, tan, and black in different combinations and with any kind of markings—are seen.

Grooming & Exercise Needs The beagle needs to be groomed with a hound glove once a week. Beagles enjoy vigorous daily walks or the chance to run in a secured area.

Origins Beagles are an ancient breed with a clouded history. Small hounds used to hunt hare existed in the British Isles for centuries, probably arriving with the Celts. Breedings to French scent hounds give us the dogs we know as beagles today.

(!) Breed-related health concerns: hypothyroidism (page 452), glaucoma (page 434), progressive retinal atrophy (page 435), cataracts (page 434), intervertebral disc protrusion (page 456), epilepsy (page 455), bleeding disorders, atopy (page 437), pulmonic stenosis (page 449).

HEIGHT 13–15"

WEIGHT 18–30 LBS.

LIFE SPAN 13–14 YRS.

English Foxhound

LARGE

HIGH ENERGY INDOORS

SPECIAL EXERCISE NEEDS

GOOD WITH KIDS

The fast, lean English foxhound can be a wonderful companion. This breed is gentle, loves children, and gets along with other dogs. Because of their strong instincts to chase small game, foxhounds are not recommended for households with cats or other small animals. They may bark (a distinctive "yodel") at strangers, but more as a greeting than a threat. Obedience-training foxhounds can be extremely difficult because they are distracted by scents and have a pack-bonding mentality. Because English foxhounds retain their hunting-dog instincts, they may bay or bark if they hear other dogs and may roam if not kept in a secured area.

Tricolored English foxhound

Appearance The coat is short, dense, and glossy. Its color is black, white, or tan—or any combination of these and various "pieds," which are composed of white and various shades of yellow and tan.

Grooming & Exercise Needs English foxhounds require only occasional brushing. They need a lot of exercise and a secured, open space in which to run. Always walk English foxhounds on a leash.

Origins The English foxhound was developed in the 13th century by crossing St. Hubert/bloodhound-type dogs with swift, light hounds, possibly including the greyhound.

(!) The English foxhound is not suitable for inexperienced dog owners, nor is it appropriate for city or apartment life.

HEIGHT 24-25"

WEIGHT 60-70 LBS.

LIFE SPAN 11-13 YRS.

Pack of English foxhounds

Harrier

MEDIUM

Harriers are affectionate and so friendly they greet strangers as if they were old friends. They love children but may sometimes be too playful for toddlers, knocking them down in their enthusiasm. Harriers are great for families that play hard. Exercise is very important—if it is lacking, these dogs may become howlers, barkers, or diggers. Harriers get along with other dogs but if not raised with cats will sometimes chase them. They usually do well in obedience training, although they can become distracted by different scents.

Harrier sniffing out a scent

HIGH ENERGY INDOORS

SPECIAL EXERCISE NEEDS

Appearance The harrier looks like a small English foxhound. Its coat is short, dense, and glossy. It is seen in all colors, especially black, tan, and white—evenly distributed.

GOOD WATCHDOG

Grooming & Exercise Needs The harrier needs to be brushed once a week. Long walks are required and runs in the country are recommended for this high-energy dog. Harriers are wonderful companions for joggers, hikers, bikers, and horseback riders—they can run all day long.

GOOD WITH KIDS

Origins The harrier was developed in England in the 12th century to hunt in packs for hare and fox.

(!) The harrier thrives in the country, but its tracking instinct makes it unsuitable for city life or even life in the suburbs if there is only a small yard.

Tricolor harrier

HEIGHT 19–21"

WEIGHT 45–60 LBS.

LIFE SPAN 11–12 YRS.

Bloodhound

LARGE

SPECIAL EXERCISE NEEDS

GOOD WITH KIDS

Bloodhounds are extremely affectionate with people and are rarely quarrelsome with other animals. They bark deeply when strangers approach their territory but are actually very friendly. They slobber, and their wagging tails may knock objects off tables. Don't expect your bloodhound to be at the top of its obedience class, but there is no comparable dog when it comes to cold scent-tracking.

The bloodhound's long ears and facial wrinkles capture scent.

Appearance The bloodhound has one of the most interesting faces in the dog world. The loose, super-abundant skin on the head and neck seems to take on a life of its own as the bloodhound walks, runs, and lies down. Its extremely long ears fall in graceful folds. Its coat is short and dense and is seen in black and tan, red and tan, or tawny.

Grooming & Exercise Needs Bloodhounds need a weekly brushing and ear cleaning. They need a lot of exercise, such as long, vigorous daily walks during which they can follow scent trails. This powerful dog must always be walked on a leash or it will follow a scent rather than its owner.

Black and tan bloodhound

HEIGHT 23–27"

WEIGHT 80–110 LBS.

LIFE SPAN 10–12 YRS.

Origins The bloodhound has been known, in some form, since ancient times, and many of today's scent hounds—such as bassets, beagles, and foxhounds—are descended from bloodhound ancestors.

(!) The bloodhound's strong instinct for following scents makes it unsuitable for city or apartment life. Breed-related health concerns: hip dysplasia (page 442), bloat (page 445), ectropion/entropion (page 434), otitis externa (page 435).

Otter Hound

LARGE

SPECIAL EXERCISE NEEDS

SPECIAL GROOMING NEEDS

Otter hounds are energetic and usually friendly with everyone. They are quite vocal—they frequently bark and bay. Bred as pack hunters, otter hounds usually get along with other dogs but may chase unfamiliar cats and small animals. They may be resistant to obedience training, and they do best in the country with experienced owners.

Appearance The otter hound's outercoat is dense, rough, coarse, and hard (softer on the head and lower legs); the undercoat is water-resistant, short, woolly, and slightly oily. All coat colors are seen; the most common are sandy, blue and white, gray, and black and tan. The feet are substantially webbed.

Sandy otter hound with black and tan puppy

Grooming & Exercise Needs Otter hounds need to be brushed daily to prevent matting. They love the outdoors and require a lot of exercise, including long daily romps in a secured area or on a leash, and frequent opportunities to swim.

Origins The otter hound, probably a descendant of rough-coated French hounds, was used to hunt otters in cold English rivers as early as the 11th century.

(!) A diligent hunter, this breed is not suitable for city or apartment living—nor is it suitable for inexperienced dog owners. Breed-related health concerns: hip and elbow dysplasia (page 442), bloat (page 445), canine thrombocytopathy (a bleeding disorder resulting from abnormal platelets).

HEIGHT 23–27"

WEIGHT 65–115 LBS.

LIFE SPAN 11–13 YRS.

Sandy otter hound

Scent Hound Mixes

Scent hound mixes are playful, even-tempered dogs that make good family pets and are generally social with other dogs. Their exceptional noses can get them into trouble. You may have to work to keep their attention at times, as they are easily distracted by the scents around them. They typically have robust appetites and can easily become overweight if owners aren't watchful. Though not prone to nonstop barking, scent hounds howl and bay (especially when left alone); it is in their nature to do so.

This basset-beagle mix shows the dwarfed body of a basset.

Appearance Scent hound mixes tend to have short legs, longish bodies, and long pendulous ears. The coat is short and often tricolored (tan, black, and white). The skin sometimes appears to be bigger than the dog, hanging in loose folds on the neck and forehead and drooping under the eyes.

This beagle-basset mix's long ears and low-to-the-ground body make him an expert tracker, easily distracted by the scents around him.

This mix of a beagle and a larger dog is leggier than the beagle and rough-coated, showing that it has another dog group in its genes.

Grooming & Exercise Needs The coat is easy to care for, needing no more than a weekly grooming with a rubber brush or a hound glove. Scent hounds generally like to run, so expect scent hound mixes to need a lot of exercise.

Jack Russell terrier-beagle mixes like this one can be spunky and easy-going with children.

A beagle mix is small and compact. Its sensitive nose is bound to lead it into trouble, although most of the time hound mixes are even tempered and playful.

Sight Hounds

Borzois, swift and powerful dogs, were bred in the Middle Ages to hunt in pairs for wolves.

Sight hounds, dogs that traditionally hunt mainly by sight, are believed to share a common ancestor—the Phoenician hound. All bear a similar silhouette: long jaw, refined head, lean muscular body, deep chest, fairly long neck, thin powerful legs, and hare feet, which have elongated middle toes that make the foot appear longer overall.

Many of the sight hound breeds can be traced back to antiquity and originated in the Middle East and Southwest Asia. Breeds that were refined in Africa and the Mediterranean region, such as the saluki, Rhodesian Ridgeback, Italian greyhound, and greyhound, have short smooth coats, whereas those developed in harsher climates such as Afghanistan (Afghan hound), Russia (borzoi), and the northern United Kingdom (Scottish deerhound, Irish wolfhound), bear longer, rougher, weather-resistant coats. The short-haired whippet is the Johnny-come-lately of the sight hounds, developed in nineteenth-century England by crossing the greyhound, the Italian greyhound, and a now-extinct English terrier.

Almost all of the dogs in this group hunt primarily by sight, taking off in hot pursuit of game at the detection of the slightest movement. The fastest dogs in the canine kingdom, they are used today in dog racing and lure coursing and are nearly impossible to catch if they get away. Their desire to capture and kill prey is paramount, thus many of them need to be carefully supervised around cats and other small mammals, especially when outdoors.

With people, the larger sight hound breeds (Afghan, saluki, Ibizan hound, and pharaoh hound) and the basenji are gentle but not particularly demonstrative. The smaller Italian greyhounds were bred to be companions and thin-skinned bed warmers, so they are naturally more outwardly affectionate.

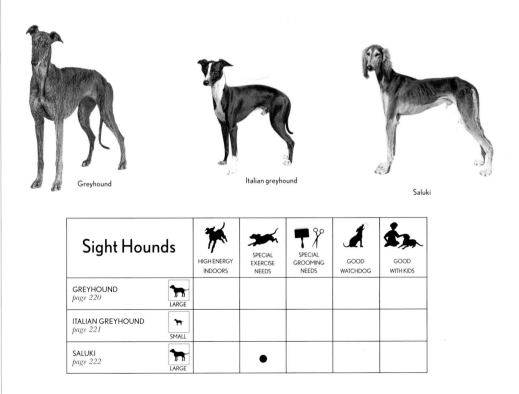

Greyhound

Italian greyhound

Saluki

Sight Hounds		HIGH ENERGY INDOORS	SPECIAL EXERCISE NEEDS	SPECIAL GROOMING NEEDS	GOOD WATCHDOG	GOOD WITH KIDS
GREYHOUND *page 220*	LARGE					
ITALIAN GREYHOUND *page 221*	SMALL					
SALUKI *page 222*	LARGE		●			

Whippet

Afghan hound

Borzoi

Sight Hounds		HIGH ENERGY INDOORS	SPECIAL EXERCISE NEEDS	SPECIAL GROOMING NEEDS	GOOD WATCHDOG	GOOD WITH KIDS
WHIPPET *page 223*	MEDIUM					
AFGHAN HOUND *page 224*	LARGE		●	●		
BORZOI *page 225*	LARGE		●			
IRISH WOLFHOUND *page 226*	GIANT					●
RHODESIAN RIDGEBACK *page 227*	LARGE		●		●	

Irish wolfhound

Rhodesian Ridgeback

Scottish deerhound

Basenji

Sight Hounds		HIGH ENERGY INDOORS	SPECIAL EXERCISE NEEDS	SPECIAL GROOMING NEEDS	GOOD WATCHDOG	GOOD WITH KIDS
SCOTTISH DEERHOUND *page 228*	LARGE					●
BASENJI *page 229*	MEDIUM					
IBIZAN HOUND *page 230*	LARGE		●			
PHARAOH HOUND *page 231*	LARGE		●			

Ibizan hound

Pharaoh hound

LARGE

Greyhound

Greyhounds, the fastest dogs in the world, are sweet, gentle, and loyal and do well in quiet households. They are generally patient with children and can be timid (but rarely aggressive) with strangers. They are usually submissive to medium- and large-size dogs, although some greyhounds can be a danger to small dogs and cats. Adopted retired racers adapt very well in a loving home.

Red and white particolor greyhound

Appearance Built for speed and endurance, the greyhound has a lean, narrow body, a deep chest, long, muscular legs, and a long, narrow head and neck. The coat is short, smooth, and firm in texture. All coat colors are seen; the most common are red, black, fawn, and brindle.

Grooming & Exercise Needs Greyhounds need only an occasional brushing. They should be taken on vigorous daily walks or jogs, always leashed since their sight hound instincts may inspire them to bolt. Allow these dogs to play off-leash only in fenced-in areas.

Origins The greyhound is an ancient breed. Similar dogs are depicted on Egyptian tombs and papyri. They were used for hunting over 4,000 years ago. Traders from the Middle East probably introduced the greyhound to Europe around A.D. 900.

HEIGHT 27-30"

WEIGHT 55-80 LBS.

⚠ Breed-related health concerns: bloat (page 445), hemophilia, sensitivity to anesthesia, tick diseases (page 439), diarrhea (page 444).

LIFE SPAN 10-12 YRS.

Red brindle greyhound

Italian Greyhound

The gentleness, beauty, and grace of Italian greyhounds have endeared them to dog owners around the world. They are ideal for city and apartment living. Quiet, sensitive, and affectionate, they need very little training, although obedience classes are recommended for fine-tuning and to expose them to different types of environments, animals, and people. Some can be difficult to house-train. They get along with children who treat them gently and are perfect companions for the elderly. They are usually submissive to other dogs and friendly with small animals, such as cats.

Fawn and white
Italian greyhound

Appearance The Italian greyhound is known for its slender, graceful appearance and unique high-stepping gait. The coat is short, soft, and glossy. All colors except for black and tan and brindle are seen; the most common are fawn, blue, black, and red. White markings may appear on the face, chest, tail tip, and feet.

Grooming & Exercise Needs Italian greyhounds need to be brushed weekly with a hound glove. They appreciate a sweater to wear outside in the winter and need a few brisk walks daily.

Black and white Italian greyhound

Origins Italian greyhounds were developed about 2,500 years ago by breeding small greyhounds with each other. They were admired by the ancient Egyptians and Romans and were favorites of the kings and queens of 17th-century Europe.

(!) Breed-related health concerns: epilepsy (page 455), dental problems (page 444), broken legs, progressive retinal atrophy (page 435), patellar luxation (page 443).

HEIGHT 13–15"

WEIGHT 7–12 LBS.

LIFE SPAN 13–15 YRS.

Saluki

LARGE

SPECIAL EXERCISE NEEDS

Salukis, superb sight hounds, are quiet, gentle dogs that exhibit a catlike aloofness. They are not demonstrative or playful, but if they are left alone for long periods without human companionship, they will become destructive. Often reserved and timid with strangers, they are usually tolerant of gentle children over eight years old, but they should not be left unsupervised with younger children. Their great speed and endurance can get them into trouble if allowed off-leash in unsecured areas, as they may not be able to resist chasing cats or other small animals (unless raised with them from an early age). They do get along with other dogs. Salukis do best in suburban or country settings. City noise and activity may make these sensitive dogs nervous.

Black and tan saluki

Appearance There are two varieties of salukis: one has slight feathering on the legs, backs of the thighs, and ears; the other has no feathering. The coat on both is smooth, soft, and silky and comes in white, cream, fawn, golden, red, grizzle, tan, tricolor (white, black, and tan), or black and tan.

Grooming & Exercise Needs Salukis should be brushed once a week. They require a lot of daily exercise, either running in large, secured areas or on a leash elsewhere.

Origins The saluki was used to hunt gazelles in ancient Egypt over 5,000 years ago and may be the oldest breed known to humans.

(!) The saluki is not suitable for inexperienced dog owners or for city or apartment living. Breed-related health concerns include: progressive retinal atrophy (page 435), hypothyroidism (page 452).

HEIGHT 21–28"

WEIGHT 40–60 LBS.

LIFE SPAN 12–14 YRS.

Saluki with feathering (left) and without feathering

Whippet

MEDIUM

The adaptable whippet can fit in anywhere—city, apartment, suburbs, or country. These gentle, mild-mannered, and affectionate dogs respond enthusiastically to obedience training. Neat, clean, and easy to train, they make great family dogs. They are friendly with children, get along with cats and other dogs, but need to be watched around pet rabbits or rodents. Some are very sensitive to sounds (such as squealing children) so should be exposed to urban noises at a young age if they are to live in a city.

Fawn brindle and white particolor whippet

Whippet puppies, about four months old

Appearance The whippet's long, lean head tapers to the nose; its small ears—called rose ears—fold over and back to reveal the inside of the ear. The whippet carries its long, tapering tail straight down or between its legs when not in motion. The coat is short, close, smooth, and firm in texture. All coat colors are seen; common ones include brindle and white or white and fawn.

Grooming & Exercise Needs Whippets shed minimally and need only a weekly brushing with a rubber brush or hound glove. They need several brisk walks and the chance to run in a secured area daily. Whippets should never be allowed to run off-leash in unsecured areas, as they can disappear in a flash, traveling at up to thirty-five miles an hour.

Origins In the 19th century the whippet, probably a cross between terriers, small greyhounds, and Italian greyhounds, was used in England for the popular gambling sport of rabbit coursing (racing) in which it would "snap like a whip" around a small field, snatching up and killing live rabbits.

ⓘ Breed-related health concerns: undescended testicles, Demodex mange (page 440), weak digestive tracts.

HEIGHT 18–22"

WEIGHT 20–30 LBS.

LIFE SPAN 12–15 YRS.

Afghan Hound

LARGE

SPECIAL EXERCISE NEEDS

SPECIAL GROOMING NEEDS

Black and tan Afghan hound

Afghans, like most sight hounds, are generally gentle dogs but are aloof and cautious with strangers. They are friendly with most other animals, although they may chase cats if not socialized with them early. They are very sensitive to strange noises. It is very important to socialize and obedience train these outstandingly graceful dogs from an early age.

Appearance The long, flowing coat ranges in color from light and dark golden blond to black. Its texture is silky, except for the short hair on its back.

Grooming & Exercise Needs Afghans require daily brushing and combing. A daily dose of vigorous exercise, such as several brisk walks, and the opportunity to run freely in a fenced-in area several times a week are necessary to avoid behavioral problems.

Origins This aristocratic dog is known in the West as a competitor in the show ring and as a fashionable companion, but its origins are more rugged and earthy. It originated as a large-game hunting and falconing dog in the mountains of Afghanistan in the 17th century.

(!) Breed-related health concerns: sensitivity to anesthesia, whole milk, and flea/tick dips and collars, hypothyroidism (page 452), hip dysplasia (page 442), juvenile cataracts (page 434).

HEIGHT 25-27"

WEIGHT 50-60 LBS.

LIFE SPAN 12-14 YRS.

Afghan hound with show coat

Borzoi

LARGE

SPECIAL EXERCISE NEEDS

This quiet, elegant, graceful dog gets along with adults and other dogs, especially if socialized at an early age. It may not, however, get along with children. Early obedience classes are recommended since the borzoi can be stubborn and sometimes snappy. While the borzoi may be tolerant of cats indoors, it will chase and perhaps kill them or other small animals when outdoors.

Black and white borzoi

Appearance The coat is long and silky and either flat, wavy, or somewhat curly on the body, but short and smooth on the head, ears, and front of the legs. The frill on the neck is thick and curly; feathering on the hindquarters and tail is long and profuse. All coat colors and combinations are seen; the most common are black and white; black, tan, and white; liver and white; tan and white; and white with orange or lemon spots.

Grooming & Exercise Needs Borzois need to be brushed every other day to prevent matting. They also need several brisk daily walks on a leash or in a fenced-in area.

Origins The swift and powerful borzoi—once known as the Russian wolfhound and thought to be descended from the greyhound, saluki, and a Russian working dog—was bred in the Middle Ages to hunt in pairs for wolves. It is now bred for its reserved companionability.

Three-month-old borzoi puppies

(!) Breed-related health concerns: bloat (page 445), hypothyroidism (page 452), sensitivity to anesthesia, progressive retinal atrophy (page 435).

HEIGHT 26–28"

WEIGHT 60–105 LBS.

LIFE SPAN 12–14 YRS.

Irish Wolfhound

GIANT

GOOD WITH KIDS

This sweet dog requires an enormous amount of love and affection, and though it needs a fenced yard for exercise, it should not be left alone outside for long periods. Irish wolfhounds are very friendly and love children, although some may be initially shy with strangers. Early socialization with adults, children, other animals, and noises help them to learn how to adapt to different situations.

Fawn Irish wolfhound

Irish wolfhounds do not shine in obedience class but will nevertheless learn when handled with patience and gentleness. They are wonderful dogs for families who live in large houses with land.

Irish wolfhounds are known as gentle giants.

Appearance The coat is rough, hard, and wiry. Its color is gray, brindle, red, black, pure white, fawn, or any other color that appears in the Scottish deerhound.

Grooming & Exercise Needs Irish wolfhounds need to be brushed and combed once or twice a week. Some stripping (removing old hair by hand) and trimming are needed twice a year to shape the coat. The Irish wolfhound needs a long walk or, preferably, a good run in a secured area, every day.

Origins This giant dog was valued by ancient Celtic chieftains for its hunting prowess against wolves, boars, stags, and the now-extinct gigantic, six-foot-tall Irish elk.

HEIGHT 30–34"

WEIGHT 105–120 LBS.

LIFE SPAN 5–10 YRS.

(!) The Irish wolfhound is not suitable for city or apartment life. Breed-related health concerns: hip and elbow dysplasia (page 442), osteochondritis dissecans (page 442), bloat (page 445), progressive retinal atrophy (page 435), osteosarcoma (page 431).

Rhodesian Ridgeback

LARGE

SPECIAL EXERCISE NEEDS

GOOD WATCHDOG

Rhodesians are good dogs in the right hands—but they must have proper training and exercise. Without this they can be undisciplined and aggressive. They may be stubborn and difficult to train if obedience school is not started early or if the owner is inexperienced. They should be socialized with children and other animals at an early age. Their caution with strangers makes them reliable watchdogs and guard dogs.

Red wheaten Rhodesian Ridgeback

Appearance The hallmark of this breed is the ridge of hair that grows forward along the center of the back. Its coat is short, dense, sleek, and glossy. Its color ranges from light wheaten to red wheaten. A little white may appear on the chest or toes.

Grooming & Exercise Needs Rhodesians need only a quick brushing once a week. They require vigorous daily exercise and so do best in the suburbs or country.

Origins The Hottentot people of southern Africa had a ridgebacked dog that 19th-century Dutch and German settlers crossed with European mastiffs, scent hounds, greyhounds, and Great Danes to produce the Rhodesian Ridgeback.

(!) The Rhodesian Ridgeback is not suitable for inexperienced dog owners. Breed-related health concerns: hip dysplasia (page 442), dermoid sinus (opening of skin on the back that can cause infection of the spinal cord), deafness (page 436).

The Rhodesian's distinctive ridge

HEIGHT 24–25"

WEIGHT 65–85 LBS.

LIFE SPAN 10–14 YRS.

LARGE

GOOD WITH KIDS

Scottish Deerhound

Scottish deerhounds are dignified, undemanding dogs that do well in obedience classes, get along with everyone, and love the attention of children, especially if socialized with them at an early age. While they are comfortable with animals, they may run after cats if not socialized with them early. They are not protective of their territory but take their time getting to

Dark blue-gray Scottish deerhound

know strangers. Although they can adjust to city life, they are better off in suburban and rural settings where they have room to exercise and stretch their long, graceful legs.

Appearance The deerhound's coat is harsh, wiry, and shaggy. Its color is gray, dark blue-gray, brindle, yellow, sandy red, or red fawn.

Grooming & Exercise Needs Scottish deerhounds need to be brushed and combed once a week. They need several long walks daily and the opportunity to run and romp in a secured area at least once a week.

Origins Scottish deerhounds were owned only by nobility in Scotland during the Middle Ages and were used to course deer. The collapse of the clan system in the mid-18th century and the introduction of guns for hunting decreased the popularity of the deerhound.

(!) Breed-related health concerns include: bloat (page 445), osteochondritis dissecans (page 442).

HEIGHT 28–32"

WEIGHT 75–110 LBS.

LIFE SPAN 8–12 YRS.

Basenji

MEDIUM

The basenji is stubborn but very friendly toward family members, most children, and other animals—although it can be aloof with adult strangers. The basenji's hunting spirit surfaces when it sees cars. To avoid car chasing, this dog must be leashed or fenced in when outside. The basenji does not bark in the typical canine way, but yodels when happy and screams when unhappy.

Five-week-old basenji puppy

Appearance The basenji's distinctive features include a wrinkled forehead, a tightly curled tail, and a swift, effortless horse-trotting-like gait. Its coat can be chestnut red, pure black, tricolor, and brindle (black stripes on a background of chestnut red), all with white feet, chest, and tail tip. The basenji may also have white legs, blaze, and collar.

Grooming & Exercise Needs The basenji sheds minimally and needs very little brushing. A vigorous daily walk or play period with other dogs will make the basenji happy.

Origins This "barkless" dog of Central Africa probably originated thousands of years ago. Images of similar dogs are seen in Egyptian tomb art.

Brindle and white basenji

(!) The basenji is not appropriate for inexperienced owners. Breed-related health concerns: pyruvate kinase deficiency (fatal enzyme deficiency causing destruction of red blood cells), immunoproliferative enteropathy (a fatal intestinal disorder), persistent pupillary membrane (strand-shaped remnants of the embryological structure that atrophy in most dogs by eight weeks of age; if present longer, they may impair vision), progressive retinal atrophy (page 435), fanconi syndrome (a hereditary disease that can produce kidney failure).

HEIGHT 16-17"

WEIGHT 21-24 LBS.

LIFE SPAN 10-13 YRS.

Ibizan Hound

LARGE

SPECIAL EXERCISE NEEDS

Ibizan hounds are clean, well-mannered, and very loyal to their families—though sometimes reserved with strangers. They are playful with children, if socialized with them at an early age. Obedience training usually goes well as long as the methods used are gentle. Ibizan hounds may chase small animals unless socialized with them when young. They love playing with other dogs and may growl and click their teeth as part of this play. City life may be too confining for these dogs.

Wire-coated Ibizan hound

Appearance The Ibizan's coat may be smooth or wiry; the wire coat often includes a generous mustache. Coats are red or lion-colored (light yellowish red) with white feet, tail tip, chest, muzzle, and blaze; pied (equal parts red and white); solid white; or solid red. The nose is a rosy color.

Grooming & Exercise Needs Ibizan hounds need only short weekly brushings. They require vigorous exercise, preferably in an area secured with high fences.

Origins This ancient breed was found depicted on the walls of Tutankhamen's tomb and is thought to have been bred as a hunting dog for the Egyptian pharaohs. Centuries later it was brought to Spain by traders and named after the island of Ibiza.

(!) Breed-related health concerns: axonal degeneration (a degeneration of cells in the nervous system that can lead to paralysis), deafness (page 436), bloat (page 445).

HEIGHT 22 1/2–27 1/2"

WEIGHT 45–55 LBS.

LIFE SPAN 12–14 YRS.

Smooth-coated Ibizan hound

Pharaoh Hound

LARGE

SPECIAL EXERCISE NEEDS

Pharaoh hounds want to please their owners and are very receptive to obedience training—which should begin early. They can be timid if not socialized with people, children, and other animals at an early age. They are wonderful additions to families that can meet their needs for space, exercise, play, and interaction. Pharaoh hounds can only be left off-leash in secured areas because they will chase small animals. They can live with cats, however, if exposed to them when young.

The pharaoh hound has a short, glossy coat.

Appearance The pharaoh hound's coat is short and glossy, ranging from fine and close to slightly harsh with no feathering. The color varies from shades of tan to chestnut; white may appear on the chest (called a star), toes, and tip of the tail, and there may also be a slim white snip on the center line of the face. The dog's nose blushes when it gets excited.

Grooming & Exercise Needs Pharaoh hounds only need to be brushed once a week. These energetic dogs need a lot of exercise, space, and owner interaction.

Origins The pharaoh hound was brought to the Mediterranean islands of Malta and Gozo from the Middle East by Phoenician traders over 2,000 years ago. The pharaoh hound resembles depictions of the ancient Egyptian dog-god, Anubis.

(!) Breed-related health concerns: cardiovascular disease, gastrointestinal disorders.

The pharaoh hound's nose blushes.

HEIGHT 21-25"

WEIGHT 45-55 LBS.

LIFE SPAN 12-14 YRS.

Sporting Dogs

Many sporting dogs, including retrievers, enjoy swimming.

Historically, hunter's companion was one of the most important canine jobs. Most of the hunting (or sporting) breeds were developed between the seventeenth and nineteenth centuries for different types of game and terrain.

Pointers and setters, the earliest sporting dogs, were bred to sniff out game and then freeze into a "point" or "set" position, alerting the hunter to the exact location of the prey. Pointers (German shorthaired and wirehaired pointers, pointer, Spinone Italiano, vizsla, weimaraner, and wirehaired pointing griffon) stiffen their bodies, stretch their necks forward, and raise a forepaw. Setters crouch down. The control these dogs display on the job gives no hint of the high-strung behavior they often exhibit when not working.

The development of spaniels and retrievers began in the 1700s, when firearms were introduced into hunting. Spaniels could flush birds up into the air or out from beneath dense underbrush; retrievers could bring downed birds back to the hunter from land or water. To this day these breeds are among the most cooperative in obedience training and are generally friendly and outgoing.

Nearly all sporting dogs are high energy. Without several hours of aerobic-level exercise daily, they may become destructive in the home. Once regarded essentially as country dogs, the sporting breeds actually adapt well to life in urban environments.

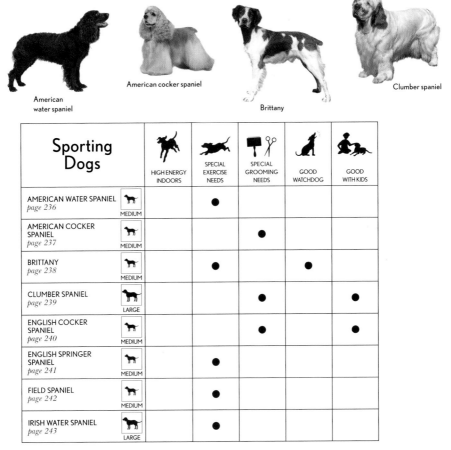

American water spaniel

American cocker spaniel

Brittany

Clumber spaniel

Sporting Dogs		HIGH ENERGY INDOORS	SPECIAL EXERCISE NEEDS	SPECIAL GROOMING NEEDS	GOOD WATCHDOG	GOOD WITH KIDS
AMERICAN WATER SPANIEL *page 236*	MEDIUM		●			
AMERICAN COCKER SPANIEL *page 237*	MEDIUM			●		
BRITTANY *page 238*	MEDIUM		●		●	
CLUMBER SPANIEL *page 239*	LARGE			●		●
ENGLISH COCKER SPANIEL *page 240*	MEDIUM			●		●
ENGLISH SPRINGER SPANIEL *page 241*	MEDIUM		●			
FIELD SPANIEL *page 242*	MEDIUM		●			
IRISH WATER SPANIEL *page 243*	LARGE		●			

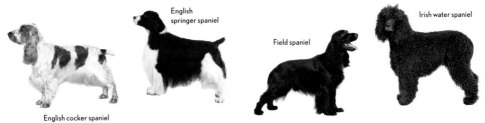

English springer spaniel

Field spaniel

Irish water spaniel

English cocker spaniel

Sussex spaniel

Spaniel mixes

Gordon setter

Welsh springer spaniel

English setter

Sporting Dogs		HIGH ENERGY INDOORS	SPECIAL EXERCISE NEEDS	SPECIAL GROOMING NEEDS	GOOD WATCHDOG	GOOD WITH KIDS
SUSSEX SPANIEL page 244	MEDIUM		●			
WELSH SPRINGER SPANIEL page 245	MEDIUM		●			
ENGLISH SETTER page 248	LARGE		●			●
GORDON SETTER page 249	LARGE		●		●	
IRISH SETTER page 250	LARGE	●	●			●
CHESAPEAKE BAY RETRIEVER page 251	LARGE		●		●	
CURLY-COATED RETRIEVER page 252	LARGE		●			
FLAT-COATED RETRIEVER page 253	LARGE		●			●
GOLDEN RETRIEVER page 254	LARGE					●

Chesapeake Bay retriever

Flat-coated retriever

Irish setter

Curly-coated retriever

Golden retriever

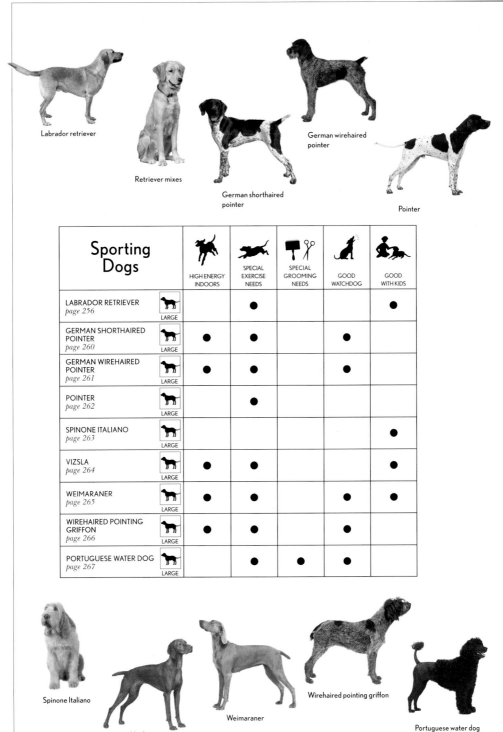

Labrador retriever

Retriever mixes

German shorthaired pointer

German wirehaired pointer

Pointer

Sporting Dogs		HIGH ENERGY INDOORS	SPECIAL EXERCISE NEEDS	SPECIAL GROOMING NEEDS	GOOD WATCHDOG	GOOD WITH KIDS
LABRADOR RETRIEVER *page 256*	LARGE		●			●
GERMAN SHORTHAIRED POINTER *page 260*	LARGE	●	●		●	
GERMAN WIREHAIRED POINTER *page 261*	LARGE	●	●		●	
POINTER *page 262*	LARGE		●			
SPINONE ITALIANO *page 263*	LARGE					●
VIZSLA *page 264*	LARGE	●	●			●
WEIMARANER *page 265*	LARGE	●	●		●	●
WIREHAIRED POINTING GRIFFON *page 266*	LARGE	●	●		●	
PORTUGUESE WATER DOG *page 267*	LARGE		●	●	●	

Spinone Italiano

Vizsla

Weimaraner

Wirehaired pointing griffon

Portuguese water dog

MEDIUM

SPECIAL EXERCISE NEEDS

American Water Spaniel

American water spaniels need room to run around.

American water spaniels, still bred primarily to work, do best with experienced dog owners who want to share an active exercise program with their animals. These dogs must be obedience trained and acclimated to being left alone or they will develop such behavior problems as barking and whining. American water spaniels get along with other animals and enjoy children as long as they are exposed to them at an early age.

Appearance The coat can be closely curled or marcel (uniformly waved). Coat color is solid liver or dark chocolate.

Grooming & Exercise Needs American water spaniels shed lightly but continually and so require weekly brushing. They need daily vigorous walks and runs in a secured area. They love to swim.

Origins The American water spaniel originated in the American Midwest. The Irish water spaniel and the curly-coated retriever are probably ancestors but little else is known about the breed's origins. This dog was bred to be a superb shooting dog, retriever, and swimmer; it was expected to retrieve from skiffs or canoes.

(!) The American water spaniel is not suitable for inexperienced dog owners.

HEIGHT 15–18"

WEIGHT 25–45 LBS.

Dark chocolate American water spaniel

LIFE SPAN 10–12 YRS.

American Cocker Spaniel

MEDIUM

SPECIAL GROOMING NEEDS

The American cocker spaniel can be a delight or a medical and behavioral nightmare. The delightful cocker loves children and is very friendly, gentle, playful, and trainable. Unfortunately, due to careless breeding, many American cockers are aggressive, nippy, intolerant of children, and difficult to train. If you want an American cocker, begin obedience classes and socialization with adults, children, and other animals early. The cocker does well in the city, suburbs, or country.

Buff American cocker spaniel with a show coat

Appearance The cocker's coat is silky and flat or slightly wavy and may be black, any other solid color, black and tan, or particolor. The ears, chest, abdomen, and legs are well feathered, the ears lobe-shaped and long.

Grooming & Exercise Needs The cocker should be brushed and combed two to three times a week and trimmed every two to three months. The ears should be cleaned weekly, and the ear flaps, which tend to end up in the food bowl, need to be wiped off daily. This dog needs brisk walks and playtime every day.

Origins The American cocker spaniel is descended from the English "cocking" spaniels that were used to flush woodcocks from their hiding places in the 19th century.

(!) It is especially important to obtain a cocker spaniel from a reputable breeder; indiscriminate breeding has resulted in dogs with some serious problems. Do not buy one from a pet store. Breed-related health concerns: deafness (page 436), skin problems, hypothyroidism (page 452), autoimmune diseases, eye and ear problems, patellar luxation (page 443), urinary tract problems.

HEIGHT 14–15"

WEIGHT 24–28 LBS.

LIFE SPAN 12–15 YRS.

Black and white particolor American cocker spaniel

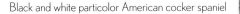

MEDIUM

SPECIAL EXERCISE NEEDS

GOOD WATCHDOG

Brittany

Friendly and affectionate with household members but wary of strangers, Brittanys make excellent watchdogs. They are fine with gentle children and usually get along with other dogs, although some males are aggressive with other males. They get along with other animals, such as cats, if socialized with them early. Without plenty of time and space for playing, these high-energy dogs will develop such undesirable behaviors as excessive barking, hyperactivity, and destructive chewing.

Brittany on point

Appearance The coat of the long-legged, stubby-tailed Brittany is medium in length, dense, and flat or wavy. The skin is fairly loose. Coat color may be a dark rich orange and white, liver and white, or black and white in either clear or roan patterns.

Grooming & Exercise Needs The Brittany needs to be brushed and combed twice a week and needs several long, brisk walks or runs in a secured area daily.

Origins The Brittany, native to and very popular in France, hunts, points, and retrieves—the dog world's equivalent to the utility player in baseball. The name comes from the French province where the breed originated in the 17th and 18th centuries.

(!) The Brittany is not suitable for inexperienced dog owners. Breed-related health concerns: hip dysplasia (page 442), epilepsy (page 455), hemophilia (a bleeding disorder).

Orange and white Brittany

HEIGHT 17 ½-20 ½"

WEIGHT 30-40 LBS.

LIFE SPAN 12-13 YRS.

Clumber Spaniel

LARGE

SPECIAL GROOMING NEEDS

GOOD WITH KIDS

The clumber is an affectionate, gentle, easygoing dog, reserved but not nasty around strangers. This dog can be stubborn during training but responds to kindness and positive reinforcement. The clumber is good with children and gets along with other animals.

Appearance The clumber's coat is dense, straight, flat, and soft, with moderate feathering on the ears, legs, and abdomen. Coat color is primarily white, with lemon or orange markings. The head is massive, the nose large and square. The eyes are dark amber.

White with orange clumber spaniel

Five-month-old white with lemon clumber puppies

Grooming & Exercise Needs The clumber spaniel requires daily brushing and ear cleaning. The hair on the bottom of the feet and the feathering should be trimmed occasionally. This dog needs brisk daily walks but is otherwise not athletic—definitely not the choice for an owner who wants to take her dog jogging. The clumber's enthusiasm is ignited by the scent of birds, although clumbers that are bred for show may be less inclined to pursue them.

Origins Clumber spaniels were developed in England and France in the 19th century, possibly from basset hound and alpine spaniel stock, and were very popular for flushing and retrieving birds for hunters.

(!) Breed-related health concerns include entropion (page 434).

HEIGHT 17-20"

WEIGHT 55-85 LBS.

LIFE SPAN 10-13 YRS.

MEDIUM

SPECIAL GROOMING NEEDS

GOOD WITH KIDS

English Cocker Spaniel

Red roan and white English cocker

English cocker spaniels are happy, playful, gentle, and loving toward everyone. They like to be included in all family activities and are usually good with children. They get along with other dogs (though males may be aggressive with other males) and small animals, such as cats, especially if socialized with them early. Although they may bark to alert the household of a visitor, they are not protective of their property. They do very well in obedience training.

Appearance The silky, medium-length coat is straight or wavy on the body, with feathering on the ears, chest, belly, and legs. Coat color is white with black, liver, blue, or red markings, roaning, or ticking; or black, liver, or red with or without tan markings. The ears are long, silky, and pendulous. The muzzle is longer—and some would say more elegant—than the American cocker's.

Grooming & Exercise Needs The English cocker should be brushed and combed two to three times a week and clipped and scissored every three months. The ears need weekly cleaning and the ear flaps, which tend to end up in the food bowl a lot, should be wiped off daily. The English cocker is an energetic dog that enjoys long, vigorous walks every day.

Red English cocker with eight-week-old puppy

Origins The English cocker was developed in the 19th century in England to flush and retrieve woodcocks from densely wooded areas.

HEIGHT 15-17"

WEIGHT 26-34 LBS.

LIFE SPAN 10-14 YRS.

⚠ Breed-related health concerns: progressive retinal atrophy (page 435), glaucoma (page 434), cataracts (page 434), deafness (page 436), ear infections, undescended testicles.

English Springer Spaniel

MEDIUM

SPECIAL EXERCISE NEEDS

The English springer is one of the tallest spaniels.

Well-bred, trained English springer spaniels are playful, trusting, loyal, and affectionate. Eager to please, they do very well in obedience training. These dogs are good with children and other animals and love to play and romp with their families, although some may be aggressively possessive. Springers that are left alone too much may become destructive and/or aggressive. They may warm up slowly to strangers but are not usually aggressive toward them.

Appearance The medium-length outercoat can be flat or wavy; the undercoat is short, soft, and dense. Coat color is liver or black with white markings; liver or black and white with tan markings; liver; or blue roan. The pendulous ears have abundant hair and the legs and chest have some feathering.

Liver and white English springer puppies, about seven weeks old

Grooming & Exercise Needs The English springer spaniel sheds very little but should be brushed two to three times a week to avoid matting on the ears, chest, and legs. The springer needs several brisk walks and runs in a secure area daily. This dog also appreciates long walks, retrieving balls from water, and jogs or runs in a secure rural setting.

Origins The English springer spaniel was developed in England in the 17th century to flush, or spring, pheasants from their hiding places and retrieve them for the hunter.

(!) It is especially important to obtain an English springer spaniel from a reputable breeder. Breed-related health concerns: progressive retinal atrophy (page 435), entropion (page 434), glaucoma (page 434), hip dysplasia (page 442), chronic ear infections.

HEIGHT 19-20"

WEIGHT 49-55 LBS.

LIFE SPAN 12-14 YRS.

Field Spaniel

MEDIUM

SPECIAL EXERCISE NEEDS

Considered the calmest and most affectionate of all the spaniels and a pleasant family companion, the field spaniel is still a relatively unknown breed. These dogs usually get along with adults, other animals, and gentle children if introduced to them at an early age. Strangers are also greeted warmly, though sometimes with barking. The field spaniel is very receptive to obedience training. Even though the field spaniel is a sporting dog, it does well in the city if exercised properly.

Appearance The field spaniel's coat is moderately long, flat or slightly wavy, silky, glossy, dense, and water-repellent, with setter-like feathering on the ears, body, and legs. Coat color is black, liver, golden, or roan, sometimes with tan markings. The ears are moderately long.

Black field spaniel

Grooming & Exercise Needs The field spaniel's coat needs to be brushed and combed two to three times a week and trimmed occasionally around the head, ears, neck, legs, and tail. These dogs need to be taken on long walks and given the chance to run in a secure area daily. They also appreciate occasional vacations in the country.

Origins The field spaniel was developed in the 19th century in England to flush birds from the underbrush and retrieve them for the hunter.

HEIGHT 17-18"

WEIGHT 35-50 LBS.

LIFE SPAN 12-14 YRS.

(!) Breed-related health concerns: hip dysplasia (page 442), progressive retinal atrophy (page 435), hypothyroidism (page 452), cataracts (page 434).

Liver field spaniel

Irish Water Spaniel

LARGE

SPECIAL EXERCISE NEEDS

Irish water spaniels can be good family dogs if socialized with people and other animals at an early age, though some attach themselves to just one person. While these dogs can be clownish around their families, some are aloof or unsociable with strangers and can be quite intimidating and protective of their property. They also can be aggressive with other dogs and do better with gentle children over five years of age. Consistent leadership and obedience training are necessary, as these dogs can be assertive, stubborn, and independent. Irish water spaniels love to have a task, such as retrieving objects from the water. They are not ideally suited for city or apartment life.

Irish water spaniels are bred to retrieve from cold water.

Appearance The Irish water spaniel's liver-colored, water-repellent coat is short, thick, crisply curled, and harsh to the touch; it is longer on the legs and chest. This breed is distinguished by a topknot of long, loose curls, a smooth face, and a smooth "rat" tail.

Grooming & Exercise Needs The Irish water spaniel needs to be brushed two to three times a week and clipped every three months. This strong dog needs long, brisk walks and runs in a secured area daily and the opportunity to swim whenever possible.

Origins There is some controversy about the origins of the Irish water spaniel. Some claim that 7th- or 8th-century skeletal remains found in Ireland are those of Irish water spaniels. Regardless of its history, the breed is certainly well suited to retrieving from the icy winter waters of Ireland.

Irish water spaniels have a liver-colored nose.

(!) The Irish water spaniel is not suitable for inexperienced dog owners.

HEIGHT 21–24"

WEIGHT 45–65 LBS.

LIFE SPAN 10–12 YRS.

Sussex Spaniel

Despite its somewhat somber expression, the Sussex spaniel is a cheerful and affectionate dog with a constantly wagging tail. These dogs get along with children if raised with them and are usually friendly with strangers. They are sociable with other dogs, though sometimes they try to dominate. They can be difficult to train, and some may bark or howl excessively. Sussex spaniels can adjust to city life as long as they are given enough exercise.

Sussex spaniels feature moderately feathered legs.

Appearance The Sussex spaniel's abundant coat is flat or slightly wavy and a rich, golden liver color. A serious expression; long, lobe-shaped ears covered with soft, wavy hair; a well-marked neck frill; and moderately feathered legs (above the hocks) distinguish the Sussex spaniel.

Grooming & Exercise Needs The Sussex needs to be brushed and combed two to three times a week and trimmed every three months. This dog needs several long, brisk walks daily.

Origins The Sussex spaniel originated in the 19th century in Sussex, England, where it was used as a field dog, bred to be slow moving so that hunters could follow on foot.

The Sussex needs to be brushed and combed at least a couple of times a week.

HEIGHT 13–15"

WEIGHT 35–45 LBS.

LIFE SPAN 12–14 YRS.

⚠ Breed-related health concerns: heart defects, intervertebral disc protrusion (page 456), ear infections.

Welsh Springer Spaniel

MEDIUM

SPECIAL EXERCISE NEEDS

Welsh springer spaniels are loyal, affectionate, and playful family companions, though they may be reserved with strangers. They are eager to please, love to work, and do very well in obedience classes. They enjoy children as long as they are treated gently and respectfully and are very sociable with other animals. Welsh springer spaniels do best in suburban or rural areas.

Welsh springer spaniels have moderate feathering.

Appearance The Welsh springer spaniel's coat is naturally straight, flat, and soft to the touch, never wiry or wavy. There is moderate feathering on the back of the legs, the chest, and the undersides. Coat color is rich red and white.

Grooming & Exercise Needs Welsh springer spaniels should be brushed and combed two to three times a week and trimmed every three months. They need long, vigorous walks and a safe place to run and play on a daily basis.

Origins The Welsh springer spaniel originated in Wales more than 400 years ago for flushing ("springing") and retrieving game birds. Today the Welsh springer spaniel is considered an outstanding sporting dog and companion.

(!) Breed-related health concerns: cataracts (page 434), glaucoma (page 434), hypothyroidism (page 452).

Adolescent Welsh springers, six to eight months old

HEIGHT 17–19"

WEIGHT 35–50 LBS.

LIFE SPAN 12–15 YRS.

Spaniel Mixes

Spaniel mixes are friend-ly, outgoing, wonderful family pets. Behavior problems common in purebred spaniels, such as possession-aggression, are often tempered in or absent from spaniel mixes, depending, of course, on the temperament of other breeds represented in the mix. The extremely high energy levels common to pure-bred field stock spaniels are also often tempered in mixed-breed spaniels, again depending on the breed mix.

The spaniel-beagle mix has well-feathered ears and a soft coat, traits of its spaniel ancestors.

A Brittany spaniel nurses her mixed-breed pups, who appear to have had a Labrador for a father. Crossbreeds usually look more like one parent than the other.

This springer spaniel or Brittany mix is a good family dog and a good watchdog. Mixing with other breeds tends to avert the behavioral problems that can beset pure-bred spaniels.

Appearance Spaniel mixes tend to be of medium height, with a stocky, somewhat hefty build, a gentle sweet face with a soft expression, and warm brown eyes. They usually have a wavy coat, in a variety of colors and markings, with feathering on ears and tail.

Grooming & Exercise Needs The ears and tails may require extra brushing in order to prevent matting problems. Although spaniel mixes tend to have more moderate energy levels than purebreds, they still need to be exercised daily.

This spaniel-retriever mix has the long wavy hair of spaniels and the larger size of a retriever.

This coal black spaniel mix has the wavy coat and dark, expressive eyes of the spaniel group. Its legginess probably comes from a nonspaniel forebear.

English Setter

LARGE

SPECIAL EXERCISE NEEDS

GOOD WITH KIDS

English setters, the gentlest and sweetest of the setters, get along with adults, children, dogs, and other animals. They do best in quiet households where they are considered important members of the family and are given regular exercise and playtime; they do not like to be left alone. English setters may bark at strangers who come to the house but more as a greeting than a threat. English setters respond well to firm but patient and gentle handling, though their hunting instincts can make obedience training (which should be started early) difficult. This dog thrives in the country, where it can get a lot of exercise.

Orange belton English setter

Appearance The English setter's flat coat is accented by abundant feathering. Coat color is black and white; black, tan, and white; lemon and white; orange and white; liver and white; lemon belton; orange belton; liver belton; blue belton; or solid white.

Grooming & Exercise Needs The English setter needs to be brushed and combed three times a week and trimmed about three or four times a year. Long, brisk daily walks are essential.

Origins The English setter was originally bred in the 16th century for bird setting and retrieving.

⊙ The English setter is not suited for city or apartment life. Breed-related health concerns: deafness (page 436), progressive retinal atrophy (page 435), hip dysplasia (page 442).

HEIGHT 24-25"

WEIGHT 50-70 LBS.

LIFE SPAN 12-14 YRS.

Warm brown eyes contribute to the English setter's sweet expression.

Gordon Setter

LARGE

SPECIAL EXERCISE NEEDS

GOOD WATCHDOG

Ten-week-old Gordon setter puppies

Gordon setters are very affectionate with their families but reserved with strangers. They need to be obedience trained and exposed early to diverse social situations to avoid behavior problems. Gordons need a firm, gentle hand and lots of praise. They can be aggressive with other dogs (but generally get along with other types of animals) and can be good barking watchdogs.

Appearance The coat is soft, shiny, straight or slightly waved, with feathering on the ears, stomach, chest, tail, and legs. Coat color is black with rich chestnut or mahogany markings over the eyes, on the muzzle and throat, on the chest, inside the hindlegs, under the tail, and on the feet. Narrow black stripes may appear on the toes and there may be a little white on the chest.

Grooming & Exercise Needs Gordon setters need to be brushed and combed a few times a week. They need daily exercise—a brisk walk, a jog, or a hike in the woods will make them happy.

Origins Gordon setters were used in 17th-century Scotland for tracking, pointing, and retrieving. In the mid-18th century, the Duke of Gordon made the breed popular for hunting.

(!) Breed-related health concerns: hip dysplasia (page 442), progressive retinal atrophy (435), hypothyroidism (page 452), cerebellar cortical abiotrophy (a congenital disease causing degeneration of cells in the cerebellum, which controls coordination), epilepsy (page 455).

Gordon setters feature well-feathered tails.

HEIGHT 23-27"

WEIGHT 45-80 LBS.

LIFE SPAN 10-12 YRS.

Irish Setter

LARGE

HIGH ENERGY INDOORS

SPECIAL EXERCISE NEEDS

GOOD WITH KIDS

Well-bred, properly trained, and socialized Irish setters make wonderful companions. They need enormous amounts of daily exercise, however, or they become nervous, hyperactive, and destructive. They are very friendly with children (although their exuberance may be overwhelming) and with other dogs. Irish Setters may bark when someone comes to the door, but they warm up quickly. They must be leashed when they are walked as they tend to run off—"come" seems to be a particularly difficult command for this breed to learn. Irish setters are happiest in an environment where they can run and play a lot.

Irish setter with a show coat

Appearance The coat is of moderate length, straight, and flat. Feathering is long, straight, and silky on the ears and legs. Color is mahogany or rich chestnut red. A very small amount of white may appear on the chest, throat, or toes.

Grooming & Exercise Needs Irish setters need to be brushed and combed twice a week and trimmed every three months. They must be allowed to run free in a secured area every day.

Origins Irish setters were developed in Ireland in the 18th century as hunting dogs. When they find hiding birds, they freeze, flush, and then retrieve the birds after the hunter has shot them.

(!) It is especially important to obtain an Irish setter from a reputable breeder. Breed-related health concerns: hip dysplasia (page 442), progressive retinal atrophy (page 435), juvenile cataracts (page 434), osteosarcoma (page 431), otitis externa (page 435), hypothyroidism (page 452), bloat (page 445).

HEIGHT 25-27"

WEIGHT 60-75 LBS.

LIFE SPAN 10-12 YRS.

Irish setters have a black or chocolate nose.

Chesapeake Bay Retriever

LARGE

SPECIAL EXERCISE NEEDS

GOOD WATCHDOG

Chesapeakes are good family dogs but can be reserved with strangers and aggressive toward other dogs. They are friendly to children if raised with them. Obedience training and socialization with other people and animals must begin early, and aggressive games should be avoided.

Chesapeake Bay retriever with a deadgrass coat

Appearance The outercoat is thick, short, harsh, oily, and wavy in places; the undercoat is dense, fine, and woolly—a unique coat that resists water and helps to keep the animal warm. Color ranges from tan to a dull straw color (called "deadgrass" in this breed) to dark brown. The eyes are yellow or amber.

Grooming & Exercise Needs Chesapeakes need to be brushed only occasionally. They require a few vigorous walks or runs daily, along with frequent retrieval and swim outings.

Origins The Chesapeake Bay retriever, considered the finest waterfowl dog, originated in early 19th-century Maryland, where it was famous for enduring mile-long swims and retrieving hundreds of ducks per day from the rough, icy waters of Chesapeake Bay. The breed probably resulted from the crossing of Newfoundland-type dogs with the curly-coated retriever, the Irish water spaniel, and possibly the otter hound.

Brown Chesapeake Bay retriever

(!) Apartment or urban living is not recommended for Chesapeakes, and they are not suitable for inexperienced owners. Breed-related health concerns: hip dysplasia (page 442), progressive retinal atrophy (page 435).

HEIGHT 21-26"

WEIGHT 55-80 LBS.

LIFE SPAN 10-12 YRS.

Curly-Coated Retriever

LARGE

SPECIAL EXERCISE NEEDS

The curly-coated retriever is devoted to its master, does well with children if socialized to them at an early age, and gets along with other animals. It may be aloof (but not aggressive) toward strangers. This hunting dog should begin obedience training early.

Appearance The unique coat is a thick mass of small, tight, crisp, close-lying curls that are dense enough to protect against weather, water, and harsh vegetation. Coat color is black or liver.

Liver curly-coated retriever

Grooming & Exercise Needs Curly-coated retrievers need to be brushed a few times a week. They love long runs and retrieving tennis balls and other objects from the water.

The curly-coated retriever has crisp curls over its entire body.

Origins The curly-coated retriever, which originated in the 19th century, is thought to be descended from a mixture of the English water spaniel, the poodle, the Newfoundland, and/or a setter. The result is a dog whose concept of heaven is swimming in cold, icy water to retrieve waterfowl.

HEIGHT 25-27"

WEIGHT 65-85 LBS.

LIFE SPAN 10-13 YRS.

(!) The curly-coated retriever is not suitable for city or apartment life. Breed-related health concerns: hair loss, hypothyroidism (page 452), Cushing's syndrome (page 451).

Flat-Coated Retriever

LARGE

SPECIAL EXERCISE NEEDS

GOOD WITH KIDS

Flat-coated retrievers are exuberant, tail-wagging dogs whose biggest faults may be overfriendliness and jumping up on people to greet them. They love children and get along with other animals. It is important to start obedience training and socialization to non-family members early, as these dogs are sometimes suspicious of strangers. Flat-coats are enthusiastic students and quick learners.

Appearance The moderately long outercoat is dense, shiny, fine, straight, and flat-lying; the undercoat is waterproof. When the dog is in full coat, the ears, chest, back of the legs, and underside of the tail are thickly feathered. Coat color is solid black or liver.

The flat-coated retriever is cheerful and eager to please.

Grooming & Exercise Needs The flat-coated retriever needs to be brushed a few times a week; feathering should be trimmed occasionally. Daily exercise, such as a run, swim, or game of fetch, is important.

Black flat-coated retriever

Origins Flat-coated retrievers originated in the 19th century and are thought to be the result of a cross between the Labrador retriever and the Newfoundland. They are superb bird flushers and land-and-water-retrievers and don't mind icy water or chilling winds as long as they are working.

(!) Breed-related health concerns: patellar luxation (page 443), osteosarcoma (page 431).

HEIGHT 22–24"

WEIGHT 60–70 LBS.

LIFE SPAN 10–14 YRS.

LARGE

GOOD WITH KIDS

Golden Retriever

There are few breeds as gentle, affectionate, playful, eager to please, and devoted as the golden retriever. These sweet dogs like people and other animals and are ideal playmates for children. They can be annoying at times because they crave so much attention and always want to be with their owners. Goldens generally do very well in obedience training, which

Golden retrievers love to retrieve. Their coats are various shades of gold.

should be started early, although some dogs may be easily distracted. Gentle, positive reinforcement is all that's needed. Goldens may bark when a stranger comes to the door but more often as a greeting rather than as a warning. A fenced yard is essential—goldens tend to follow their noses and wander. These dogs can live in the city as long as they are exercised daily and given a lot of attention.

The golden competes successfully in agility, Flyball, tracking, and obedience; excels in narcotics detection and search and rescue; and is

HEIGHT 21½–24"

Golden retriever
in a show pose

WEIGHT 55–75 LBS.

LIFE SPAN 12–14 YRS.

regularly chosen to work as a therapy dog as well as with the physically challenged and visually impaired.

Appearance The outercoat is dense, shiny, wavy or flat, and water-repellent; the undercoat is dense and waterproof. Feathering is heavy on the front of the neck, back of the thighs, and underside of the tail, and moderate on the back of the front legs and the underbody. Color is various shades of rich, lustrous gold.

Golden retriever puppy with its mother

Grooming & Exercise Needs Goldens shed a lot and need to be brushed and combed a few times a week. They are happiest when they are taken on several brisk daily walks and are given the opportunity to play with other dogs. Fetching Frisbees or balls and swimming are favorite activities.

Origins Developed in England and Scotland in the 19th century, the golden retriever resulted from the breeding of a Newfoundland-derived yellow retriever with the Tweed water spaniel and the occasional out-crossing of this new dog with the Irish setter, bloodhound, and other water spaniels. The advent of the breech-loading shotgun enabled hunters to down enormous quantities of ducks, and a large-bodied dog was needed to both locate and retrieve game. Until the golden retriever's arrival, setters and pointers located the game, and spaniels flushed and retrieved.

(!) It is especially important to obtain a golden retriever from a reputable breeder. Bad breeders and pet stores often sell aggressive, hyperactive, or timid goldens with serious medical problems. Breed-related health concerns: hip and elbow dysplasia (page 442), cataracts (page 434), hot spots (page 438), hypothyroidism (page 452), lymphoma (page 432), subaortic stenosis (page 449).

Goldens have heavy feathering on the front of the neck, back of the thighs, and underside of the tail.

LARGE

SPECIAL EXERCISE NEEDS

GOOD WITH KIDS

Labrador Retriever

Chocolate Labrador puppies, four- to five-weeks old

Labrador retrievers are among the most appealing dogs. They are very trainable—always ready to work and to please their owners. They are also kind, outgoing, intelligent, adaptable, and friendly to humans and to other animals. They love children and want to be involved in all of their activities. The Labrador excels in field trials, as a service dog, and in narcotics detection.

Appearance The outercoat is short, straight, and very dense; the undercoat is soft and weather-resistant. Coat color is black, yellow, or chocolate, sometimes with a small white spot on the chest. The tail is otterlike, thick at the base, tapering gradually to the tip.

Grooming & Exercise Needs Labrador retrievers need to be brushed one to two times a week. They need a lot of exercise—daily vigorous walks and an opportunity, preferably daily, to romp and retrieve balls in a secured open area. They love

HEIGHT 21½-24½"

WEIGHT 55-75 LBS.

LIFE SPAN 10-12 YRS.

Yellow Labrador retrievers should never be called "golden labs."

Black Labrador retriever

water and, in all fairness, should be taken to swim and retrieve in a safe area on a regular basis. Field stock is generally much higher in energy than show stock.

Origins The Labrador retriever originated in the 19th century in Newfoundland (not Labrador), where it was used by fishermen to pull in fish-filled nets by retrieving the attached cork floats.

(!) It is especially important to obtain a Labrador retriever from a reputable breeder. Breed-related health concerns: hip dysplasia (page 442), osteochondritis dissecans (page 442), hypothyroidism (page 452), progressive retinal atrophy (page 435), cataracts (page 434), epilepsy (page 455).

Labrador service dog helps to pull a wheelchair.

Retriever Mixes

Retriever mixes are generally sweet, gentle, tolerant dogs that respond well to children. They love outdoor activities, especially fetch, and are among the easiest dogs to train.

Appearance Retriever mixes can range from medium to large in size. Their coats are typically water-resistant (water beads up on the fur); hair length ranges from short (indicating Labrador blood) to longish and fluffy

This golden retriever mix is exuberant, playful, quick to learn, and eager to please.

Golden mixes show the same range of tones as purebred golden retrievers: deep red, like this dog, to pale blond.

This retriever mix displays the high energy and enthusiasm for play found in purebred retrievers.

with feathering around the tail and ears (indicating golden or flat-coated retriever blood). Coat colors vary, as in purebred retrievers, and can be gold to red or black to chocolate, sometimes with white markings on the toes, legs, and chest.

Grooming & Exercise Needs Mixed-breed retrievers with long, feathered coats need regular brushing to prevent mats from forming, especially around their ears and tails. Daily exercise is essential.

A golden retriever mix, leggier and thinner than the breed standard, shows the soft expression and outgoing personality of the purebred dog.

These Labrador mix puppies love to chew on each other, a sign of the mouthiness (page 401) sometimes associated with retriever mixes.

LARGE

HIGH ENERGY INDOORS

SPECIAL EXERCISE NEEDS

GOOD WATCHDOG

German Shorthaired Pointer

German shorthaired pointers love their families and other dogs and will accept cats if raised with them from an early age. They require early, gentle, firm obedience training. They usually bark when a person comes onto their property. They generally warm up to strangers easily, but some can be excessively protective. This hunting dog is a superb tracker, pointer, and retriever.

Four-month-old German short-haired pointer puppy

Appearance The German shorthaired pointer's coat is short, thick, tough, and harsh to the touch. The color is liver and white or solid liver. The eyes are large and deep brown.

Grooming & Exercise Needs The German shorthaired pointer needs only a quick brushing with a rubber brush once a week. This highly energetic dog needs vigorous activity to prevent such behavioral problems as house destruction or constant barking when left alone.

Origins The German shorthaired pointer was developed in Germany in the 19th century; its ancestors were probably a Spanish pointer and some English or German scent hounds.

(!) This breed is unsuitable for city or apartment living. Breed-related health concerns: hip dysplasia (page 442), von Willebrand's disease (a common disorder that causes excessive bleeding during or after surgery), lymphedema (an obstruction in the lymphatic system that prevents draining of fluids, which can lead to swelling), hypothyroidism (page 452), subaortic stenosis (page 449), entropion (page 434).

HEIGHT 21–25"

WEIGHT 45–70 LBS.

LIFE SPAN 12–14 YRS.

German shorthaired pointer in show pose

German Wirehaired Pointer

LARGE

German wirehaired pointers are more aloof and wary of strangers than their shorthaired cousins. They can be stubborn and easily distracted, making obedience training a challenge. While they are generally good with children, they should be introduced to them at an early age. Early socialization with people and exposure to different noises and places

Liver and roan German wirehaired pointer

HIGH ENERGY INDOORS

SPECIAL EXERCISE NEEDS

may help them to become more adaptable. They can be aggressive with other dogs and protective of their property but get along with other animals, such as cats, if raised with them.

Appearance The distinctive outercoat is straight, harsh, wiry, one to two inches long, and close-lying, and protects against rough cover, such as thorny bushes; the undercoat is thick in winter and thin in summer. Coat color is solid liver, liver and white, or liver and roan. There may be spots, roaning, or ticking. Facial features include bushy eyebrows, a medium-length beard and whiskers, and a large brown nose with wide-open nostrils.

GOOD WATCHDOG

Grooming & Exercise Needs The German wirehaired pointer needs to be brushed and combed twice a week. This breed is only suitable for those who can give the dog vigorous, daily exercise, such as long runs or jogs.

Origins The Germans developed this breed in the 19th century for endurance and versatility—to track, point, and retrieve all types of game in even the most difficult terrain and weather conditions.

⚠ This breed is not suitable for inexperienced dog owners or for city or apartment living.

The German wirehaired pointer's coat is virtually water-repellent.

HEIGHT 22-26"

WEIGHT 45-70 LBS.

LIFE SPAN 12-14 YRS.

Pointer

LARGE

SPECIAL EXERCISE NEEDS

Pointers are hard-driving hunting dogs known for their stamina, courage, and single-minded impulse to find birds and are bred primarily for field work. Pointers bred for show may be calmer than those bred for hunting, but both still require a lot of exercise and space. They are reserved but get along well with children and animals. Although they can be stubborn, they do respond to firm and patient obedience

A sleek coat accentuates the pointer's shapely outline.

training. They may bark occasionally when a stranger comes to the door, but they are by no means guard dogs or watchdogs.

Appearance The coat is short, dense, and smooth with a sheen. Coat color is liver, lemon, black, or orange, usually in combination with white.

Grooming & Exercise Needs The pointer needs only a quick weekly brushing. The pointer's enormous energy must be channeled into productive work, such as agility trials or other dog sports. It needs a lot of exercise—long jogs and romps in secured areas.

Origins The pointer probably originated in the Middle Ages in England, where it was used to find hare and then freeze in a point (an immovable stance to indicate location of game) for the hunter.

(!) The pointer is not suitable for city or apartment living. Breed-related health concerns: entropion (page 434), cataracts (page 434), progressive retinal atrophy (page 435), deafness (page 436), umbilical hernia (page 441).

HEIGHT 23–28"

WEIGHT 45–75 LBS.

LIFE SPAN 12–14 YRS.

A white coat with ticking and liver-colored spots is common among pointers.

Spinone Italiano

LARGE

GOOD WITH KIDS

Spinone Italianos are affectionate, intelligent, and patient family companions that adore children and get along with other animals. They may be cautious but not unfriendly toward strangers and will bark when someone comes to the door. They are naturally obedient and do well in training classes. They can adapt to urban and rural environments. The Spinone Italiano is an enthusiastic, hardy, and fearless hunting dog and a friendly, easygoing family dog.

White Spinone Italianos with yellow patches (left) and brown patches (right)

Appearance The coat is short, rough, hard, and wiry. Coat color is all white, or white with yellow or light brown patches. Distinguishing features include bushy eyebrows, a profuse mustache and beard, and typical hound ears—large, dropped, and hanging close to the cheeks.

Grooming & Exercise Needs Spinone Italianos should be brushed a few times a week. They need to run daily in safe, secured areas or be taken for long, brisk walks. They may also enjoy retrieving balls.

Origins The Spinone Italiano, descended from griffon stock from the Piedmont region of Italy, has been around since the Middle Ages and is considered one of the best pointing griffons and a superb retriever, in part because of its "soft" mouth (which means that the dog doesn't damage the game when retrieving it).

(!) Breed-related health concerns: hip dysplasia (page 442), hypothyroidism (page 452).

White Spinone Italiano

HEIGHT 20–26"

WEIGHT 56–80 LBS.

LIFE SPAN 12–14 YRS.

Vizsla

LARGE

HIGH ENERGY INDOORS

SPECIAL EXERCISE NEEDS

GOOD WITH KIDS

Vizsla on point

Vizslas are very friendly, devoted dogs that must be included in family activities. Some can be stubborn and easily distracted, making obedience training a challenge. Training and socialization must begin early and should be ongoing. To counteract their hypersensitivity they need to be taken to noisy, busy areas at a young age. Vizslas get along with children, although their energy level can be overwhelming. They are friendly toward strangers and other animals. Vizslas retain their hunting-dog spirit and must be made to feel useful. They are best suited for life in rural or suburban areas with a lot of space.

Appearance The coat is short, smooth, dense, and close-lying. Coat color is different shades of solid golden rust, sometimes with small white spots on the chest and toes.

Grooming & Exercise Needs Vizslas need to be brushed once a week. They are extremely energetic and want to run, explore, and work all the time. To prevent behavior problems such as house destruction, these dogs need long walks or the chance to run daily.

Origins The vizsla is descended from dogs that accompanied the nomadic Magyar people across Europe over a thousand years ago and settled with them in the region now known as Hungary. In the 19th century the vizsla became an outstanding pointer and retriever.

(!) It is especially important to obtain a vizsla from a reputable breeder. The vizsla is not suited to city or apartment living unless properly exercised. Breed-related health concerns include hemophilia (a bleeding disorder).

HEIGHT 19 ½-25 ½"

WEIGHT 45-60 LBS.

LIFE SPAN 12-14 YRS.

Vizsla with an identification tattoo on the thigh

Weimaraner

LARGE

Weimaraners are friendly, playful, and highly energetic. They can also be stubborn and require an experienced owner willing to work with the dog in early and ongoing obedience classes. They are friendly with children, although they may be too energetic for toddlers, and may be reserved or very friendly to strangers, depending on their genetics, training, and socialization. They get along with other dogs but may chase cats if not raised with them. The weimaraner, a study in grace, speed, stamina, energy, and endurance, is used as a pointer and retriever by bird hunters.

HIGH ENERGY INDOORS

SPECIAL EXERCISE NEEDS

GOOD WATCHDOG

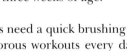

Weimaraner with amber eyes

GOOD WITH KIDS

Appearance The coat is short, smooth, and sleek. Coat color is shades of mouse gray to silver gray, sometimes with a small white mark on the chest. The unusually colored eyes are shades of light amber, gray, or blue-gray. Puppies are born with dark stripes running down the length of their bodies. The stripes disappear at three weeks of age.

Grooming & Exercise Needs Weimaraners need a quick brushing once a week. They must be given long, vigorous workouts every day or they will become unmanageable and destructive.

Four-month-old weimaraner puppy

Origins The weimaraner, affectionately known as the Gray Ghost, was developed in Germany in the 19th century for large-game hunting.

(!) The weimaraner is not suitable for inexperienced owners. Breed-related health concerns: hip dysplasia (page 442), hemophilia (a bleeding disorder), bloat (page 445), eye problems.

HEIGHT 23–27"

WEIGHT 55–85 LBS.

LIFE SPAN 10–12 YRS.

Wirehaired Pointing Griffon

LARGE

HIGH ENERGY INDOORS

SPECIAL EXERCISE NEEDS

GOOD WATCHDOG

Wirehaired pointing griffons are gentle, responsive, and obedient but need early socialization and obedience training to prevent timidity. They are respectful with strangers and easygoing with most other dogs, but they like to chase cats. The griffon's temperament is best suited to an adult home in the country. Its reputation as a supreme hunting dog is well earned.

Chestnut roan wirehaired pointing griffon

Appearance The outercoat is medium in length, straight, and wiry; the undercoat is an abundant, fine, thick down. Coat color is gray, chestnut, roan, steel gray with chestnut markings, white with chestnut markings, or dirty white mixed with chestnut. Distinguishing features include bushy eyebrows covering large yellow-brown eyes and a thick, harsh beard.

Grooming & Exercise Needs Wirehaired pointing griffons need to be brushed and combed weekly. If this country dog does not get an enormous amount of exercise, behavior problems, such as excessive barking and house destruction, may occur.

Origins The wirehaired pointing griffon was developed in France by a Dutchman, Eduard K. Korthals, in the 1870s for pointing and retrieving in all types of weather and rough terrain.

(!) The wirehaired pointing griffon is not suitable for city or apartment life or for inexperienced owners. Breed-related health concerns include hip dysplasia (page 442).

Steel gray wirehaired pointing griffon with chestnut markings

HEIGHT 20-24"

WEIGHT 45-60 LBS.

LIFE SPAN 10-12 YRS.

Portuguese Water Dog

LARGE

SPECIAL EXERCISE NEEDS

SPECIAL GROOMING NEEDS

Portuguese water dogs are very intelligent, playful, and active. They require early obedience training and socialization to become accustomed to different types of people, animals, and noises. They may bark excessively to guard their territory, communicate with other dogs, or get attention. They also may be "mouthy," wanting to chew or hold household objects in their mouths.

Portuguese water dogs need occasional swims.

GOOD WATCHDOG

Appearance Their profuse, thick coat comes in two varieties: curly with lusterless, compact, cylindrical curls; or wavy with gently falling curls and a slight sheen. Color is black, white, various tones of brown, and combinations of black or brown with white. There are two common clips: the lion (face and hindquarters shaved) or the retriever (evenly trimmed all over). The tail is usually shaved with a plume on the end.

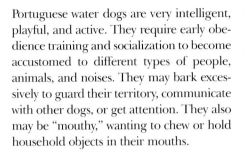

Black Portuguese water dog with a lion clip

Grooming & Exercise Needs Portuguese water dogs need to be brushed and combed a few times a week and trimmed every month or two. They need to be taken on at least one long walk or run every day and given the occasional opportunity to swim.

Origins The Portuguese water dog, an exceptional swimmer and diver, originated in the Middle Ages and for centuries helped fishermen by retrieving broken nets, herding schools of fish, and carrying messages from boat to shore.

! This breed is not suitable for inexperienced dog owners. Breed-related health concerns: progressive retinal atrophy (page 435), glycogen storage disease (a rare and fatal nervous system disorder), congenital kidney problems that may lead to kidney failure, Addison's disease (page 452), cardiomyopathy (page 450), follicular dysplasia (a condition caused by abnormally formed hair follicles that results in hair loss).

HEIGHT 17-23"

WEIGHT 35-60 LBS.

LIFE SPAN 10-14 YRS.

Terriers

The terrier group includes descendants of bullbaiting breeds and of dogs bred to exterminate vermin.

Terra, the Latin word for "earth," is the basis for the name "terrier," given to a group of dogs bred to tunnel into the earth—or "go to ground"—to exterminate vermin. Most terriers recognized today were developed in the British Isles, some as long ago as the fifteenth century. These were working dogs, bred for their abilities rather than for consistent looks, and the majority of them weren't recognized as purebreds until the eighteenth and nineteenth centuries, when The Kennel Club in Great Britain began to set breed standards for them. Physical characteristics of terrier breeds differ based on the county in which they were developed and the attributes that were needed to capture native vermin.

The smallest, short-legged terriers—cairn, Norfolk, Norwich, West Highland white, Australian, toy fox, Manchester, and miniature schnauzer—were bred to be excellent "ratters" in fields and on farms. The slightly leggier terriers—Border, fox, and Jack Russell—accompanied fox hunters on horseback. Vocal and alert, they also served as watchdogs. The bulkier terriers—Kerry blue, Lakeland, Scottish, Skye, Dandie Dinmont, and Bedlington—were used to hunt badgers and otters, while the tallest of terriers—Airedale, soft-coated wheaten, and standard schnauzer—made excellent watchdogs and family guardians. The bull and terrier dogs—American Staffordshire, American pit bull, Staffordshire bull, bull, and miniature bull—are descendants of a long-ago cross between terrier and bullbaiting breeds, and were created primarily as dog-versus-dog pit fighters.

Early terriers were bred to fight to the death, to never back down even in the face of a physically superior competitor. These traits are still evident in the scrappy, high-energy terriers of today. As a group, terriers are the most difficult dogs to obedience train, and they require daily aerobic exercise.

Many terriers do not shed but need to be hand-stripped or clipped in order to rid them of dead hair. Often this makes them a good choice for people who have mild canine allergies.

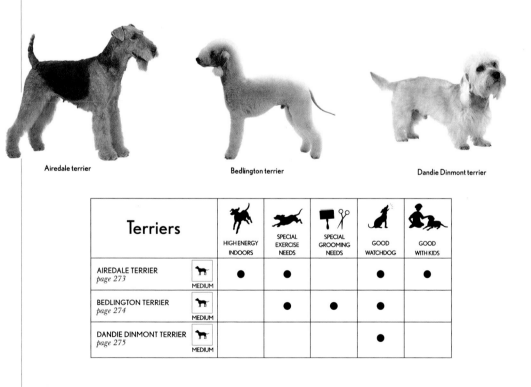

Airedale terrier

Bedlington terrier

Dandie Dinmont terrier

Terriers		HIGH ENERGY INDOORS	SPECIAL EXERCISE NEEDS	SPECIAL GROOMING NEEDS	GOOD WATCHDOG	GOOD WITH KIDS
AIREDALE TERRIER *page 273*	MEDIUM	●	●		●	●
BEDLINGTON TERRIER *page 274*	MEDIUM		●	●	●	
DANDIE DINMONT TERRIER *page 275*	MEDIUM				●	

Fox terrier

Irish terrier

Kerry blue terrier

Lakeland terrier

Terriers		HIGH ENERGY INDOORS	SPECIAL EXERCISE NEEDS	SPECIAL GROOMING NEEDS	GOOD WATCHDOG	GOOD WITH KIDS
FOX TERRIER *page 276*	SMALL	●	●		●	
IRISH TERRIER *page 278*	MEDIUM		●		●	
KERRY BLUE TERRIER *page 279*	MEDIUM		●		●	
LAKELAND TERRIER *page 280*	SMALL	●	●		●	
SCOTTISH TERRIER *page 281*	MEDIUM	●	●		●	
SEALYHAM TERRIER *page 282*	MEDIUM				●	
SKYE TERRIER *page 283*	MEDIUM			●	●	
SOFT-COATED WHEATEN TERRIER *page 284*	MEDIUM		●	●	●	●

Scottish terrier

Sealyham terrier

Skye terrier

Soft-coated wheaten terrier

American pit
bull terrier

Bull terrier

American Staffordshire terrier

Miniature bull terrier

Terriers		HIGH ENERGY INDOORS	SPECIAL EXERCISE NEEDS	SPECIAL GROOMING NEEDS	GOOD WATCHDOG	GOOD WITH KIDS
AMERICAN PIT BULL TERRIER *page 285*	MEDIUM	●	●		●	
AMERICAN STAFFORDSHIRE TERRIER *page 286*	LARGE	●	●		●	
BULL TERRIER *page 287*	MEDIUM	●	●		●	
MINIATURE BULL TERRIER *page 288*	SMALL	●	●		●	
STAFFORDSHIRE BULL TERRIER *page 289*	MEDIUM		●			●
AUSTRALIAN TERRIER *page 292*	SMALL	●	●		●	
BORDER TERRIER *page 293*	SMALL					●
CAIRN TERRIER *page 294*	SMALL	●	●		●	

Staffordshire bull terrier

Australian terrier

Cairn terrier

Pit bull mixes

Border terrier

Jack Russell terrier

Manchester terrier

Miniature schnauzer

Norwich terrier

Norfolk terrier

Terriers		HIGH ENERGY INDOORS	SPECIAL EXERCISE NEEDS	SPECIAL GROOMING NEEDS	GOOD WATCHDOG	GOOD WITH KIDS
JACK RUSSELL TERRIER *page 295*	SMALL	●	●		●	
MANCHESTER TERRIER *page 296*	SMALL MEDIUM	●	●		●	
MINIATURE SCHNAUZER *page 297*	SMALL	●	●		●	
NORFOLK TERRIER *page 298*	SMALL	●	●		●	●
NORWICH TERRIER *page 299*	SMALL	●	●		●	●
STANDARD SCHNAUZER *page 300*	MEDIUM	●	●		●	
TOY FOX TERRIER *page 301*	SMALL	●	●		●	
WELSH TERRIER *page 302*	MEDIUM	●	●		●	
WEST HIGHLAND WHITE TERRIER *page 303*	SMALL	●	●		●	

Standard schnauzer

Toy fox terrier

Welsh terrier

West Highland white terrier

Terrier mixes

Airedale Terrier

MEDIUM

HIGH ENERGY INDOORS

SPECIAL EXERCISE NEEDS

GOOD WATCHDOG

GOOD WITH KIDS

Three-month-old Airedale puppy

The Airedale terrier is known for its playfulness and courage, as well as its love of and patience with children. It can, however, be stubborn and may challenge its owners for dominance in the "pack." It may also be aggressive with other dogs. Obedience training and socialization are highly recommended at an early age. The Airedale is a first-class watchdog, wary of strangers at first but ready to befriend them if encouraged by its owners.

Appearance The Airedale's outercoat is wiry and its undercoat is soft. The color can be tan and black or tan and dark gray. The head, ears, and beard are always tan.

Grooming & Exercise Needs Grooming requirements are minimal. Show dogs need stripping (removing old hair by hand) and pets require occasional clipping. Daily vigorous exercise, such as a few long, brisk walks and a couple of aerobic play sessions, will help keep the Airedale happy.

Origins The Airedale terrier originated in the 19th century in Yorkshire, England, along the Aire River, when a black-and-tan terrier (now extinct) was crossed with an otter hound. The result was a fearless, tenacious dog (terrier) that loved cold water (otter hound).

(!) Breed-related health concerns: malignant tumors, such as lymphoma (page 432), hypothyroidism (page 452).

An Airedale's permanent coloring emerges with maturity. A black "saddle" is very common.

HEIGHT 22–23"

WEIGHT 45–50 LBS.

LIFE SPAN 12–14 YRS.

Bedlington Terrier

The Bedlington is a loyal companion and gets along with children and other animals if socialized with them at an early age, but it may be cautious with strangers. Some are high-strung and can be snappish when irritable. To avoid behavioral problems, such as excessive barking and house destruction, proper obedience training, regular exercise, and play are necessary.

Appearance The Bedlington terrier looks like a lamb. Its coat is a mixture of coarse and soft hair that stands well out from the skin and is crisp to the touch. It comes in blue, sandy, liver, blue and tan, sandy and tan, or liver and tan.

Adolescent Bedlington with a pet clip

Grooming & Exercise Needs
Bedlington terriers don't shed but need weekly combing and a professional grooming every two months to keep their coats, which tend to curl, in good shape. This high-energy dog needs several vigorous walks and aerobic play sessions daily.

Origins The Bedlington was developed in England in the late 18th to early 19th centuries to hunt fox and badger, to work as a ratter in coal mines, and to be a dogfighter.

(!) This dog is not suitable for inexperienced dog owners. Breed-related health concerns: copper toxicosis (a hereditary disease in which copper accumulates in the liver and can lead to liver failure), retinal dysplasia (conditions resulting from improper retina development that in rare cases cause blindness), congenital kidney problems.

HEIGHT 15-17"

WEIGHT 17-23 LBS.

LIFE SPAN 12-14 YRS.

Bedlington terrier with a show coat

Dandie Dinmont Terrier

MEDIUM

GOOD WATCHDOG

Pepper Dandie Dinmont

The properly socialized and trained Dandie Dinmont is a delightful dog. It can be protective of its property, wary of strangers, dominant, and independent, but also gentle if treated kindly and with respect. It is very important to start obedience training and to socialize this dog with adults, children, and other animals at an early age.

Appearance The Dandie Dinmont's coat, a mixture of coarse and soft hair with a crisp texture, is about two inches long. Its color is pepper or mustard. The head and the soft, silky topknot on the head may be creamy white. The rich, dark hazel eyes are large, round, and bright.

Grooming & Exercise Needs Dandie Dinmonts need to be brushed and combed two to three times a week and trimmed every three months. Vigorous exercise will reduce this dog's tendency to dig holes and bark excessively.

Origins The Dandie Dinmont was developed in England in the 17th century to hunt badgers, foxes, rats, and weasels. In the 19th century it was named Dandie Dinmont after a country gentleman in Sir Walter Scott's 1815 novel *Guy Mannering*. Dinmont, who lived on the border between England and Scotland, kept six of these playful, affectionate terriers on his farm. This breed has been popular with gypsies as well as aristocracy at various times in its history.

(!) Breed-related health concerns: hip dysplasia (page 442), patellar luxation (page 443), intervertebral disc protrusion (page 456), ear infections, lymphoma (page 432).

Mustard Dandie Dinmont

HEIGHT 8-11"

WEIGHT 18-24 LBS.

LIFE SPAN 14-15 YRS.

Fox Terrier

SMALL

HIGH ENERGY INDOORS

SPECIAL EXERCISE NEEDS

GOOD WATCHDOG

Ten-week-old wirehaired
fox terrier puppy

The popular fox terrier is lively and fun-loving, gets along with respectful children over about five years old, and can live in the city or the country. Other animals can be a problem. For instance, fox terriers may chase cats that are not family members. Obedience training and socialization must begin early. Fox terriers can be distracted easily when excited by other animals or peripheral events, so firm and consistent handling is required. Without training, they may also develop some behavioral problems, such as excessive barking, hole digging, or possessiveness with their toys or food bowls. Aggressive games, such as tug-of-war, should not be played with these dogs.

Appearance The fox terrier has a flat, narrow head and a long muzzle that slopes to a black nose. There are two different coats, the smooth and the wirehaired. The smooth coat is short and flat-lying. The wirehaired coat is moderately long and has a dense, wiry texture; the hairs twist together, making it difficult to part them in order to see the skin. Fox terriers are white with black or black and tan markings. Wirehaired puppies are black and white or all white at birth; the black on the face and some of the markings on the shoulders, hips, and tail will turn tan.

HEIGHT 14-15 ½"

WEIGHT 15-19 LBS.

LIFE SPAN 12-14 YRS.

Smooth fox terrier

Grooming & Exercise Needs The wirehaired should be brushed and combed twice a week and clipped or stripped (removing old hair by hand) to preserve the texture and luster of the coat every three months. The smooth only needs a short brushing once a week. Fox terriers are extremely energetic and need daily exercise—long, vigorous walks and/or ball playing—as well as human interaction.

Black and tan wirehaired fox terrier

Origins The fox terrier, both the smooth and wirehaired, was developed in England in the 18th century for "bolting"—or driving out—foxes from their dens. These fearless hunters would dig, crawl, and squirm their way into a fox hole and attack unrelentingly until the fox bolted.

① Breed-related health concerns: deafness (page 436), Legg-Perthes disease (page 443), mast cell tumors (page 431).

Fox terriers display a wide variety of markings, with color often concentrated on the head.

Irish Terrier

MEDIUM

SPECIAL EXERCISE NEEDS

GOOD WATCHDOG

Irish terrier in a show pose

Irish terriers are loyal, lively, and affectionate. They are good family dogs and like to play with children but may behave aggressively if their property—toys, food bowls—is touched. Some lines can be highly protective and may snap at anyone they perceive as a threat to their family. They can do well in obedience class but may be aggressive toward other dogs and may mistake cats as prey. Secure the yard with a fence and always walk Irish terriers on a leash. When properly trained, the Irish terrier is a good companion in the city, suburbs, or country.

Appearance The Irish terrier has bushy eyebrows and a beard. Its coat is short, dense, and wiry. Its color is solid bright red, golden red, red wheaten, or wheaten.

Grooming & Exercise Needs The Irish terrier should be brushed and combed twice a week and trimmed every three months. To avoid behavioral problems, such as nonstop barking or digging, this energetic dog needs long walks, hikes, and vigorous play in a secured area.

Origins The Irish terrier is one of the oldest terrier breeds. It was developed in the 18th century for hunting rats, small and big game, and as a land and water retriever. During World War I this fearless terrier was used as a patrol and messenger dog.

HEIGHT 17-18"

WEIGHT 25-27 LBS.

LIFE SPAN 12-15 YRS.

(!) The Irish Terrier is not suitable for inexperienced dog owners. Breed-related health concerns include cystine stones (bladder stones caused by an inability of the kidneys to absorb the animo acid cystine).

Irish terriers have a distinctive beard.

Kerry Blue Terrier

MEDIUM

SPECIAL EXERCISE NEEDS

GOOD WATCHDOG

Kerry blues are loyal to their owners but may not be tolerant of young children. They are aggressive toward other dogs as well, and they will chase small animals, such as cats, if not introduced to them at an early age. Obedience training is difficult but mandatory, and must be ongoing, for these are very stubborn, assertive dogs.

Kerry blue terrier herding a goat

Appearance The Kerry blue's ears fold forward and its beard is thick. Its coat is soft, dense, and wavy. The color ranges from light blue-gray to deep slate; pups are born black. The head, muzzle, ears, tail, and feet are darker than the rest of the body.

Grooming & Exercise Needs Kerry blues need to be brushed and combed twice a week and trimmed every three months. They require a lot of exercise and must be kept on a leash around other dogs.

The Kerry blue terrier has a soft, dense coat.

Origins The Kerry blue terrier, developed in County Kerry, Ireland, has been used for many types of work, including water retrieving, trailing, and herding.

(!) The Kerry blue is not suitable for inexperienced dog owners. It may not be tolerant of young children. Breed-related health concerns: hip dysplasia (page 442), hypothyroidism (page 452), eye problems.

HEIGHT 17-20"

WEIGHT 33-40 LBS.

LIFE SPAN 12-15 YRS.

Lakeland Terrier

SMALL

HIGH ENERGY INDOORS

SPECIAL EXERCISE NEEDS

GOOD WATCHDOG

Lakelands are fearless, gregarious, and loyal companions. They are friendly with family members—though they may guard their toys and food bowls—but they may be suspicious of strangers and scrappy around other dogs. They are usually fine around familiar cats but may need to be watched around cats outdoors and other small animals. They enjoy the company of children, especially those who are at least eight years old and gentle. If left alone for long periods they may develop behavioral problems, such as excessive barking, digging, and dominance and territory issues.

Wheaten Lakeland terrier

Appearance The Lakeland's distinctive ears fold forward; it also has characteristic bushy eyebrows, a substantial beard, and a mustache. The outercoat is short, hard, and wiry; the undercoat is close to the skin and soft. Coat color is blue, black, liver, red, or wheaten. The saddle may be black, liver, blue, or shades of grizzle.

Grooming & Exercise Needs Lakeland terriers need to be brushed and combed twice a week. They should be allowed to romp in a secured area and taken on vigorous daily walks.

Origins The Lakeland terrier was originally bred in the 18th century in the rugged shale mountains of England's Northern Lake District to "bolt" (drive out), catch, and kill the foxes that preyed on farmers' livestock.

⚠ Breed-related health concerns: Legg-Perthes disease (page 443), undescended testicles.

HEIGHT 14-15"

WEIGHT 15-17 LBS.

LIFE SPAN 14-15 YRS.

Lakeland terrier with a black saddle

Scottish Terrier

MEDIUM

Brindle Scottish terrier

Scotties are self-assured, spunky, fearless, and independent. They require early socialization and on-going obedience training. They are devoted to their families and get along with children if exposed to them at an early age. Some, however, can be snappish and irritable at times, so they may not be the best choice for a family with young children. They may be aggressive with other animals, including cats and dogs, if not raised with them. They bark a lot and are natural watchdogs. Scotties can live anywhere as long as they are given daily exercise. They must be limited to safe, enclosed areas when off-leash, as they are likely to chase small animals.

HIGH ENERGY INDOORS

SPECIAL EXERCISE NEEDS

GOOD WATCHDOG

Appearance The Scottie's eyebrows are long, its beard ample. Its weather-resistant coat is hard and wiry with a soft and dense undercoat. The coat color is black, sandy, wheaten, steel or iron gray, brindled or grizzled. A small amount of white may appear on the chest and chin.

Grooming & Exercise Needs Scotties need to be brushed one to two times a week and trimmed every three months. They need several brisk walks and daily playtime with their owners.

Origins This compact, sturdily built dog originated in the 19th century in the Scottish Highlands, where it was used to hunt vermin.

(!) Breed-related health concerns: von Willebrand's disease (a common disorder that causes excessive bleeding during or after surgery), craniomandibular osteopathy (a bone disease causing excessive growth of head bones in young dogs), allergies, lymphoma (page 432), Scottie cramp (a disorder appearing at around one year characterized by muscle stiffness when the dog is excited), elbow dysplasia (page 442), intervertebral disc protrusion (page 456).

Wheaten Scottish terrier

HEIGHT 10"

WEIGHT 18–22 LBS.

LIFE SPAN 12–14 YRS.

MEDIUM

GOOD WATCHDOG

Sealyham Terrier

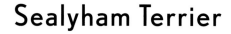

The independent, fun-loving Sealyham makes an excellent urban companion. Although comfortable with gentle children over eight years old—they won't tolerate rough handling—Sealyhams are naturally cautious with strangers. They can be aggressive with other animals if not socialized early and require early obedience training with owners who are able to maintain dominance. Their deep bark, which makes them seem more aggressive than they actually are, emphasizes their watchdog talents. Sealyhams, like Scotties, do well in apartments and cities if their exercise needs are met.

White Sealyham terrier with tan markings

Appearance The Sealyham's weather-resistant coat is firm and wiry on top and soft and dense underneath. The dogs are all white or white with lemon, tan, or badger markings on the head and ears. Distinctive features include bushy eyebrows, a beard, and round-tipped ears that fold down.

Grooming & Exercise Needs Sealyhams should be brushed and combed twice a week and trimmed every three months. They need brisk daily walks and occasional romps in secured areas.

Origins The Sealyham terrier was developed in Wales in the 19th century to be a bold, tenacious rat and badger hunter.

HEIGHT 10½"

WEIGHT 22-24 LBS.

LIFE SPAN 12-14 YRS.

⚠ Breed-related health concerns: allergies, deafness (page 436), hereditary eye problems including glaucoma (page 434).

Sealyhams have bushy eyebrows and beards.

Skye Terrier

MEDIUM

Skye terriers are physically powerful, strong-willed, bold, and loyal. They require a lot of individual attention. Early socialization and obedience training, preferably with an experienced owner who can maintain leadership, should make them less cautious with strangers, less nippy with children, and less hostile toward other animals. They are fine city dogs if exercised daily.

Blue Skye terrier with a show coat

SPECIAL GROOMING NEEDS

GOOD WATCHDOG

Appearance The Skye's well-feathered hair falls like a veil over its forehead and eyes, a feature that protects this hunter from brush and briars. The outercoat is firm, flat, straight, and about five inches long; the undercoat is short, close, soft, and woolly. Coat color is black, blue, light or dark gray, silver platinum, cream, or fawn.

Grooming & Exercise Needs Skye terriers need to be brushed and combed every other day to avoid matting. Some trimming may be necessary every three months. They need long walks daily and occasional runs in safe, secured areas.

Origins The Skye terrier originated in the 16th century on the rugged, harsh islands of northwest Scotland—one of which is the Isle of Skye. The breed displayed stamina, courage, strength, and agility in pursuit of small game. It was a favorite of royalty; Queen Victoria fell in love with the breed. The story goes that in the 19th century an ever loyal Skye terrier named Greyfriar's Bobby mourned and visited its master's grave for ten years—until its own death.

(!) This breed requires an experienced owner. Breed-related health concerns: hypothyroidism (page 452), atopy (page 437), copper toxicosis (a hereditary disease in which copper accumulates in the liver and can lead to liver failure).

Skye terriers need to be brushed every other day.

HEIGHT 9-10"

WEIGHT 23-28 LBS.

LIFE SPAN 12-15 YRS.

Soft-Coated Wheaten Terrier

MEDIUM

SPECIAL EXERCISE NEEDS

SPECIAL GROOMING NEEDS

GOOD WATCHDOG

GOOD WITH KIDS

Fourteen-week-old wheaten puppy

The most sedate of the terriers, the soft-coated wheaten makes a first-rate companion with its happy, steady personality. Wheatens are wonderful, playful family dogs that can adapt to city or suburban living as long as they are exercised daily and given the human companionship they need. They are eager to please and do well in obedience training. They love children who treat them gently, get along with other animals, and are generally friendly with strangers. They may bark as an alarm—but unlike other terriers, the wheaten is not yappy.

Appearance The wheaten's soft, single, golden coat is more abundant than the coats of other terriers. Pups may be black at birth and young dogs display black tipping up to one year of age.

Grooming & Exercise Needs The wheaten should be brushed and combed daily and trimmed every three months. It is an energetic breed and requires long, brisk daily walks and romps and playtime with its family in a safe, secured area.

Origins The soft-coated wheaten terrier originated over 200 years ago in Ireland, where it was used as an all-purpose worker—guarding, droving, herding, and hunting.

(!) It is especially important to obtain a soft-coated wheaten terrier from a reputable breeder. Breed-related health concerns: progressive retinal atrophy (page 435), congenital kidney problems, allergies.

HEIGHT 17-19"

WEIGHT 30-40 LBS.

LIFE SPAN 13-15 YRS.

Soft-coated wheaten with a show coat

American Pit Bull Terrier

MEDIUM

Despite its reputation, the extraordinarily muscled American pit bull terrier can be a wonderful family companion if bred for gentle temperament and trained at a young age. The breed can also be stubborn and aggressive, so early socialization with all kinds of people and animals is crucial.

HIGH ENERGY INDOORS

Appearance The muscular pit bull terrier has a bricklike shape and powerful jaws. Its short, glossy coat comes in all colors and markings, including brindle, white with patches of color, black, and red.

SPECIAL EXERCISE NEEDS

Grooming & Exercise Needs The pit bull's short coat needs to be brushed once a week with a rubber brush. This active dog needs a few long walks and some playtime in a secured area daily.

GOOD WATCHDOG

Origins The American pit bull terrier, a cross between Staffordshire bull terriers and an extinct fighting bulldog, was bred in the 19th century for dogfighting.

(!) The American pit bull terrier is not suitable for inexperienced dog owners. It can be especially aggressive with other dogs. Prospective owners should avoid selecting puppies from fighting stock. It is especially important to obtain an American pit bull terrier from a reputable breeder, as there are, unfortunately, some who choose to breed the most aggressive animals and then train them to maim or kill. Avoid puppies under seven weeks of age that are sold off the street.

Red American pit bull terrier
with a red nose

HEIGHT 18-22"

WEIGHT 30-70 LBS.

LIFE SPAN 11-13 YRS.

LARGE

HIGH ENERGY INDOORS

SPECIAL EXERCISE NEEDS

GOOD WATCHDOG

American Staffordshire Terrier

Fawn and white American Staffordshire terrier with six-week-old puppy

The American Staffordshire terrier is very affectionate to family members, including children, and to most strangers. Because of its fighting background, however, it should always be walked on-leash and kept in a fenced area when playing. Aggressive games like tug-of-war are ill-advised with dogs from fighting stock, and they should be supervised around other animals. Early socialization and obedience training is advised.

Appearance The short coat is glossy and stiff to the touch. Any color in the solid, particolor, or patched pattern is possible. Brindle, white with patches of color, black, and red are the most common.

Grooming & Exercise Needs Although the American Staffordshire terrier needs only minimal brushing, bathing three to six times a year is important for a healthy skin and coat. This dog needs a few long walks and aerobic-level play sessions daily.

Origins The American Staffordshire terrier, a descendant of an English bulldog crossed with an unidentified terrier, was created in the 19th century primarily for pit fighting.

! The American Staffordshire is not suitable for inexperienced owners. Breed-related health concerns: anterior cruciate rupture (page 442), progressive retinal atrophy (page 435), hip dysplasia (page 442), skin allergies (page 437).

HEIGHT 17-19"

WEIGHT 50-65 LBS.

LIFE SPAN 12-14 YRS.

Brindle American Staffordshire terrier with natural (uncropped) ears

Bull Terrier

MEDIUM

Bull terriers are sweet, energetic, playful dogs that require a lot of attention and love to frolic with their families. If they are ignored, behavioral problems may develop. Early obedience classes and socialization with children, adults, and other animals are recommended. Bull terriers are rarely stars at obedience school, but if handled with leadership and praise, they will succeed. Don't play aggressive games with bull terriers. They are usually friendly to strangers, but always walk them on a leash to avoid confrontations with other dogs. If provoked, they may cause serious injury or death to other dogs.

White bull terrier

HIGH ENERGY INDOORS

SPECIAL EXERCISE NEEDS

GOOD WATCHDOG

Appearance The head of a bull terrier has a distinct egg shape and, in profile, gently curves downward from the top of the skull to the tip of the nose. The short, flat coat is harsh to the touch and has a slight luster. Its color is white, brindle, red, or fawn. White bull terriers may have colored markings on their heads.

Grooming & Exercise Needs Bull terriers need only an occasional brushing. They require a lot of play and exercise, including several long walks daily.

Origins Bull terriers, the offspring of a bulldog and a now extinct white terrier, were bred for dogfighting in England in the 19th century.

① The bull terrier is not suitable for inexperienced owners. Breed-related health concerns: deafness (page 436), spinning disorder (a neurological disorder that causes dogs to "spin" in circles), acrodermatitis (a hereditary and fatal disorder in which dogs cannot properly metabolize zinc).

Six-week-old brindle bull terrier puppies

HEIGHT 21-22"

WEIGHT 50-60 LBS.

LIFE SPAN 11-13 YRS.

Miniature Bull Terrier

SMALL

HIGH ENERGY INDOORS

SPECIAL EXERCISE NEEDS

GOOD WATCHDOG

Miniature bull terriers are energetic, courageous, and strong-willed companions that require early obedience training. They love children but may be suspicious of strangers. Most get along with other animals if exposed to them at an early age. They are happy as long as they are exercised, played with, and included in family activities. If isolated, however, these dogs will develop behavioral problems. They are as sweet and spunky as the standard bull terrier but smaller, making them a good choice for city or apartment dwellers who have time to enjoy and exercise their dogs.

Brindle and white miniature bull terrier

Appearance The strongly built, square-bodied miniature bull terrier is known for its distinctive egg-shaped head. The coat is short, flat, and harsh to the touch, with a fine gloss. It can be any color, the most common being white or brindle.

Grooming & Exercise Needs Miniature bull terriers need only quick weekly brushings. They also need a lot of exercise and attention, or they may dig holes, chew, and become destructive in the house. They enjoy brisk long walks, ball games, and the chance to play with other dogs.

Origins Miniature bull terriers originated in England in the 19th century.

⚠ Breed-related health concerns include deafness (page 436).

HEIGHT 10-14"

WEIGHT 25-35 LBS.

LIFE SPAN 12-14 YRS.

White miniature bull terrier

Staffordshire Bull Terrier

MEDIUM

SPECIAL EXERCISE NEEDS

Staffordshire bull terriers are devoted family members and adore children. They are friendly to strangers, especially if a dominant family member is present, and get along with other family pets as long as they are exposed to them while young. Note, however, that two male dogs in the same household may continually challenge each other for dominance. Staffordshires may not get along with strange dogs and should always be walked on a leash because of their tendency to fight. They become restless if they don't get a lot of exercise. Never play aggressive games with them. These powerful and athletic dogs respond well to early socialization and obedience training when handled by experienced owners.

Red and white Staffordshire bull terrier with brindle and white puppy

GOOD WITH KIDS

Appearance The Staffordshire's smooth coat lies close to the skin. Color is red, fawn, black, blue, any of those colors with white, solid white, brindle, or brindle and white.

Grooming & Exercise Needs Staffordshire bull terriers need to be brushed once a week and taken on several brisk long walks daily.

Origins The Staffordshire bull terrier was developed in Staffordshire, England, in the 19th century for dog fighting and ratting. It is thought to be descended from the larger, old-fashioned bulldog and a terrier similar to today's Manchester terrier.

Red Staffordshire bull terrier

HEIGHT 14-16"

WEIGHT 24-38 LBS.

(!) Breed-related health concerns include cataracts (page 434).

LIFE SPAN 11-13 YRS.

Pit Bull Mixes

This five-year-old pit bull-sporting dog mix has a solid, muscular build.

Pit bull mixes vary in temperament according to their parentage and how well they have been socialized as puppies with other dogs and people. Some grow up to be one-person dogs that will accept only their owner, while others can be friendly and accepting of all people. Like other dogs, pit bull mixes can be either extremely aggressive and prone to fighting or exuberant, playful, and sociable. They are sure to be high-energy dogs with tremendous strength. Common in many urban shelters, pit bull mixes are recommended for experienced owners only and are not suitable for households with children under seven years of age.

Appearance Pit bull mixes have short-haired coats in a range of colors and patterns. They have broad-backed skulls, wide mouths, and extremely strong jaws.

Grooming & Exercise Needs Brush these dogs once a week with a rubber brush. Because pit bull mixes are very active and have tremendous energy, they will develop such behavior problems as inappropriate chewing and jumping if they are not exercised frequently. They need at least three walks daily plus aerobic-level exercise in a secured area.

With proper socialization and training, many pit bull mixes make gentle companions.

Pit bull mixes generally have the wide mouth and broad-backed skull that are common features of pit bulls.

Brindle is a common coat pattern of both purebred and mixed-breed pit bulls.

The body shape of pit bull mixes can range from stocky to tall and leggy, like this dog.

Australian Terrier

SMALL

HIGH ENERGY INDOORS

SPECIAL EXERCISE NEEDS

GOOD WATCHDOG

Blue and tan Australian terriers

Australian terriers are affectionate, entertaining, and energetic little dogs. They do fine with young children if raised with them and if they are not teased. Although originally bred to kill small vermin, they may be able to live peacefully with cats if raised with them, but pity the poor dog that picks a fight with an Aussie. These terriers are pugnacious and tenacious—they will not back down.

Appearance The outercoat is harsh and straight, about two to three inches long; the undercoat is short and soft. Coat color is blue and tan, solid red, or sandy.

Grooming & Exercise Needs This dog needs to be brushed two to three times a week. Daily exercise should include a romp in a secured area and a few brisk walks.

Origins The spirited Australian terrier is descended from cairn, Skye, and Yorkshire terriers, among others. It was used as a ratter in 19th-century Australia.

(!) Breed-related health concerns: diabetes mellitus (page 451), undescended testicles, yeast dermatitis (a skin infection caused by an overgrowth of yeast).

HEIGHT 10-11"

WEIGHT 12-14 LBS.

LIFE SPAN 12-15 YRS.

Australian terriers have black nails.

Border Terrier

SMALL

The Border terrier, the most easygoing and affectionate of the terriers, is an ideal companion. It loves children and is very playful with them. The Border terrier accepts feline family members if raised with them but will chase (and possibly kill) strays or other small animals if not controlled by its owner. It may also be scrappy with other dogs unless socialized when young. As with most other dogs, Border terriers do best with early obedience training.

Grizzle and tan Border terrier

GOOD WITH KIDS

Appearance The Border terrier has a broad, otterlike head and a dark, short muzzle. Its undercoat is short and dense; its outercoat is very wiry and close-lying. Coat color is red, grizzle and tan, blue and tan, or wheaten. A thick but loose-fitting hide enables this dog to move through bushes and brush without getting cut or tangled up.

Grooming & Exercise Needs If the Border terrier is groomed regularly—slicker brushing weekly and stripping (removing old hair by hand) every six weeks—the coat won't mat and shedding will be minimal. The Border terrier enjoys daily walks, jogs, and hikes but can adapt to a more relaxed, easygoing lifestyle.

Origins Native to Great Britain and Scotland, the Border terrier was bred in the 18th century to chase and "bolt" (drive out) foxes from their hiding places. This superb, hard-working hunting dog will cross any terrain or obstacle in any type of weather.

HEIGHT 10-12"

WEIGHT 11½-14 LBS.

LIFE SPAN 13-15 YRS.

The Border terrier has a broad, otterlike head.

Cairn Terrier

SMALL

HIGH ENERGY INDOORS

SPECIAL EXERCISE NEEDS

GOOD WATCHDOG

Three-month-old cairn terrier puppies with wheaten, gray, and red coats

The cairn terrier is assertive, cheerful, eager to please, and loves to play but can be nippy with children and may chase cats if not socialized with them at an early age. The cairn is an ideal companion for a single person or a couple without children and adapts well to city or apartment living. It is a good watchdog, but excessive yapping should be controlled at an early age. Cairns always want to dominate—they won't pick fights but will be happy to finish them. These dogs do well in obedience class.

Appearance The cairn terrier has a broader head than most terriers, a short, dark muzzle, and a well-muscled body with enough leg to allow maneuvering over rocky terrain. The coat is water-resistant with a firm outercoat and soft, woolly undercoat. Coat color is cream, wheaten, red, gray, or nearly black; brindling is possible.

Grooming & Exercise Needs Cairn terriers need to be brushed, combed, and stripped or clipped three to four times a year. They need a couple of good daily walks on a leash and, if possible, some vigorous play in a secured area.

Origins The cairn terrier originated in 16th-century Scotland on the Isle of Skye, where it searched out cairns (rocky cliff dens) for foxes.

Wheaten cairn terrier

(!) Breed-related health concerns: globoid cell leukodystrophy (an untreatable hereditary disease causing progressive paralysis and death), allergies.

HEIGHT 9½-10"

WEIGHT 13-14 LBS.

LIFE SPAN 13-15 YRS.

Jack Russell Terrier

SMALL

HIGH ENERGY INDOORS

SPECIAL EXERCISE NEEDS

GOOD WATCHDOG

Jack Russells make very enjoyable companions when raised in the right setting—roomy suburban or country areas. They were bred as runners and are not suited for city or apartment life. Because they retain their working instincts and may chase and kill cats, rabbits, and other small animals, they should always be leashed or exercised in a secured area. Obedience training must start early because these dogs are easily distracted by surrounding activities and scents. They enjoy children and other dogs if exposed to them at an early age. They will bark when someone comes to the door but are not usually aggressive. They can, however, be protective of their property—toys and food bowls and such.

Wiry-coated Jack Russell terrier

Appearance The Jack Russell's distinctive ears fold forward. Its coat can be smooth or wiry and is mostly white with some black and/or tan markings.

Grooming & Exercise Needs Jack Russells need to be brushed weekly. They need vigorous play and exercise daily.

Origins The Jack Russell terrier was developed in England in the 19th century to run with horses in pursuit of foxes.

⚠ Breed-related health concerns: Legg-Perthes disease and patellar luxation (page 443), deafness (page 436).

Smooth-coated Jack Russell puppies, about six weeks old

HEIGHT 12-15"

WEIGHT 9-15 LBS.

LIFE SPAN 14-15 YRS.

STANDARD

MEDIUM

HIGH ENERGY INDOORS

SPECIAL EXERCISE NEEDS

GOOD WATCHDOG

Manchester Terrier

Manchesters are affectionate with their families but reserved with strangers and can be nippy and protective of their food bowls. They are accepting of gentle children over about eight years old and, if socialized with them early, small animals such as cats. Although they usually get along with other dogs, some may try to be dominant or aggressive. Therefore, they must be obedience trained and socialized early. They will definitely bark when strangers knock on the door. These low-maintenance dogs are ideal for city or apartment living.

Manchester terrier with natural (uncropped) button ears

Toy and standard Manchester terriers

Appearance There are two Manchester varieties: toy and standard. Both have coats that are smooth, short, and glossy, never soft to the touch. Coat color is jet-black and rich dark tan with well-defined boundaries. There is usually a black "thumbprint" patch on the front of each "wrist" area on the forelegs and narrow black stripes called pencil marks on the top of each toe.

Grooming & Exercise Needs Manchesters require only a quick weekly brushing. They need brisk daily walks or vigorous romps and playtimes with other dogs or their owner in a secured area.

Origins The Manchester was developed in England in the late 19th century to control rats and to track small game.

(!) Breed-related health concerns: glaucoma (page 434), sensitivity to immunization, skin irritations and infections.

HEIGHT
TOY 10-12"
STANDARD 15-16"

WEIGHT
TOY 7-12 LBS.
STANDARD 12-22 LBS.

LIFE SPAN 15-16 YRS.

Miniature Schnauzer

Miniature schnauzers with pet coats

Miniature schnauzers are spirited yet obedient family dogs. They usually enjoy—and are responsive to—early socialization and obedience training. Miniature schnauzers enjoy the company of children and other animals, especially if raised with them from an early age. Some schnauzers are outgoing with strangers and others are more reserved. Excessive barking can become a problem if not corrected when the dog is young.

Appearance The miniature schnauzer has a dense, profuse beard and bushy, bristly eyebrows. Its outercoat is hard and wiry; the undercoat is very short. Coat color is salt-and-pepper, black and silver, or solid black.

Grooming & Exercise Needs The miniature schnauzer should be brushed and combed twice a week and trimmed every two to three months. The beard needs to be cleaned daily. This dog loves long walks but may forgo exercise on rainy days.

Origins The bushy-muzzled miniature schnauzer —named after the German word for nose or muzzle—was developed from affenpinscher, giant schnauzer, and miniature pinscher bloodlines in the 19th century in Germany for its ratting ability.

Miniature schnauzer with a show coat

ⓘ It is especially important to obtain a miniature schnauzer from a reputable breeder. Breed-related health concerns: bladder stones (page 453), follicular dermatitis (inflamation of the hair follicles), kidney disease, allergies (page 437), high cholesterol, seizures (page 455), pancreatitis (page 446), juvenile cataracts (page 434), progressive retinal atrophy (page 435), hypothyroidism (page 452), atherosclerosis, von Willebrand's disease (a common disorder that causes excessive bleeding during or after surgery), Legg-Perthes disease (page 443).

Norfolk Terrier

SMALL

HIGH ENERGY INDOORS

SPECIAL EXERCISE NEEDS

GOOD WITH KIDS

GOOD WATCHDOG

Norfolk terriers are great small dogs—with large-dog attitudes. They are high-spirited, assertive, energetic, and bark at the arrival of strangers. Norfolks are very playful and love children if socialized with them at an early age and treated gently. They learn quickly in obedience class as long as their exuberance is gently and patiently controlled. They get along with other animals, including cats, though they may not be able to resist chasing them sometimes. Indefatigable in the field, Norfolks are always ready to go into tunnels and holes to "bolt" (run out) a fox or tackle other small animals. For this reason it is important to keep Norfolks on a leash when walking.

Black and tan Norfolk terrier. The folded ears distinguish it from the Norwich terrier.

Appearance The Norfolk's small ears fold forward and are carried close to the cheek. The outercoat is short, wiry, and straight; the undercoat is shorter. Norfolks come in all shades of red, wheaten, black and tan, or grizzle, sometimes with dark points.

Grooming & Exercise Needs Norfolks need a quick brushing and combing once or twice a week and clipping twice a year. They need a lot of exercise. Long walks, runs, or hikes are ideal. They should not be left alone in a fenced yard because they will dig or bark excessively.

Origins Norfolks originated in England in the 19th century, where they were used to control the rat population and hunt foxes. They became popular as pets with students at Cambridge University.

(!) Breed-related health concerns include summer eczema.

HEIGHT 9-12"

WEIGHT 11-12 LBS.

LIFE SPAN 13-14 YRS.

Red Norfolk terrier

Norwich Terrier

SMALL

Except for its erect ears, the Norwich terrier is identical to the Norfolk, and the breeds share the same ancestors. Fearless, loyal, and affectionate, Norwich terriers make good companions and live harmoniously with other pets. They are at home in rural and urban surroundings. They love children (if socialized with them early) and do well in obedience classes. Because of their energy and eagerness to chase small animals, these dogs should be walked on a leash. Norwich terriers are good watchdogs and will bark if strangers appear at the door.

Black and tan Norwich terrier

HIGH ENERGY INDOORS

SPECIAL EXERCISE NEEDS

Appearance Compact and short-legged, the Norwich has medium-size erect ears and an almost weatherproof coat. The topcoat is hard, wiry, and straight, with a shorter undercoat. This breed can be found in all shades of red, wheaten, black and tan, or grizzle, sometimes with dark points.

GOOD WITH KIDS

Grooming & Exercise Needs The Norwich terrier needs to be brushed or combed a couple of times a week and clipped twice a year. They need a lot of exercise, so long walks and runs are essential. They should not be kept in a fenced yard, for they will dig or bark excessively if left alone for too long.

GOOD WATCHDOG

Origins Norwich and Norfolk terriers—bred from Irish, Border, and cairn terriers—developed in the 19th century in England. Originally bred to be ratters, they were later used to hunt foxes. The breeds began to develop independently in the 1930s. These small terriers have been recognized as two separate breeds since 1964 in England and 1979 in the United States.

(!) Breed-related health concerns include summer eczema.

Wheaten Norwich terrier

HEIGHT 9-12"

WEIGHT 11-12 LBS.

LIFE SPAN 13-14 YRS.

Standard Schnauzer

MEDIUM

HIGH ENERGY INDOORS

SPECIAL EXERCISE NEEDS

GOOD WATCHDOG

Standard schnauzers are quick learners and love to be in the middle of family activities. They get along with children and small animals, such as cats, if socialized with them at an early age. They usually get along with other dogs but are fearless and will not back down if challenged and will bark when visitors arrive at the door; males may try to dominate other dogs. Early socialization and obedience training are required to control this dog's high energy level.

Salt-and-pepper standard schnauzer with a show coat

Appearance The standard schnauzer's face has thick, arched eyebrows and a bristly mustache. The outercoat is harsh, wiry, and thick; the undercoat is soft and tight. Coat color is salt-and-pepper or black.

Grooming & Exercise Needs The standard schnauzer needs to be brushed and combed two to three times a week and clipped or stripped three to four times a year. These dogs need several long, brisk walks and vigorous playtime in a secured area daily.

(!) Breed-related health concerns: hip dysplasia (page 442), hypothyroidism (page 452).

The standard schnauzer has arched eyebrows and a mustache.

HEIGHT 17½–19½"

WEIGHT 32–40 LBS.

LIFE SPAN 12–14 YRS.

Toy Fox Terrier

SMALL

HIGH ENERGY INDOORS

SPECIAL EXERCISE NEEDS

GOOD WATCHDOG

The toy fox terrier, also called the American toy terrier, is spunky, loyal, and sometimes protective. Early socialization and obedience training are important to counteract this dog's tendency to be a little scrappy with other dogs and to chase cats. The toy fox is usually comfortable with gentle children eight years of age or older. Because of its small size, it is well suited to apartment living.

Appearance The toy fox terrier's short, smooth coat is satiny to the touch. Color is predominantly white on the body, sometimes with black spots; the head is black, with tan on the cheeks and in spots over the eyes. White and black (without tan) and white and tan (without black) are also seen. Among the breed's distinguishing features are relatively large, erect ears.

Grooming & Exercise Needs The toy fox terrier needs to be brushed once a week and bathed occasionally to keep its coat shiny. This frisky entertainer needs several short, brisk walks as well as a play session in a secured area daily.

The toy fox terrier is a big dog in a little body.

Origins The toy fox terrier was produced by breeding together runts of the smooth fox terrier. Still adept at ratting, these bright, energetic dogs are more likely to be used today as service dogs for the deaf or family companions than as vermin exterminators.

(!) Breed-related health concerns include patellar luxation (page 443).

HEIGHT 10"

WEIGHT 3–7 LBS.

LIFE SPAN 13–15 YRS.

Welsh Terrier

MEDIUM

HIGH ENERGY INDOORS

SPECIAL EXERCISE NEEDS

GOOD WATCHDOG

Welsh terriers are very loyal family companions with high energy levels. They are not as enthusiastic about strangers and will bark to announce their arrival. They are intelligent and do well in obedience training. Some Welsh terriers are happy to play with other dogs, while others will take on dogs of all sizes. They see cats as prey, though they may tolerate them if socialized with them at an early age. Some Welsh terriers can be possessive of their food bowls and toys. Welsh terriers can live in cities as long as they are given enough exercise. This tough, tenacious dog has limitless energy to run and play.

Black and tan Welsh terrier

Appearance The Welsh terrier's outercoat is hard, wiry, and dense with a close-fitting thick jacket; the undercoat is short and soft. The jacket is black or grizzle, spreading onto the neck, down onto the tail, and into the upper thighs. The legs, hindquarters, and head are a clear reddish tan. Distinctive features include bushy eyebrows, a beard, and small V-shaped ears. Welsh terrier pups are born black.

Grooming & Exercise Needs Welsh terriers need to be brushed and combed twice a week and trimmed every three months. They have a lot of energy and need the chance to run and play in a secured area on a daily basis.

Origins This scrappy terrier originated about 300 years ago in North Wales to hunt otter, fox, and badger and is still used on farms today to control vermin.

HEIGHT 15–20"

WEIGHT 19–22 LBS.

LIFE SPAN 10–14 YRS.

The Welsh terrier has bushy eyebrows and a beard.

West Highland White Terrier

SMALL

HIGH ENERGY INDOORS

SPECIAL EXERCISE NEEDS

GOOD WATCHDOG

West Highland white terriers are good family dogs adaptable to life in the cities, suburbs, or country. They are more high-strung than cairn terriers but still respond well to obedience training. They love to romp with children if socialized with them at an early age and will accept strangers after an initial inspection. Westies are good watchdogs. They usually get along well with other dogs but may fight for dominance. They get along with cats that are raised in the home but may chase strays.

Westies have small, erect ears and black noses.

Appearance The outercoat is straight, hard, and about two inches long, shorter on the neck and shoulders; the undercoat is short, soft, and tight. Coat color is pure white. Among the breed's distinguishing features are small, erect ears with sharp tips and a black nose.

Grooming & Exercise Needs The West Highland white terrier needs to be brushed and combed twice a week and trimmed every three months. Several walks and some playtime daily suit this dog well.

Origins The West Highland white terrier originated in the 19th century and probably shares a common Highland ancestry with the Scottie, cairn, and Dandie Dinmont. They were used for ratting and for "going to ground" after game in their burrows.

West Highland white terrier with a pet clip

(!) It is important to obtain a West Highland white terrier from a reputable breeder. Breed-related health concerns: Legg-Perthes disease (page 443), craniomandibular osteopathy (a disease characterized by excessive growth of skull bones), atopy (page 437), cataracts (page 434), copper toxicosis (a hereditary disease that can lead to liver failure), inguinal hernia (page 441), deafness (page 436), pyruvate kinase deficiency (a fatal enzyme deficiency).

HEIGHT 10-11"

WEIGHT 15-20 LBS.

LIFE SPAN 12-14 YRS.

Terrier Mixes

Terrier mixes are wonderfully spirited, playful, mischievous dogs. They often display the quick-to-bark watchdog qualities for which terriers are so well known. These high-energy dogs can be stubborn and difficult to train. Some may be nippy, especially with children.

Appearance Terrier mixes range in size from small to large. Their coats are usually wiry and medium length, but some can be soft and wavy or short, smooth, and shiny. Their ears can range from small prick ears to larger, semiprick ears to flap down, fold-over ears—virtually any type except long and pendulous.

Grooming & Exercise Needs Mixes with long, wavy coats will need brushing several times a week to avoid matting. A professional trim several times a year will keep the coat in prime condition. Terriers have notoriously high energy levels indoors and out and demand an owner with a strong commitment to exercise.

Terrier mix with a beard and a wiry coat

Wiry-coated Jack Russell mix with a compact square body and an alert stance

This cairn mix is ever-watchful from its perch, ready to enter the chase and small enough to trap vermin in tight corners.

This terrier mix with a gray and tan coat resembles many terrier breeds that have earth-toned coats. Its terrier genes are also apparent in its beard and mustache and its slightly wiry coat.

This mischievous Airedale mix is always looking for new ways to make its owners laugh.

III

What Makes a Dog a Dog?

The more you understand about what makes a dog a dog, the more interesting and rewarding an experience it is to live with your canine companion, and the more responsible a pet owner you can be. This section opens with an overview of the long history of the relationship between dogs and humans, followed by a guide to how dogs are built and how they work. The last chapter is an exploration of how dogs express themselves.

This introduction to the inner life of your dog is followed by the section Taking Care of Your Dog, a comprehensive guide to keeping your dog healthy and happy throughout her life.

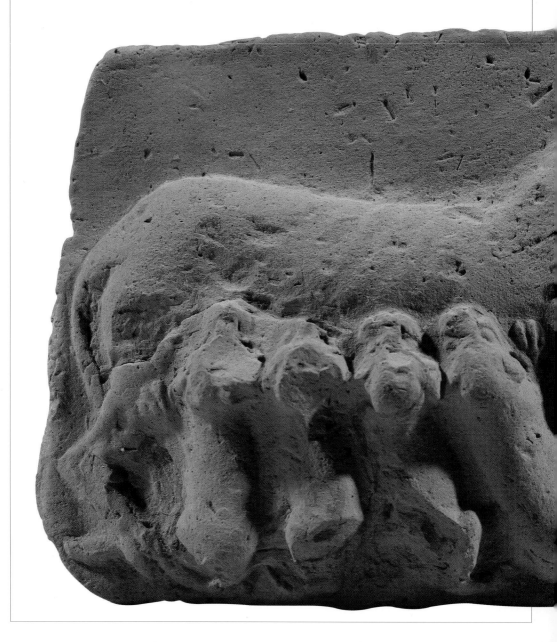

Neo-Sumerian terra-cotta carving of a mother
dog and pups, 2000 B.C.

How the Dog
Came to Be Man's Best Friend

In all of nature, few relationships between two species are more complex and personal than the bond between humans and dogs. To anyone who loves dogs, it seems only natural that such a relationship should exist. But does our emotional connection with dogs make sense? Why should two predators—potentially competitors in the struggle for survival—cooperate with each other, much less become fast friends? The answer may lie in our similarities. While humans and dogs look very different, beneath the surface, humans are deeply social animals who share the need to be part of something bigger than ourselves—pack, family, society.

Ancestors of the modern dog first crossed paths with human hunters in prehistoric times. What kind of animals were the dog's ancient canine forebears? We still see their kind today: dogs are almost certainly descended from wolves. There are more than thirty subspecies of wolves, varying in size, coat, color, and other physical characteristics, as well as in behavior. This diversity probably laid the foundation for some of the broad differences we see among dogs today.

Echoes of the pack behavior of wolves can be seen in today's dogs.

How Wolves Became Dogs

No one can say when dogs emerged as a distinct species. The earliest known remains of dogs are not quite 15,000 years old, but the archaeological record provides a tantalizing hint that wild canines may have had significance for humans much earlier: at ancient Stone Age shelters in France dating back 125,000 years, archaeologists have found wolf skulls positioned at the entrances.

We will probably never know when and where the domestication of dogs took place—it was surely a gradual process that spanned thousands of years—but we can easily envision how the lives of humans and wolves became intertwined. The two shared similar hunting techniques, using teamwork to bring down their quarry, and probably chose the same prey and territories. Humans may have killed wolves for food and used their skins for clothing, but they also probably kept live pups. They may have planned to kill and eat them, but very likely some of these puppies endeared themselves to their captors, grew tame, and were adopted by humans. Domestication probably began when "home-raised" wolves began mating with one another.

If humans and wolves competed for the same quarry, perhaps they both learned that cooperation, even if unintentional, had its advantages. Packs of wolves could have accidentally chased game into hunters' range. Humans might have realized that wolves, with their keen senses of smell and hearing, could locate the next potential meal more effectively or could alert them to potential threats, such as larger, more ferocious predators. It is also possible that wolf packs used humans, treating them as part of their territory and protecting them from other predators, perhaps because they appreciated the edible scraps humans threw away or left behind. Once early humans started feeding these animals, they probably couldn't get rid of them and (quite understandably to us) grew to like them.

The genetic changes that transformed the tame wolf into the domesticated dog occurred gradually over many centuries. Domestication depended on humans keeping tame wolves from mingling with wild ones and breeding the tame wolves selectively for desirable traits, including hunting skill and obedience. Certain pups probably showed a special aptitude for tracking prey, and by breeding them, humans ensured that they would be good hunting partners.

By the dawn of agricultural societies (about 7000 B.C.) dogs had been genetically isolated from their wolf brethren for thousands of years—and looked distinctly different from them. Rock art found in Iraq, site of the earliest known agricultural societies, depicts humans hunting large game accompanied by animals that look like dogs with curled tails. By this time, domesticated dogs were also probably being bred for guarding herds and flocks—ironically, from wolves.

Dogs Through the Ages

Since antiquity, dogs have virtually always had a role in human society. Until recently, the role was most often a rather arduous one. For every dog that led a life of leisure, a great many more toiled for their keep. Following is a look at the wide variety of roles dogs have had in different cultures through the ages.

Friends of the Pharaohs in Ancient Egypt

Dogs resembling modern sight hounds (breeds developed to track by sight rather than by scent), such as salukis, greyhounds, pharaoh hounds, and Ibizan hounds, appear on ancient Egyptian wall paintings and sculptures. Tomb paintings often show the deceased with his or her dog—loyal and loving unto death and beyond.

Greyhound-like dogs were probably part of Egyptian life as early as 4500 B.C. Statues of the god Seth from that period often depict him as having the body of a greyhound. Lean, long-legged dogs such as these lived well; their owners were typically nobles with a fondness for both the hunt and hunting dogs.

But other dogs in ancient Egypt led more difficult lives. Historical records show that large numbers of dogs roamed

Dogs in ancient Egypt were revered by their owners and portrayed with honor in the culture's art and artifacts.

the streets of Egyptian cities without homes or caretakers. Certain dogs, especially the powerful, mastiff-like breeds introduced to the region around 1650 B.C., became useful as warriors. They were trained to attack enemy soldiers, and fiercely defended their kingdom against intruders.

Whether a dog was a worker or simply a companion, public displays of grief for a departed canine friend—including shaved eyebrows—were an ordinary rite of Egyptian life, as was the mummification of cherished family dogs. Most dogs that were mummified, however, had never known much human love: they were bred by the tens of thousands to be sacrificed, often as puppies, to the jackal-faced god Anubis, gatekeeper of the afterlife.

DNA from the dog mummies of ancient Egypt may help scientists determine if modern breeds such as salukis and greyhounds are truly descendants of Egyptian dogs, as many people believe.

"Cave Canem" (Beware of Dog) appeared in this Pompeii mosaic to warn visitors to be careful of the dogs loose on the grounds.

Valued Workers in Ancient Greece

Dogs without status—strays and what we might call mutts today—were sacrificed in large numbers, hundreds at a time, to appease or honor the gods. But even for dogs that "mattered," life could be hard. The Greeks valued dogs for hunting and for guarding property, but there is little in their writing or art to suggest that they loved them the way the Egyptians did. The philosopher Aristotle (384–322 B.C.) named three "useful" dogs (Epirotic, Laconian, and Molossian) and classified them by their use—and by the social status of those who used them. Alexander the Great (356–323 B.C.) had an abiding fondness for dogs, if not for people. When his favorite Molossian (a mastiff-like war dog) died, Alexander was inconsolable. The dog had reputedly killed an elephant and a lion in one-on-one fights, a source of great pride for Alexander, and he ordered that an annual holiday be celebrated in her honor.

For dogs in ancient Greece, rank had its privileges.

Status Symbols in the Roman Empire

Roman dogs were as diverse as the lands their owners conquered. As the Empire grew and absorbed the many cultures of Europe, the Middle East, and North Africa, the Romans interbred the dogs of these far-flung regions. In some cases, this gave rise to dogs similar to modern breeds. The Empire was home to dogs resembling bloodhounds and greyhounds (these were used for hunting), curly-coated dogs like poodles, chunky ones like beagles, and lapdogs that looked like bichons and Italian greyhounds. Powerful and wealthy Romans, including Julius Caesar himself, adored lapdogs, dressing them up with bejeweled collars and lavishing great affection on them. Unlike the prized hunting dogs of ancient Egypt, these nonutilitarian little pooches didn't have to do anything to win their owners' affection. Roman affluence had produced a new phenomenon: the dog as pure status symbol.

But Rome wasn't built by tenderhearted dog lovers. The most famous dogs of the Empire were the Molossians, the ubiquitous battle mastiffs of the ancient Mediterranean. Outfitted with iron collars with spiked blades, they were trained to knock enemy cavalrymen off their horses and disembowel or dismember them and their mounts. They were also used as public executioners, dispatching prisoners in Rome's Circus Maximus, and they served as bodyguards par excellence for prominent citizens. One house excavated from the ruins of Pompeii displays a mosaic of a huge, snarling Molossian and some good advice: *cave canem* (beware of the dog).

Julius Caesar was also fond of Celtic hunting dogs. The Romans learned much from the Celts about dog training and the hunt. The Celts reveled in the chase and took great pleasure from watching their dogs pursue prey in the field. When Celtic hounds were crossed with Roman dogs that guarded flocks, the union produced gentler dogs resembling retrievers and pointers. Like most peoples of antiquity, the Celts also trained dogs for war, and though lanky, these hounds were terrifying. Perhaps their greatest advantage over the human foe was that they bore not the slightest fear of death. In one reported instance, perhaps apocryphal but still revealing, it took a few hours for Roman legionnaires to slaughter a Celtic army and two days to subdue their dogs.

During the Han dynasty in China, dogs were used for protection and hunting.

Prized Pets in Imperial China

Lucky were the dogs who lived in the court of a Chinese emperor. These pets were treated with exceptional devotion—one account describes male palace dogs being given official court titles, with their female mates elevated to the level of court wives. The signature dog of China is the Pekingese, one of the oldest breeds in the world. Historical records show that small, square-faced dogs similar to the Peke were already coveted by members of the Chinese court 3,000 years ago. Around A.D. 620, Roman Maltese dogs were presented to the Chinese emperor as a gift from the Byzantine emperor. These probably contributed their genes to the development of the modern Pekingese, perhaps the first and only dog to achieve the status of state secret: the Chinese imperial court was so jealously protective of it that the breed was unknown in the West until the mid-nineteenth century.

But the status of the dog has been as varied in China as it has elsewhere in the world. During the Chou dynasty (about 1027–256 B.C.), emperors prized hunting dogs. Statues from the Han dynasty (202 B.C.–A.D. 220) show curly-tailed progenitors of the chow chow, probably a distant descendant of the Chinese wolf, employed as guard dogs and wolf hunters. The huge Tibetan mastiff, which arrived in China during the Han dynasty, probably descended from the much-

Dogs were both status symbol and necessity on a medieval nobleman's hunt.

traveled Molossian and was used for guarding flocks, occasionally for hunting, and as a war dog. These and other dogs are also known to have been used as a food source.

Expert Hunters in Medieval Europe

Especially in the Middle Ages, a dog's lot in life depended on that of its owner. During this time, European society was dominated by nobles and knights, among whom sport hunting was very popular. A single nobleman might own hundreds of hunting dogs, while many commoners

Aside from the possible trauma inflicted by a wild boar, medieval hunting dogs lived relatively well.

This detail of a fifteenth-century Renaissance painting by Andrea Mantegna depicts grooms with greyhounds (right) and mastiff types (left) of the time.

toiled at manufacturing and maintaining the trappings of the hunt and caring for the dogs. Commoners' dogs, however, were less fortunate. Like their owners, they were treated callously by the aristocracy, which brutally punished any poacher, human or canine. Herding dogs and other large working dogs of common folk were hobbled to make them incapable of going astray.

As in other times and places, dogs of the Middle Ages were categorized by size and use. Medium-size dogs called brachets, adept at pursuing small game such as rabbits, were very popular among nobility. Levriers were larger and stronger than the brachets and were used for hunting deer. Alaunts were huge, powerful Molossian-type dogs that were used for pursuing and bringing down dangerous game such as wild boar. The alaunts were to be important in the development of the large, powerful mastiff-like breeds of the Renaissance.

Pampered Breeds of the Renaissance

During the great cultural reawakening of Europe (around 1300–1600), the breeding of dogs by the aristocracy and the well-to-do flourished. The dogs of the privileged class were pampered, with special meats to eat, elaborate collars, and public displays of affection, something not seen in Europe since Roman times. Hunters prided themselves on breeding the fastest, strongest, and smartest dogs, including progenitors of modern greyhounds, pointers, and terriers. Women of the Renaissance favored small, dainty dogs such as the English toy spaniel, Italian greyhound, Maltese, and bichon frise, breeds immortalized by painters of the time. A new sporting breed, the Hound of St. Hubert, was developed in Belgium. It was slower and less muscular than the levrier and alaunt, but its superb sense of smell, endurance, and determination made this gentle dog very popular among hunters. With its pendulous ears and loose folds of skin, the Hound of St. Hubert seems a likely progenitor of today's basset hound and bloodhound.

For all the luxury enjoyed by the preferred breeds, others served grim lives as laborers or competitors in what was known as blood sport. This savage form of entertainment pitted mastiffs and other large breeds against other dogs or adversaries such as bulls or bears, with spectators and owners laying bets on which animal would survive.

From the Renaissance onward, companion dogs living among the upper classes enjoyed a pampered life, as captured here by painter Joseph Caraud.

The lot of the working-class dog was a hard one, as depicted by this heavily laden cart dog in Flanders.

The Canine Elite of the Industrial Revolution

With the advent of the Industrial Revolution (around 1759–1900), the new urban middle class, and the old upper class, now needed dogs far less for their working abilities. Instead, people developed an interest in selective breeding and the owning of purebred dogs as status symbols. That interest, called "the fancy," produced most of the modern dog breeds.

The first formal dog show, designed to display "dog aristocracy" of elite lineage, was held in Newcastle upon Tyne in England in 1859. The sixty dogs in the show were divided into just two categories: pointers and setters. From that simple beginning, the dog-show circuit grew rapidly, and it was quickly overtaken by corruption: judges showed open favoritism to the dogs of influential owners, while owners bred dogs with dubious credentials. In response, The Kennel Club of Great Britain was created in 1873 to police the show circuit, to improve and maintain British dog breeds, to recognize foreign breeds, and to use foreign breeds to improve British stock.

In North America, the American Kennel Club was founded in 1884, bringing the number of dog breeds recognized on both sides of the Atlantic to 300 by the turn of the century. Many large kennels rose to prominence at this time. By the 1930s, obedience schools had been founded in the United States, patterned after British models. Unlike the hard-working dogs of the Associated Sheep, Police, and Army Dog Society in England, however, the first American obedience trials featured poodles—to prove that they were just as intelligent and hardy as other breeds, despite their fancy haircuts.

Coinciding with the interest in dog breeding was the rise of humanitarian activism on behalf of the dog. The nineteenth and early twentieth centuries saw the freeing of many dogs from the hard labor that had been their lot from feudal times. New animal-protection organizations, including the ASPCA (founded in 1866), were established in the nineteenth century and successfully lobbied for anti-cruelty legislation, including the "emancipation" of cart dogs.

Loyal Companions of Modern Times

In the more developed parts of the world, the twentieth century has been a good time for dogs, although problems remain in the areas of overpopulation, poor breeding practices, and animal abuse and testing. The majority of the approximately 60 million dogs in the United States today live in good homes where they are appreciated and well cared for.

In fact, many dogs now serve their owners not merely as companions but as healers. Studies have demonstrated the significant benefits of canine companionship for human health. Having a dog in your life can help prevent or alleviate loneliness, anxiety, depression, and stress-related diseases, including heart disease and high blood pressure. Some dogs continue their centuries-old work as herders, hunters, and guardians. Others help the blind, deaf, and wheelchair-bound to lead full and independent lives. Still others help police and other agencies detect explosives or drugs and rescue people lost or buried in the rubble of disasters. Much has changed for the dog in the past hundred years, but one thing remains a constant—the dog's unparalleled loyalty.

Today's working dogs, like this golden retriever, help people with disabilities lead independent lives.

The dog's anatomical framework makes possible
a wide range of motion and good endurance.

How the Dog Works

Although modern dogs retain some of the physical qualities that made their ancestors successful hunters thousands of years ago, many of today's dogs probably couldn't catch anything more exotic than a few extra hours' sleep.

Selective breeding over the centuries has created an awesome variety of shapes and sizes of purebred dogs—compare the tall, powerful Irish wolfhound to the diminutive and feisty Yorkshire terrier—tailor-made for everything from hunting to companionship. Yet the basic anatomy of dogs is remarkably alike, from the most exquisitely pedigreed show dog to the humblest mixed-breed mutt.

This chapter explains the basic workings of the dog: the strong yet flexible framework of bones and muscles; the powerful heart and lungs; the efficient digestive and urinary systems; the formidable teeth; the complex reproductive system; the specialized skin, whiskers, and coat; the sturdy claws; and the eyesight, hearing, and smelling capabilities closely adapted to the dog's every need. Understanding how this canine machinery works is an important and enlightening part of caring for and appreciating your dog.

Framework: Bones and Muscles

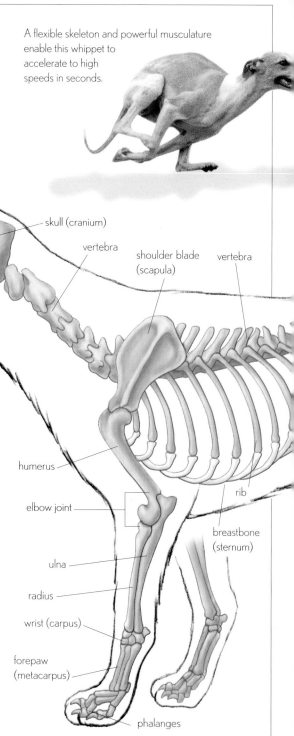

A flexible skeleton and powerful musculature enable this whippet to accelerate to high speeds in seconds.

As in other mammals, parts of the dog's skeleton such as the rib cage, the shoulder blades, the skull, and the spinal column (collectively called the axial skeleton) serve to protect vital organs. The rest of the skeleton provides a framework of levers for movement. The power for movement comes from the dog's considerable skeletal muscles.

The dog skeleton is a flexible structure well designed for the chase. A dog's shoulder blades are loosely attached to its axial skeleton, giving the dog a great range of motion and allowing long, loping strides.

The dog's skeletal muscles are those of an endurance athlete, made for sustained effort such as pulling a sled or chasing prey over long distances. Modern dog owners can attest to the powers of canine endurance; few games of fetch ever end because the dog runs out of energy.

Though most dogs are built for endurance rather than great speed, some—the greyhound and the borzoi, for example—have been bred to sprint, and can run faster than thirty miles an hour (about as fast as a horse). Thanks to their very long legs and flexible backs, they have the mechanical advantage of being able to put their hind paws down in front of their forepaws when running. For short-legged breeds like basset hounds, such a ground-gobbling stride is impossible; their hind

skull (cranium)

vertebra

shoulder blade (scapula)

vertebra

eye socket (orbit)

humerus

elbow joint

rib

breastbone (sternum)

ulna

radius

wrist (carpus)

forepaw (metacarpus)

phalanges

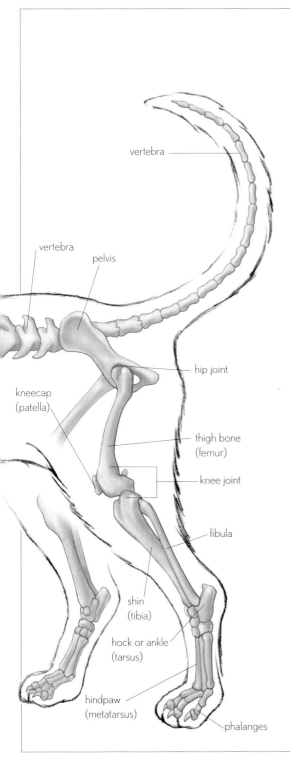

vertebra

vertebra

pelvis

hip joint

kneecap
(patella)

thigh bone
(femur)

knee joint

fibula

shin
(tibia)

hock or ankle
(tarsus)

hindpaw
(metatarsus)

phalanges

Selective breeding by humans has created a huge variation in the scale and proportions of the dog skeleton. Miniaturized dogs like the Yorkshire terrier retain the proportions of a larger dog and are simply scaled down. In dwarf breeds like the dachshund, the long leg bones have been shrunk by breeding and are no longer proportional to the rest of the skeleton.

paws can't travel very far before having to touch down again. For the dog, running speed is a useful accessory. But in the end, the dog's hallmark as a predator remains its dedication to getting the job done no matter how long it takes. Canine tenacity has even added a word to the language: the adjective "dogged," signifying determination, comes from the Middle English *dogge* for "dog."

The dog's bones and muscles are a marvel, but its nervous system must orchestrate the contraction and relaxation of the muscles. That orchestration begins in the dog's brain, just as it does in our own. In less than two-thousandths of a second, voluntary nerve impulses travel from the brain via the spinal cord and activate muscles to contract.

Skull

Centuries of selective breeding by humans have produced three basic skull types in dogs: long-nosed (dolichocephalic), medium-nosed (mesocephalic), and short-nosed (brachycephalic).

Long-nosed dogs have the most wolflike appearance, with their eyes positioned far back along the sides of the head (not surprising, considering that many of the long-nosed breeds—such as afghans and greyhounds—are among the oldest breeds).

Because each of their eyes points at the world at a slightly outward angle (rather than forward like human eyes), long-nosed dogs have outstanding peripheral vision—they can see not only straight ahead of them but also far to the left and right. But because the visual fields of their two eyes do not overlap very much, the depth perception of long-nosed dogs is not as refined as their peripheral vision. They are not as adept at determining how close or far away objects are as shorter-nosed dogs (or cats or humans).

Short-nosed dogs, on the other hand, are as non-wolflike in appearance as dogs can get. Their skull shape gives them an endearing babylike look in toy breeds such as the Pekingese and a handsomely pugnacious look in larger breeds such as the boxer.

Because the eyes of short-nosed dogs are positioned toward the front of the face and are pointed forward, much like our own, short-nosed breeds have the best depth perception in the canine world. Their visual field is narrower than that of the long-nosed breeds, but still much wider than our own meager 135 degrees.

In between the wolflike long-nosed dolichocephalic breeds and the short-nosed brachycephalic breeds are the dogs with medium-nosed mesocephalic skulls, such as the golden retriever and the springer spaniel. When it comes to peripheral vision and depth perception, they split the difference between their long-nosed and snub-nosed brethren.

The boxer (left), a brachycephalic breed, and the borzoi (right), a dolichocephalic breed, illustrate the extremes found in canine skull shapes.

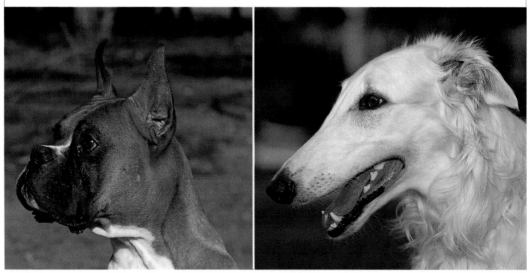

Heart and Lungs

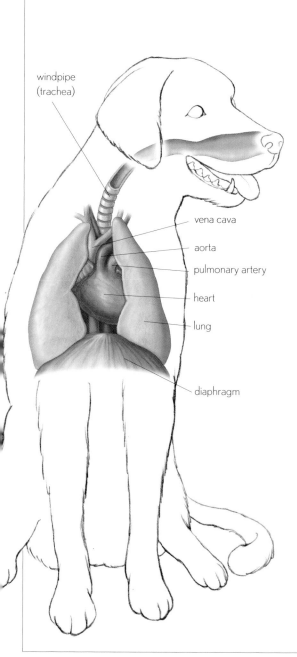

windpipe (trachea)

vena cava

aorta

pulmonary artery

heart

lung

diaphragm

Dogs have the typical mammalian respiratory and circulatory systems. The oxygen they take in through the mouth and nostrils travels down the trachea (windpipe) to the lungs. Encased in the protective rib cage and separated from the digestive system by the diaphragm, the heart and lungs then work together to circulate the oxygen, via the blood, throughout the body. Conducted along an intricate system of arteries and veins, blood distributes oxygen, nutrients, and disease-fighting agents and takes up carbon dioxide. When the blood makes its way back to the lungs, the blood vessels of the circulatory system and the branches of the respiratory system (called bronchi and bronchioles) make a vital exchange of newly inhaled oxygen and carbon dioxide to be exhaled. The key blood vessels involved in this exchange are the pulmonary veins, which carry freshly oxygenated blood to the heart; the aorta, the major artery that leaves the heart with fresh blood for the body; the vena cava, which brings oxygen-poor blood back to the heart; and the pulmonary artery, which shunts blood back to the lungs at the end of the cycle.

Dogs are natural "nose breathers." They breathe through the mouth when they need to—during heavy exertion, to pull in additional air and keep their body temperature down, and when the weather is very hot, in order to cool off. The dog's nasal cavity contains thin scroll-like structures that warm and humidify the air flowing into the nose and produce mucus that filters the air and contains antibodies against viruses and bacteria. (Humans have these scrolls, too, but they are much smaller than a dog's.) For more on the dog's amazing nose, see page 333.

Digestive and Urinary Systems

The dog's digestive system works much the same as a human's: Food is broken down in the mouth by the teeth, made soft and slippery by saliva, and then swallowed. It travels down the esophagus to the stomach, where acids and enzymes break it down further. It then passes through the small and large intestines, where water and nutrients are absorbed and enter the bloodstream. The remaining undigested solid waste material is carried out of the body (via the large intestines and anus) in the form of feces.

The liver contributes to the digestive process by secreting bile into the small intestine where it breaks down fats. Nutrients absorbed in the blood return from the intestines and pass to the liver, where they are converted into forms the body can use. The pancreas produces digestive enzymes and some hormones.

The urinary system is responsible for vital functions such as helping to maintain the proper amount of water in the body and helping to keep the body's overall chemistry in balance. The kidneys filter various waste products into urine, which is carried via the ureter to the bladder, where it is stored transiently, and out of the body via the urethra.

The dog's wild ancestors often had to go for long stretches between meals, then gorge themselves when the opportunity to hunt or scavenge arose. Still equipped with a big stomach and fairly short intestines, today's domestic dog remains a gastronomic opportunist, often eagerly overeating whenever food (or material mistaken for food) is available—even if it means scavenging from the trash.

rectum
colon
ureters
kidneys
spleen
stomach
urethra
bladder
small intestine
liver

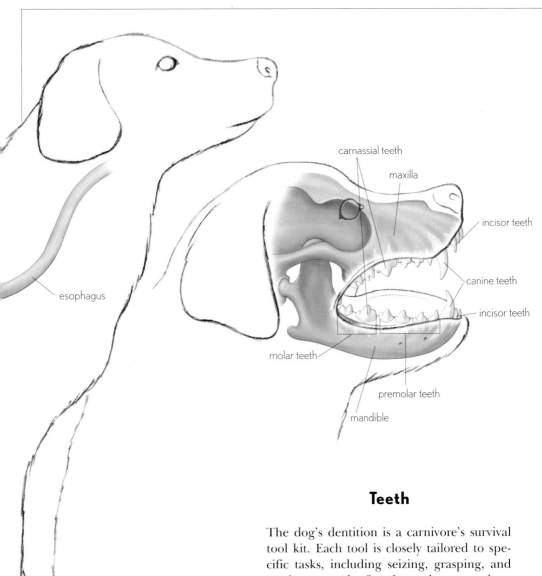

carnassial teeth

maxilla

incisor teeth

canine teeth

incisor teeth

esophagus

molar teeth

premolar teeth

mandible

Teeth

The dog's dentition is a carnivore's survival tool kit. Each tool is closely tailored to specific tasks, including seizing, grasping, and tearing prey (the four long, deep-rooted canine teeth); nibbling to clean the coat or remove flesh from the bones of prey (the twelve small incisors); and cutting meat and grinding gristle and roughage (the array of sixteen premolars and ten molars, including four deep-rooted carnassials for ripping flesh). Teeth that have a more strenuous workload (holding, tearing, ripping) have long roots to anchor them securely in the jaw.

Reproductive System

Dogs reproduce sexually, as all mammals do, and have the standard mammalian reproductive system. Like other domestic animals, the female dog goes into a period called estrus (commonly known as heat) at the time in her reproductive cycle that she is fertile and ready to mate. The female may release up to twenty eggs, so if she mates with multiple males, puppies born in the same litter may have different fathers. Puppies are born about sixty-three days after the eggs are fertilized. (See the Beginning and End of Life: Times for Special Care on page 479 for more on mating, pregnancy, and birth.)

Dogs of both sexes become reproductively mature at about six to twelve months of age. Unlike female dogs, which usually go into heat about twice a year and will

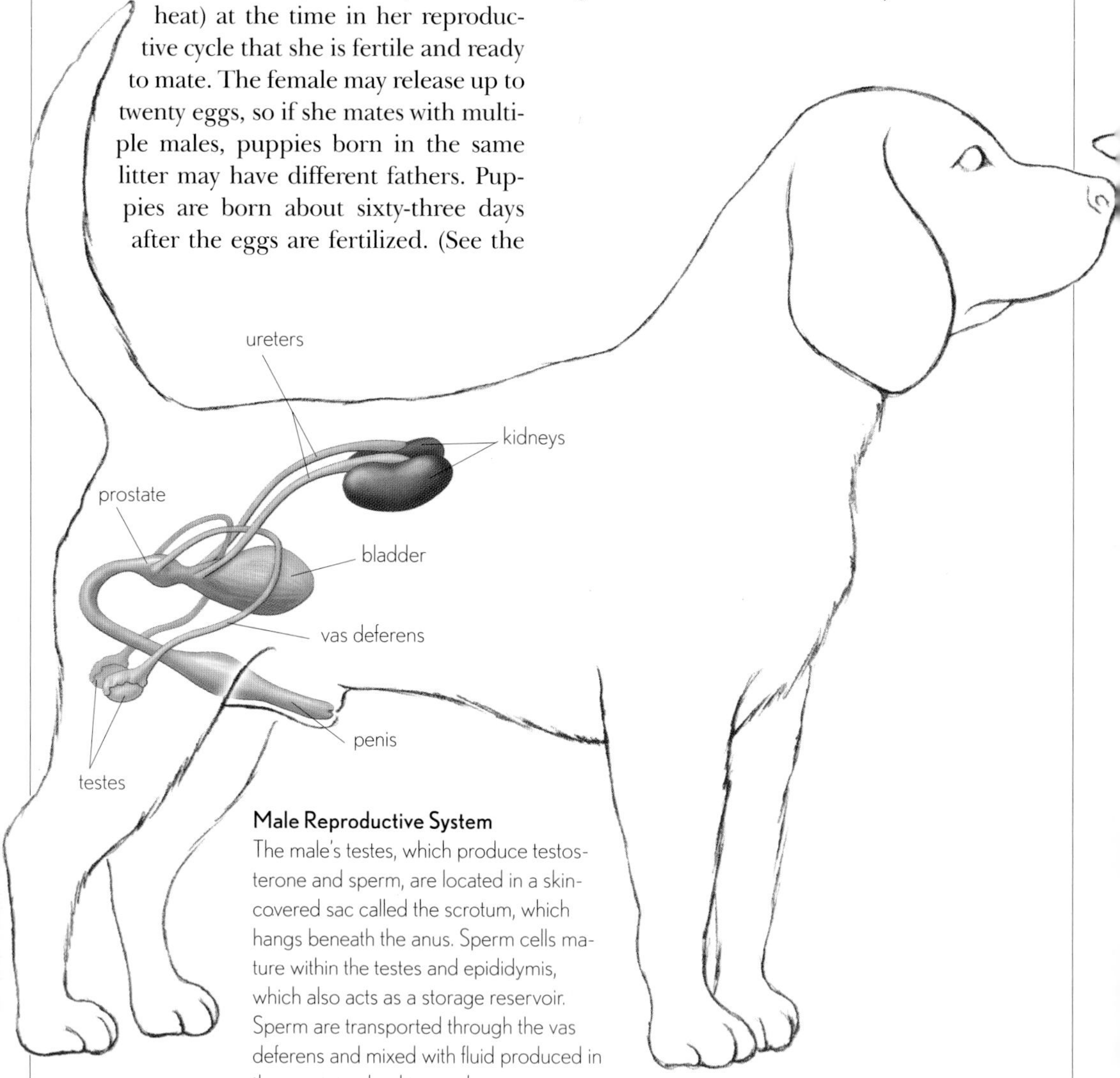

ureters

kidneys

prostate

bladder

vas deferens

penis

testes

Male Reproductive System
The male's testes, which produce testosterone and sperm, are located in a skin-covered sac called the scrotum, which hangs beneath the anus. Sperm cells mature within the testes and epididymis, which also acts as a storage reservoir. Sperm are transported through the vas deferens and mixed with fluid produced in the prostate gland to produce semen. Sperm production begins at puberty and continues throughout the dog's life.

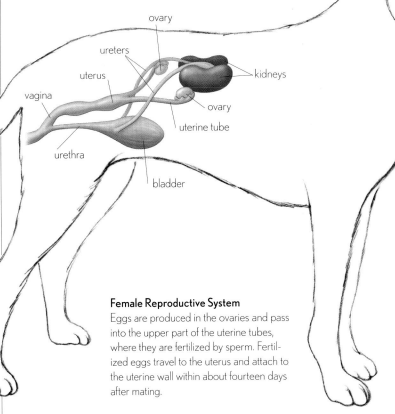

Mating

The canine penis contains a bone (baculum) that lies above the urethra. During mating, the area around this bone swells, temporarily locking the male to the female in order to aid fertilization.

ovary

ureters

uterus

kidneys

vagina

ovary

uterine tube

urethra

bladder

Female Reproductive System

Eggs are produced in the ovaries and pass into the upper part of the uterine tubes, where they are fertilized by sperm. Fertilized eggs travel to the uterus and attach to the uterine wall within about fourteen days after mating.

allow mating only at that time, male dogs are always sexually ready. During heat, which lasts approximately twenty-one days, a female will signal her fertility by being playful and inviting males to inspect and sniff her rear end. This behavior allows the male to determine the female's hormonal stage, although he can also determine this from the smell of pheromones (sex hormones) in her urine. The scent of a fertile female stimulates the male dog to produce more sperm cells and to attempt coitus.

Neutering

When male dogs are neutered, the testicles are removed and the spermatic cords are tied. Neutering the female, a more complex operation, means removing the ovaries and uterus (nearly the whole reproductive system is removed to reduce the chances of health problems later in life). Both procedures are performed under general anesthesia, usually at around five to six months of age, but can now safely be done as early as two months of age.

Senses

Like many animals, dogs have sensory abilities that put their human counterparts to shame. With eyes calibrated to see well at night, ears developed to pinpoint a sound source, and a nose so refined it can detect a human being's emotional state, dogs are sophisticated sensory beings.

Eyesight

Dogs see more of the world at a glance than we do, thanks to their better peripheral vision (see discussion of the dog's skull, page 324), but the world they see is blurrier. They see the world differently in other ways as well, because their eyes, while similar to ours, contain features that ours do not.

In all mammals, the part of the eye that is sensitive to light is called the retina. Located at the rear of the eye, the retina contains two types of light-sensitive cells: rods and cones. Each converts light into electrochemical impulses that travel to the vision center of the brain via the optic nerve. Rods can gather visual information in very dim light, but they do not distinguish colors. Cones need better lighting in order to work, but they are sensitive to color. (We see the world in shades of gray at dusk because our rods are doing all the work, while our cones have, in effect, called it a day.)

Of the more than 100 million light receptors in the dog's retina, only about five million are cones. Our own eyes have an even smaller percentage of cones (about

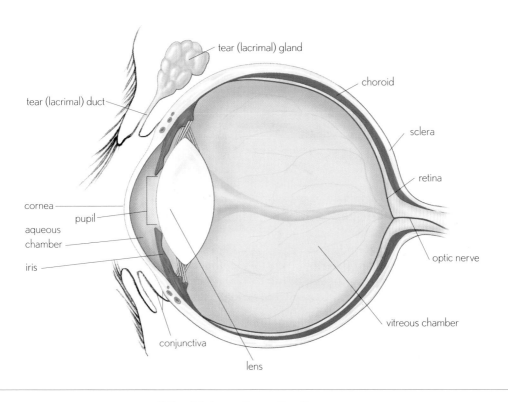

tear (lacrimal) gland
choroid
tear (lacrimal) duct
sclera
retina
cornea
pupil
aqueous chamber
iris
optic nerve
vitreous chamber
conjunctiva
lens

An estimation of how dogs see stationary objects (left) compared to how humans see stationary objects (right)

six million cones to 130 million rods), but they are clustered in areas specialized for color vision. A dog's cones aren't distributed as purposefully as ours. Thus to a dog, the world is a pretty drab place, mostly gray, black, and white. At best, the dog sees hues such as reds and greens only faintly. To see things the way your dog probably does, fiddle with the controls on a color TV until you've "washed out" all but the most dilute amount of color.

Thanks to their abundant supply of rods, however, dogs have good night vision—far better than our own (but not as good as that of cats, which are nocturnal hunters par excellence). Their ability to see in the dark is enhanced by the *tapetum lucidum*, reflective tissue in the choroid coat behind the retina. The tapetum concentrates light and reflects it back to the rods for a "second look." Cats and many other nocturnal animals have similar reflective tissue behind the retina. That's why their eyes seem to glow in the dark when seen in a beam of light.

Another predatory advantage dogs enjoy is an enhanced ability to detect movement, especially in the distance and to the sides. Despite that specialized gift, because the lens of the canine eye adjusts poorly to different focal distances, a dog spends its life somewhat nearsighted. Humans have much sharper vision than dogs; we see stationary objects much more clearly. Perhaps that was useful to us long ago, as omnivorous hunter-gatherers, since not everything we ate moved. It may also help explain our excellent color vision (many fruits are colorful). But for hunting carnivores like the wolf and the dog, if an object didn't move, there would be little point in noticing it—let alone what color it was. The differences between a dog's vision and our own, then, may have a lot to do with our species' different survival strategies.

An approximation of how dogs see colors (bottom) compared to how humans see colors (top)

Hearing

While a seeing contest between a dog and a human might not produce a clear winner, when it comes to hearing, the dog has us beat in just about every way. If a human can barely hear a radio playing at a distance of fifty feet, a dog will hear the same radio, at the same volume, from a distance of 200 feet.

Dogs also hear a wider range of sounds than humans do. At lower frequencies—such as the sound produced by a passing truck—our hearing compares favorably with a dog's, but at higher frequencies a dog's hearing is far superior. Dogs can tell the difference between one high-pitched sound and another better than we can, and they can detect such sounds at much lower volume. The dog can also hear sounds so high-pitched that the human ear misses them altogether.

A dog's ear, like a cat's, can swivel to locate the source of a sound, and the two ears can move independently of each other. This enables a dog to home in on noises with lightning speed and great accuracy: within about a half-second after the first sound waves strike its eardrum, a dog can determine the location of a sound. While the earflaps, or pinnae, come in all shapes and sizes, a dog's hearing apparatus is the same from breed to breed and—except for the L-shaped ear canal—is constructed very much like a human's. Erect pinnae, such as a German shepherd's, resemble the original, ancestral dog ear. Floppy ears result from selective breeding by humans.

As in humans, the vibrations of the eardrum are picked up and amplified by a series of three interconnected bones in the middle ear: the malleus (hammer), the incus (anvil), and the stapes (stirrup). These bones transmit the vibrations to the cochlea in the inner ear, which converts the vibrations into nerve impulses. These are then carried to the brain via the vestibulocochlear nerve.

Housed in the inner ear is the balance mechanism, which consists of the vestibule and the three semicircular canals. Functioning in a manner similar to a carpenter's level, these devices detect any change in motion of the head and evaluate the head's position relative to the ground. The data gathered by these structures is conveyed via the vestibulocochlear nerve to the brain, which then sends instructions to the muscles of the limbs, the neck, and the eyes to help the dog stay upright.

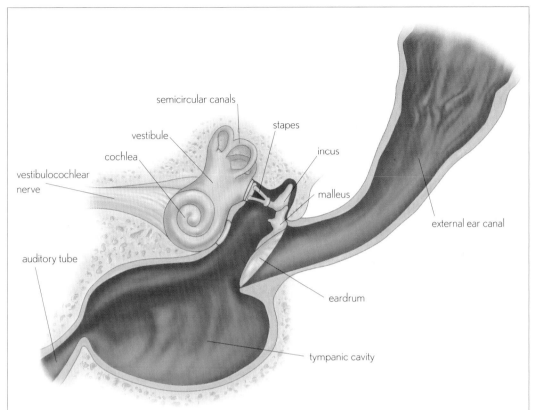

semicircular canals

vestibule

cochlea

stapes

incus

vestibulocochlear
nerve

malleus

external ear canal

auditory tube

eardrum

tympanic cavity

A sampling of canine ear shapes includes (from left) a pug with button ears, a borzoi with rose ears, a miniature pinscher with uncropped erect ears, and a beagle with long, pendulous ears.

Smell

Of all the dog's senses, none is more highly developed than its sense of smell. Dogs' noses help them identify who was in an area before they arrived and who is approaching. Smell also alerts dogs to the presence of pheromones (sex hormones). Released by both sexes in the urine and used to mark territory, pheromones announce a dog's presence to the opposite sex. (Male dogs announce their presence purposefully and repeatedly, as anyone who has ever walked one can attest. Females tend to deposit their pheromones as an afterthought to the main objective: emptying their bladders.)

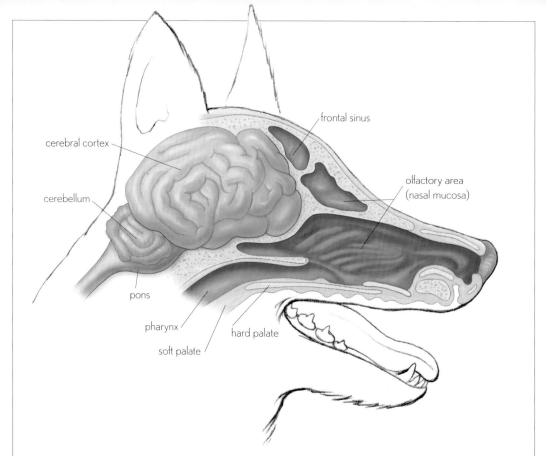

cerebral cortex

cerebellum

pons

pharynx

soft palate

hard palate

frontal sinus

olfactory area
(nasal mucosa)

When dogs sniff each other, they gather a great deal of useful information such as the unique olfactory "signature" of the other dog, its age, sex, stage of the sexual cycle (if the other dog is a female), and even odors that can help two dogs sort out dominance issues without raising a hackle. Many experts think that dogs learn a lot about humans when they sniff us as well. Besides memorizing our unique odor, dogs may be able to perceive our emotional states—including fear—through smell. (Our body language and tone of voice also give a dog valuable clues as to our confidence and dominance, or lack of same.)

The dog's powers of scent detection border on the unbelievable. For example,

if a concentration of butyric acid (an active ingredient of human sweat) just strong enough for a human to smell were dissolved in one million quarts of water, a dog would still be able to detect the scent. To a dog, every human it encounters is an absolute riot of odors, even fresh out of the shower. We may think we don't smell, but we are always pungent to a dog. How do they do it? Dogs have extraordinary physical equipment for smelling, starting at the cold, wet tip of the nose, which stays moist for one main reason: to capture and dissolve molecules of scent. From there, scents travel into the olfactory area within the nose, where a staggering number of smell receptors, called olfactory cells, await. Humans have five

The German shepherd's exceptional sense of smell is put to use sniffing out survivors in rubble.

Once captured in the olfactory area, a scent is converted to electrochemical impulses by the olfactory cells and transmitted by the olfactory nerve to the smell center of the brain. Not surprisingly, a large portion of a dog's brain is dedicated to interpreting smells; dogs have forty times more cells in the olfactory center of their brains than we do.

With so much of the animal's brainpower devoted to sense of smell, it follows that dogs have a good memory for odors. Once they've registered the scent of other dogs or humans—certainly those who are significant in their lives, but also those who merely live in their neighborhood—they're not likely to forget it. Moreover, if a smell (such as that of its owner) has particular meaning for a dog, it will be able to pick that smell out of the "olfactory noise" of thousands of other, possibly stronger, smells competing for its attention. Your dog would know that you had arrived the minute you walked into a building, whether it was a stable or a perfume factory.

Having evolved as some of nature's most effective smelling machines, dogs now put this vital hunting asset to work for us in many ways, even using their noses to save human lives. Specially trained dogs are often employed in search-and-rescue work, while others sniff out bombs, drugs, and contraband agriculture for law-enforcement agencies.

A dog's scent is his calling card.

million of these cells. Dogs have anywhere from 150 million to 250 million. Moreover, dogs have fifteen times more cilia (hairlike structures that can capture scent) on their olfactory cells than we do.

It takes a lot of room to accommodate that many structures for smelling; even from the outside, we can see that canine noses are bigger than our own. But hidden inside is a truly remarkable feature: closely packed folds of specialized mucous membranes called the olfactory area (nasal mucosa). Resembling a blanket doubled over on itself repeatedly, this convoluted structure, whose surface area measures twenty square inches or more, traps odors and holds them for "inspection" by the dog. The human olfactory area is tiny by comparison. In addition to the extra acreage, a dog's olfactory area crams in many more smell receptors per square inch than a human's, further ensuring that a whiff of something interesting won't escape the dog's notice.

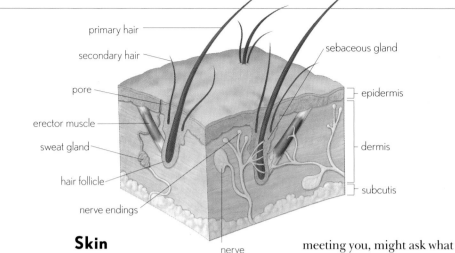

primary hair
secondary hair
pore
erector muscle
sweat gland
hair follicle
nerve endings

sebaceous gland
epidermis
dermis
subcutis

nerve

Skin

The dog's skin is its largest organ, just as our skin is for us. Moreover, it serves many of the same functions as ours does—such as keeping germs and toxins out of the body—but it also contains structures and operates in ways that are distinctly canine.

The visible part of the skin, composed of layers of dead cells, is called the epidermis. Beneath the epidermis is the dermis, made up of living skin cells. Within the dermis are sweat glands; sebaceous glands, which produce oils that coat the dog's skin and hair; and follicles, pits in which the hairs of the coat grow. Nerve endings in the dermis near the hair follicles assist in sensory perception; they can detect pressure on or movement of the hairs.

Among the most important of skin structures, to a dog, are the two anal sacs and the glands associated with them. Consisting of specialized skin and located on either side of the anal opening, the sacs hold a fluid with a scent unique to its owner, enabling the dog to mark territory by imprinting its personal signature on its feces. (Cats have these glands, too, and they serve the same basic function for them.) The odor from the sacs also serves as an icebreaker. While strangers, upon meeting you, might ask what you do for a living, dogs couldn't care less. They are born to sniff. If dogs conversed, their first question would be: What do you smell like? As it is, they skip the formalities and find out, each one sniffing under the other's tail. What they're inhaling is the unique odor produced by the glands in and around the other dog's anal sacs. (At the same time, they are very likely checking out the other dog for smells indicating fear, submission, or sexual interest.)

The pads on a dog's paws are also made of modified skin—a very thick, tough variant of the dog's normally thin epidermis (thinner in dogs than in humans). The pads are excellent shock absorbers, built to take a lifetime's pounding and to protect the dog's feet on hot or cold surfaces. Sweat glands in the pads also produce a secretion that keeps the pads from drying out and cracking.

Dogs perspire head to tail, but not to cool down the way humans do, through the evaporation of sweat. The sweat glands of dogs seem mainly designed to enhance a dog's personal odor through their fatty secretions; the smellier a dog, the more interesting it is to its peers. (This is probably why dogs love to roll in things we wouldn't touch with a ten-foot pole.) To stay cool in hot weather, a dog pants, using the respiratory system to do the work of cooling through evaporation.

Whiskers The dog's vibrissae, or whiskers, are yet another specialized skin structure. These long, stiff hairs have great sensitivity to touch and are found on a dog's muzzle, upper eyelids, cheeks, and legs, serving in each location as feelers that help that dog navigate at night or in dark areas.

Coat While smells produced by glands in the skin are a dog's canine calling card, the first impression a dog makes on humans has a lot to do with its coat. The dog's fur is composed of two different kinds of hair. Strong, coarse primary hairs form the topcoat. Each primary hair can have several finer, smoother secondary hairs surrounding it. The follicles that hold the primary hairs have tiny

On very cold days, a dog's topcoat "sits up," creating larger insulating pockets that can hold more warm air.

erector muscles that can pull the hairs upright (for example, when a dog raises its hackles in a warning display). Lacking such muscles, secondary hairs never stand up. Coarse-haired dogs such as wirehaired terriers have many primary hairs and relatively few secondary hairs. In a soft-haired breed like the smooth-haired fox terrier, secondary hairs predominate and make the coat smooth to the touch. In between are breeds like the German shepherd, which are abundantly supplied with both kinds of hair. The coat texture of such double-coated dogs is like that of the wolf (and the very first dogs). Extreme coarseness or smoothness developed later, as dogs branched

Canine coats are tremendously varied. Clockwise from top left: Tibetan terrier with a long outercoat; Border terrier with a short, wiry outercoat; pharaoh hound with a short, glossy coat; Australian cattle dog with a weather-resistant and moderately short outercoat.

out geographically and were bred for specific tasks. Soft-coated, shorthaired dogs, for example, may trace their ancestry back to places like Egypt, where the weather is warm year-round. Coarsehaired dogs may descend from hunting dogs whose thick coats were a shield against nettles and thorns.

Dogs shed in the spring to rid themselves of their thick winter coat. As each winter approaches, they doff their light summer topcoat to make way for a warm winter coat. Year-round the dog's fur acts as an excellent temperature regulator, trapping a layer of air between the coat and the skin. Air is a good insulator, and it protects the dog from temperature extremes. In summer, it keeps hot air away from the skin. In winter, it traps body heat under the coat.

Strong claws and powerful front legs enable this Jack Russell terrier to go after vermin.

Claws

The dog's claws are formed from modified skin, in the same way our toe- and fingernails are. They give the dog traction and serve as effective tools for digging, and they can also help the dog protect itself. But compared to the dagger-like claws of the cat, a dog's claws are butter knives. A dog's claws cannot be retracted, or pulled in, as a cat's can; they are permanently in the "out" position.

High on the inner side of their front paws, all dogs have a small dewclaw, an evolutionary memento that might once have been larger and more functional but now serves no real purpose. Because it is particularly vulnerable to getting caught and broken, some owners choose to have it removed. Except for the dewclaw, however, one would be hard put to find anything impractical about a dog's skin or the hair and claws that it produces. The organ that worked so effectively as a bodysuit for the dog's ancient ancestors still serves our own dogs admirably today.

Dewclaws, such as those seen on the forepaws of this four-week-old terrier-collie mix puppy, serve no purpose and are usually removed to prevent injury.

Owners can learn to recognize the difference between harmless dog play and more aggressive behavior.

Understanding Your Dog

Getting to know your dog means coming to a better understanding of the behaviors that express a canine's state of mind. Different canine body postures and vocalizations offer clues to a dog's level of anxiety or contentment. Reading these signals will help you tell whether your pet is naturally dominant or submissive or whether a dog will be wary or affectionate around children. It is also wise to learn the "tell-tail" warning signals, such as raised hackles and defiant eye contact, that indicate when a dog is likely to show aggression.

This section will help you interpret your dog's body language and will give you suggestions for modifying extremely aggressive or submissive behaviors (for more on correcting canine behavior problems, see page 397). Just as shy humans can learn to improve their self-confidence, so can a submissive dog be coaxed out to play. And if you've ever wondered what a dog is trying to say with a yelp or a howl, this section explores these special canine communications, as well as your dog's propensity to play, sniff, and sleep.

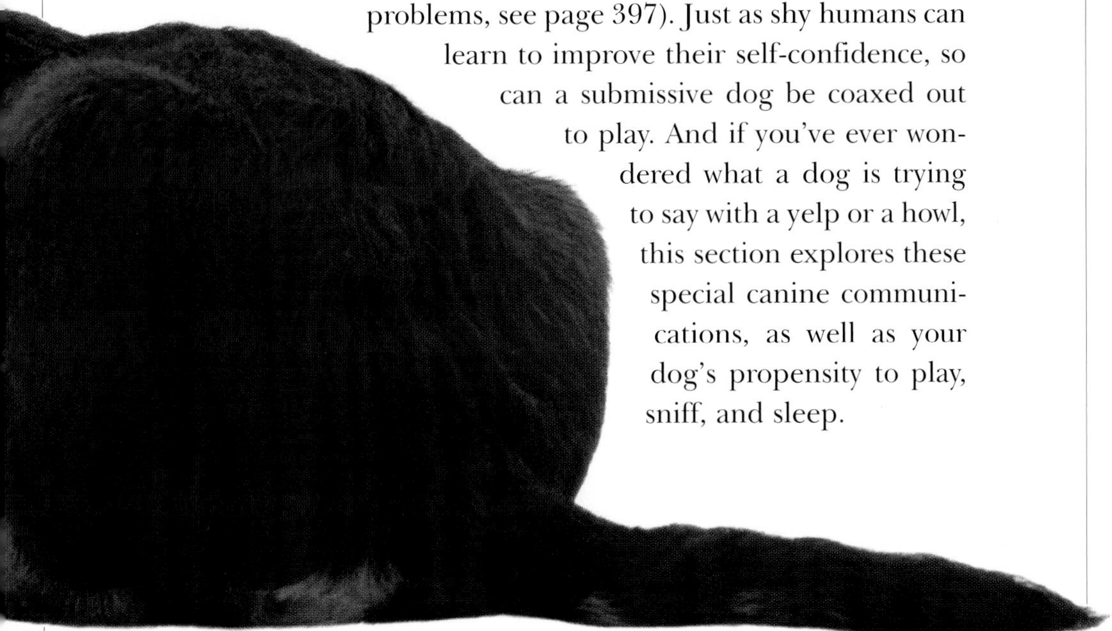

Canine Body Language

By the wag of a tail, a shift in posture, or a sudden grimace, a dog can express feelings of joy, fear, or aggression to both human and canine observers. As pack animals, dogs need to be able to communicate their state of mind to fellow pack members. In the past, this communication brought success in group hunts and communal rearing of young. Nowadays, domestic dogs no longer need to band together to hunt large prey, but they do need to send messages to other dogs to avoid fights or invite play. They also send signals to their human pack members—as anyone who has ever been insistently pawed under the dinner table knows—as means of manipulating humans into doing their bidding. Deciphering canine body language will give you the tools to read your dog's messages—to his peers and to you—loud and clear.

Not unlike most humans, this dog is starting her day with a stretch.

At Ease

When at ease, the normal dog carries his weight evenly distributed over all four feet, giving a sturdy table-like appearance. His facial muscles are relaxed and his mouth may be closed or hanging slightly open. Depending on breed type, the tail may be hanging down with a slight curve to it or may be curled and resting on the back.

Curiosity is conveyed by the tension of this greyhound's ears.

At Attention

If something catches the dog's attention, he will move into an alert posture. Body muscles will tense and the dog will draw up in height. Light tension in the facial muscles will give the dog a watchful expression. His ears will tense

Speak to a fearful dog in a normal tone of voice; coddling will reward his behavior and sternness will aggravate his condition.

and shift forward. He will begin to wag or quiver his tail depending on level of excitement and breed of dog. If the dog is both excited and wary, a ridge of fur may rise up over his shoulders or down his spine (also known as "getting his hackles up" or piloerection).

Fear

If something catches the dog's attention and causes him to feel afraid, he will draw back and in doing so will appear to carry his weight over his rear legs. He will slouch closer to the ground while turning his head away, averting his gaze. His pupils will become big, black saucers, and you may even see some of the white in the corners of his eyes. He will pull his ears closer back to his skull, and the tail may hang down or be tightly pulled between the dog's rear legs and pressed up against his belly.

Should the dog feel intimidated, he may act in a submissive manner. His body will crouch low to the ground, and his ears will be pulled back as far as his ear set allows. He may paw at the ground with a front paw in a puppylike gesture while moving his body in a slight, low wiggle. A softness will be noticeable in his face, but tension in his facial muscles may result in an open-mouthed, submissive grin. Don't mistake this for a snarl, as there will be no accompanying growly vocalizations. The dog may dart his tongue out or he may lick his lips in nervousness. It is also common for a fearful dog to squat and release a small amount of urine or, if strongly intimidated, to roll onto his back, display his belly, avert his eyes, and even urinate on himself as an act of total surrender.

Happiness

If the object of interest is pleasurable, the dog may begin to lean forward and wag—not merely his tail but his entire body. Some dogs express sheer happiness or uncontainable excitement by leaping off the ground with a wide grin.

Flight, Fight, or Freeze?

When frightened by a noise, object, or stranger, a dog may respond by fleeing, fighting, freezing, fainting, or fooling around. The most common response in a young dog is to flee. Whether under a coffee table, into another room, or behind the owner's legs, the dog is looking for a safe haven from which she can observe the fearful stimulus. As the frightened pet gets used to the noise, object, or stranger in her environment, she will cautiously approach. It is important to allow the dog as much time as she needs to acclimate.

Do not force a reluctant dog toward the object of her fear. A dog that cannot escape may feel forced to fight or bite. If menacing a stranger with a growl or snap gets the scary person to retreat, the dog feels instantly rewarded and is likely to try the behavior again when in a similar situation (see advice on fear aggression, page 404).

The dog that freezes is temporarily caught in a situation she believes she cannot face or retreat from. She stiffens into a freeze posture while taking in more information to determine the next course of action. From there, the dog can swiftly move into another response without warning. Be cautious around a dog in freeze position because her next move may be a quick bite.

Fainting, very seldom seen in dogs, is most likely to happen when a dog feels that she is trapped and cannot escape the fearful stimulus. As sometimes happens to humans, a dog becomes so overwhelmed by fear that she faints.

For a dog that is very anxious or highly excited, the urges to fight or flee may feel evenly balanced or blocked altogether, and

The hard stare and display of sharp white teeth show that this rottweiler is ready to take on any aggressive challenge.

Offensive Aggression

If the dog feels the need to intimidate or threaten to become aggressive, he will pull himself erect and appear to be practically walking on his toes. His body will stiffen and his weight will appear to be loaded over his front legs as he leans toward what he wishes to intimidate. Ears are brought forward and the tail will be up above back level and wagging in an agitated manner. Tensed facial muscles cause wrinkling between the eyes and pull back the cheek muscles, resulting in a snarling appearance. The eyes deliver a hard stare, a challenge to fight to the animal or human in question. If the intimidating posture alone does not cause the challenger to back off, a bite will ensue.

the dog may cope with the stress by engaging in an activity that under the circumstances seems bizarre, such as yawning, scratching, grooming, or chasing after imaginary critters. This is known as "displacement behavior." Human examples of this behavior include people who whistle when they are uneasy.

Dogs and Social Status

Two dogs meet. First they stand nose-to-tail with one another to gather information on gender and reproductive status. They then turn face-to-face, eyeing each other while sniffing mouths, ears, and anything else that draws their attention. Within moments it is decided who is the dominant partner and who is the submissive partner in this new relationship. At that point body language will take over.

Few dogs are dominant or submissive in every social situation. Their response is conditional—based on the dog (or human) before them in a specific instance. Factors such as health, age, and conditioning play an important role in pack hierarchy. A young puppy or malnourished stray may not appear to be dominant at first, but as she matures or gains weight she may jockey with her owner or other household dogs for leadership of the family pack.

Age, health, and sexual status are gleaned from a posterior sniff.

Dominance Behaviors

Leaning forward, placing the head over another dog's shoulders, mounting from the rear, and sustaining eye contact are all dominant gestures. Dominance gestures toward people may take many different forms, including barking for attention, mounting, and nudging with the nose or smacking with a forepaw to demand petting or play. A dog expressing dominance may growl or snarl when asked to move or to relinquish valuable property. Some dogs will even go as far as grabbing at clothing or body parts, purposefully demonstrating their power. Others will frequently throw a paw over their leash, play tug-of-war, pull ahead while on-leash, or resolutely balk or refuse to move. You may effectively quash this "palace revolt" by following the leadership guidelines given on page 384.

Strutting out ahead of her handler, this dog makes it clear who's in charge.

The dog lying on her back with her tail tucked as she paws and licks her elder's muzzle is displaying submissive behavior. The older dog's dominance is evident in her tail held up and over her back, her raised hackles, and her head hanging over the other dog.

Submissive Behaviors

Dogs that lack confidence often display submissive body language toward their "betters." Submissive behavior can include lowering the forepaws and chest into a play bow, averting the gaze, pawing at the ground, ducking away from being touched, submissive grinning, or shaking. Some dogs will lick nervously, especially at the lips of the leader, in what is sometimes called an appeasement gesture. Others will avert their eyes, lower their body into a slouching posture, urinate nervously, or roll over on their backs, exposing their bellies.

These are the behaviors of a dog that has no desire to challenge pack order or move up in the world. While such a dog will seldom have any problem with his peers, a pet owner may wish to boost the dog's confidence level around people by increased socialization and training.

For a shy or submissive dog, both obedience and agility classes are wonderful for improving confidence levels. While an excessively submissive dog can be trying to live with, a mildly submissive dog displays a desire to please. This kind of dog will be particularly good at taking direction, even from young children—a healthy trait for a family dog.

Dog Talk

Dogs communicate extensively with one another and with their family pack through vocalization. Even the barkless basenji has plenty to say through whining,

Howling with your dog can be quite amusing, as this Alaskan malamute's buddy can attest.

growling, yelping, and a breed-specific vocalization called yodeling. All other dogs bark and howl as well.

The most often heard canine vocalization is, of course, barking. Dogs use barking to summon their pack, warn of an intruder on their territory, frighten an interloper away, or demand attention. The meaning of the bark is conveyed through intensity, frequency, and volume.

Whining is a sound of stress and the first sound most pups ever make. If separated from the mother, a puppy only a few hours old is capable of signaling his distress and helping Mom pinpoint his location. Many adult dogs will whine when separated from their owners, especially if they are on unfamiliar territory.

Yelping is employed by dogs when they are in distress. It can be an indicator of pain, such as the loud, shrieking yelps emitted when a dog is hit by a car, or a short, startled response, such as the sound given when the family cat jumps on a napping dog.

Howling is a locator sound. Scent hounds will howl (called "baying" or "giving tongue" in different breeds) when they are on an animal's trail or have treed game so their handlers can locate them. Dogs of many breed types can be heard howling when left alone, trying to aid their families in finding the way back home. Howling can be contagious. One dog starts and others are likely to join in. Sirens or sounds on television can set off an entire neighborhood in a group howl.

Growling is used as a warning. Deep, throaty growls are used to scare away strangers or threaten others that if they come closer or challenge the dog in any way, a bite will ensue. Usually the deeper the growl, the more serious the threat.

Sniffing and Marking

The canine nose knows few equals. The dog's ability to catch and follow a particular scent has been put to use to serve humans in hunting for thousands of years and in areas like search and rescue and bomb detection in more recent times. It is little wonder that when taken outdoors, the dog's focus is on the myriad smells scattered throughout the neighborhood or backyard. The dog picks up information detailing the animal traffic through the area by smelling the urine, feces, vomitus, hair, and even dander left behind.

The urine of other dogs will often prompt a dog to lift his leg and mark on top of it, adding his own scent—an act akin to signing the neighborhood guest registry. The target for this squirt is often a vertical object, such as a tree, fire hydrant, or fence post. Unneutered males most often exhibit marking behavior, but neutered males and many females mark too—albeit less frequently. While females will not cock their

Canines glean neighborhood information via scents left behind.

hindlegs in male fashion, some will slightly elevate one of their rear legs while marking. Females in heat show an increase in marking behavior, as they use their pheromone-laced urine to attract suitors.

A dog uses his nose to track animal traffic through the area.

Why Dogs Mount

Mounting behavior is commonly seen in litters of puppies as young as three or four weeks of age. In these young dogs, mounting is play and investigatory behavior without any sexual intent, although it does serve to orient them to proper positioning later in life.

At puberty and beyond, mounting is done to accomplish sexual penetration of a female in heat or to display dominance over another individual. While there is no need to interrupt such behavior between dogs unless you fear a fight may break out or an unspayed female in heat is involved, you should strongly discourage a dog from any attempt to mount humans with a sharp "no" and a few minutes of social isolation. Be aware that some older males can get quite nasty when their "fun" is interrupted. Neutered dogs are much less likely to engage in mounting behavior than unneutered dogs.

A cooperative game of tug-of-war between two German shorthaired pointer puppies.

Canine Play

There are few things more enjoyable than watching a playful pack of hounds cavorting around in a fenced yard. As pack animals and social creatures, most dogs enjoy the company of other dogs. While most dogs are friendly, their styles of play can differ according to breed type, age, and conditioning. The bull breeds are known as body slammers, running headlong into the side of another dog. Herding dogs like to chase and nip at the heels of other dogs, while retrievers engage in mouth-wrestling games.

Dog play can be a terrific outlet for excess energy, but make sure to supervise play sessions carefully. When dogs get too excited, play can become dangerous as it evolves in the dog's mind from just a game into an actual hunt or fight. Avoid this by diffusing the intensity: call the dogs away from each other, involve them in one or two minutes of obedience work, and then send them back to play.

Play with Humans

Engaging your dog in play helps to expend her energy and strengthen the bond between you. As you get to know your dog, you will discover her play preferences. Some dogs are born retrievers, while others live to pounce on their squeakies and stuffed toys. Often play preferences are determined by breed type, but individual differences exist as well. Some dogs seem not to know how to play. This may be the result of early social isolation, and such a dog can usually be enticed to play using the techniques described below.

How you play with your dog depends on your day-to-day relationship with her. If yours is a bossy dog, confidence-building games such as tug-of-war or wrestling are not recommended. Exerting your leadership through a retrieving game that demands she deposit the toy directly into your hand in order for the next round to begin is more beneficial to the relationship, yet still a lot of fun.

Tug-of-war can be a fine game for submissive to even-tempered dogs as long as it is played by the rules. Humans control this game, not dogs. The tug toy is brought out, the dog is called over to play, and the game begins. Do not allow the dog to put her mouth on the human.

Playing games with your dog—according to your rules—will help to strengthen the bond between the two of you.

When the command "drop it" is issued, the dog must do so or the game ends. Do not worry about the growling vocalizations the dog makes while tugging on the toy. These are merely play vocalizations. However, if you have commanded the dog to drop the toy and she stares you in the eye and growls, this is a serious infraction. Once the toy is safely removed, reconsider the wisdom of engaging this particular dog in tug-of-war. She may have some possession-aggression issues to resolve first.

Sleeping Dogs

Dogs spend the better part of their days asleep. Just how many hours depends on the age of the dog and the stimulation level of her environment. Young puppies that are learning and growing with every second will spend much of their day napping, interspersed with high-intensity play periods. Adolescents will spend more time awake looking for ways to expend their seemingly limitless

energy and curiosity. As dogs age, they tend to sleep more. Geriatric dogs sleep longer and deeper than others but not necessarily at nighttime. Some older dogs will wander the halls at night and howl, whine, or bark for you to get up and join them.

Upon selecting a suitable place to nap, many dogs will circle a few times before actually lying down. This is probably a throwback to life in the wild, when dogs would trample down grasses to make a safe, snug bed. Nowadays it suffices to rearrange the comforter or the throw rug on the kitchen floor. The dog then lies down and assumes her favorite sleeping position, curled up into a tight little ball with tail over nose, on her side with legs outstretched, or on her back with legs sprawled out in all directions.

When comfortably deep in slumber, do dogs dream? While little is written on the subject, the whimpering vocalizations, limb jerks, and rapid eye movement all seem to indicate that the sleep of dogs—like that of their human caretakers—is indeed filled with dreams.

After euphoric play, puppies and their owners need time to recover.

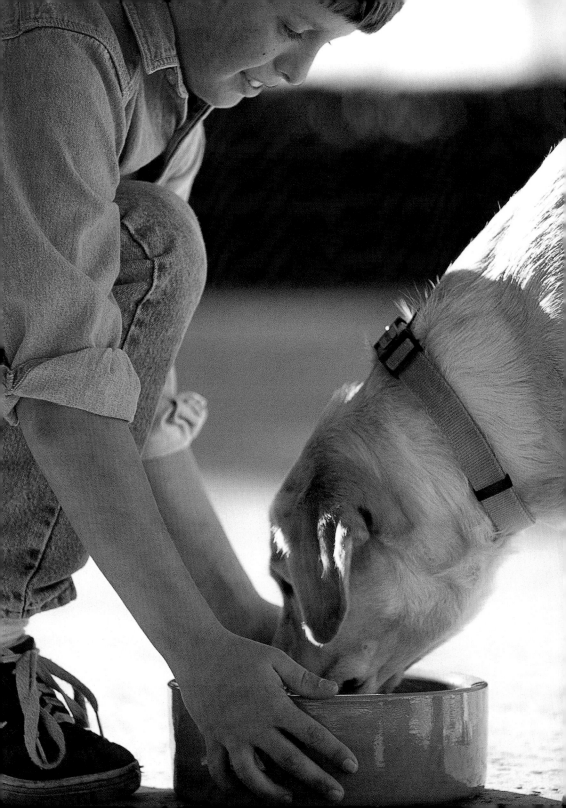

IV

Taking Care of
Your Dog

For a new dog owner, each day is filled with novel experiences, some of which can be challenging. This section is a comprehensive reference guide to caring for your dog—in sickness and in health, in youth and in old age. It takes you through the everyday routines of feeding, grooming, and training; the steps toward maintaining your dog's health; and the procedures of emergency care. Special features on household poisons and on caring for sick dogs, pregnant dogs, and aging dogs will help prepare you for any eventuality.

Within this section there are six chapters on caring for your dog:

Everyday Care for Your Dog

How to Bring a Dog into Your Life covered the basics of choosing a dog, welcoming a puppy or adult dog into your home, house training, and early socialization. Now you need to undertake the daily care essential to your new best friend's long-term health and happiness. This chapter offers guidance on providing your dog with optimum nutrition and exercise, including organized dog sports, to build muscle tone and expend excess energy. The grooming needs of various breed types are detailed, along with directions for nail trimming, tooth brushing, and other maintenance requirements. Segments on obedience training and solving behavior problems provide step-by-step instructions to help you educate your dog. After all, a well-trained dog is welcomed in the homes of friends and relatives, on hiking trails in many public parks, and even in some of the best hotels. The travel tips near the end of the chapter will help you get wherever you may want to go.

Dogs thrive on consistency, so the sooner you set up routines for feeding, exercising, grooming, training, and traveling with your dog, the better off everyone involved will be.

Feeding Your Dog

Although dogs generally aren't too picky about their food, like humans they have varying nutritional needs governed by age, metabolism, activity level, and the amount of time they spend outdoors in cold weather. The next few pages offer advice for figuring out what to feed your dog, how much to feed him, and how often.

Choosing the Right Food

When selecting a food, you must consider your dog's age, health, and lifestyle. A growing or active dog needs more calories than an older or sedate dog. A dog with food allergies or gastrointestinal, urinary, heart, or obesity problems needs a special diet; ask your veterinarian to recommend one. Pregnant, lactating, and elderly dogs also have special nutritional needs (see pages 483 and 490). If your dog's weight is appropriate for her breed and size, if she is alert and active and has a glossy coat, she is probably getting an adequate diet in both quantity and quality.

Dog Food Brands Stick with dog foods manufactured by the major pet food companies. Generic brands may lack essential ingredients, and thus cause serious nutritional deficits and can be difficult to digest. The premium brands are always made with the same recipe, whereas ingredients in some of the less-expensive brands may be changed based on cost to the manufacturer. Some dogs' digestive tracts are sensitive to such changes. Premium foods are more efficiently digested and produce less stool than some generic and supermarket brands—which can be a significant consideration if you have a large dog.

Dry or Moist? A good-quality dry food is nutritionally equal to a good-quality canned or semi-moist one. Such factors as your dog's age, pickiness, and tendency to obesity and dental problems can make one type of food more suitable, but the choice is usually a matter of owner preference. Dogs accustomed to eating canned or semi-moist food may be reluctant to switch to dry kibble. Changing foods can also cause gastrointestinal upset. Once you find a food that your dog seems to like and that is keeping him in good health, it's best not to change it unless directed to by your veterinarian.

Choose a good-quality food appropriate to your dog's age and state of health and stick with it unless advised otherwise by your veterinarian.

Dry food is the most economical option. It is easy to use, can be left out for the dog to eat at will, and can be stored in large quantities since it doesn't need to be refrigerated. The abrasive action of dry dog food against the teeth also helps reduce and retard tartar formation. Some dogs find dry food less palatable than semi-moist and wet foods.

Semi-moist food is more expensive than dry food. As with dry food, it does not need

Reading Dog Food Labels

The most important information to look for on a dog food label is that the food meets the nutritional standards set in feeding trials by the Association of American Feed Control Officials. The label should also indicate if the product is complete and balanced for all life stages or for a particular life stage. If not complete and balanced, the label should say "not to be fed as sole diet" or "for intermittent feeding only." The Guaranteed Analysis printed on most labels is of questionable usefulness because it does not separate the digestible protein, fat, and fiber in the food from the indigestible; the percentages offered are for the crude protein, fat, and fiber, which means they are combinations of both digestible and indigestible components. The ingredients in a dog food are listed in descending order of predominance by weight. Meat, fish, or poultry, as well as cereal grains and soybean meal, should be near the top of the list.

Dog Food Basics

Your dog needs the proper quantity, quality, and balance of carbohydrates, proteins, fats, vitamins, minerals, and water to stay happy and healthy.

Carbohydrates Sources: well-cooked grains, cellulose, starches, sugars. Uses: for energy; for bulk (indigestible cellulose) to prevent constipation, since fiber absorbs water and stimulates intestinal movements; to spare proteins (since carbohydrates are used for quick energy) so they can be used for body growth and repair.

Proteins Sources: meat, eggs, fish, legumes (especially soybeans), milk and milk products, yeast. Uses: for growth; healthy tissue repair and maintenance; formation of antibodies that fight infection; formation of enzymes and hormones that are essential to the body's chemical reactions.

Fats Sources: poultry, beef, lamb, fish by-products, meal. Uses: provide energy; transport vitamins A, D, E, K (fat-soluble vitamins); provide fatty acids for a healthy skin and coat; enhance flavor.

Vitamins and Minerals Sources: meat, eggs, fish, vegetables, milk and milk products, yeast. Uses: for normal body functioning, including vision, growth, reproduction, and blood clotting.

Water Sources: obtained from metabolism of the foods (especially of fats) and liquids the dog ingests. Uses: integral to every function and every cell in the body.

to be refrigerated, so it is easy to use and store. It is highly palatable, which can lead some dogs to overeat. The high sugar content in semi-moist food may cause dental problems for some dogs.

Canned food is also more expensive than dry food. Leftovers must be refrigerated, as they will spoil if left in the dog's bowl all day. Canned food has a higher water content than other formulations, so dogs that eat it may need to urinate more frequently. As with semi-moist food, dogs find canned food especially tasty, so it is not the most sensible choice if your dog has a weight problem.

How to Feed Your Dog

Whether you are feeding your dog dry, semi-moist, or canned food, divide the daily ration into two equal feedings. Canned food can be mixed with dry food (be certain to count calories from both when determining

how much to feed). Dry and semi-moist foods don't need refrigeration and can be left out for your dog to snack on at will. However, if your dog isn't housebroken or if rodents or insects are a problem, pick up the food after fifteen minutes. If untouched, store it in an airtight container; if your dog has drooled on it, throw it away.

Most dogs thrive on routine—being fed in the same place, in the same bowl, at the same time. However, if dogs learn to be flexible during puppyhood, they are less likely to be upset if the routine is changed—for example, if they have to stay at a kennel. Most adult dogs do well when they are fed twice a day. Puppies should be fed three times a day (in the morning, early afternoon, and late afternoon or early evening) until six months of age, then twice daily thereafter. (Regular feeding schedules can help with house training.) Dogs that are prone to bloat (page 445), such as large, deep-chested

Weight	Calories Needed	
in pounds	by puppies	by adult dogs
5	500	250
10	850	450
15	1,200	600
20	1,400	700
25	1,600	800
30	1,800	900
40	2,300	1,200
50	2,700	1,400
60	3,200	1,600
70	3,600	1,500
90	–	2,100
120	–	3,000

A Saint Bernard (left) can eat the same food as an Italian greyhound (right). He'll just need to eat a lot more of it.

breeds (Saint Bernards, Great Danes, German shepherds, Irish setters, Doberman pinschers), should be kept on a two- to three-meal-a-day schedule throughout their lives.

The calorie chart (above) offers general guidelines for the caloric needs of your puppy or dog. However, each dog is different. Follow the directions on the dog food package and adjust according to how your dog responds. If she consistently leaves food in the bowl, feed less. If she is gaining too much weight, cut back her food by 10 to 25 percent. If she is too thin or continually searches for more food, increase her ration by 10 to 25 percent. Be sure to consult your veterinarian if your dog is gaining or losing significant amounts of weight.

Changing Food If you want to change your dog's food to a different brand, you must do it gradually so your dog does not suffer digestive upset. Start by replacing a small portion of the old food with the new, then gradually increase the proportion until the dog is eating only the new food.

Water

Make sure your dog has access to fresh, clean water at all times. Most dogs need about one cup of water per ten pounds of body weight daily. Factors that will increase your dog's need for water include lactation, fever, hot weather, exercise, and water loss from vomiting or diarrhea. The type of food you give your dog also affects how much water he will drink. Dry foods (only 10 percent moisture) will increase your dog's water intake, while canned foods (75 percent moisture) will decrease intake.

The Overweight Dog

Your dog is probably overweight if there is not a clearly visible distinction between the ribcage and the abdomen, or if you can't feel the ribs when you run your hands down the sides of the dog's body from shoulders to flanks. Obesity is a common problem often attributable to genetics, overeating, or a sedentary lifestyle. It is less frequently caused by medical conditions such as hypothyroidism (a lack of thyroid hormone), a condition sometimes seen in Dobermans, Irish setters, spaniels, dachshunds, and golden retrievers. If you think your dog might be overweight, consult with your veterinarian. If all medical tests are normal, the vet will probably recommend a special diet and increased exercise. Though it may take a long time—sometimes more than six months—to see significant weight loss, it is definitely worth the effort. Obesity increases the risk of serious health problems, such as diabetes and diseases of the heart, skin, and joints.

Treats

Dog biscuits can contain a lot of calories, sometimes as many as fifty to seventy-five calories each. If your dog gains weight easily, limit the number of daily biscuits. Some dogs like to chew on low-calorie vegetables like carrots, which help keep the teeth clean and are a good source of vitamin A. If your dog is on a special diet or has food allergies, speak to your veterinarian before offering the dog any treats. Some dogs may experience gastrointestinal upset when new treats are introduced. It is always wise to start out with a very small amount and increase it slowly.

Chewies Dogs love to chew, and there is a huge assortment of animal-based dog chewies on the market, including rawhide, pig ears, and cow hooves. Some dogs have difficulty with these chewies, and may experience choking, vomiting, diarrhea, internal irritation, or blockage. The first time you offer your dog one of these items, watch carefully as she consumes it and monitor any changes in behavior or excretion. If your dog has trouble or tends to swallow large chunks of animal-based products, you may want to try safer options. Nylon or rubber chewies or those made out of hardened vegetable proteins do not break up into chunks.

Bones Many experts believe that the only bones appropriate for dogs are synthetic bones. Others believe that beef knuckle and leg bones are acceptable. However, all experts agree that poultry, pig, and steak bones are unsafe because they can splinter and cause obstruction or penetration of the gastrointestinal tract, which can lead to peritonitis (infection of the abdomen) and death. Before giving a dog a bone, remove the excess fat, which can cause diarrhea. Freshness is crucial to avoid harmful bacteria; refrigerate fresh bones until use. Make sure there are no sharp edges that can hurt the dog's mouth. Take the bone away from your dog if it begins to splinter. Some dogs can be very possessive of their bones. To avoid fights in a multidog household, separate the dogs while they are feasting on their bones and take the bones away before the dogs are reunited. Be especially alert when young children are around, as even a very friendly dog may snap at a child who reaches for her bone.

Exercise and Play

Physical exercise is as important for your dog as it is for the rest of the family. In addition to improving the dog's muscle tone, joint flexibility, digestion, and cardiovascular fitness, exercise increases the production of brain chemicals, called endorphins, that contribute to a feeling of well-being and relaxation. (These chemicals are also released in human brains during exercise.) Dogs that are given regular exercise appropriate for their breed, age, and state of health seem to have fewer medical and behavioral problems, such as destructive chewing or excessive barking. Exercise and dog sports strengthen the bond between dog and owner and give many dogs the satisfying opportunity to "work" in ways similar to those for which they were originally bred. Exercise should be a playful, enjoyable experience for your dog. Twenty to forty-five minutes of moderate exercise, such as brisk walking, twice a day will keep the average adult dog vital and alert. This will suffice for most mixed breeds (herding breed mixes and pit bull mixes will demand more exercise) as well as many purebreds, such as collies, golden retrievers, and most sizes of poodles. More athletic breeds, such as pharoah hounds and Norwegian elkhounds, need one to two hours of vigorous exercise daily. For purebred dogs, see the Reference Guide to Dog Breeds for information on each breed's exercise needs—those needing a great deal of exercise are marked with the Special Exercise Needs icon . Puppies and adolescents up to about eighteen months old are more demanding in their exercise needs. Puppies play wildly for short periods of time, then crash, then play wildly again, repeating this scenario dozens of times a day. Adolescents play for hours, nap for fifteen minutes, then get up and start all over again.

How Much Exercise Does Your Dog Need?

When trying to estimate how much exercise a dog will need, you must consider several variables: breed type, physique, age, amount of stimulation within the home environment, and the condition and health of the dog. Some breeds were created to work from sunup to sundown. Kept as pets, they need an owner tremendously committed to exercising them; otherwise they get bored and can become destructive. The short-legged, long-bodied physiques of such dogs as basset hounds and Pekingese are not built for high-energy activities, so these breeds have moderate exercise needs. Dogs that are compact and built for speed or agility, like Border collies and dalmatians, have much more demanding exercise requirements.

All breeds are at their most active during adolescence (generally around six to eighteen months of age). Very active breeds such as pointers and pit bulls have adolescent-like energy levels until they are nearly geriatric. Dogs raised in a home where there is a lot of activity will tire themselves out by following everyone around, wrestling with the kids, and racing to the door to see who has come in or gone out. A dog that lives in an all-adult household in which everyone is away at work ten hours a day will need more structured exercise periods to tucker him out.

As for condition and health, the better shape a dog is in, the more exercise he can handle. A dog with a weight problem (either

too fat or too thin) will not have the stamina of a healthy, well-toned dog. Heart, lung, and skeletal problems will also put limits on a dog's activities. Some dogs just need more exercise than their littermates or others of their breed type or age group. When your dog throws himself down on the ground, flops over on his side, and takes a long nap, you know you have met his exercise needs.

Starting a New Exercise Program

Before embarking on a new exercise regimen with your dog, visit your vet so that she can verify that your dog is up to the task.

The veterinarian will check the dog's weight and his heart, kidney, and joint status. If your dog has medical problems, is at high risk for cardiomyopathy—an enlargement of the heart caused by a thickening or thinning of the heart muscle (Dobermans and boxers are among the breeds at risk)—or is six years old or older, your veterinarian may recommend blood tests, X rays, urinalysis, electrocardiograms, or echocardiograms. Tell your veterinarian if you will be training your dog at high altitudes, where the blood's oxygen-carrying capacity changes.

Before engaging in a new sport or activity, it is also important to consider what commands your dog should know to make the activity safe and enjoyable for both of you (see Basic Commands, page 386). For instance, jogging will be much more pleasant if your dog responds to the heel command and will run at your side instead of tangling you in the leash as he crosses in front of or behind you. When swimming with your dog, a recall (responding to the come command) is essential because you will need to call him back to you to prevent him from swimming out too far.

Start an exercise program with fifteen-minute sessions three or four times a week and slowly increase to thirty minutes or longer. Include both a warm-up and a cool-down period to avoid injuries or muscle strain. It takes at least eight weeks of increasing activity for a previously inactive dog to reach peak conditioning. During this time the capacity of the heart to pump

Above: High-energy dogs like these well-trained dalmatians can run for miles without tiring. They need warm-up and cool-down periods.

blood increases, the dog's ability to metabolize food and distribute energy increases, and the dog's muscle tone and respiratory capacity increase. The foot pads also get tougher.

To avoid weather-related complications, such as heatstroke, hypothermia, or frostbite, be extra careful in very hot and very cold weather. On cold days, exercise your dog around midday when the temperature is at its highest and stop right away if your dog starts shivering or becomes exhausted, or if the ear tips, tail, or scrotum look pale or are red, hot, or swollen and seem painful to the touch. On hot days, exercise your dog in the morning or evening when the temperature is at its coolest. Stop the workout immediately if the dog begins panting excessively, falls behind, seems weak, or doesn't want to go on.

Walking Probably the most popular way to exercise a dog is walking. It is easy on the joints and ligaments of both the dog and the walker and also gives both the chance to "smell the roses" and visit with neighbors. Try to choose routes that include uphills, downhills, and turns so that your dog's entire body is exercised. Always walk your dog on a leash.

Over time, you may wish to speed up from a walk to a slow jog or trot. Gradually increase your speed from walking to jogging over a four- to six-week period. Jogging on a leash is fine for a large dog but can be treacherous for a small dog, who might unwittingly run into your jogging path. Jog with a small dog only if you have leash trained her extremely well.

Running If you and your dog are properly conditioned, you have an athletic breed or mix, and you follow safety rules, then running is a good exercise choice. The best

running partners are medium to large dogs (twenty-five to ninety pounds), such as retrievers, pointers, and greyhounds, that are between one and seven years old. With the possible exception of boxers, which are a high-energy breed, dogs with pushed-in faces, such as pugs and bulldogs, are not well suited to running because they may have difficulty breathing.

For safety's sake, increase from a walk to a jog gradually.

To start a running regime, gradually increase from a walk to a jog to a run over a six- to eight-week period. You can allow your dog to run off-leash if you are in a secured area (such as a sports stadium or fenced field) and your dog is well trained. Avoid hot pavements and areas with broken glass or sharp rocks. Do not push your dog beyond her limits. Rest or stop completely if your dog slows down or pants a lot. Be careful that your dog doesn't run in your path, which can cause injury to both of you. Don't feed your dog before running or for an hour after running as this may cause an upset stomach or bloat (see page 445). Don't run on very hot days. Give your dog small amounts of water during the cool-down period.

Many dogs don't mind carrying their own gear.

Hiking If you observe the following rules, hiking can be fun and safe for your dog. Start slowly if your dog isn't in good condition. Stop and rest if your dog gets tired. Carry water for the dog unless you know there is water on the trail. Train your dog to walk behind you on the trail. Let him walk off-leash only if it is permitted, he is well trained, and you are in a secured area. During warm weather, avoid hot surfaces and apply an insect repellent (talk to your veterinarian about safe products to prevent fleas, ticks, and mosquitoes from biting your dog). During cold weather, check your dog's paws for iceballs and frostbite. Always avoid areas with broken glass, sharp rocks, or burrs. For long hikes, consider equipping your dog with a backpack so that he can carry his own food, treats, water (and bowl), and first aid kit. The dog's pack should fit snugly without irritating the skin and should not weigh more than 10 to 15 percent of the dog's weight. The contents should be distributed evenly on both sides of the pack.

Retrievers and other sporting dogs are keen on swimming and fetching things from the water.

Swimming A perfect sport for humans and dogs, swimming improves stamina and is easy on the ligaments and joints. A five-minute swim gives you a workout equivalent to that gained by a thirty-minute walk. Some dogs, such as retrievers and Irish water spaniels, are natural swimmers; others have no interest in the water and should not be forced to go in. Many dogs enjoy swimming and, if they are introduced to it gently and with reassurance, take to it naturally with the traditional "doggy paddle." If your dog doesn't jump in independently but seems interested, try going into the water together, keeping the first session just a few minutes long. Praise your dog softly and stay on the dog's side so that he won't thrash and claw at you. Move forward at a slow pace, then show your dog where to get out. It is safe for dogs to swim in backyard chlorinated pools under supervision. Afterwards, bathe or rinse your dog thoroughly to remove chlorine from the coat. Remove cloth and leather collars while your dog is drying to prevent fungus from growing underneath.

Playing with Other Dogs Playing with other dogs provides a great workout and also improves a dog's social skills. The best playmates are dogs that have been well socialized with other dogs at an early age. Different breed types have differing styles of play. Sporting dogs often engage in mouth wrestling, sight hounds chase each other at high speeds, and the bull and terrier breeds are champion body slammers. The exertion and excitement of such activity may be dangerous for certain sizes and builds of dogs.

A flexible flying disk is easier on a dog's mouth than the hard kind made for human play.

When playing fetch with a stick, be sure the stick has no pointy ends that could scratch or puncture the dog's mouth.

Retrieving Some breeds are natural retrievers, but even those to whom retrieving does not come naturally can almost always learn how to fetch a toy and return it. When choosing what to throw, consider your dog's size and the textures he prefers. Rubber bumpers, tennis balls, or soft fleece toys work with most dogs. Beware of sticks that have sharp edges or pointed ends and balls that are too small and could become lodged in the dog's windpipe.

Before you go out to exercise, check your dog's equipment (replace frayed leashes and collars that are too loose or too tight) and make sure his ID tags are attached.

Carry water (dog canteens or squirt bottles are ideal), especially when exercising in warm weather or for long periods of time.

Make sure the weather is suitable for exercising your dog. Northern and snub-nosed breeds do not do well in hot, humid weather. Short-haired sighthounds cannot tolerate cold.

Choose dog-friendly surfaces like grass or dirt rather than asphalt or cement. Avoid exercising in areas with broken glass, sharp metal edges, chemical salts, thorns, and foxtails.

When taking long walks or jogs, check your dog's pads from time to time for blisters.

Disks and Frisbees Dogs love to catch moving objects. Running, leaping, and grasping a saucerlike disk floating in the air is the ultimate game for many dogs. If you want to introduce your dog to disk playing, make sure that she is in good physical shape first. Buy a disk made for human play or a nylon disk made for dogs. Try different kinds to see which ones you and your dog like best. Let your dog feel the disk in her mouth. Throw the disk about two feet at first, then gradually increase the distance. Play with the disk on grass or soft ground to prevent the injuries that can occur on hard surfaces. If you plan to play in or around water, be sure to get a disk that floats. Alex Stein and his dog, Ashley Whippet, launched the sport of canine Frisbee in 1974 at Dodger Stadium in Los Angeles. For information and event schedules for competing in canine Frisbee contests, contact the Disc Dog Quarterly (see the Organized Sports and Showing appendix).

Indoor Exercise

You don't have to cancel your dog's daily exercise routine because of inclement weather. Try some indoor exercises, such as retrieving, hide-and-seek, and running up and down the stairs. Hide a ball or a dozen pieces of kibble and watch your dog find them.

During inclement weather, try hide-and-seek or retrieving games with soft toys.

Organized Sports and Shows

Organized sports are a wonderful way for you and your dog to bond, exercise, and meet like-minded human–canine teams. Children involved in sports with their pets develop high self-esteem and confidence and learn the value of working toward a goal. Information on organized group sports can be obtained from the American Kennel Club, the United Kennel Club, and local 4-H, breed, and kennel clubs, as well as the organizations specified below (see the Organized Sports and Showing appendix for addresses).

Flyball The object of Flyball competition is for each dog on a four-dog relay team to jump over four hurdles, release a tennis ball from a Flyball box by stepping on a spring-loaded platform, retrieve the ball, and race back over the four hurdles. The team that successfully completes the relay race in the fastest time wins. Border collies perform especially well in this sport, but any dog that enjoys retrieving and jumping over hurdles can participate. For more information, contact the North American Flyball Association.

Agility Trials Dogs in agility trials negotiate complex courses—jumping hurdles, weaving through poles, ducking through tunnels, and navigating A-frames, balance beams, and seesaws—with their enthusiastic handlers running alongside and urging them on. Many breed and obedience clubs offer agility training and competition. Border collies and Shetland sheepdogs are natural competitors because they are quick and athletic, but any dog can participate. For more information, contact the United States Dog Agility Association.

Herding Tests and Trials During these events, herding breeds (see the breed descriptions beginning on page 152) demonstrate their ability to herd livestock under the direction of a handler (often the owner). Sheep, cattle, goats, or ducks are used at the trials. For more information, contact the International Sheep Dog Society or the American Herding Breed Association.

Agility training is invaluable for building confidence and burning up energy.

Herding sheep comes naturally to this Old English sheepdog.

Dogsledding and Skijoring These sports are great fun for medium to large dogs with caretakers who love the great outdoors in winter. The northern breeds (see the breed descriptions beginning on page 182) are particularly well suited for these activities, but any thick-coated, muscular dog can take part. Skijoring involves dogs pulling a person on cross-country skis, while dogsledding teams pull sleds either on runners or wheels, depending on the season and the terrain. For more information, contact the International Federation of Sleddog Sports.

Sight hounds, such as this Afghan, fly across fields in hot pursuit of mechanical lures.

Lure Coursing If you own a sight hound (see the breed descriptions beginning on page 216), you and your dog may enjoy lure coursing, an activity in which dogs sprint across a course at blinding speed after a high-speed artificial lure. The dogs are scored on speed, enthusiasm, agility, endurance, and their ability to follow a lure. For more information, contact the American Sighthound Field Association or the American Kennel Club.

Water Trials Newfoundlands and Portuguese water dogs have a long tradition of working in the water—rescuing drowning victims, setting fishermen's nets, and delivering messages from ship to ship. Water trials demonstrate the dog's enthusiasm and ability to retrieve floating or underwater objects; tow a boat (usually a rowboat); retrieve off a boat; or jump overboard, swim to a person in the water (usually the handler), and tow the person fifty feet to shore. For more information, contact the Newfoundland Club of America or the Portuguese Water Dog Club of America.

Dog Shows Taking part in dog shows can be an enjoyable activity for owners of purebred dogs. When your puppy is approximately five to six months of age, take him to a reputable breeder to find out if he has any disqualifying faults and if the breeder deems him show quality. If the puppy is up to the task, he will need show-handling classes to prepare him for the showring. Show coats demand much more care than the average pet dog coat, so you will need to learn how to groom your dog for the ring as well.

Traveling, competing, and meeting other dog owners can be lots of fun. However, it is important to make sure that the dog is enjoying the experience as much as you are. Some dogs love the extra attention they get when they are in the spotlight; others prefer to stay home and play ball in the yard. Your desire to win in the ring should come second to the desire to make your dog happy. For more information, contact the American Kennel Club, the United Kennel Club, and the national club for your dog's breed.

Facing page: A prize-winning keeshond

Bathing and Grooming

Regular grooming, which includes combing and brushing, nail trimming, and ear and teeth cleaning, will keep your dog clean, attractive, and healthy, and will deepen the trust and comfort level between the two of you. In addition, if you groom your dog regularly you are more likely to spot signs of illness in their early stages, when they are usually easiest to treat.

The sooner you begin grooming your dog, the sooner he will become comfortable with the handling and touching involved and the easier it will be. Keep sessions short at first—to about five minutes.

While working, speak softly and reassuringly to your dog. If necessary, trim one nail at a time or just handle a toe gently. Brush the teeth for only a few seconds at first, if that is all your puppy can handle. Begin bathing your puppy at fourteen weeks of age— sooner if he gets dirty. Offer treats during grooming and bathing.

Grooming tools (clockwise from top): hound glove, scissors, flea comb, chamois glove, pin brush, bristle brush, wide-toothed comb, slicker brush, rubber brush

Brushing and Combing

Most dogs should be brushed and combed in the direction in which the hair grows. All dogs should be flea combed regularly during flea season (ask your veterinarian what time of year this is in your region), and all dogs need more frequent brushing during shedding season (generally fall and spring).

Otherwise, brushing and combing needs vary depending on the dog's coat type and length.

The tools you need for grooming your dog's coat are fairly basic and inexpensive. Different coat types require different equipment, as specified in the instructions on the following pages.

During warm weather, kids can have fun bathing the family dog in the yard.

Grooming Short, Glossy Coats If your dog's coat is very short and glossy (as in boxers, Doberman pinschers, and greyhounds), brush every week or two with a rubber brush or hound glove to remove loose hair and dry skin. Follow with a spritz of coat conditioner, then "polish" with a chamois cloth if you want your dog to glisten. If you have a dog with somewhat longer short hair (such as a Labrador retriever or a rottweiler), groom every week or two with a rubber brush and then follow up with a bristle brush.

Grooming Medium-Length Coats If your dog's coat is thick and medium in length (as in golden retrievers, corgis, and New-foundlands), use a slicker brush to remove loose hairs from the fluffy undercoat. Follow with a comb-through using a wide-toothed metal comb to finish off any small knots and snarls. Pay extra attention to areas prone to matting—behind the ears, on the backs of the rear legs, and in the tail feathering. If you need to cut out a mat, be careful not to cut the dog's skin. As a precaution, hold a comb between the dog and the scissors. How often these types of dogs need to be groomed depends on the types of activities they engage in and the time of year. During shedding season (usually in fall and spring), they need to be groomed daily. During the rest of the year, a couple of times a week will suffice. They should also be groomed after such activities as hiking in the woods, swimming, and playing in dusty dog runs.

Grooming Wire Coats Wire-coated dogs (such as Airedales, wirehaired fox terriers, and wirehaired dachshunds) need to be brushed with a slicker brush, then combed a couple of times a week. Two or three times a year, take the dog to a professional groomer to have dead hair removed. If you want your terrier to resemble a show dog, you will have to find a hand-stripping specialist to pluck out the dead hairs (which will keep the texture of the dog's coat "hard"). Many pet owners have their dogs machine-clipped, which is more economical; the result is a neat, albeit softer-textured, coat.

Grooming Curly Coats Many of the curly-coated breeds (such as poodles, Portuguese water dogs, and Kerry blue terriers) shed minimally. These breeds need to be clipped at a grooming salon every six to ten weeks. In between, the curls need to be brushed out every few days to prevent matting. Use a slicker brush on the shorter-haired areas and a pin brush on long hairs. Then comb the dog with a wide-toothed metal comb to make sure all snarls are gone.

Grooming Long Coats If you have a long-haired breed (such as a Lhasa apso, Tibetan terrier, Pomeranian, or Afghan hound), use a slicker brush to get out snarls, mats, and loose hairs. Divide the coat into small sections and brush from the skin out to the end of the hair. Next, go over the coat with a wide-toothed metal comb to get out any small snarls you may have missed with the brush. You may need to cut some hair under the tail region, between the paw pads, and around the eyes. Finish off long silky coats with a bristle brush; use a pin brush for dogs with puffier coats (such as Pomeranians). Dogs with long hair need to be brushed out every day or two. When grooming the thicker-coated longhaired breeds, make sure to thoroughly brush out the undercoat, not just the topcoat, or matting will result. If the dog has more than a few mats, take him to a professional groomer who will be able to determine if the mats can be broken apart or have to be cut out. Since the untangling of knots and mats is painful to the dog, the groomer may suggest shaving him down to the skin and allowing the hair to grow anew.

Dogs come in a multitude of coat types. Top row, from left: The Labrador retriever has a short, glossy coat; this dachshund is wire-haired; the Pomeranian has a long coat. Bottom row, from left: The Newfoundland has a medium-length coat; the poodle's curly coat is one of its hallmarks.

Flea Combing Your Dog

If your dog goes outside during flea season (check with your local veterinarian to find out when this is in your area) or plays with other dogs, she is at risk for picking up fleas and should be combed with a flea comb (a special narrow-toothed comb designed to pick up live fleas and flea debris). When flea combing your dog, pay particular attention to the areas around the ears, armpits, and base of the tail, as these are the areas most likely to become infested. The presence of flea debris, black pepper-like flecks that bleed red or orange when placed on a wet paper towel, indicates a problem needing treatment (speak to your veterinarian about options). If you catch live fleas in the teeth of the comb, dispose of them by dipping the comb in a jar of soapy water or by crushing the fleas between the comb and a hard surface. Fleas are very hardy parasites with tremendous jumping abilities, so dispatch them immediately or they will most certainly invade your home (see page 439 for more about fleas).

Bathing

Generally speaking, there is no limit to the frequency with which a dog can be bathed, since the oils come back into the hair and skin within twenty-four hours. However, too frequent bathing or the use of harsh or improper shampoos will dry the skin and cause flaking and itching. A bath every month or two is usually adequate unless the dog has a tendency to get dirty more often.

During the bath, stroke and reassure your dog frequently. Check for infections, parasites, or lumps by examining the dog's ears, eyes, and mouth, in between her paws, and all over her skin. If your dog is frightened by running water, use a spray hose or pour water from nonbreakable containers prepared ahead of time instead. Give her small treats during the bath.

- Brush your dog. Remove loose hairs and untangle mats. Mats that are not combed out before bathing are impossible to comb out afterward and must be cut out.
- Place cotton balls in the dog's ears to prevent soap and water from getting inside. If desired, place a mild ophthalmic ointment in her eyes.
- If using a tub, place a rubber mat in it to prevent slipping.
- If indoors, close the door to the room so the dog cannot run out.
- Lift the dog into the tub or basin, or place a platform near the tub so the dog can step in by herself.
- Wet the coat thoroughly with a soft spray hose or garden hose (if outside), or by pouring tap water from a cup or bucket onto the dog. Do not fill the tub.
- Lather the dog's body with shampoo. Wash the face with a soft cloth.
- Rinse thoroughly; do not let soapy water seep into the eyes.
- Squeeze excess water from the coat and towel dry.
- Remove cotton balls from the ears.
- Let the dog air-dry in a warm room or use a hair dryer set on warm. Be careful not to burn the skin or coat. Do not use a dryer if it frightens the dog.
- Brush the dog while drying. This is especially important with longhaired breeds.

Bathing can be an enjoyable and relaxing time, especially if the dog is acclimated to the process during puppyhood.

Nail Trimming

Begin trimming your dog's nails when he is ten to twelve weeks of age. The nails should be trimmed when they grow long enough to touch the ground, which can range from once a week to once a month, depending on how much exercise the dog gets (running around wears down the nails), how slowly or quickly the dog's nails happen to grow, and the surfaces on which the dog walks (some dogs that spend a lot of time on pavement need to have only their dewclaws trimmed). If present, the dewclaws (high up on the inside of the front and back paws) need to be trimmed more frequently than the other nails because they do not touch the ground and so do not get worn down. If left untrimmed, dogs' nails can get caught in carpeting, grow into the footpad, or cause the dog to stand improperly, which can lead to osteoarthritis.

The two types of dog nail clippers—guillotine clippers and standard scissors-style clippers—both work well. If you feel unsure about trimming your dog's nails, ask your vet or groomer to demonstrate the correct procedure during your next visit. As with all grooming, the earlier you start the easier it will be. If your dog resists nail clipping despite your conscientious efforts to acclimate him to the procedure, consider purchasing electric nail grinders, which are more expensive than clippers but may be more tolerable for your dog (though some dogs are upset by the noise or vibration), or have the nails clipped by your veterinarian or professional groomer.

Trim your dog's nails when he is tired. Use a small room with the door shut (so the dog can't make a quick escape). If possible, have someone help you hold the dog. Begin by talking softly to your dog and holding one paw. You may offer a treat or chew toy when holding the paw. When the dog is comfortable with a paw being held, trim one or more nails a day following the instructions in the captions on page 379 until the dog will allow you to trim all the nails in one sitting.

Nail trimming tools (left to right): grinder, standard clipper, styptic powder, guillotine clipper

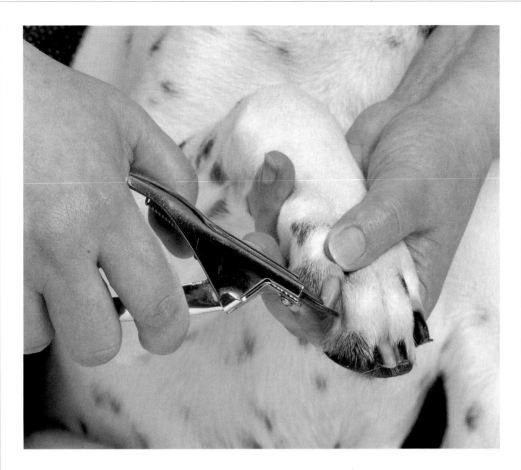

If your dog's nails grow too long, the blood vessels will grow as well, in which case extra care must be taken not to cause bleeding by cutting the nails too short. If a nail starts to bleed, which means you clipped through the quick, put styptic powder (an astringent) on the nail tip or apply direct pressure with a tissue. If bleeding continues for more than a couple of minutes, alert your veterinarian—your dog may have a clotting disorder. For dogs with such conditions, it is safest to have the nails trimmed at the veterinarian's office.

One at a time, clip the nails with the clipper in front of the pink area, or quick, which contains nerves and blood vessels. If the nail is too dark and you cannot see the pink area, shine a penlight through the nail to see where the quick begins. Otherwise, just trim the tip of the nail. Until you gain experience, clip small bits at a time, clipping the same nail a few times if necessary.

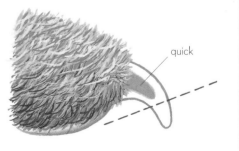

quick

Cleaning the Eye Area

Dampen a cotton ball with water and gently wipe any discharge from the eye area (wipe outward from the corner of the eye). Keeping the area around the eye clean helps prevent the sensitive skin there from getting irritated. Pay attention to the amount and consistency of discharge—excessive or thick discharge can be a sign of disease (see page 433).

Wiping discharge from the eye area helps to prevent irritation and infection.

Checking Between the Toes

If your dog is limping or chewing at her feet, check between the toes for any inflammation and for splinters or other foreign bodies that need to be removed.

If you routinely walk your dog in a tick-infested area, you may need to check daily between the pads for ticks.

Cleaning the Ears

Dogs with long, pendulous ears, such as Irish setters, cocker spaniels, and basset hounds, seem to be more prone to ear infections than dogs with short, erect ears. Signs of infection include head shaking, an unpleasant odor coming from the ears, and redness in the ears. Moisture and poor ventilation in the ear (caused by the L shape of the ear canal), hypothyroidism, and allergies can all cause ear infections. Some dogs inherit a tendency to get ear infections. Inspect your dog's ears once a week. If they look clean, and there is no visible dirt or noticeable odors, leave them alone. If you suspect an ear infection, see the veterinarian right away.

When cleaning your dog's ears, wipe only the exterior portion; do not insert anything into the ear canal.

After a dog romps through the woods, paws should be checked for ticks, burrs, and foxtails.

To clean visible dirt out of healthy ears, soak a cotton ball in baby oil or hydrogen peroxide, lift the earflap, and gently wipe the area that is visible. It can be helpful to place the cotton on the end of your index finger. Don't insert anything into your dog's ear canal. Cotton-tipped swabs and other implements can irritate the canal and pack debris against the eardrum. If your dog is prone to ear infections or swims a lot, your veterinarian can provide products that clean and dry the ear canal and make the canal environment inhospitable to bacteria and yeast. Ask your veterinarian to demonstrate the correct method for using these products. Consult with your veterinarian before plucking any hairs from your dog's ears.

Brushing your dog's teeth may take getting used to. The younger the dog is when you start, the better.

Brushing Teeth

It is important to keep your dog's teeth clean to avoid cavities, receding gums, periodontal disease, tooth loss, and bacterial infections that weaken the immune system, heart, liver, and kidneys. Although the formation of some plaque and tartar can be slowed down by feeding your dog hard, dry food and giving him toxin-free rawhide, nylon, and rubber toys to chew on, it is still necessary to brush your dog's teeth, ideally every day. Make toothbrushing a quick and pleasant experience.

To begin to accustom your dog to regular home dental care, massage the dog's lips with your finger in a circular motion for thirty to sixty seconds once or twice a day for a few weeks. Next massage the dog's teeth and gums in a circular motion for thirty to sixty seconds once or twice a day for a few weeks. Once the dog is comfortable with lip and gum massage, start regular brushing.

Use a human toothbrush with soft, round-tipped bristles that fits into the dog's mouth easily, a special dog toothbrush, or soft gauze wrapped around your finger. Buy a specially formulated canine toothpaste (available at pet stores) or make a paste of baking soda and water. Some canine toothpastes contain fluoride or pyrophosphate, which inhibit tartar formation and retard cavity formation. Do not use fluoride with dogs under six months of age because it can interfere with enamel formation on the teeth. Avoid human toothpaste as it may upset the dog's stomach.

Working in one area of the mouth at a time, and lifting up your dog's lip as necessary, place the brush or gauze-wrapped finger at a 45-degree angle to the teeth and gum line, and clean the teeth and the gums with small circular motions. Finish each tooth with a downward stroke from the gum to the end of the tooth to remove plaque and food from between the teeth. Repeat until all of the teeth have been cleaned. The side of the teeth next to the cheek is easier to clean and usually has the most plaque and tartar. Your dog may resist having her mouth opened to brush the inner surfaces; don't fight it. Usually very little tartar accumulates on the inner surfaces and, if need be, the vet can remove it during a professional cleaning.

Puppies have short attention spans. They respond best to short, upbeat training sessions.

Training

The greatest gift you can give your dog is early socialization and training. Your dog learns his place in the "pack" and what kind of behavior is expected of him both in private and in public, and as a result the two of you can build a strong bond based on trust and kindness. Unfortunately, many people do not take training seriously and then abandon their dogs when their poor behavior proves overwhelming.

If your new dog is a puppy under sixteen weeks of age, his attention span and retention capacity will be short and bladder control will be lacking. However, a puppy is as close to a blank slate as you can get, and there is a lot of work that can and should be done early, starting at eight weeks of age (or as soon as your puppy starts living in your home). See Guidelines for Early Training, below. Some formal training classes will not take dogs until they reach four to six months of age; sign up for classes well in advance since they often fill quickly.

An older dog comes with some learning. He may be housebroken, finished with the teething and puppy mouthing stage, and able to stay alone quietly for the average workday. He may also have fears and learned reactions that do not make sense to you, his new owner. Contrary to a popular misconception, it is never too late to train a dog. It may be a challenge and take a little time, but all problems except the most severe can be remolded into acceptable behaviors.

While most dogs and their owners can learn what they need to know in group classes, in some cases it's necessary to supplement classes with private training. Dog owners who could best be helped by a private trainer include those whose dogs have household-based behavior problems, those whose dogs are aggressive with or over-stimulated by other dogs or people, and those whose schedules are too chaotic to commit to one or two months of weekly classes. See Finding a Trainer on page 403.

Most importantly, training for all dogs must be ongoing. Just as the dominant dog in a pack must reassert its authority on a regular basis to keep the social order intact, you must continually reinforce the skills learned in obedience classes. Agility classes and dog sports (see page 368) also help to reinforce the bond between owner and dog.

Guidelines for Early Training

It's never too early to begin laying the groundwork for training. The following tips will help you to make training an enjoyable, productive part of your relationship with your dog. Instructions for basic commands begin on page 386.

For consistency, which is crucial in dog training, gather all household members together and agree on a list of commands the dog will learn. Use short, clear commands, and give them with a friendly expression.

Always keep the training fun, relaxed, and positive, offering your dog lots of enthusiastic encouragement, including food treats, petting, and verbal praise. Begin teaching new commands in a quiet, comfortable environment where the dog cannot be easily distracted. Use your dog's name to get her attention and work to improve eye contact (see page 386).

Motivate your dog to learn by conducting short training sessions before meals (but after the dog has eliminated and been exercised). She will work harder for food treats when she is hungry and not distracted by the need to eliminate or blow off steam. To keep the dog from getting bored, limit the length of the training sessions (several three- to ten-minute sessions a day is ideal) and end with a few minutes of play.

Rather than pushing your dog into position, use positive methods that lure the dog into the correct position (such methods are shown on the following pages). As soon as a command is achieved, reward the dog with a smile, warm praise, and the food treat or favorite toy that has served as a lure. Over time, the movement of the hand that held the lure becomes a hand signal, and the reward can be delayed and randomized—saved for only the quickest responses or for exercises accomplished in very distracting circumstances.

Work commands into all interactions with your dog: have her sit-stay during food preparation or elevator trips, shake paw to wipe off muddy feet, down-stay during the family's dinner, and come when it's time to put on the leash to go out for a walk.

If your dog does not respond to a command, do not repeat the command over and over, which can be counterproductive and confusing. Instead, try to show the dog what you want by luring her into position.

It is said that the majority of dogs think their name is "No" because their owners use this word so often when interacting with them. When your dog truly misbehaves, immediately use a stern "no" or disruptive noise like "ech," "phooey," or "uh-uh." But remember, dogs—like humans—usually respond better to praise and rewards than they do to punishment. Never hit your dog or one day your dog just might hit back—with her teeth.

How to Become a Benevolent Leader

As a pack animal, your dog is prepared to live in a structured society in which each member holds a certain position. If human members of the dog's family do not demonstrate leadership, the dog will take over the role. Such a dog may become aggressive if he feels his position is being challenged. To avoid this potentially dangerous situation, become a benevolent leader by enforcing the following rules.

Leaders control space. Do not step over the dog lying in the doorway. Tell him to get up and out of your way. Do not let the dog dash out of the door ahead of you. Command him to sit-stay while you walk through first, then call him to follow.

Leaders eat first and eat as much as they want. Feed the dog after the humans in the household have finished their meals. Control his eagerness by giving the sit-stay command while you are preparing his meal. When the meal is ready, make the dog wait until you verbally release him before allowing him to dive into the food bowl. During puppyhood, interrupt the dog's meal occasionally by asking him to move aside while you add something else to the bowl. For safety's sake, do not try this with a newly acquired adult dog.

Leaders control valuable property. If the dog is allowed to sit on furniture, tell him to get off several times a week for no particular reason. If compliance isn't immediate, or if the dog stiffens or growls in response, take away all furniture privileges for at least thirty days. Outfit a grouchy dog who has lost furniture privileges with a ten-foot-long, ¼-inch-wide lightweight nylon house lead so that you can remove him from sofas and beds without having to reach for the collar, an action that might provoke aggression.

Leaders control play and set the rules. Just because a dog drops a soggy tennis ball in your lap and swats you with a big hairy paw does not mean that you should engage in a game of fetch. If you feel like playing at that moment, make sure the dog does something for you before you do something for him. Ask him to sit-stay while you throw the ball, then verbally release him to fetch it. Insist that the dog return the ball to your hand. If he does not, declare the game over and ignore him. If you want to play tug-of-war with the dog, take the tug toy off the shelf and call the dog to play. Whenever you feel like it, tell the dog to release the toy by using whatever command you used in training (such as "out," "drop it," or "off"). If you do not get immediate compliance, take the toy from the dog and put it away. If the dog clamps down on the toy or stares at you while growling (not to be confused with the play vocalization "grrring" that goes on when tugging), verbally express your disgust with this behavior, leave the room, and shun the dog for the next five to fifteen minutes, ignoring any attention-seeking behavior. When the dog leaves the tug toy, put it away. Before attempting the next bout of tug-of-war, teach the dog how to release the toy on command by using the trading-up method described in Take It/Leave It/Drop It on page 392. If a dog cannot play tug-of-war by the rules, then it should not be played at all.

Leaders are obeyed without question. Build your dog's obedience repertoire and practice daily so she learns to obey every command without challenge. Practice long down-stays several times a week. Work up to a thirty-

Play tug-of-war only with dogs that play by your rules; dogs must drop the tug object on command.

minute down-stay on a comfortable surface like carpeting or a pet bed. Put her through repetitions of push-ups by having her sit, then lie down, then sit up, then lie down in quick succession. This type of exercise will enable the dog to excel in obedience, and your leadership will prevail unchallenged.

Basic Commands

The following commands should be taught in a gradual progression. Once your dog grasps the first concept, go ahead and introduce the next one. In each training session take time to review previous training sessions. Keep training sessions short and break them up with playtime.

Establishing Eye Contact Eye contact is a crucial part of training. A dog who frequently checks in by looking at her handler is a dog most apt to be attentive to commands. Some breeds, like Border collies and golden retrievers, are very comfortable with eye contact; other breeds, most notably chow chows, are not. However, all dogs can learn eye contact on command.

To teach eye contact, stand facing the dog. Hold a tasty tidbit between your thumb and middle finger and draw a straight line from the dog's nose to the outside corner of your eye, pointing to your eye with your forefinger. As the dog's gaze travels up to meet yours, state the command "watch me." Lock eyes for a few seconds and then bring the treat back to the dog's nose and let the dog gobble it up. After several repetitions, the movement of pointing up toward your eye paired with the verbal command will be all that is needed to get the desired behavior. This command is invaluable when you need to keep your pet's focus on you and the job at hand, as when teaching other commands.

Above and right: Eye contact is taught by drawing a treat from the dog's nose up to the outer corner of your eye while saying "watch me."

Sit and Sit-Stay For most dog owners, teaching the sit command is the first foray into obedience training. Teaching the dog to stay in that position is the next step. The well-behaved dog that sit-stays in elevators, on street corners, and at check-out counters is a joy to take out in public. The one that sit-stays while dinner is being prepared and while the leash is being attached is a pleasure to live with.

Teach your dog to sit by luring him into position. Stand facing the dog with a food lure between your thumb and forefinger. Hold the lure an inch from your dog's nose and then slowly move it back over his nose toward the skull. The dog is likely to follow the treat by raising his chin and tipping his

Lure a dog into a sit by holding a treat in front of her nose, then up and slightly over her head.

Once the dog is sitting, say "stay" and flash a flat palm in front of her eyes to serve as the stay hand signal.

head back, which will cause him to tuck into a sit. If the treat is held up too high, the dog may jump up to get it. The treat may be held close enough for the dog to nibble on it while it is moved up and back. If, instead of sitting, the dog is scooting backward to follow the treat, set up the exercise in a corner so that the dog will be compelled to sit. Repeat this exercise a few times before adding the sit command at the beginning of the exercise, so the dog will be able to figure out what sit means and can succeed.

Once you are sure the dog understands what sit means, add stay to the sit command. First, give the sit command. When the dog's rear end touches the floor, release the treat so that he can chew and swallow it, flash a flat, open hand, with your palm facing the dog and a few inches from him at eye level (the hand signal for stay), and say "stay." Praise the dog while he is holding the stay, and after a few seconds, say "okay" to release the dog. If the dog gets up during the stay, just say "no" and command him—or lure him if necessary—to sit again. If the dog does not get up when you say "okay," clap your hands or call him to you to entice him to get up. Soon the dog will understand that "okay" means that his work is finished until he hears the next command.

Since dogs do not generalize, you will initially need to teach the sit-stay command anew in different situations. Vary locations, distractions, lengths of time, and your positions in relation to him.

If the dog loses focus while holding a sit-stay, get his attention back by giving the eye contact command. As with all training, timing is important. Utter a warning noise (such as "ech" or "phooey") when you think the dog is about to break position, not after the dog is up and six steps away.

Down and Down-Stay Lying down is a comfortable position for many dogs and one that most dogs can hold considerably longer than a sit. Practice down and down-stay on a surface that is comfortable for the dog. The best place to start training a dog to lie down on command is in a quiet carpeted room in your home where the dog feels relaxed and comfortable. Thin breeds with little hair and body fat such as greyhounds, whippets, and miniature pinschers will resist lying down on cold, hard surfaces or wet grass, and if you work on surfaces like these, training will be nearly impossible.

Down is a very subordinate posture, and both dominant and timid canines may initially have problems with this command. First, ask your dog to sit, then kneel next to the dog at her right side. Lightly rest your left hand on her back at the shoulders. Do not apply pressure. With a treat between the thumb and forefinger of your right hand, starting at the dog's nose level, slowly draw the treat straight down to the floor and then straight away from the dog (an L-shaped movement). The dog should follow the treat with his nose, lowering her head to the ground and then creeping forward to follow the food into the down position. As the chest and elbows hit the floor say "down," release the treat, and say "stay" while flashing the stay hand signal.

If the dog stands up to follow the treat, it's likely that either your left hand was not resting on the dog's shoulders or the lure was not drawn into a sharp right angle but rather made a slanted line to the ground. For some dogs, drawing a reverse L—with the bottom section drawn between the front feet toward the belly instead of away from the dog—works better. As the treat approaches, the dog will bunch up her front end, kick back her rear legs, and collapse into the down position. This is particularly effective with smaller, long-backed breeds. Once your dog has learned the down-stay command, practice building up the length of the stay as well as steadiness around distractions and distance from the handler.

The down-stay command can be quite useful in problem solving. Begging at the

As the dog nibbles a treat while in a sitting position, draw the tidbit straight down to the ground and away from the dog to lure him into a down position. Finish with a stay command.

table can be prevented by putting the dog on a long down-stay on her bed in a corner of the dining room. You can benignly teach a pushy dog who's boss by using thirty-minute down-stays three to five times a week as part of a leadership program. Commanding a barking dog to down-stay generally silences the dog, since it is uncomfortable for a dog to vocalize from the down position. If you have gone to the trouble of teaching your dog a fast down-stay from a distance, it just may save the dog's life one day as you prevent her from running head-on into trouble.

Come All dogs need to be taught to come to their owners when called. In order to get a swift, attentive recall, make sure that what follows the come command is not displeasing to the dog. What is the impetus to come when called if the result is being given a pill, having your nails trimmed, or having your playtime ended? If you need to do something the dog may perceive as negative, retrieve him without using your recall command so that negative associations are not established.

Start recall training outdoors with the dog on a six-foot leash. As the dog gets distracted by a smell or noise, say "come" and move swiftly backward, away from the dog. As you move away, gesture to the dog by extending your arm out to the side and then drawing your hand in toward your chest. This is the hand signal for come. As the dog runs toward you, have a treat at his nose level as a target for his approach. As the dog arrives to within arm's length, say "sit" while raising the treat above his nose and slightly back over the head. When the dog sits, say "stay" while issuing the hand signal, grab the collar with the other hand, and then release the treat. The collar grab is important to practice because many dogs dash away when their caretakers reach for them. In an emergency, this could be a costly mistake.

When the dog is easy to handle on a six-foot leash, progress to a long line or retractable leash and a wide-open space, such as a ball field, playground, or large backyard. Increase the distractions. Will he come if he spies picnickers, ballplayers, or squirrels? Will he come when busy playing with other dogs?

If the answer to these questions is yes, then you may be ready to try off-leash recalls in fenced-in areas. If the answer is no, as the handler you will need to find ways to be more enticing and rewarding than the distractions—better treats, more animation, whatever works for the two of you. If this does not work for you, progress to using lighter and lighter leashes until the dog is unaware of the handler's control yet there is still a safety mechanism to help him be successful if necessary.

A no-questions-asked recall could one day save your dog's life. Perfecting this command is worth every minute of practice it takes.

When teaching controlled walking, execute a quick about-turn any time the dog pulls ahead enough to jerk your arm.

Controlled Walking Is there anything more pleasant on a warm, sunny day than a stroll through the park with your dog? Some dog owners would find a root canal more pleasant because their dogs are not trained to walk nicely on a leash. The urge to pull out ahead or lag behind is common, particularly in young, untrained dogs. All dogs must be taught acceptable street manners. Most people don't need their dog to learn a

precision heel, in which the dog's right ear lines up with the outer seam of the walker's left pant leg. It is enough for the dog to take as much leash as you care to give without pulling it taut. A loose leash is the goal.

Start teaching controlled walking in a hallway, basement, or garage with the dog on a six-foot leash. You can train the dog to walk on your left side, which is the traditional position, or on your right, whichever suits you best. Be sure to be consistent and to arrange your equipment correctly for the side you have chosen.

Begin walking at a brisk pace to maintain the dog's interest. Praise the dog when she is in the appropriate place; if she begins to build up steam, warn her, using "easy" or "ech," before she hits the end of the leash. If the dog pulls out ahead enough to jerk your arm, execute an about-face (U-turn) while leaning into the leash. Now, for at least the moment, you have taken the lead. As the dog returns to a position near your side, praise her. If she is looking at you, reward

Introduce the recall (come) when the dog is on a leash. Move backwards away from the dog while calling "come" and command him to sit within arm's reach. Reward the dog after you have grabbed his collar.

her with a treat. Every time the dog pulls out ahead, respond with a sharp about-face. After approximately four to six such turns, the dog may stop and stare at you as though she is wondering if you have lost your mind. Believe it or not, this is your goal. In the dog's mind, you are no longer predictable and therefore bear watching.

From time to time, hold a treat by your side at the dog's nose level. When the dog checks in, notices the treat, and returns to heel position to retrieve it, verbally praise the dog and reward her. The dog will soon recognize the area by your side as the site of wonderful rewards and will want to spend more time there.

Work your way up to busier streets and places where kids and other dogs congregate. When you have leash control around these distractions, that pleasant stroll in the park will be yours.

Take It/Leave It/Drop It Dogs don't have opposable thumbs, so they tend to explore their world by putting everything in their mouths. To avoid having to reach into your dog's mouth and pull objects out, put his mouth on command by teaching take it, leave it, and drop it. Take it gives the dog permission to put something in his mouth. Leave it means look away, and denies the dog permission to put something in his mouth. Drop it orders the dog to spit out whatever is in his mouth. When teaching these commands, it is important to keep in mind how the dog perceives what is happening. Teaching these commands improperly can inadvertently make your dog feel that he needs to protect his possessions from you, which can lead to aggression problems.

Take it is one of the easiest commands to teach. Put the dog in a sit-stay, present the

dog with something he wants, and say "take it." Smile, praise the dog, and give him the object. This works with toys, treats, food bowls, and chewies.

If your dog leaps toward the item and bears down hard on your fingers in the process, teach a wait command, which will

"Leave it" is an important command for a dog to understand and obey when getting ready to grab an inappropriate, unsafe, or unsanitary object.

between your thumb and forefinger, look into the dog's eyes, and say "wait." If the dog moves his head back, reward him by issuing the take it command and releasing the treat. If the dog moves forward to try to snatch the treat, cover it with your fist and say in a firm, no-nonsense voice, "no, wait." Repeat these steps until the desired behavior is achieved.

When you say "leave it" (some people prefer the command "off"), the dog is expected to look away from whatever he is focusing on. This command is useful when you are passing any distraction that may provoke an undesired reaction in the dog, such as garbage, a barking dog, or running children. By commanding a dog to leave it, you tell him that he will not get to have that item but that you will provide something better for obeying the command.

To train your dog to respond to the leave it command, place an item in the middle of a large room. Select an item that is never given to the dog but is safe for him to have if you don't manage to get it back from him. A three-day-old bagel is a good choice. After placing the item on the floor, put the dog on a leash and bring him into the room. As the dog dives for the object, say "leave it" as you snap the leash and move away from the object. At the exact moment the dog looks away from the object, praise and reward him with something better than what he just passed up. Repeat this step until the dog locks eyes with you immediately after the command is issued. Practice both indoors and outdoors so the dog will understand that no matter where he is, no matter whom he is with, leave it always means look away.

Drop it is one of the more difficult commands for dogs to learn because they often already understand it to mean that someone is going to swoop down and take away a

help him control his excitement. A dog that understands the wait command will move his head a few inches away from the desired object until directed to take it. To teach wait, command the dog to sit-stay, hold the treat

valued possession. In such cases the dog's response is to swallow quickly, protect aggressively, or head in the opposite direction and thus instigate a game of keep-away.

If your dog has no negative associations with the command, teach drop it by presenting him with a twelve-inch rawhide retriever stick and saying "take it." Let the dog chew on one end while you hold the other. After thirty to sixty seconds, say "drop it" and take it out of the dog's mouth. If the dog bears down on the stick, use the stick as a lever to open his mouth. If he withdraws from the stick, praise him verbally and ask him to take it again. After the third repetition, allow the dog to have the retriever stick indefinitely. The goal is to build up an association in the dog's mind that when he complies, he is rewarded with the item. Too many repetitions will frustrate the dog. Once you no longer need the stick to act as a lever to pry open a resistant mouth, you can use other toys and treats.

To teach the drop it command to a suspicious dog that already has a tendency to clamp down on goodies when he hears "drop it," make a list, in order of preference, of all the objects the dog holds dear and practice drop it by trading up the list. For example, if the dog's preferences are, in ascending order, vinyl squeakies, tennis balls, and rawhide in the top position, then use these items to trade up. Give the dog a squeaky, command him to drop it, and bring out a tennis ball. As the dog drops the toy to grab for the tennis

ball, say "good, drop it" and reward him with the ball. Do the same with the rawhide. This method is safe, fair, and builds up trust. If the right associations are made in the dog's mind, when the dog does seize something dangerous, such as a chicken bone off the street or out of the garbage, he will comply with the drop it command because he knows something better will follow.

"Drop it" is taught by returning the dropped object to the dog after she releases it or by replacing it with a more desirable object.

Shake is a simple trick that almost any dog can learn quickly.

Teaching Tricks It's not necessary to teach a dog tricks, but it can be a lot of fun. Start out with tricks that suit your dog's physical attributes. Square-bodied dogs, like most terriers, are terrific at sitting up. Poodles and bichons dance circles around most other breeds—on their hindlegs, no less. Most scent hounds are natural winners at the canine shell game (hide a treat under one of three paper cups, shuffle them, and have the dog paw the cup that has the treat beneath it). Retrievers can conquer roll over in no time flat.

Training your dog to do tricks is no different from training her to respond to obedience commands: lure the dog into position and reward the best effort. When teaching a complex trick, break it down into several parts. Teach them separately and then link them together. It can be helpful to start teaching the last parts of the trick first, so that the dog works toward the parts with which she is most familiar.

Shake paw is an easy trick to teach. First, put the dog in a sit-stay facing you. Hold a treat in a closed fist, palm up, several inches off the ground. The dog will start nuzzling and licking at your fist—keep it closed. When the dog paws at your fist, open your hand to release the treat. Repeat this exercise, saying "shake paw," until the dog responds to the verbal command by immediately pawing your hand. The next step is to extend your closed fist without a treat and give the command. If the dog complies, reward her from your pocket or other hand. Finally, extend a flat hand, palm up, issue the command, and reward compliance. Your dog has just learned her first trick!

Bringing a Baby Home

While many dogs can adjust to a new baby without much of a fuss, all dogs need to be prepared well in advance of the new arrival. The following guidelines should help ease the transition. If you are concerned that there will be a problem, do not hesitate to consult with a professional trainer or behaviorist.

- Make sure that the dog responds to basic obedience commands. If she has gotten rusty, begin a refresher course. Sit, down, come, heel, and no jumping are essential.
- Play a cassette recording of babies crying while the dog is eating dinner or engaged in a favorite activity to help her develop positive associations with baby sounds. Start out at a low volume and gradually increase to a real-life noise level as the dog becomes comfortable with it.

Socialization to infants and young children should be continued throughout a dog's lifetime in preparation for the day a new baby may join the household.

- Put baby powder or baby lotion on your hands and then take the dog for a walk or play a game with her, so that she connects baby smells to pleasant times.
- Set up the nursery a month or two in advance in order to give the dog time to get used to it.
- Make any necessary changes in exercise or feeding schedules several weeks before the baby is due so that the dog will be comfortable with the new changes before the big event happens.
- Walk around the house with a doll or stuffed toy in a front-of-the-body baby carrier or in a blanket. Coo to it the way you would to a real baby. If the dog jumps up to see what the fuss is all about, correct her, then praise or reward her for behaving properly (sitting or lying down on command).
- On the big day, enter the house without the baby and greet the dog. Once the dog has settled down and you are seated, have someone else bring in the baby and give the baby to you. Let the dog come and sniff the baby. If you are unsure how the dog will react, put her on a leash. Talk to the dog softly and praise and reward her for behaving properly.
- Help the dog establish positive associations with the baby by offering the dog a special treat, such as a hollow rubber ball stuffed with peanut butter or cream cheese, to chew as you feed the baby nearby.
- Make sure the dog's needs continue to be met and that she gets enough exercise.

Solving Behavior Problems

Your new dog won't stop chewing on furniture. She barks day and night. She urinates in the house. What do you do? This section will help you recognize the most common behavior problems and learn how to solve them. The problems described here are divided into two groups: those that you can probably solve on your own and those that will require the help of a specialist. Start working on solving a behavior problem as soon as it becomes apparent. Do not hope that your dog will grow out of it—or that it will simply go away. Your dog is trying to tell you something with her behavior. It is important to listen and respond.

Common Causes of Behavior Problems

The first step in solving a problem is identifying its cause. Canine behavior problems usually arise from one or more of the following causes: a medical condition, genetic predisposition, improper socialization, pack separation or dominance issues, or mental and physical deprivation.

Medical Condition Always check with your veterinarian if there is a change in your dog's behavior. A friendly dog may become snappish if he doesn't feel well or is in pain because of an injury.

Genetic Predisposition Many breeds are still genetically linked to their working past, and this drive and desire to work must be satisfied. For example, a Border collie or Jack Russell terrier that is left home alone all day without a job to do may become destructive or bark constantly.

Improper Socialization A dog that was not well socialized—exposed to various noises, people of all sizes and colors, and other animals—as a puppy or is not obedience trained is more likely to develop behavior problems.

Pack Separation and Dominance Issues Dogs are social animals that feel secure when they know their place in the hierarchy of the pack or the family. Dogs may try to challenge family members for dominance. When left home alone, a dog may act out because of discomfort at being separated from the family pack.

Mental and Physical Deprivation Dogs that sit home all day without mental stimulation and physical activity tend to develop behavior problems. Exercise appropriate to a dog's age and breed type and a variety of toys (including food-dispensing items) can help avert destructive tendencies that stem from boredom.

Common Behavior Problems

Most canine activities that we view as problems are actually normal dog behaviors done in the wrong place or at the wrong time. Elimination is necessary, just not in the house, please. Barking and digging are

Shoes are common victims of puppy teething indiscretions.

both common canine activities that need to be channeled to an appropriate place and time. It is the pet owner's job to teach the dog where and when certain behaviors are acceptable. Normal dog behavior and the instincts that drive it are discussed in Understanding Your Dog, beginning on page 341.

House Soiling If your dog is urinating in inappropriate places in the house and you are giving him enough opportunities to go outside, consult with a veterinarian. Inappropriate urination can indicate a medical problem, such as a bladder infection, diabetes, kidney disease, or incontinence. The veterinarian may suggest a physical exam, blood tests, urinalysis, X rays, or an ultrasound exam. Some medications can increase a dog's thirst and result in accidents if the dog is kept on his usual schedule.

If you are not able to take your dog outside as often as the dog needs to go, consider either asking a neighbor to help you or hiring a dog-walking service.

If your dog has urinated in an inappropriate place, clean the area, then spray it with an odor neutralizer designed for this purpose. Otherwise, the scent remains detectable to the dog, and he may be inspired to urinate in that spot again.

Once you are aware that your dog is having trouble with inappropriate urination, restrict him to a small area, such as a dog crate or the kitchen, until the problem is solved.

Improper urination can also be a sign of submission (see page 346), as some submissive dogs will urinate when greeted. Such dogs do better if you greet them quietly, down at their level—without eye contact. Or, ignore the dog when you first enter the house and wait until he settles down to greet him.

Male dogs will lift their legs and urinate on vertical objects to mark their territory. If this is done in inappropriate areas, such as indoors, neutering may solve the problem. However, if this is a long-standing problem, the dog may need additional training to curb the problem.

Always see a veterinarian if your dog is defecating inappropriately despite having enough opportunities to do so in the proper place. Inappropriate defecation can indicate a medical problem, such as intestinal parasites, colitis, tumors, or, in old dogs, an enlarged prostate. Your veterinarian may recommend blood tests, urinalysis, X rays, ultrasound, endoscopy, or fecal exams and cultures.

If there is no medical problem, the solution may be as simple as changing the dog's food (your veterinarian may recommend a low-residue or more efficiently digested dog food), giving the dog a stool softener, or changing the time at which you feed your dog. Some dogs need to defecate immediately after eating—this is called the gastro-colic reflex—so they must be fed only when someone is home to take them out afterward.

Excessive Barking Dogs bark for many reasons, such as to protect their property, to communicate with neighbor dogs, to relieve boredom, and to play. Some breeds, such as terriers and scent hounds, have a greater tendency than other dogs to bark and

A dog that barks excessively can create hostility among neighbors.

howl. Barking can be useful at times, alerting you to the arrival of a visitor or to the presence of smoke or fire. Excessive barking can become a serious problem, especially if it is bothersome to neighbors.

Many dogs become overstimulated by wildlife, neighborhood kids, and other dogs they see, hear, or smell through a backyard fence or outside the windows. If your dog is barking because she is left alone in a yard all day, keep her inside the house. When leaving a dog alone indoors, create a calm, restful environment by drawing the curtains, turning off the lights, and playing relaxing music or the television at moderate volume to mask other noises.

A humane and effective way to silence a dog that barks too much is to fit the dog with a training collar that releases a burst of citronella when she barks. If frantic barking is accompanied by diarrhea or bloody paws or nose (caused by trying to dig out of the house), the dog may be suffering from separation anxiety (see page 403). In that case, the anxiety must be relieved in order for the barking to subside.

Jumping Up Dogs jump up when they are excited or want affection or to show their dominance. If your dog looks as though he is getting ready to jump up, avoid eye contact and don't wave your arms or speak in an excited tone. Instead, give the sit-stay command, then bend down, avoiding eye contact, and pet the dog on his forechest or sides (not the top of the head) and praise. If your dog jumps up, quickly side-step him so that he has no place on your body to land and his front paws will fall to the floor. Alternatively, try turning away from a jumping dog and facing the wall. Dogs are social creatures, and most do not like to be shunned. As the dog pauses in response to your turning away, command him to sit-stay and reward compliance by turning back around and offering low-key praise and petting—down at his level.

Some breeds, such as the Jack Russell terrier and the Italian greyhound, need to express their enthusiasm in leaps of joy. Teach such dogs to jump straight up and down without bouncing off people, and make jump a command so that it can be "turned off" when not appropriate. (To teach this, rev the dog up to jump, but don't allow him to land on you.)

To condition your dog not to jump on visitors, engage the help of a friend. Arrange for the friend to visit at a specific time, treats in hand. Before the friend arrives, put your dog on a leash so that you can maintain control during the exercise. When the friend enters your home, give the dog the sit command. When your dog sits, have the friend give him a treat. Repeat often, with several different friends, until the dog stops trying to jump on them.

Jumping up is a normal canine greeting. Teach your dog to sit-stay when saying hello.

A beach that allows dogs is a good place for digging.

Digging Dogs that dig holes in the yard are usually not getting enough attention or exercise. The cure, of course, is more of both. Accompany your dog out into the yard and when it looks as though the dog is going to start digging, say "No dig" and engage in a game of fetch or Frisbee chasing instead.

Some dogs, particularly the thick-coated northern breeds, will dig cooling pits for themselves on hot days. Prevent hole digging by keeping these dogs cool. During periods of hot weather, keep them inside with the air conditioning turned on or set up a plastic wading pool in which they can cool off outside. Take them out for exercise in the early morning and early evening.

Dogs originally bred to tunnel in the ground, such as small terriers, are genetically prone to digging. Some of these dogs engage in digging to catch animals such as moles and woodchucks. Others dig merely for pleasure. Channel their instincts by teaching them to dig solely in a designated digging pit—a four-foot-square area of soil and sand created just for their burrowing pleasure.

If a dog is digging along the fence line, it may be an effort to break out of the yard to go exploring and possibly looking for mates. The desire to roam is particularly strong in unneutered males. In such cases, monitor the dog whenever he is outside and call him away from the fence line whenever he approaches it. If need be, create a chicken-wire barrier running from about one foot up the fence to six inches below the soil line and extending a few feet into the yard. When the dog digs through the sod and his paws make contact with the wire, digging will be unpleasant and he will be forced to stop.

Household Destruction Puppies and adolescents are notorious for committing "creative" acts of household destruction when left unsupervised—furniture gets moved, pillows lose their stuffing, books are shredded, and garbage gets strewn about the house—all in a quest to eliminate boredom and relieve stress caused by social isolation or teething.

All puppies chew, especially when they are teething. The adult teeth emerge between four and six months of age. From seven to ten months of age, adolescent puppies seek out rawhides, bones, or table legs to satisfy chewing urges and alleviate boredom. During this time, try to keep shoes and other eminently gnawable possessions out of your puppy's reach, and provide a large supply of toys and chewies. (Never give puppies old shoes to chew on; they are unable to distinguish between old and new ones, so they won't understand which ones are off limits.) A soothing toy for a teething puppy is a knotted cotton-rope toy that has been dampened with water and then placed in the freezer. A frozen hollow rubber ball stuffed with peanut butter is also appreciated. To keep your puppy from chewing on furniture, try spraying cloth areas with an antichew spray or rubbing the woodwork with an antichew cream. (Both products are available from pet supply stores; test them on small, hidden areas to make sure they won't stain.)

If you catch your puppy chewing on something inappropriate, say "no" once and substitute an allowable object, such as a chewie or a toy. When you leave the house, place a teething puppy or rowdy adolescent in a crate or a room blocked off from the rest of the house with two toys and a chewie. Rotate toys and chewies so that you are not leaving your puppy with the same ones each time you go out; you want to keep the puppy from losing interest in the toys.

Adult dogs usually won't chew if they are trained well when they are young. If your adult dog has a chewing problem, follow the same training methods as for puppies, and consider providing him with more exercise.

Inquisitive and adolescent (six- to eighteen-month-old) dogs not exercised enough by their owners are known to "redecorate" the home by herding the couch cushions into the middle of the room, dispersing dirty laundry throughout the house, or pulling down venetian blinds to get a better look at the mail carrier. Canine adolescence is a time of high energy levels, boundary testing, and generally inconsistent behavior. To protect your home, you can provide your dog with energy-burning aerobic-level exercise before leaving the house and confine the dog to a crate or dog-proofed space while you are gone. Toys that dispense kibble when they are moved can make a dog work for his food and, in the process, provide both entertainment and mental stimulation in the caretaker's absence.

Puppy Mouthing Puppies use their mouths to explore their world, running everything—including your hands and any other body part that comes within reach—past those brand-new, needle-sharp pearly whites. There are several ways to stop mouthing behavior. For young puppies (under twelve weeks of age), yelping like a wounded littermate is often enough to get the puppy's mouth off you. If that fails, or if the puppy is older, offer a chew toy as soon as the mouthing begins (always keep chew toys within arm's reach for such situations).

Redirect inquisitive puppy teeth off human hands and onto dog toys and chewies.

rewarding to the dogs. Among stray or feral dogs, eating stool may be a dietary necessity: they may not be getting enough to eat, or they may be compensating for a nutritional deficiency. But the average healthy dog will eat stool for different reasons: boredom, a taste for food remains that are in the stool, or a desire to hide the proof of a house-training indiscretion.

There are products on the market that can be added to a dog's food to make his own stool less palatable, but the success rate of such products is mixed. Controlling coprophagy is primarily a management issue. Puppies need to be put on a house-training schedule appropriate for their developmental stage and must not be overpunished for accidents. Dogs of any age should be kept on a leash when being taken out to eliminate; their feces should be cleaned up before they have the chance to turn around, much less eat. If you have a yard, be diligent about cleaning up after the dog. When hiking in pastures or woods, keep the dog on a long line or retractable leash to prevent opportunities to snack on farm-animal or wildlife dung. If you have a cat, keep the litter box in a place the dog cannot reach or use a covered litter box. Keep a dog left home alone occupied by providing a rotating assortment of food-dispensing toys, stuffed bones, and other chew toys (rotating them will sustain their desirability).

For the bold puppy that gets excited and comes back for another nip, try a gruff "no bite" and a few minutes of social isolation in a time-out space like the crate or on the other side of a puppy gate away from all the fun. An excessive mouther may need a stronger impetus to stop. For those pups, a squirt of aerosol breath spray in the mouth works wonders. It tastes unpleasant but is totally safe. Best of all, puppies quickly make the connection between the breath spray and the undesirable behavior, and the mouthing ceases. It is crucial to nip mouthing in the bud, while the dog is still young, because a mouthy adolescent is a serious problem. Stopping mouthing in adolescence—usually a signal of troublesome dominance and control issues—often requires work with a trainer.

Eating Stool (Coprophagy) Many dogs will eat either their own feces or those of another animal. This behavior is particularly revolting to caretakers but clearly is

Problems for the Specialist

Dogs exhibiting behaviors that can cause harm to themselves or to humans need to be treated by a canine behavior specialist—an applied animal behaviorist, a veterinary behaviorist, or a dog trainer who is experienced in advanced problem solving.

Separation Anxiety Separation anxiety stems from overbonding and is seen more frequently in re-adopted dogs than in dogs placed in permanent homes as puppies. When left alone, dogs that suffer from separation anxiety may panic and try to eat or dig their way through crates, walls, doors, and window moldings. They may shriek and bark in an attempt to call their owners back home. Because of the stress of the situation they may develop diarrhea or urinate in the house. In the worst cases, they may try to follow their owners by jumping through screens or even plate-glass windows. Severe cases of separation anxiety require a combination of desensitization to the owner's comings and goings, behavior modification, appropriate exercise, and, possibly, anti-anxiety drugs.

Dogs that suffer from separation anxiety panic when they are left alone, whining, barking uncontrollably, soiling excessively, and destroying windowsills and doors.

Finding a Trainer

You may wish (or need) to enlist the help of a dog trainer, animal behaviorist, or veterinary behaviorist. Trainers may have advanced degrees in animal behavior, but more likely they learned their craft through apprenticeships, seminars, and hands-on experience. Applied animal behaviorists and veterinary behaviorists have obtained doctorates (Ph.D.s) and/or degrees in veterinary medicine (D.V.M.s) and have done advanced academic work in the field of animal behavior. Behaviorists specialize in problems that require behavior modification along with medication.

Training usually takes place in one of three venues: in the home, at a training center, or at a board-and-train kennel. Before signing up for group classes, ask if you can observe a class to see that the training space is clean and well maintained, how the instructor runs the class, and what methods are employed. Before hiring a private in-home trainer, inquire about credentials and ask for references. Before using a board-and-train facility, check out the premises and ask to observe a training session. Make sure you are comfortable with any facility before leaving your pet there.

Call your veterinarian, local animal shelter, or SPCA for a referral to a reputable trainer or behaviorist. The Association of Pet Dog Trainers (800-PET-DOGS) can also refer you to member trainers in your area.

Phobias of thunderstorms, fire-crackers, or other loud noises often provoke cowering, shaking, and other signs of terror.

Fears and Phobias Dogs can exhibit fearful responses to a number of stimuli, from common ones like thunderstorms or fireworks to idiosyncratic ones like striped umbrellas, basement steps, or men with beards. Responses range from panting, pacing, and shaking to freezing and bolting or worse. Some dogs are so fearful that, in a fit of panic, they do grave bodily harm to themselves.

If your dog has any fears or phobias exhibited by more than shaking a bit and hiding temporarily, consult with a behavior specialist who can assess your dog's condition and set up a protocol for recovery. Treatment may include a combination of habituation, desensitization, and counter-conditioning as well as anti-anxiety or antidepressant drug therapy. The behaviorist will also make sure that you are not inadvertently doing anything to worsen the situation. For example, attempting to soothe the dog with stroking and comforting words rewards the dog's fearful behavior, reinforcing rather than curbing it.

Aggression Protection of home and the family "pack" is an acceptable canine response only if it is controlled. For example, if a dog barks at the door when a visitor arrives but stops when called off, you probably do not have a problem.

However, an aggressive dog—one that menaces and bites and cannot be controlled easily—can cause serious injury. Aggression problems are the most difficult behavioral problems to resolve. Aggressive dogs that are not kept under strict control stimulate antidog sentiment in many communities, thus limiting freedom for well-behaved dogs. Every year, thousands of dogs are euthanized because of aggression problems.

If your dog shows any signs of aggression, seek the help of a behavior specialist immediately and do everything possible to keep the dog out of potentially injurious situations. When handling an aggressive dog, remember that aggression begets aggression. Resist any temptation to hit the dog, for it can only make the problem worse—and be wary of any trainers whose treatment protocol involves corporal punishment.

Keep in mind that many aggressive dogs are young, unneutered males. The first steps in prevention are early socialization (page 73), early training (page 383), and early neutering (page 75).

Most forms of canine aggression fall into one of the following categories: dominance aggression, fear aggression, protective aggression, territorial aggression, interdog aggression, play aggression, possessive aggression, pain aggression, and predatory aggression.

In dominance aggression, the dog challenges the leader of the pack, human or canine, in an aggressive manner that may include snarling, growling, or biting. Punishing the dog only worsens the situation.

Most dogs exhibiting dominance aggression are confident, bossy, take-charge males of a dominant breed type, such as chow chows, rottweilers, Airedales, Lhasa apsos, Akitas, and Shiba Inus, although dogs of either sex or any breed or mix may display dominance aggression if they perceive their owner to be weak and not in charge of the family "pack." Dogs begin to exhibit this behavior at one and a half to three years of age. Whenever it presents itself, dominance aggression must be dealt with promptly.

In cases of fear aggression, a dog lacks confidence, was probably improperly socialized as a pup, and may also be the offspring of a fearful parent (fearfulness can be an

Any dog showing signs of aggression should be seen by a behavior specialist promptly. The longer the problem is allowed to continue, the more dangerous it is likely to become.

inherited trait). Dogs exhibiting fear aggression may shake, tremble, or cower before biting, or they may go in for the bite once the threat has passed (biting the threat from behind). They may warn by growling.

Protective aggression occurs when a dog perceives a human or another dog as a threat to the person whom she has designated herself to protect. The dog stands between the "protected" and the "threat" and snarls, growls, barks, or bites.

Territorial aggression occurs when a dog believes that she must protect property, such as houses, cars, and yards. The snarling, growling, and barking get more intense as the "threat" gets closer, and will usually subside if the "threat" moves away from the dog's territory. Otherwise, biting may ensue.

Interdog aggression is usually expressed in the form of a dogfight between two males or two females. It may be in response to a sexual situation (two males may fight over a female in heat, two females may be aggressive toward each other if either or both are in heat). Dogs in the same household may fight for control of a chew toy or bed. Even neutered dogs can exhibit interdog aggression, just not as commonly as intact males do.

The puppy or adult dog exhibiting play aggression will in the course of play growl, bark, and bite at a person's hands, arms, legs, or clothing. This behavior is sometimes seen in adult dogs that were not exposed to play situations when they were pups or that are allowed to play roughly with their owners.

Dogs exhibiting possessive aggression feel the need to protect their valuables. These dogs may growl or bite if a person or dog approaches or is in sight while they are eating or in possession of treats, toys, bones, or stolen objects.

Pain aggression is exhibited when a dog bites a person (sometimes not bearing down hard) because what the person is doing is painful to the dog or is perceived by the dog as something that may lead to pain. For example, having the ears cleaned could provoke pain aggression if a dog's ears are tender because of an infection or if a dog suffered pain in a previous ear cleaning.

Long ago, all dogs were predators, killing other animals for sustenance. Some pet dogs still exhibit this instinct, called predatory aggression. Through selective breeding, most breeds no longer run down game and go in for the kill—although terriers and sight hounds are probably closer to their predatory past than most other breed types. In particular, rottweilers and pit bull terriers have been implicated in a number of predatory aggression incidents involving young children. In many rural areas, dogs that worry livestock or game can legally be shot on sight. A dog with predatory inclinations is the blight of the urban dog run. Predatory aggression is difficult to resolve and must be carefully managed so that humans and other animals are not harmed.

Certain breeds, like rottweilers and other guardian dogs, are more apt to be overprotective or territorial.

Traveling with a dog has its own set of special complications and requires a considerable amount of preparation.

Traveling with Your Dog

Whether you and your dog are traveling by car or by plane, you must have the proper equipment, prepare for the trip itself, and anticipate how you will accommodate your dog's needs upon arrival at your destination.

Preparing for a Trip

Before embarking on any trip, confirm that the hotels, motels, or campgrounds where you will be staying allow dogs. Always make reservations. If you are staying with friends or family, make sure that they know you are bringing your dog and that they will be accommodating. To ensure a warm welcome, crate train your dog prior to the trip so he can feel safe and secure left in his "own room" when you go out. Bringing along your dog's bedding or blanket from home as well as a few favorite playthings will help keep him at ease while away from home.

If your dog eats a hard-to-find food, is on a restricted diet, or has a sensitive stomach, pack enough food for the entire trip. Because the mineral content of regional waters can sometimes cause diarrhea, pack a few gallons of water from home to help ease the transition to the new water.

Make sure that your dog has proper identification on his collar or harness. Ideally, your dog should also be marked with a tattooed identification number or have a microchip implant (page 59). The identification tag on the collar should bear your dog's name as well as your name, address, and telephone number. If you are going far from home for an extended period, it is also a good idea to attach a second, temporary tag marked with your destination address and telephone number. A current rabies tag with a vaccination identification number and your veterinarian's name, address, and telephone number is also important. Just in case, bring along a current photograph of your dog that can be photocopied for emergency "lost dog" posters.

Bring copies of current health and vaccination certificates as well as a copy of your dog's health records in case medical treatment is needed while traveling. If you are crossing an international border, check with the consulate of the country you are visiting beforehand to find out which medical records you may need, whether there is a quarantine period, and whether you may have to file paperwork.

Travel Checklist

✓ dog first aid kit (see next page)
✓ dog food
✓ bottled water
✓ food and water bowls
✓ soap for cleaning bowls
✓ can opener and spoon (if food is canned)
✓ collar and/or harness
✓ leash
✓ plastic bags for picking up feces at rest stops
✓ identification tags
✓ crate
✓ familiar bedding or blanket
✓ toys and treats
✓ paper towels
✓ grooming brush and comb
✓ current photograph of the dog
✓ your veterinarian's phone number
✓ health and vaccination records

Air travel requires a hard-sided, USDA-approved carrier if your dog will not be traveling with you in the cabin.

Pack a dog first aid kit that includes:

- medications prescribed by your vet
- canine antidiarrhea medicine
- a rectal thermometer
- antibacterial skin ointment
- cotton swabs
- tweezers
- scissors
- gauze bandages
- nonstick gauze pads
- adhesive tape

Car Travel

Dogs make good travel companions provided they get used to riding in cars when they are puppies. Some puppies will acclimate easily; others will resist.

Start acclimating a dog to car travel at an early age (eight to twelve weeks). On several occasions before the first car ride, let the dog sniff around inside the parked car. Occasionally dispense treats or feed the dog in the parked car to establish positive associations.

Take the dog for short rides around the block at first. Be sure to praise him for proper behavior during the ride. Work up to slightly longer drives to places the dog will enjoy: to the pet supply store for a toy or treat or, if the dog has had all of his vaccinations (which should be the case once a puppy has reached about sixteen weeks of age), to the park for a walk.

Take drives with the dog in the backseat of the car and accompanied by another person he likes. While you are driving, have the other person pet the dog and praise him in a jolly, upbeat tone of voice. Avoid driving alone with an unrestrained dog in the front seat, as this could divert your attention and cause an accident.

Once your dog is comfortable with short trips, begin car crate training (assuming the dog is already crate-trained in the home). First let the dog sniff around inside the crate, then take short drives with the dog in the crate until he is acclimated. Give the dog a chew toy to hold his attention while he is in the crate. Instead of a crate, a metal barrier can be set up to restrict the dog to the back of the car. Keep in mind that such barriers do little to protect dogs in car accidents. Another option is a canine seat belt or harness. Before using any of these devices, be sure to read the manufacturer's instructions.

To reduce motion sickness, refrain from feeding your dog for three to four hours before any car trip. Consult your vet for other options if acclimation exercises have not alleviated your dog's car sickness.

On the Road Keep your dog in a crate or secured with a canine seat belt whenever you are in transit. Stop every few hours so your dog can eliminate. Make sure that you attach the leash to your dog's collar before opening the car door and always walk your dog on a leash. If possible, wait to feed your dog until after you have completed all travel for the day. Offer only water and treats while in transit.

On hot or cold days, never leave your dog unattended in the car, even for just a few minutes. Changes in body temperature leading to heatstroke or hypothermia can occur quickly. In mild weather, leave your dog alone in the car only for short periods, and always leave windows partially open (not wide enough for the dog to jump out) for ventilation.

Air Travel

Make arrangements for your dog with the airline in advance to avoid last-minute complications. Get a list of the airline's rules and regulations regarding dog travel.

The United States Department of Agriculture requires that all dogs be older than eight weeks and fully weaned before flying. Most airlines require health and vaccination certificates from a veterinarian; the health certificate must be issued less than ten days prior to the outbound flight. Many airlines do not transport very large dogs.

If you are traveling internationally, check with the consulate of the country you are visiting for specific regulations. You may be required to file extensive paperwork, to acquire an importation certificate, and to show proof that a rabies vaccine was administered between thirty days and one year prior to your departure date. Some countries have extensive (one- to six-month) quarantine requirements.

If you have a small dog, ask the airline if you can carry her in a carrier under your seat. Airlines typically allow one animal in a carry-on bag in the cabin.

If your dog must travel in the cargo hold (which is a pressurized compartment beneath the passenger compartment), you must obtain a heavy-duty USDA-approved pet carrier. Contact the airline for specific requirements. It should have side bars to allow for adequate ventilation even when surrounded by crates and boxes, and it should be large enough for your dog to stand, lie down, and turn around.

Be sure that the crate has the words "live animal" written on it in letters at least one inch tall and prominent arrows that indicate the upright position of the carrier. Line the carrier with a towel, plus something with your smell on it and a favorite toy for comfort.

Attach to the outside of the pet carrier a permanent waterproof label on which you have printed the following information: your dog's name and your name, address, and telephone number (at your home and place of destination). Also attach a plastic sleeve in which you have placed a copy of your dog's health certificate and your veterinarian's name and telephone number. Be sure that your dog is wearing up-to-date identification tags.

If the flight travel time is longer than eight hours and there is a layover, a water bowl should be firmly attached to the inside of the carrier and positioned so that airline personnel can fill it without opening the door. Close the carrier door securely, but leave it unlocked so that airline personnel can open it if necessary. If the flight is more than twenty-four hours, attach both food and water bowls (again, inside the carrier but accessible from the outside); also attach a cloth or mesh bag filled with dry dog food to the outside of the carrier. During the layover, speak to airline personnel to make sure that your dog is being cared for.

The USDA, through the Animal Welfare Act, oversees the way all animals are handled when traveling by plane out of their owner's custody. Mishaps are uncommon, but you should still take precautions. Travel on direct, nonstop flights whenever possible. Transfers and delays can be problematic, especially in extremely hot or cold environments and when the dog is left in the plane on the tarmac for long periods. Try to avoid traveling with your dog on holidays, weekends, or at other busy times.

Ask the airline about its policy on unsafe conditions for animal transport. For example, if the temperature is too hot (above 85°F) or too cold (below 45°F) at the point of departure or destination, the airline may restrict the times when you and your dog can fly. Early morning or early evening flights are best if flying through hot places.

Do not give your dog a tranquilizer

before traveling unless specifically recommended by your veterinarian. Your dog may not be able to regulate body temperature and other important functions if sedated. To avoid motion sickness, don't feed your dog or offer water for four hours before traveling. If your dog is prone to motion sickness, ask your veterinarian to prescribe medication or to suggest an over-the-counter medication.

Exercise your dog at the airport on a leash as close to the flight time as possible to allow her time to eliminate. After a flight of less than four hours on cool days, let the dog calm down for about thirty minutes before offering water. After flights of more than four hours or any flights on hot days, offer the dog a small amount of water right away. Some excited dogs may gulp the water, then vomit.

Leaving Your Dog at Home

When you travel without your dog, it is best for the dog's comfort and well-being—and for your own peace of mind—to arrange for a relative or trusted friend to stay in your home and care for your dog. Ideally, the caretaker should be someone who has spent time with the dog on previous occasions. If you can't find a friend or relative to care for your dog, you'll need to find a reliable pet sitter or a good kennel.

Be sure to provide any caretaker with an adequate supply of the food the dog is accustomed to eating, as well as any chewies and treats you would like your dog to have in your absence. The caretaker also needs to have the following vital information

Ideally, a dog should be looked after by an in-home caretaker, such as a trusted friend or relative, when her family goes away. Other options include pet sitters and kennels.

about your dog: feeding, elimination, and exercise schedule; a list of commands he reliably responds to; descriptions of any allergies or special sensitivities (such as noises that alarm the dog or body parts that the dog doesn't like touched); descriptions of neighborhood rivals and where to be on the lookout for them; and telephone numbers for you, your next of kin, and your veterinarian.

Pet Sitters They work in one of three ways: they visit your dog a predetermined number of times a day for walks, playtime, and feeding (least expensive option); they stay with your pet in your home (most expensive option); or they care for your pet in their home while you are gone.

Drop-by care will do when you have to be away for one to three days, as long as your dog is mature, housebroken, and placid. This arrangement can work quite well when the dog is part of a multianimal household, in which the animals have one another for company when the pet sitter isn't there. The dog gets to sleep in his own bed, exercise in his own neighborhood, and stay comfortable in his own environment.

Drop-by care is not an option for puppies and adolescent dogs because of the amount of attention they need each and every day. It is also unsuitable for dogs with separation anxiety or health conditions that need to be watched carefully. For these dogs, consider hiring a pet sitter who can stay in your home or who can accommodate your dog in his home.

Get recommendations for pet sitters from your veterinarian, other pet-service providers (such as a trainer or groomer), or pet-owning friends. Check the sitter's references and discuss with the sitter his level of expertise. Find out if the sitter is bonded and insured and a member of trade organizations, such as Pet Sitters International—these are signs of professionalism. Ask the sitter how he generally works. The sitter should want to meet the dog in your presence in advance. This is important for dogs that show territorial protectiveness. Go through a dry run with the sitter to make sure he knows how to attach a leash, brush a dog, and provide any other necessary care. If the dog is staying in the sitter's home, find out if there will be children or other animals present. If so, decide whether your dog will be able to manage under those conditions.

When you hire a pet sitter you should feel completely confident that he will follow your directions, respect your community's dog ordinances, and make your dog's well-being and safety a top priority. If you do not feel confident, seek out other options.

Once you have chosen a sitter, provide him with the vital information listed at the top of this page. Explain all of your dog's likes, dislikes, and idiosyncrasies.

Kennels It is very important to research boarding facilities in advance; you don't want to find out when you drop your dog off at a new facility, perhaps on your way to the airport, that it is unsanitary or otherwise unsafe. To narrow down your choices, get recommendations from your veterinarian, trainer, groomer, or friends, and choose a kennel that is a member of the American Boarding Kennel Association. Some vets board dogs for clients, an appealing option if your dog needs medical treatment that can be administered while you are away, such as a professional dental cleaning.

Before making reservations, visit the boarding facility to be sure it is cleaned daily, well lit, well ventilated, and free of offensive odors and noises. Reservations often need to be made weeks in advance, especially during holidays and summer.

Make sure that your dog will have the opportunity to eliminate away from her bed three to six times a day. To lessen the chance that your dog will pick up a contagious disease, check that animals from different households are housed individually, not allowed to run freely with others. Ask if a health certificate and certain vaccinations are required. If proof of vaccinations against rabies, DHLPP, and bordetella are not required, find another facility.

If necessary, find out if the facility operators are willing to feed a special diet or administer medications. Some kennels require that you provide food for your dog; others feed all dogs the same food, which is provided as part of the kennel fee. To keep the dogs occupied, kennels usually offer indoor/outdoor runs, walks on a leash, or play sessions in a yard. Choose the options that you think will suit your dog best. When dropping off your dog, leave, if allowed, a familiar object (such as a favorite blanket, pillow, or toy). Also provide a phone number at which you can be reached in case of emergency, as well as your veterinarian's phone number.

At pickup time, carefully assess your dog's kennel experience. Observe the dog's behavior and appearance and speak to the kennel operators. If your dog seems depressed, lethargic, or especially frantic or fearful; has lost a lot of weight; or has a dull coat and is shedding a lot, he was extremely distressed by the experience and other options should be explored next time. If the kennel operators report that your dog barked or menaced the whole time or wouldn't eat even after a couple of days, kenneling probably isn't a good option in the future.

When leaving your dog, keep farewells brief and upbeat to avoid distressing the dog.

Bright eyes, alertness, and good appetite
are signs of good canine health.

Keeping Your Dog Healthy

One of the best ways to safeguard your dog's health is to be on the lookout for physical and behavioral changes at all times. For example, incorporate a mini–physical exam into your grooming routine; pay attention to how your dog moves when you walk and exercise her; keep track of how much she eats; notice if her demeanor changes. This will allow you to catch most illnesses in their early stages, when they may be most easily cured. In addition, schedule regular veterinary checkups. Your veterinarian will tell you how often your dog needs to be scheduled for well-pet visits, which will include vaccinations and dewormings, based upon your dog's age, risk of disease exposure, and state of health. Of course, your veterinarian will want to see your dog whenever any medical problems arise. The more observant you are and the better your communication with your veterinarian, the healthier your pet is likely to be.

The Mini-Physical Exam

Make the home checkup an extension of the normal attention you pay your dog, and he will not even know that he is being "examined." It doesn't matter where you perform the exam, as long as both you and your dog are comfortable.

Skin and Coat

Weekly grooming provides a good opportunity for evaluating the health of the skin and coat. Pass your hands over your dog's body, feeling for swelling, asymmetry, or sensitive areas. Call the veterinarian if you discover patches of hair loss, the black flecks that signal the presence of fleas (see page 439), scabby or reddened areas, or skin bumps. With your dog facing away from you, gently lift the tail and take a quick peek at the rear end. If you see tan-colored rice-size objects, you are probably looking at packets of tapeworm eggs (page 447), which require veterinary treatment. Next, use a moist paper towel to clean away any feces. In long-coated dogs in particular, feces can get caught in the fur and, if trapped against the skin, can cause serious problems. If the hair has become matted, use scissors to carefully cut out the mats yourself, or, better yet, take your dog to a vet or groomer, who can use clippers to remove them.

Ears

With your dog facing you, gently pull up on the earflap and look at the inner surface and down into the ear canal. The ears should be clean and light pink in color. Any discharge, redness, swelling, or odor is abnormal. Never insert anything into your dog's ear canal—doing so can aggravate an ear condition or even cause trauma or infection.

Eyes

Face your dog head-on and examine the eyes. They should be bright, and both pupils should be of equal size. There should be little if any tearing at the corners of the eyes, and the inner eyelids should not protrude. Gently roll down the lower eyelid with your thumb; the tissue lining the lid should be pink, not white or red. Be sure your dog is not squinting with either eye.

Mouth and Nose

With your dog facing you, lift up the lips to examine the gums and teeth. The gums should be pink, not white or red, and should show no signs of swelling. The teeth should be clean, without any brownish tartar. Sniff your dog's breath; while a dog's breath is never pleasant, a strong, fetid odor is abnormal and may indicate a problem. Excessive drooling can also be a sign of oral disease. There should be no nasal discharge.

Early Signs of Illness

Dog illnesses are almost always easier to treat if they are caught early. Since your dog cannot tell you in words that he is not feeling well, you need to watch closely and learn to identify the early signs that something might be wrong. Contact your veterinarian right away if your dog exhibits any of the following signs:

- decrease in activity level
- withdrawal from other members of the household
- change in appetite that lasts longer than a day or two
- change in water intake
- diarrhea that is severe or lasts longer than 36 hours (see page 444)
- straining to defecate
- urinating more or less than normal
- straining to urinate
- vomiting that is severe or lasts longer than 36 hours (see page 444)
- uncharacteristic mouth odor
- excessive eye discharge
- nasal discharge
- coughing
- excessive head shaking
- excessive scratching or licking
- indications of pain, such as limping, crying, hiding, irritability, and sensitivity to touch
- uncharacteristic behavior changes

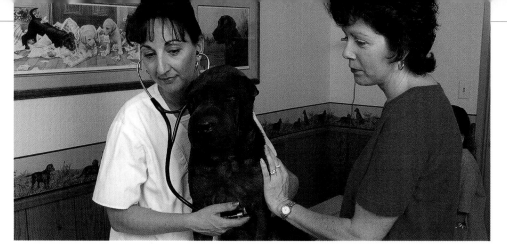

Keeping a dog in prime condition requires collaboration between her caretaker and her veterinarian.

You and Your Veterinarian

Your veterinarian will be your ally throughout the life of your dog, someone you'll depend on to help maintain your dog's health from puppyhood through old age. As your dog matures, your vet can serve as both knowledgeable advisor and compassionate friend, helping you to understand how your dog is aging and eventually to come to terms with his death. The following pages provide advice on finding and choosing the right veterinarian for you and your dog and on establishing a good working relationship with that vet. Also included is a brief overview of what to expect from a routine veterinary examination.

Finding a Veterinarian

Finding and choosing the right veterinarian is extremely important. But how do you go about it? Dog-owning friends are a good source of referrals, as is the shelter or person from whom you adopted or purchased your dog.

In your search for a veterinarian, you may come across different types of practices. Some owners prefer solo practitioners to a group practice because they like the consistency of care and the familiarity that the vet develops with each pet's case. Veterinarians in a group practice regularly consult with one another about their patients and are also able to cover for each other during vacations and other times when they are not working or on call.

Referral hospitals employ board-certified specialists. Typically they treat only patients referred to them by general practitioners.

Pet health insurance is a fairly recent development. Some policies require owners to use only participating veterinarians; others allow owners to use their veterinarian of choice. When shopping around for insurance, check references, read policies carefully, and ask your veterinarian to review any policies you are seriously considering. Make sure you understand the range of services covered. Some, for example, do not cover well-pet visits.

Evaluating a Veterinarian

Once you have narrowed down your choices in veterinarians, arrange to visit the facilities that interest you. Schedule such visits during relatively quiet times, and keep the following factors in mind.

A veterinary clinic should be neat, clean, and well-equipped, and should not have any unpleasant odors. The condition of the office and examining rooms will give you a good indication of the conscientiousness of the doctors and staff.

Good communication is important. The doctors and staff should encourage you to ask questions, and they should answer them in an understandable way without using excessive medical jargon. Lack of communication is the most common problem in the veterinarian-owner relationship.

Doctors and staff should always treat the pets in their care gently. There is no need for rough or aggressive handling; however, for everyone's protection, some dogs may need to be muzzled or tranquilized during certain procedures.

Find out whether veterinary specialists or referral centers are available in the area and if your veterinarian utilizes them. It is impossible to be proficient and up-to-date in all areas of veterinary medicine; a good veterinarian should not be reluctant to seek the advice of other veterinarians or to refer difficult cases to a specialty center if necessary.

When an emergency happens, every second counts. Find out how after-hours emergencies are handled. Some hospitals prefer to attend to their own emergencies, while others may refer them to a special emergency facility in the area.

Don't be afraid to talk about rates, fees, and accepted methods of payment. The veterinarian should be willing to provide running estimates on all services before they are rendered.

Working with Your Veterinarian

Keeping your dog healthy is much easier if you and your veterinarian work well together. Following are some ways that you can help your veterinarian to give your dog the best care possible.

If you have adopted a new dog or puppy, schedule an appointment for a physical examination, preferably within twenty-four hours after purchase or adoption. Give the veterinarian as much information as possible about the new dog, including date of birth and medical record.

Schedule puppies for their first visit to the vet at about six to eight weeks of age. At this time they should be given a complete physical and initial vaccinations. Bring along a fresh stool sample so that your vet can check for internal parasites.

If your dog is sick, use the checklist on page 420 to keep track of all the symptoms so you won't forget them when you are speaking with the doctor. For example, if the dog has diarrhea or is vomiting, the doctor will want to know when the problem started, how often it occurs, and at what times of day.

Bring a paper and pen with you and write down (or have your veterinarian write down) all important information and instructions. If you must administer medication or other treatments at home, make sure you understand how to do so. Ask the veterinarian or a staff member to show you, then have them observe while you perform the procedure to make sure you are doing it correctly.

Follow your veterinarian's instructions carefully and faithfully return for any recommended follow-up visits. If you don't understand something, ask questions! Veterinarians like to know that pet owners are interested and concerned. If you are uncomfortable speaking with your veterinarian, it may be a good idea to try to find a different one with whom you can communicate better.

Helping Your Dog Feel Comfortable at the Veterinarian's Office

To get your dog used to the veterinarian's office, it's a good idea to visit once or twice when no procedures are scheduled. Go in, sit in the waiting room, have the receptionist give your dog a biscuit, and leave. Before an official visit, call the office and tell the staff about any idiosyncrasies your dog might have. For example, some dogs are more docile when examined standing on the floor rather than on a table. Take your dog for a walk before entering the office so she can eliminate. Bring along a favorite toy or treats. Keep the dog on a leash at all times. If your dog is friendly, let her greet the staff. Ask the veterinarian or staff to offer your dog a treat and praise after the visit, if they don't do this as a matter of course.

The Veterinary Examination

Your dog should be given a complete physical examination whenever he goes in for a well-pet visit. Through annual or semiannual exams, many diseases can be detected before they start to cause obvious problems. Some veterinarians prefer taking a complete medical history before even touching the dog, while others prefer to ask questions during the examination. Each veterinarian has his or her own order for performing an examination— some start by taking the temperature, others by evaluating the coat—but the typical complete physical exam should include at least the components listed on page 421.

Checklist for Veterinary Visits

Present Medical Problem(s)
If you think your dog might be sick, make a list of the following information so that you can provide your vet with a full account of the dog's condition:
✓ date of onset
✓ changes in behavior, appetite, water intake, activity level, urinating, or bowel movements
✓ medication(s) the dog was taking before illness began
✓ medication(s) the dog is currently taking

Past Medical Problems
If you are seeing a new veterinarian, either obtain your dog's records from previous care providers or make a list of the following information for all of your dog's past health problems:

✓ date
✓ tests administered
✓ diagnosis
✓ treatment
Also include the dog's complete vaccination history and the type and date of any surgery the dog has had.

Remember to ask the vet the following questions: What is wrong with my dog? What tests are needed for diagnosis? How will the condition be treated? Are there alternative treatments? Will hospitalization be necessary? What will the costs be? What is the expected outcome? Do you have any literature on this subject?

Observation Veterinarians make an initial "hands-off" observation of the dog's demeanor, posture, gait, and general physical condition.

Weights and Measures A physical exam includes a recording of body temperature, weight, pulse rate, respiratory rate, and state of hydration.

Skin and Coat Veterinarians examine the skin and coat on all parts of the body; this includes a thorough evaluation of the mammary gland area. They check for parasites as well as for changes in the skin and coat that might warn of illness.

Head and Neck The vet palpates (examines by touch) the neck and throat to evaluate symmetry and to check the salivary glands, lymph nodes, and thyroid gland for nodules or swelling.

Face Veterinarians make an evaluation of facial symmetry by sight and touch.

Ears The ears are examined for discharge, odors, masses, color, and pain. The ear canal is examined with an otoscope; if a more thorough ear examination is necessary, the dog may have to be sedated.

Eyes Examination of the eyes includes

Ears are examined with an otoscope.

checking pupil size, response to light, clarity, color, and condition of tissues; checking the eyelids for swelling, squinting, and discoloration; and looking for masses. An ophthalmoscope is used to view the inside of the eye.

Nose The nose is examined for swelling, discharge, and color.

Mouth Examination of the lips and mouth for tooth and gum health includes an open-mouth exam for foreign bodies, growths, or disease, and a check of gum color.

Limbs The paws and limbs are examined for symmetry, muscle tone, joint flexibility, reflexes, and painful areas or swelling. The lymph nodes are palpated for enlargement.

Heart and lungs are examined with a stethoscope.

Chest Examination of the chest includes palpation for symmetry, a chest auscultation (listening with the stethoscope) to evaluate heart and lung sounds, and sometimes a chest percussion (sharp taps on the chest to detect areas of increased or decreased resonance).

Abdomen Palpation of all parts of the abdomen enables the doctor to evaluate internal structures.

Rear End Examination of the pelvis, back, and tail includes palpation for symmetry, swelling, pain, and flexibility. The rectal and external genital area as well as the anal glands are inspected.

Vaccination

Vaccines are indispensable weapons in the battle against infectious disease for animals as well as humans. Vaccines contain antigens that to the immune system "look" like the disease-causing organism but that don't cause disease. When a vaccine is given to a healthy animal, the immune system mounts a protective response to fight the disease. If the dog is then exposed to the disease-causing virus or bacteria, the immune system is prepared and either prevents infection or reduces the severity of the disease.

Vaccinations for Puppies
Colostrum, the first milk a mother dog produces, contains antibodies that help protect puppies from infectious disease until their own immune systems are more mature. These antibodies also interfere with a vaccine's ability to stimulate the puppy's immune system. Therefore, veterinarians administer vaccines every three or four weeks beginning when the puppy is around six to eight weeks of age and continuing until the puppy is about sixteen weeks of age. (See the sample vaccination schedule on page 423.) In some cases, as with the rabies vaccine, the initial vaccine is not given until puppies are twelve weeks old. It is very important that the puppy receive the whole series of vaccinations and boosters in a timely fashion. When obtaining a puppy, be sure to find out exactly which vaccinations have been administered and when they were administered so that you can give this information to your veterinarian and she can proceed accordingly.

Vaccinations for Adult Dogs
Adult dogs need boosters of vaccines to maintain sufficient protection from disease. Your veterinarian will probably send you reminders, but it is a good idea to mark your calendar ahead of time to remind you when the boosters are due.

Safety Factors
Your veterinarian will help you decide which vaccines are appropriate for your dog and how often they should be given. The choice depends on a number of factors, including the following:
- your dog's risk of exposure to the disease-causing organism (this depends in part on the health of the other dogs to which yours is exposed and the environment in which your dog lives);
- the consequence of infection;
- the risk an infected dog poses to human health;
- the protective ability of the vaccine;
- the frequency or severity of reactions the vaccine may produce;
- the age and health of your dog;
- reactions to vaccines that your dog may have experienced in the past.

Generally speaking, vaccines are very safe. In most cases, the risk of having a vaccination is much smaller than the risk of the dog contracting disease if vaccines are not given. But to minimize the risk, before your dog is vaccinated, inform your veterinarian of any health problems the dog is experiencing, any medication he is receiving, and any reaction he has experienced in the past.

Following is a brief list of reactions that may occur after vaccination. If you think your dog is experiencing a problem associated with his vaccines, call your veterinarian right away.

Mild Reactions Any of the following reactions are fairly common and may appear within hours to several days after vaccination and last no more than a few days:

- discomfort at the site where the vaccine was given;
- mild fever;
- diminished appetite and activity;
- sneezing (four to seven days after an intranasal vaccination);
- development of a small, firm, nonpainful swelling under the skin at the site where the vaccine was given. The swelling usually goes away after several weeks, but if you notice such a swelling, contact your veterinarian.

Serious Reactions These reactions occur very rarely:

- a potentially life-threatening allergic reaction within several minutes to an hour after vaccination, manifested as hives, severe vomiting and diarrhea, and/or collapse and death;
- a kind of tumor called a sarcoma developing at the vaccine site several weeks, months, or even longer after vaccination.

Sample Vaccination Schedule

The following sample schedule is followed by many veterinarians. However, your veterinarian may recommend an alternative schedule based upon your dog's age, his potential exposure to diseases, and the risk of particular diseases in your geographic area. There is some controversy within the veterinary community about puppy vaccination schedules. Speak with your vet about her views, then, together, decide what is best for your dog.

Vaccines

6–8 weeks of age	DHPPLC*
6–8 weeks of age or older	Bordetella bronchiseptica
9 weeks of age	DHPPLC, Lyme disease
12 weeks of age	DHPPLC, Lyme disease, Rabies
16 weeks of age	DHPPLC
20 weeks of age	DHPPLC

Boosters

Every 6 to 12 months	Bordetella bronchiseptica
Annual	DHPPLC, Lyme disease
Every 1 to 3 years, depending on state law	Rabies

*DHPPLC is an abbreviation for a combination vaccine that includes distemper, adenovirus 2 (hepatitis virus), parvovirus, parainfluenza, leptospirosis, and coronavirus. Some veterinarians recommend that only dogs at risk of contracting leptospirosis be vaccinated against it, and others recommend that the leptospirosis portion of the vaccine be given only to puppies older than 14 weeks. Some veterinarians consider the coronavirus portion of the vaccine optional as well. Consult your veterinarian for recommendations for your puppy.

Common Canine Health Problems

The following pages present basic information on a wide selection of common canine health problems. A few uncommon conditions, such as rabies, are also included because they are important for dog owners to know about. (For more comprehensive coverage of canine health problems, consult the Recommended Reading appendix.)

Most of the conditions are grouped according to the anatomical system they tend to affect most directly. Diseases that are likely to affect a wide variety of body systems and display a broad range of symptoms are covered separately, within the categories Viral Diseases, Systemic Bacterial Diseases, and Cancer.

Dogs are complex, highly evolved creatures and, like all mammals, can be afflicted with a number of diseases.

Viral Diseases

Viruses cause disease by damaging or killing the cells in organs, by changing normal cells into cancerous ones, or by stimulating an immune response that ultimately harms the dog. The signs of viral disease vary tremendously.

Distemper is a disease that suppresses the canine immune system. The virus is shed in the secretions and excretions of infected animals and is transmitted through the air. The most common signs are fever (103 to 105°F or 38 to 40°C), depression, loss of appetite, pus-filled eyes, nasal discharge, coughing, breathing difficulties, vomiting, and diarrhea; there may also be convulsions or uncontrollable twitching of a body part, such as the head, neck, or leg. Veterinarians can provide supportive and symptomatic treatment—antibiotics, antivomiting and antidiarrheal medications, anticonvulsants (for seizures), intravenous fluids, oxygen, bronchodilators (drugs to expand the breathing passages)—with the hope that the dog's immune system will rally to overcome the virus and secondary bacterial infections.

Sadly, many dogs with distemper die, and dogs that do survive may suffer permanent neurological problems such as convulsions or muscle twitching. Unvaccinated puppies are at greatest risk. All puppies should be vaccinated every three to four weeks from six or eight to sixteen weeks of age and should then be revaccinated annually.

Canine parvovirus, primarily seen in puppies from weaning to six months of age, attacks the intestinal tract. It also damages the bone marrow, lymphoid tissues, and sometimes the immune system and heart muscle. Common signs are fever, loss of appetite, depression, vomiting, severe diarrhea (often bloody), rapid dehydration, and weight loss. If the heart is involved, coughing, labored breathing, or even sudden death may occur. Left untreated, severe dehydration, electrolyte loss, and secondary bacterial infections can also lead to death. Prompt veterinary intervention—with intravenous fluids, electrolytes, and antibiotics—is crucial.

The virus is shed in the feces of infected dogs and transmitted through mouth contact with contaminated organic debris (feces, dirt, hair) or objects, such as food and water bowls, and can survive and remain infectious for months. To prevent spreading, remove organic debris from surfaces and clean objects that may be contaminated with hot water and soap and disinfect with a diluted bleach solution. Dogs should be vaccinated for parvo every three to four weeks from six to twenty weeks of age, and revaccinated once every year. Rottweilers, Doberman pinschers, and pit bulls may be more susceptible to parvovirus than other breeds.

Infectious canine hepatitis (ICH) targets the liver, kidneys, eyes, and the cells lining the inner surfaces of blood vessels. In the most severe "peracute" form, which tends to strike puppies between two and six weeks of age, the animals die within a few hours or a day, sometimes before owners even notice a problem. The more common "acute" form is usually seen in puppies six to ten weeks of age. Signs include fever, vomiting, diarrhea, a hunched-up appearance due to abdominal pain, tonsillitis, enlarged lymph nodes in the neck, and hemorrhaging (from the nose, gums, and gastrointestinal tract, and under the skin), as well as disorientation, depression, stupor, coma, and seizures if encephalitis or severe liver disease occurs. Swollen corneas may cause the eyes to appear cloudy and blue.

In some victims, a fever that lasts a day or two with lethargy, malaise, and decreased appetite will be followed by recovery. Some dogs with partial immunity may develop a chronic, persistent hepatitis. Death may occur in other cases if the dogs are not given supportive treatment. If there is bleeding or neurological signs (such as depression, seizures, or wobbling), blood transfusions or medication may be necessary.

Dogs become infected by inhaling or ingesting the highly contagious virus, which is shed in the urine of infected dogs for up to a year. All dogs should be vaccinated every three or four weeks from six or eight to sixteen weeks of age, then yearly thereafter.

Parainfluenza/kennel cough (canine infectious tracheobronchitis) is a highly contagious disease caused by organisms that inflame and damage the larynx, trachea (windpipe), and bronchial tubes. Despite this disease's common name, "kennel cough," dogs do not have to be in a kennel to get it, although the risk of infection increases when they are brought together in large groups. The disease can be transmitted, sometimes by dogs that are showing no signs of infection, by coughing and sneezing, or by contact with contaminated objects, such as food and water bowls. Often the only sign of infection is a distinctive high-pitched, dry, honking cough followed by a gagging, retching sound. The dog may also bring up a white frothy-looking fluid. Bouts of coughing are exacerbated by excitement, barking, walking on a leash,

and exposure to cold air. Fever, lethargy, and a decreased appetite may occur if pneumonia or a more serious secondary bacterial infection develops. Occasionally there will be discharge from the eyes and nose. Recovery may take up to three weeks and treatment may not be needed if there is no loss of appetite, fever, or decrease in activity level. If the dog shows signs of pneumonia or bacterial infection, antibiotics, cough suppressants, and bronchodilators may be prescribed. The veterinarian may also recommend discontinuing vigorous exercise, replacing the collar with a harness, and using a cool-mist vaporizer or steam from a shower to help clear the breathing tubes.

To prevent kennel cough, puppies should be vaccinated against parainfluenza and adenovirus 2 every three to four weeks from six or eight to sixteen weeks of age, then yearly thereafter. Vaccines against *Bordetella* are considered optional by many veterinarians. They are often recommended for dogs that are at high risk of exposure, such as show dogs, sporting or hunting dogs, and those that are boarded.

Rabies travels through the nervous system to the brain and spinal cord, where it destroys tissue and causes fatal inflammation. It can afflict any warm-blooded animal, including humans. The virus is present in the saliva of infected animals (often raccoons, foxes, skunks, and bats) and is usually transmitted through bite wounds. Rabies can also be transmitted if the infected saliva contacts a fresh preexisting wound or a mucous membrane, such as the lining of the mouth or nose, though this means of transmission is rare. The incubation period is usually two to eight weeks, but may last six months or

Dogs suspected of having rabies must either be held in quarantine for observation or be euthanized.

form doesn't usually bite, and indeed is often incapable of biting, humans can be exposed to the virus when they examine the dog's mouth. Soon after signs of paralysis begin in the head area (usually within hours), the limbs become paralyzed; coma and death from respiratory paralysis follow.

Dogs with "furious" rabies will be restless, often roaming over a large area. Aggression toward people, other animals, and even inanimate objects are characteristic, leading to the term "mad dog." The dog will attack anything in his path, thereby spreading the fatal virus. Disorientation, a wobbly gait, and convulsions develop, followed by death from respiratory paralysis.

No treatment or cure for either form exists once signs appear; death usually occurs within two to ten days.

If your dog is up to date on his rabies vaccination and is bitten by an animal that you suspect may be rabid, bring him to a veterinarian immediately for a booster shot. Stay away from any animal that is acting strangely, and report the behavior to animal-control officers. If you are bitten by an animal that may be rabid, consult a doctor immediately for a series of injections that will save your life. Because rabies poses such grave danger to humans, any dog that is not protected by a current rabies vaccination and is exposed to a suspicious animal or bites a human must be quarantined for six months under the direction of the local health department, or must be euthanized. (There is no accurate test for rabies that can be done while the dog is still alive.)

Owners may be fined for having an unvaccinated pet. Dogs should be vaccinated at twelve weeks of age, then either

longer. Early signs are often marked by changes in behavior. Wild animals may act tame, while previously affectionate pets may act fearful. After one to three days, the affected dog will show signs of either paralysis (the "dumb" or "paralytic" form of rabies) or will be aggressive (indicating "furious rabies").

The signs of "dumb" rabies are caused by muscular paralysis. Throat and mouth muscles are usually affected first, resulting in changes in the sound of the bark, breathing difficulties, excessive drooling ("frothing of the mouth"), and what appears to be an avoidance or fear of water (hydrophobia) but is actually an inability to drink. The lower jaw frequently hangs open. Although a dog with the dumb

yearly or once every three years depending on state laws.

Canine coronavirus, a virus that causes damage to the intestinal wall, is spread when a dog's mouth comes into contact with infected feces. Most dogs either exhibit no signs or mild ones and require no treatment, but some suffer loss of appetite, vomiting, and diarrhea, with soft or watery stools containing mucus or blood. Dogs with severe diarrhea need supportive care and must be fed an easily digested diet such as chicken and rice once any vomiting ceases. Most dogs recover quickly; others may have diarrhea for three to four weeks. Deaths are rare and limited to puppies one to two weeks of age. Because the disease is usually mild or asymptomatic (without symptoms), vaccination is considered optional by many veterinarians. However, dogs that are at high risk of exposure—such as show dogs, sporting or hunting dogs, and those that are boarded—might benefit from the vaccine, which should be administered at six to eight and ten to twelve weeks of age, and yearly thereafter.

Systemic Bacterial Diseases

There are many bacteria that are capable of causing diseases in dogs. Covered here are three significant bacterial diseases that afflict a range of body systems. Bacterial diseases that primarily afflict a single system are covered within that system.

Lyme disease can lead to arthritis and neurological and cardiac complications if left untreated. The bacteria are transmitted by infected deer ticks and related tick species. Signs include joint pain (reluctance to move, limping, and pain when the joint is manipulated), fever, loss of appetite, lethargy, and enlarged lymph nodes. A positive blood test can aid in the diagnosis of Lyme disease, but it is possible for an infected dog to test negative. Lyme disease is treated with antibiotics. Dogs in areas with high incidences of the disease are vaccinated initially with two vaccines given three to four weeks apart beginning as early as nine weeks of age, then yearly thereafter.

Leptospirosis is spread by wild and domestic animals that shed the organisms in their urine for months or years after they are infected. Dogs can contract the disease directly from other animals or from contamination of water, soil, or vegetation in the environment. Most infections go unnoticed, and some dogs manage to clear the bacteria from their systems without treatment. However, the bacteria can cause inflammation of the kidneys, with signs that include fever, loss of appetite, lethargy, vomiting, diarrhea, reluctance to move, dehydration, and reddening of the mucous membranes, including those around the eyes. If the liver is affected, the gums and eyes may appear yellow, and there may be hemorrhaging (nosebleeds, vomited blood, black, tarry stools). Miscarriage, stillbirth, and inflammation of the irises can also occur, and untreated infections can result in kidney or liver failure, or both. Treatment may involve diuretics, therapy to treat shock and restore fluid losses from vomiting and diarrhea, blood transfusions, and antibiotics.

Currently vaccines exist for only a few of the types of leptospires that cause leptospirosis. Controversy exists regarding whether all dogs or only those at high risk should be vaccinated and at what age vaccinations should begin. Because humans can contract leptospirosis, infected dogs should be walked in a confined area, and areas contaminated with their urine should be disinfected with a diluted bleach solution.

Salmonellosis is caused by salmonella bacteria and is usually transmitted when a dog ingests contaminated food or water. This disease is most often seen among young dogs or those that live in crowded or unsanitary conditions. Infected dogs generally become asymptomatic carriers, but in some cases infected dogs show signs such as acute watery or mucusy diarrhea (with occasional blood), chronic intermittent diarrhea, vomiting, fever, lethargy, loss of appetite, a hunched-up appearance due to abdominal pain, and dehydration. Salmonella may be treated with fluids, electrolytes, and/or antibiotics. Without treatment, the disease can be fatal.

Because salmonellosis can affect humans, owners of infected dogs should dispose of their pets' feces, disinfect with a diluted bleach solution any surfaces contaminated with feces, and wash their hands after handling their animals or their feces.

Cancer/Tumors

Cancer is the uncontrolled growth of cells, and may be localized (confined to a single area) or generalized (spread throughout the body). The incidence of a dog getting cancer increases with age. Signs of cancer vary according to the organ affected. A veterinarian should be consulted any time a dog exhibits any of the following signs: a lump or swelling, persistent sores, abnormal discharge from any body opening,

foul breath, lack of energy, or unexplained weight loss. Since the cause of most cancers is unknown, prevention is difficult. One exception is breast cancer, the likelihood of which can be greatly reduced by spaying female dogs before their first heat. Diagnosis of cancer usually involves a biopsy in which a small piece of tissue is removed for examination under a microscope. A biopsy should be performed on any persistent lump or nonhealing wound no matter how small or insignificant. Treatment varies depending on the type of cancer detected. It may include surgery, chemotherapy, radiation, cryosurgery (freezing), or hyperthermia (heating).

Mammary gland tumors/breast cancer is the most common type of cancer in female dogs. About half of all mammary gland tumors are malignant, meaning they have the potential to spread to other organs. Even benign mammary gland tumors (which don't usually spread to other areas) can grow and rupture, causing bleeding and infection. Mammary gland tumors are most common in unspayed female dogs over six years of age. The cause is unknown, but most cases can be prevented by having the dog spayed before her first heat. The dog's risk of developing a mammary gland tumor increases significantly with each of the first two heats.

The most common sign of a mammary gland tumor is a mass or swelling in the mammary gland area, possibly associated with abnormal discharge from the nipple. Labored breathing or lameness may occur in advanced cases that have spread to the lungs or bones. Most veterinarians treat mammary gland tumors by removing them surgically. Any growth on or near the mammary glands should be biopsied or removed as early as possible. The larger the tumor, the grimmer the prognosis.

Mast cell tumors are solitary masses on the surface of the skin and in the tissue immediately under the skin. Some breeds, such as boxers, golden retrievers, and Boston terriers, are predisposed to developing mast cell tumors. Their cause is unknown. Most are located on a dog's trunk and extremities. Less common sites are the neck and internal organs, such as the spleen, liver, and small intestines. Fast-growing tumors in the groin area, between the anus and genitals, or on the prepuce (the tube of skin covering the penis) tend to be malignant, as are about half of all mast cell tumors. They can cause gastrointestinal ulcers, symptoms of which are loss of appetite, vomiting, diarrhea, and black, tarry stools. An untreated benign mast cell tumor may ulcerate and become infected; if it is not removed at that point the infection may spread. A malignant mast cell tumor can spread to the lymph nodes, spleen, liver, and bone marrow.

Veterinarians usually treat mast cell tumors by removing them surgically. Radiation, chemotherapy, or both may be used for those tumors that have spread to other organs or that cannot be completely removed. Survival time depends on the degree of malignancy of the tumor.

Squamous cell carcinomas are malignant tumors that may look like red, smooth, firm growths or inflamed masses with open sores. They appear most frequently on a dog's digits, legs, scrotum, abdomen, lips, nose, gums, tongue, and tonsils. Overexposure to the sun's ultraviolet rays is one certain cause of these tumors. Without prompt medical attention the tumors tend to invade surrounding tissue and bone and spread to the lymph nodes and lungs.

A veterinarian will usually choose aggressive surgical excision—amputation of the digit, for example—if the tumor is on the toe or nail bed. If part of the jawbone is involved, the vet will recommend its removal or, if that won't work, radiation therapy. The average survival time for dogs is four to ten months after surgery; without surgery the average survival time is one to three months.

An **osteosarcoma** is a malignant bone tumor. It develops most frequently in young dogs (six months to two years old), although it can occur at any age. Large and giant-breed dogs, such as Great Danes and Saint Bernards, are predisposed to developing osteosarcomas. Leg bones are the most commonly affected. The tumor destroys the bone and has a tendency to spread rapidly to the lungs and other areas. The main signs of an osteosarcoma are lameness and swelling at the site of the tumor.

Treatment includes amputation of the affected limb; fortunately, most dogs can walk well on three legs. For dogs with already compromised mobility, veterinarians may opt for a limb-sparing procedure that involves removing the tumor and replacing the bone defect with bone from a bone bank; this procedure is generally reserved for cases in which the osteosarcoma is near the lower end of the foreleg. Chemotherapy following surgery is very effective in prolonging life but can be expensive. Survival times average two to four months with amputation and ten to eighteen months with amputation plus chemotherapy or bone replacement.

Testicular tumors come in three types: Sertoli cell tumors, seminomas, and interstitial cell tumors. These tumors, common in older dogs, are usually benign if they are in the scrotum; malignant tumors are more likely to be found in dogs with "undescended" testicles (located within the abdomen instead of in the scrotum). The cause of testicular tumors is unknown.

One sign of a tumor is the painless swelling of a testicle. Benign interstitial cell tumors secrete testosterone and are thought to contribute to prostate enlargement and the formation of benign tumors near the anus. Benign Sertoli cell tumors can secrete estrogens, which may cause bone marrow destruction and signs of feminization, such as enlargement of the mammary glands, non-itchy symmetrical hair loss with darkening of the skin, shrinking of the penile sheath, squatting to urinate, and attraction to other male dogs. Seminomas may also secrete estrogen, but this is not common. Malignant Sertoli cell tumors and seminomas will spread to other organs and become life-threatening if left untreated. Interstitial cell tumors are nearly always benign.

Veterinarians usually treat testicular tumors by surgically removing both of the dog's testicles; the survival rate is good. Occasionally Sertoli cell tumors and seminomas spread to the lymph nodes and liver months after the testicles have been removed.

Transmissible venereal tumors are passed from dog to dog by sexual contact or licking. The main sign is bleeding, cauliflower-like growths on the penis or vulva. Tumors may also appear near the mouth or in the nasal cavity. Occasionally the tumors disappear spontaneously. More commonly, without treatment, additional growths form and the dog experiences more irritation, bleeding,

and, in some cases, infection. The growths can also obstruct urination. Most transmissible venereal tumors are benign. Nearly all transmissible venereal tumors can be cured with chemotherapy.

Lymphoma is a proliferation of malignant lymphocytes (a type of white blood cells). Golden retrievers and Saint Bernards seem particularly susceptible. The disease affects middle-aged and older dogs more often than young ones. The cause of lymphoma is unknown.

There are four types of lymphomas: multicentric (the most common), alimentary, mediastinal, and cutaneous. Multicentric lymphoma occurs at multiple sites simultaneously and usually causes all of the lymph nodes in the body to become enlarged. In cases of alimentary lymphoma, malignant lymphocytes invade the dog's digestive tract, lymph nodes, liver, and spleen, causing diarrhea and marked weight loss even though the dog's appetite may be normal. In the mediastinal form, lymphatic tissue in front of the heart enlarges, causing coughing, labored breathing, and swallowing difficulties. Cutaneous lymphoma is characterized by raised red skin lesions and open sores. With all forms of lymphoma, signs that the dog's overall health is compromised, such as poor appetite, weight loss, and lethargy, eventually develop.

Lymphoma cannot be cured but the multicentric form can be controlled for an average of ten to twelve months with chemotherapy (some dogs live as long as two years). The mediastinal and alimentary forms are rarely controllable for longer than four to six months. Cutaneous lymphoma is not responsive to any type of treatment and is rapidly fatal.

Eye Problems

Some signs of canine eye disease include squinting, pawing, or rubbing of the eye; redness of the tissue lining the eyelid; excessive tearing; unequal pupil sizes; a visible third eyelid; cloudiness or color changes on the surface or inside of the eye; and, of course, blindness.

Conjunctivitis, an inflammation of the lining around the eye, can be caused by bacteria, viruses, fungi, mycoplasma (microscopic organisms capable of causing disease), tear deficiency (keratoconjunctivitis sicca, see below), foreign bodies (hair or plant, metallic, or synthetic materials), chemical irritants (lye, ammonia), environmental irritants (dust, sand, tobacco smoke, household sprays, wallpaper, formaldehyde from new rugs), allergies, trauma, or tumors. Other causes are distortions in the shape of the eyelid, such as ectropion, entropion, and glaucoma (page 434). The signs are red eyes; a watery, mucus, or pus discharge; excessive blinking; squinting; or holding the eyes closed. The third eyelid may also protrude. If left untreated, conjunctivitis may lead to keratoconjunctivitis sicca, corneal ulcers, and vision loss. Treatment includes removing any underlying cause, whether foreign material or offending allergens; medicating allergies and relieving tear deficiencies; and controlling secondary infections.

Keratoconjunctivitis sicca (KCS), or dry eye, is a common cause of conjunctivitis in dogs. Miniature schnauzers, cocker spaniels, West Highland white terriers, pugs, Yorkshire terriers, English bulldogs, and beagles are particularly vulnerable. The condition is commonly caused by an abnormality in the immune system

Even a healthy cocker spaniel like this one is predisposed to tear duct disorders and abnormalities.

whereby the tear glands are incorrectly recognized as "foreign" and are destroyed. KCS can also be caused by certain drugs, chronic untreated conjunctivitis, viral infections, or trauma. Signs include chronic mucus or pus discharge, conjunctivitis, squinting, crust around the eyes, rubbing of the eyes, and inflammation of the cornea. Without treatment KCS can lead to corneal ulcers or blindness. If medical treatment is not effective, surgery can be performed.

Cherry eye is a condition in which the tear gland that occupies the inner base of the third eyelid enlarges, for unknown reasons, forming a protruding cherrylike mass. Occasionally the gland returns to normal size; more commonly it remains enlarged and causes recurrent conjunctivitis. Any dog can be affected, but cocker spaniels, beagles, bloodhounds, bulldogs, Boston terriers, bull terriers,

Lhasa apsos, Saint Bernards, and shar-peis are most at risk. Treatment may include topical antibiotics and steroids, although surgery is usually necessary.

Epiphora is an overflow of tears down the face that leaves facial hair stained. It can be caused by abnormal eyelashes, entropion (a rolling in of the lower lid edge, discussed at right), inflammation and obstruction of the tear duct, congenital blockage of the tear duct (commonly seen in cocker spaniels), or malposition of the tear duct in dogs with protruding eyes, such as the Lhasa apso or Boston terrier. Epiphora can also be a sign of eye pain. Topical antibiotics and steroids are used to treat tear duct inflammation and obstruction; surgery can correct duct obstruction and entropion; and abnormal eyelashes can be removed surgically. To treat mild cases, owners can try applying diaper rash ointment to the stained area (avoiding the eyes) after cleaning it with a no-tears baby shampoo and water.

Glaucoma is often hereditary among breeds that are predisposed to it, such as cocker spaniels, miniature poodles, beagles, basset hounds, Siberian huskies, Norwegian elkhounds, Samoyeds, malamutes, chow chows, shar-peis, and Afghans. Symptoms include inflammation of the iris, lens dislocation, tumors, cataracts, and bleeding resulting from trauma, high blood pressure, or a bleeding disorder. Squinting and rubbing of the eye due to pain, swollen blood vessels in the white of the eye, a cloudy cornea, a dilated pupil (even in bright light), poor vision, and an enlarged eyeball are characteristic. Immediate, aggressive treatment with medication is needed to prevent damage to the retina and optic nerve and blindness. In some cases, surgery is necessary.

Ectropion and *entropion* seem to be hereditary and are typically seen in the young of certain breeds, such as the Saint Bernard (ectropion) and the chow chow and shar-pei (entropion). Ectropion, a turning outward of the edge of the eyelid, causes the lower eyelids to droop, leaving the conjunctiva and cornea exposed and prone to inflammation, tearing, and redness. Entropion, a rolling in of the edge of the eyelid, can lead to conjunctivitis with mild eye discharge, severe eye pain, corneal ulceration, excessive tearing, and white or green pus draining from the eyes. A spastic entropion results when the pain associated with a corneal ulcer causes the eyelid muscles to contract and the eyelid to roll in; healing the ulcer may correct the condition. Ectropion and entropion can be corrected surgically.

Cataracts are white opacities in the lenses of the eyes that impair vision or cause blindness. They may be present at birth, or they may develop in young dogs (juvenile cataracts) or in old individuals (senile cataracts). Cataracts due to heredity, the most common kind, affect more than seventy breeds. Other causes include an inflammation in the eye that blocks nutrition to the lens and impedes removal of metabolic waste products; diabetes mellitus (see page 451); direct injury to the lens; nutritional deficiency, such as when puppies are fed milk-replacement formulas lacking the amino acid arginine; and the toxic effects of an electrical shock, certain drugs, or radiation therapy affecting the eye. The degree of visual impairment depends on the extent of the cataract.

The only ways to correct cataracts are to fragment the lens with ultrasonic vibrations or to remove the lens surgically. In addition to restoring vision, cataract removal may prevent such complications as lens displacement, glaucoma, or inflammation of the inside of the eye. Senile cataracts (also known as nuclear sclerosis) are a normal consequence of aging and are common in dogs over six years of age. It appears in both eyes as a translucent bluish gray haze, does not impede vision, and does not need to be treated.

Progressive retinal atrophy (PRA), in most cases hereditary, is caused by a degeneration and loss of retinal tissue. Early-onset PRA, seen during the first year of life, affects breeds such as collies, Irish setters, miniature schnauzers, elkhounds, and miniature dachshunds. Late-onset PRA, noticeable after one year of age, affects miniature poodles, cocker spaniels, and Labrador retrievers. Night blindness is usually the first sign of PRA. The dog may not like to go out at night, may be reluctant to go up and down dimly lit stairs, and may prefer to stay close by human companions. In the early stage, lighting hallways and yards will help the dog get around, but eventually the dog will go blind. There is no effective treatment for PRA. The only way to prevent it is to make sure that affected dogs and carriers do not breed. All breeding dogs should be registered with the Canine Eye Registry Foundation and should be evaluated before being bred, and then yearly thereafter by a board-certified ophthalmologist.

Blindness in one or both eyes can be caused by any disorder that blocks the movement of light through the eye. Inflammation, infection, tumors, or bleeding in the brain can lead to blindness. Signs are fairly obvious: dogs bump into objects, and their pupils don't respond to light. Without treatment, permanent blindness is likely.

Ear Problems

A dog's ear provides a perfect environment—dark and damp, with poor ventilation—for the growth of bacteria and yeast. To prevent infections, examine the ears on a regular basis, and, when necessary, clean with a cotton ball dampened with baby oil, hydrogen peroxide, or a commercial ear-cleaning preparation available from veterinarians (see page 381 for instructions on how to clean a dog's ears). Dogs with ear infections may shake their heads and scratch their ears. Owners may see redness and pus, and the ears may give off a bad odor. Basset hounds, cocker spaniels, and golden retrievers are especially prone to ear infections. Ear mites can also cause inflammation and itching. Both conditions can lead to more serious problems if left untreated.

Ear mites, tiny organisms that live in the ear canal, are highly contagious to other dogs and cats and cause a dry reddish brown or black waxy ear discharge and intense itching and head shaking. Microscopic examination of the ear debris reveals the ear mites or their eggs. Treatment involves cleaning out the debris, administering a miticide in the ears (see page 461 for instructions on how to administer ear medications), and applying a topical insecticide to kill mites on the skin and hair. If untreated, infestation can lead to skin or ear infections and aural hematomas (see page 436) due to excessive scratching and head shaking. Dogs of any age can get ear mites, but they are most common in puppies.

Otitis externa, inflammation of the external ear canal, can be caused by bacteria or yeast, ear mites, allergies, foreign bodies (such as plant material), hypothyroidism, autoimmune diseases, trauma, cancer, polyps, or disorders that cause dry or greasy flaking of the skin. Excessive moisture in the ear canal caused by too frequent bathing can also predispose a dog to developing this condition. It is most commonly seen in dogs with either hanging or floppy ears, such as cocker spaniels; dogs with narrow ear canals like shar-peis; and dogs with a large amount of hair in the ears, such as poodles. Signs include head shaking, scratching and rubbing of the ears, a foul ear odor, ear discharge, and sometimes deafness. If left untreated, inflammation can spread to the middle and inner ear. Treatment varies with the cause. Anti-mite, antibacterial, antiyeast, or anti-inflammatory medication may be prescribed along with ear-cleansing and ear-drying solutions. Flushing the ears with a bulb syringe and then drying on a regular basis may be recommended. Severe infections may require ear flushing in the hospital, often with sedation. If the otitis externa is severe and chronic, surgery might be recommended.

Otitis media is an inflammation that usually occurs when otitis externa extends into the middle ear. It has the same symptoms as otitis externa but may also cause a dog to avoid opening her mouth fully due to pain. Injury to nerves in the area may cause a drooping of the upper lip or ear and drooling on the affected side. Other signs of otitis media include Horner's syndrome, characterized by a protrusion of the third eyelid; a tiny, unresponsive pupil that does not dilate when light is directed on it; and a droopy eyelid. If otitis media is left untreated, it can extend to the inner ear and result in a head tilt, circling, rolling to the affected side, and mild to severe gait changes. Occasionally bacteria can extend into the brain. Otitis media is treated with antibiotics, flushing of the ear canal with a warm saltwater solution, and surgery.

Aural hematomas, collections of blood between the cartilage and skin that appear as soft swellings in the ear flaps, may result from scratching and head shaking associated with ear mites, trauma to the ear flap (from rough play, for example), external parasites (such as fleas and ticks), and insect bites. An untreated hematoma usually grows and then shrinks, leaving the ear flap cauliflower-like in appearance. If the underlying cause is left untreated, the hematoma may worsen or recur, and the other ear may also develop a hematoma. Surgery is the most effective treatment, although if not performed early, the appearance of the ear may remain distorted.

Deafness may be congenital or caused by ear infections, drug toxicity, or aging. Boxers, collies, dalmatians, English setters, Old English sheepdogs, and Shetland sheepdogs are some of the breeds affected by congenital deafness. Ear infections can destroy nerve cells or the structures that conduct sound. Some drugs and antiseptics used to treat inflammation of the ear can cause deafness. The aging process can cause degeneration of the sound-receptor cells and structures.

The most noticeable sign of deafness is a lack of response to verbal interaction. Hearing loss in puppies may not be noticed until an effort is made to teach them verbal commands. A brain stem auditory-evoked response (BAER) test, which requires specialized equipment usually available only at university veterinary hospitals, is useful for screening dogs for hearing loss. Treating ear infections, cleaning the ear canal, or surgically correcting an ear canal that has been narrowed by a chronic infection may cure a problem thought to have been deafness.

Skin Problems

There are just a few ways that a dog's skin responds to disease: by getting red and itchy; by developing scabby bumps, lumps, pimples, or open sores; by losing hair; and by flaking. Because the repertoire of signs is so limited, different skin diseases often look exactly the same. Also, the same disease may appear completely different from dog to dog. Only rarely can a veterinarian ascertain the cause of a skin condition by just looking at it; diagnostic tests are almost always necessary.

Allergies occur when a dog's immune system becomes supersensitive to foods or foreign particles, such as flea saliva, pollen, house dust, and wool. In response, the system produces chemicals that cause an allergy, a severe inflammatory reaction.

Atopy (allergic inhalant dermatitis) is seen in many breeds, including miniature schnauzers, Irish setters, golden retrievers, German shepherds, dalmatians, and beagles. It is caused by a supersensitivity to certain particles in the air, such as pollen from trees, ragweed, grass, and other plants, house dust, feathers, and wool. The allergy follows a predictable course: It is inherited and seasonal (signs appear at the same time every year), and it reveals itself between six months and three years of age. Signs include severe biting and scratching or rubbing of the face, ears, or feet, paw licking, sneezing, and generalized redness of the skin (often including

the ears). Treatments include avoidance of the allergens, administration of antihistamines and steroids, and/or allergy shots.

Food allergies don't seem to be as common in dogs as atopy. Signs include severe itching and skin lesions that may appear on the dog's whole body or be limited to the face, feet, and ears and may be accompanied by diarrhea. A veterinarian may prescribe a hypoallergenic diet for a minimum of eight weeks. If the dog shows dramatic improvement within that time, the veterinarian will recommend that the dog remain on the diet indefinitely. If there is no improvement or only moderate improvement, the vet may test for other causes, such as a bacterial infection or atopy (discussed at left).

Allergic contact dermatitis is the least common dog allergy. Hairless or thin-coated areas, such as the abdomen, armpits, inner thighs, chest, the area between the toes, or the scrotum become red and itchy. Common irritants are soaps, insecticides, flea collars, wool (particularly wool rugs), dyes (particularly in nylon carpets), paint, wood preservatives, poison ivy, poison oak, pollens, and grasses. Treatments include anti-inflammatory medications and avoidance of the offending allergen if it can be identified.

Flea allergic dermatitis is a very common condition. Fleas inject their saliva into dogs when they take their blood meals, and the saliva can cause some dogs to itch and bite themselves. Even as few as one or two fleas can cause a reaction. Hair loss, usually a triangular patch from the middle of the back to the tail base, with patches on the neck and on the inner thighs, and skin infection in some areas are characteristic. Moving fleas may be visible in these areas. Flea droppings (digested blood) are found primarily on the hairs of the lower back. To differentiate droppings from dirt, place what you believe to be droppings on white paper and moisten them with water. If they turn red, they are flea droppings. Treatment involves eliminating fleas, administering steroids to control itching, and addressing any bacterial skin infections that may have developed from scratching. (See page 439 for more information on fleas.)

Hot spots are areas of bald, reddened, moist, well-demarcated skin infections that can enlarge rapidly. An allergic skin reaction, especially one caused by flea or tick bites, can initiate this itchy condition, which is common in golden and Labrador retrievers. Treatments may include soothing shampoos, oral antibiotics, steroids, and topical antibiotic-corticosteroid creams, as well as insecticides or miticides to kill any external parasites if present.

Fly bite dermatitis happens in warm weather when biting flies can cause serious irritation and infection of the ears. Especially susceptible are dogs with erect ears like German shepherds. Common signs are head shaking and ear scratching, scabs, and bleeding. Left untreated, the ears can become severely infected. To eliminate the flies, the yard must be treated with pesticides and the dog kept indoors when not being walked or exercised. A medicated shampoo to use on the dog's ears, topical antibiotic-corticosteroid ointment, and oral antibiotics may be recommended. If the dog must stay outdoors, a canine fly repellent should be applied to the tips of the ears and the skin on the ear flaps.

Acral lick dermatitis (lick granuloma) develops as a thick, firm, ulcerated sore from excessive licking or biting of the skin. The lower fore or hindlegs are commonly affected. The cause is usually unknown, although some dogs will lick an area because of a foreign body in the skin, boredom, lack of exercise, or an obsessive-compulsive disorder. Doberman pinschers, German shepherds, Great Danes, and golden retrievers seem to be more prone than other breeds to this condition.

Treatments are prescribed according to the degree of inflammation, the size of the lesion, and the underlying cause. Lick granulomas that are not treated vigorously and early may enlarge and become infected, at which point radiation or surgery may become necessary.

Anal gland sacculitis involves the sacs located on either side of a dog's anus that accumulate secretions normally released when the dog exercises vigorously or moves his bowels. If the secretions, which have an unpleasant musklike odor, are not emptied, the sacs become impacted (overfilled with material) and infected. This impaction is more common in toy and miniature dogs than in other breeds. The dog will lick the anal area and slide it along the ground, and the area adjacent to the anus will become red, swollen, and painful.

Veterinarians treat anal gland sacculitis by squeezing the secretions from the impacted sac, flushing it with saline solution, instilling antibiotics, and prescribing oral antibiotics. If left untreated, the anal sac will rupture, which may lead to a more serious or chronic infection. If a dog's anal glands become impacted frequently, this treatment is repeated monthly. When treatment is ineffective, the anal glands are removed.

External Parasites

Fleas—wingless, brown, flattened insects with three pairs of elastic, powerful legs—have been plaguing their hosts for more than 100 million years. They live on their hosts' coats anywhere from two weeks to two years, depending on the temperature and humidity—ideally for the fleas, 60 to 90°F (15 to 32°C) and 65 to 85 percent humidity. The most common problems they cause are flea allergic dermatitis (see page 437), tapeworms, and anemia (mainly seen in severely infested puppies).

Fleas are usually diagnosed when they or their droppings are found in a dog's coat (see Flea Combing Your Dog on page 376). If you find substantial flea debris or more than one or two fleas on your dog, treat your dog, any other dogs or cats in the household, and the home environment. It is important to discuss with your vet what combination of products to use, because the wrong one can be deadly for your pets or simply ineffective. In regions with heavy infestations or year-round flea seasons, vets may recommend such preventive measures as monthly pills or topical insecticides.

Ticks are external parasites that bury their heads in the skin of their hosts and suck blood until they look like fat beans. When the ticks can't hold any more blood, they fall off the host and lay 5,000 eggs or more, which hatch in one or two months. Different tick species have different requirements for completing their life cycle. Some ticks need up to three hosts in order to develop from egg to adult.

Heavy tick infestations can cause anemia, severe skin irritations, and infections. Ticks can also transmit Lyme disease, Rocky Mountain spotted fever, and ehrlichiosis, a potentially chronic infectious

The Amazing Flea

Fleas do not get tired. When looking for a host they have been known to jump 10,000 times in succession without stopping, totalling the length of three football fields. Their elastic, powerful legs are equipped with specially adapted "rakes" that help them hang onto the hair of their hosts.

The female flea can consume a daily blood meal equivalent to 15 times its body weight. Seventy-five fleas (not an extremely large infestation) can consume 1 milliliter of blood (about a fifth of a teaspoon) per day, which may not seem like a lot in the short term but can add up quickly. An infestation of 220 fleas can consume 5 percent of a 2-pound puppy's blood volume in a day. Fleas can live up to two years without feeding.

The flea's body is flattened laterally so that it is higher than wide, designed for quick movement through fur.

disease that can affect the bone marrow. Ticks can be found anywhere on the dog's body, though they are most common on the ear flaps, head, neck, shoulders, and between the toes. To remove a tick from a dog's skin, using tweezers (not your fingers), grasp the tick as near the skin as you can and pull it out with a gentle tug. Do not squeeze the tick when removing it to avoid injecting more disease-causing organisms into the dog. Sometimes the tick's jaw or head remains in the skin, in most cases not a cause for concern since the dog's body usually rejects these parts.

Clean the area where the tick was imbedded with a cotton ball dampened with alcohol. After a tick is pulled out, a scab may form over the area.

Ticks can be controlled with a veterinarian-recommended insecticide. Check your dog often, especially during tick season. Although dogs cannot transmit Lyme disease, ehrlichiosis, or Rocky Mountain spotted fever to people, ticks do. Take care while removing ticks and check yourself for ticks if you find them on your dog.

Lice are small, flat, wingless insects with six legs, each leg bearing one or two claws. The adult lays sticky white eggs (nits) that become cemented to the hair of the host. Nymphs hatch from the eggs, undergo three molts, and become adults, a cycle that takes fourteen to twenty-one days. There are two types of lice: sucking and biting. Sucking lice suck the host's blood and cause itching, hair loss, and inflammation of the skin. A large infestation can cause anemia. The adult lice (and their eggs) are spread by direct contact with infected animals or by contaminated brushes, combs, or bedding. Biting lice cause itching, hair loss, and inflammation but not anemia. To diagnose, the veterinarian examines a hair sample under a microscope. Infected dogs are treated with insecticides. In addition, the dog's bedding and grooming implements must be cleaned with an insecticide or soap and very hot water. Dog lice do not spread from dogs to humans and are different from the types of lice that infect humans.

Demodex mites, which can be seen only under a microscope, live without causing any problems on the skin of many dogs; however, some dogs cannot tolerate them and develop a disease called demodicosis or Demodex mange. In these cases, the mites cause hair loss and sometimes redness on the face, around the eyes, or at the corners of the mouth. In a few instances, demodicosis spreads all over the body. Some breeds seem to have a higher incidence of juvenile-onset demodicosis. They include Afghan hounds, American Staffordshire terriers, Boston terriers, boxers, Chihuahuas, shar-peis, collies, dalmatians, Doberman pinschers, English bulldogs, German shepherds, Great Danes, Old English sheepdogs, pit bull terriers, and pugs.

Most dogs outgrow localized demodicosis. However, generalized demodicosis needs to be treated more aggressively with a combination of medications specially formulated to kill the mites, as well as antibiotics, benzoyl peroxide shampoos, and whirlpool baths or soaks.

Sarcoptes mites—microscopic white, eight-legged mites that burrow into a dog's skin—cause canine scabies (also known as sarcoptic mange), a highly contagious skin disease. Infected dogs scratch vigorously and develop crusty skin lesions, especially on the edges of the ears, elbows, hocks, and face. Scabies is usually diagnosed through an examination of a skin scraping under a microscope. Treatment involves bathing all dogs in the household in a special insecticidal dip or administering a miticide. Antibiotics, steroids, and medicated shampoos may also be necessary to control secondary infections and the severe itching. This parasite is very contagious to other dogs; all dog bedding and grooming implements must be cleaned with an insecticide or soap and very hot water. If left untreated, dogs with scabies will lose most, if not all, of their hair and become severely debilitated, taking months to recover. Sarcoptes mites can live for up to three weeks on humans—causing itchy red bumps, usually on the abdomen—but can be treated with a miticide prescribed by a physician.

Cheyletiella mites cause a mildly itchy skin disease known as cheyletiellosis. The disease is also referred to as "walking dandruff " because these mites are large enough to be seen, as small white specks, by the naked eye. The infected dog's skin becomes scaly and crusty. To diagnose, skin scrapings are examined under a microscope. Treatment involves bathing dogs and cats in the household with special miticidal dips and medicated shampoo. In addition, the home should be cleaned and treated with an insecticide effective against fleas. These mites can cause an itchy rash in humans that needs to be treated by a physician.

Musculoskeletal Problems

Dogs are more prone than cats to diseases of the bones, joints, and muscles, partly because some of the most severe canine joint problems are hereditary. Also, the physical size and structure of the domestic dog breeds varies widely, and in some cases unusual stresses and strains are placed on structures ill-equipped to handle them. (Information about breed-specific hereditary disorders is included in the Reference Guide to Dog Breeds, which begins on page 81.) The signs of musculoskeletal disease can be obvious, such as swelling or lameness, but can also be quite subtle. For example, elderly dogs with degenerative arthritis may simply become less active or avoid climbing stairs.

Hernias (abdominal, perineal, inguinal) are caused by a weakening of muscles and a corresponding protrusion of organs or tissue. They can be present from birth in the abdominal area (umbilical hernias) or can occur later in the perineal (between the anus and genitals) and inguinal (groin) areas.

Hernias cause swelling in the areas they affect. If an organ is trapped within the hernia, other signs will appear. For example, if a perineal hernia entraps the bladder, the dog may strain to urinate. Entrapped organs require immediate life-saving surgery; if there are no entrapped organs, surgery to correct the hernia is still necessary but can be scheduled at the owner's convenience. Neutering decreases the recurrence of perineal hernias.

Lameness can indicate a variety of problems. If a dog's leg seems unable to bear weight, if it is crooked or shortened or swelled, or if you can feel bone rubbing on bone, it may be broken; see a veterinarian right away. Likewise if there is sudden lameness or weakness in both hindlegs, as the dog may be suffering from a dislocated disc in the back, instability in the neck bones, or a pelvic fracture. Lameness can be caused by something as easily treatable as tar, paint, or a laceration in the foot pad or between the digits. Clean away any foreign substance with cooking or baby oil (not turpentine or other harsh paint-removing chemicals). If there is a laceration, apply direct pressure with a gauze pad or clean cloth to stop the bleeding, then clean the wound with soap and water. If the laceration is shallow, clean and treat it with an antibiotic ointment daily. If signs of infection (redness, swelling, or discharge) develop or if the laceration is deep, see the veterinarian right away.

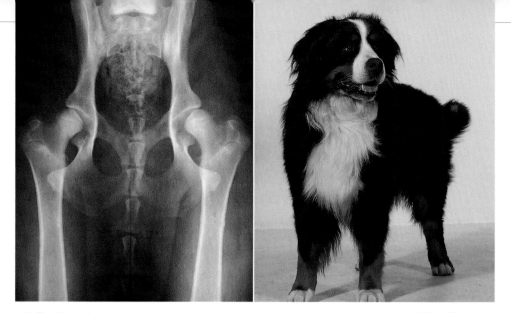

Left: This X ray of a dog's pelvis shows signs of hip dysplasia, abnormal looseness of the hip joint. Right: This Bernese mountain dog has healthy hips, but large dogs are especially prone to developing hip dysplasia.

Hip dysplasia, a painful malformation of the hip joint, has been diagnosed in almost all breeds of dogs but is most common in large breeds, such as Newfoundlands, golden retrievers, Bernese mountain dogs, and rottweilers. The condition is caused by many inherited traits, including poor position and weak attachment of the ball of the hipbone in the hip socket and insufficient muscle mass in the hip area. Overfeeding a puppy can contribute to the problem because extra weight stresses the hips. Dogs with hip dysplasia develop varying degrees of lameness. In some, the hip joint may be obliterated, whereas in others there may be only a small change in the ball-and-socket joint. Early diagnosis by X ray is helpful. Dysplasia of the elbow joint is also relatively common. Treatment depends on the severity of the condition; surgery is sometimes recommended.

To prevent hip dysplasia, make sure that affected dogs and carriers do not breed. All dogs should have their hips X-rayed and then evaluated by the Orthopedic Foundation for Animals (OFA) or PennHip prior to breeding.

Panosteitis, pain in the leg bones, most commonly occurs in young male German shepherds but can develop in other fast-growing large-breed puppies as well. The condition is diagnosed with X rays; medication can alleviate the pain. Fortunately, dogs usually outgrow panosteitis by twenty months of age.

Osteochondritis dissecans (OCD), a defect in the cartilage—usually in the shoulder but sometimes in the elbow, knee, or hock—afflicts large and giant breeds such as the Great Dane, golden retriever, and rottweiler. Limping is the most obvious sign; X rays are helpful in diagnosing the condition. The best treatment is surgical removal of the defective cartilage and joint fragment.

An *anterior cruciate rupture* happens when the anterior cruciate ligament, which prevents the bones in the knee joint from rubbing together, becomes stretched or torn during exercise or, more commonly, from stress on the joints in older, obese dogs. Immediately following the injury the dog will be reluctant to use the affected leg. After several weeks the dog may begin to use it again. However, without treatment, most affected dogs will develop arthritis in the knee and become permanently lame. Anterior cruciate rupture is best treated with surgery, but some dogs do well with anti-inflammatory drugs, limitation of exercise to walks on a leash, and restriction from stair use for six to eight weeks.

In *degenerative joint disease* (arthritis), joint movement is disrupted, cartilage breaks down, and the bone structure is re-shaped in a painful way. The main sign is lameness that worsens after inactivity and that sometimes improves after a light walk. Dogs that suffer from degenerative joint disease may be given dietary supplements to help the cartilage in the joints replenish itself and, sometimes, anti-inflammatory drugs to reduce pain.

Osteomyelitis is a bacterial or fungal bone infection caused by direct penetration of the bone itself (i.e., a bite, gunshot wound, or open fracture), an extension of tooth and gum disease into the surrounding bone, or the spread of an infection through the bloodstream from elsewhere in the body. Symptoms include pain, swelling, and redness around the affected area; loss of appetite; lethargy; and lameness if a limb is involved. Dogs with chronic osteomyelitis may also suffer muscle atrophy and enlarged lymph nodes. If osteomyelitis is not treated, the bone is likely to fracture. Treatment usually involves one or more of the following: antibiotics, surgically draining the infected area, removing any

bone that has no blood supply, and stabilizing any fracture. Sometimes amputation is necessary.

Spondylosis is a compression of nerve roots that go through the lower back. Dogs can be born with it or they can develop it later in life as part of a degenerative process caused by another condition. Middle-aged or older large-breed dogs have a higher incidence than other breeds. Signs are hindlimb lameness and back pain (the dog dislikes being touched on the back, is reluctant to move, stands rigidly with back arched, and may cry out while moving or when touched), muscular atrophy of the hindlimbs, scuffing the hindlimb toenails, reluctance to jump, difficulty climbing stairs, loss of bowel or urine control, and excessive chewing on the tail or the side of the hind feet. Treatment usually involves confining the dog to a crate and administering nonsteroidal anti-inflammatory drugs for four to six weeks. Surgery may be needed if the dog's condition does not improve.

Patellar luxation (dislocation of the kneecap) and *Legg-Perthes disease* (degeneration of the head of the femur) are found primarily in smaller breeds such as Jack Russell terriers and toy and miniature poodles. Both conditions can be diagnosed with a physical exam and X rays. With patellar luxation, the kneecap may slip in and out of place so the dog limps intermittently on the hindleg. Surgery is almost always necessary. Legg-Perthes may affect one or both hindlegs. Medical treatment may be attempted first, but surgery is usually required.

Mouth Problems

Problems in the mouth can not only be quite painful, causing some dogs to refuse to eat, but can also "seed" other parts of the body with harmful microorganisms and cause life-threatening illnesses. To maintain your dog's oral health, clean her teeth several times a week (see Brushing Teeth on page 382) and schedule annual dental examinations. Some veterinarians may also recommend using a special canine mouthwash and feeding dry food. Signs of oral disease include particularly bad breath, drooling, and difficulty eating. An abscess under your dog's eye might actually be the result of a tooth infection. Dogs that exhibit these symptoms should be checked by a veterinarian promptly.

Gingivitis is an inflammation of the gums caused primarily by the accumulation of plaque, tartar, and disease-producing bacteria above and below the gum line. Signs include bleeding; infected gums; red, swollen gum margins; and bad breath. Gingivitis is reversible with regular annual or biannual dental cleaning by a veterinarian and conscientious, daily dental care at home. If gingivitis is not treated, inflammation eventually affects the periodontal tissues (supportive tissues surrounding the teeth), and periodontal disease results. Periodontal disease is indicated by loose teeth, bad breath, tooth pain (manifested by a chattering or grinding of the teeth, failure to chew on the affected side, and avoidance of hard food), sneezing, and nasal discharge (on one side). Progression of the disease can result in tooth loss, tooth abscesses, jaw fractures, jawbone infections, and nasal bleeding. Treatment of periodontal disease begins with a general scaling of the teeth to reduce or eliminate disease-producing bacteria. In some cases root planing, which involves cleaning the periodontal pockets and smoothing the root surface to discourage plaque, tartar, and bacteria from reforming, may be necessary.

Digestive Problems

The canine digestive system is affected by a large number of diseases, signs of which include weight loss, vomiting, diarrhea, and/or loss of appetite. Thankfully, because of the high quality of today's commercial dog foods, nutritional problems in dogs are becoming increasingly rare. Following is an overview of common or significant disorders that specifically involve the stomach and intestinal tract, including those caused by internal parasites.

Diarrhea and/or *vomiting* commonly occur when a dog's diet is changed suddenly, when a dog overeats, or when he eats something he should not have, such as grass, garbage, or bones. Internal parasites (see page 446) also cause diarrhea and, occasionally, vomiting. Diarrhea or vomiting caused by a problem with the diet usually lasts twenty-four to thirty-six hours.

Because diarrhea and/or vomiting are important indicators of some serious disorders that most commonly affect young dogs, and because a puppy's physical condition can deteriorate rapidly, puppies under six months old should be examined promptly if they are experiencing either or both of these conditions.

Diarrhea in dogs over six months old can often be treated at home by replacing the dog's regular food with a diet of boiled boneless, skinless chicken and white rice. An over-the-counter antidiarrheal medication should never be administered without the approval of a veterinarian, who will specify the proper dosage. If the diarrhea is severe, lasts longer than thirty-six hours, or if there is blood in the feces, contact a veterinarian. Additional danger signs associated with diarrhea and vomiting include a hunched-up appearance due to severe abdominal pain, loss of appetite, lethargy, fever, and dehydration. (To determine whether a dog is dehydrated, lift the skin on the back of the neck; if it does not spring back immediately, the dog is probably dehydrated.)

Vomiting in dogs over six months of age can often be treated at home by offering the dog only small amounts of water or ice chips at frequent intervals. If no vomiting occurs during the next twelve hours the dog can be fed small, frequent meals of boiled, boneless chicken and white rice. If vomiting recurs or if the dog vomits pure blood or exhibits any of the danger signs listed under Diarrhea (previous page), contact a veterinarian. If the dog does not vomit after two days on the bland diet, the normal diet can be resumed by gradually adding more of the regular food and less of the bland.

Constipation may result from ingestion of undigestible materials, such as bones or rocks, or an unsettling change in the dog's environment or daily routine. Other causes include obstruction in the area of the colon and rectum due to prostate enlargement or tumors, neuromuscular dysfunction due to spinal disease or hypothyroidism, hernias, dehydration, and the use of certain drugs. The dog may fail to defecate for a few days or may make frequent, strained attempts, managing to pass only small amounts of mucus and

The causes of bloat are not known, but large, deep-chested dogs such as Saint Bernards, Irish setters, boxers, and German shepherds (above) are most commonly affected.

blood or liquid feces. There may also be loss of appetite, lethargy, vomiting, dehydration, and a hunched-up appearance due to abdominal discomfort.

Constipation caused by ingested bones may result in a fatal perforation of the colon, and a tumor of the colon may become inoperable if it is not diagnosed early. However, mild constipation may resolve itself or may be corrected with oral or suppository laxatives and dietary changes. More severe cases may require enemas or other veterinary procedures. Make sure that dogs that seem constipated can urinate; straining is also a sign of urinary tract disorders (page 453), some of which can be fatal if not treated promptly.

Bloat, or gastric torsion, is a very serious condition in which air and fluid accumulate in the stomach, causing it to distend or swell. Dogs exhibiting signs of bloat—unsuccessful attempts to vomit, a swollen abdomen, excessive salivation, restlessness, and labored breathing—should be taken to a veterinarian quickly or they will die. Treatment includes insertion of a stomach tube to decompress the stomach and administration of intravenous fluids and medications to control infection and any cardiac irregularities. If the stomach has rotated, surgery will be necessary. After treatment, affected dogs should be fed three to five small meals per day and exercise and water consumption should be restricted.

Pancreatitis, inflammation of the pancreas, often occurs after a dog consumes a large, fatty meal. Other causes include trauma, drugs (particularly those used for chemotherapy), infection, and diabetes. All dogs may be affected but obese, middle-aged, or older dogs are most at risk. Some miniature schnauzers have an elevated fat level in their blood and are prone to pancreatitis. Signs include depression, anorexia (loss of appetite), abdominal pain, vomiting, fever, and, in some cases, diarrhea. In severe cases, shock and death may occur. Bloodwork, X rays, and/or ultrasound examination aid in the diagnosis. Treatment requires hospitalization, intravenous fluids, and witholding food and water until vomiting ceases. Severe cases may require antibiotics, pain relievers, medication to control vomiting, and even plasma transfusions. Following recovery, dogs should be placed on a low-fat diet, and access to garbage, table scraps, and food for other pets in the household must be avoided. Weight reduction for obese pets is also recommended.

Internal Parasites

A parasite is an organism that lives off its host and gives nothing in return except, possibly, illness. Parasites can live in or on a dog's body. Many internal parasites spend a portion of their life cycles in the dog's digestive tract, and for that reason are included here, though the diseases they cause may also affect other parts of the body. (Heartworms are discussed on page 450 in the Heart and Blood Problems section.)

Roundworms, which resemble three- to four-inch pieces of spaghetti, are sometimes visible in a dog's vomit or stool. Most puppies are infected by larvae transmitted through mother's milk or in the womb. Signs include a potbelly, weight loss, increased or lost appetite, dry coat, vomiting, diarrhea, coughing, and seizures. Adult dogs can become infected when they ingest eggs or larvae when playing in dirt, but they may not show any signs of illness. Young children can also ingest roundworm eggs while playing in dirt. The eggs hatch into larvae, which migrate throughout the body and cause a rare disease called visceral larva migrans. Blindness, pneumonia, or other problems may result. It is important to keep children away from soil that may be contaminated with dog or cat feces.

Roundworms are diagnosed by examining stool samples under a microscope for evidence of eggs. Infected dogs are given a medication that kills the adult worms in the intestines. Two or more of these dewormings may be necessary to kill the entire worm population. Prevention measures include deworming all puppies at two, four, six, and eight weeks of age and keeping the dog's environment clean by removing feces from yards and washing concrete runs often with rock salt, a one-percent bleach solution, or sodium borate (borax). Note that the chemicals used for washing concrete runs can damage or kill grass and other vegetation. A monthly heartworm preventive given year-round will also prevent roundworms. Veterinarians should check stool samples annually and supervise dewormings.

Hookworms are tiny worms that commonly infect puppies through mother's milk, though dogs of any age can be infected when larvae are swallowed or penetrate the skin. (Hookworm larvae can also tunnel through human skin and cause a condition called cutaneous larval migrans, which results in extreme itchiness.) Hookworms cause severe anemia, weakness, bloody diarrhea, and death, especially in puppies. Diagnosis and treatment are identical to the measures described for roundworms on page 446.

Whipworms are very thin and threadlike, shaped like whips. A dog can pick up the eggs by licking infected ground. Whipworms can cause weight loss, anemia, and diarrhea. Diagnosis may require microscopic examination of several stool samples. Even if no eggs are found, the veterinarian may prescribe medication to treat whipworms based on signs observed. Treatment includes deworming medication as well as medication to treat diarrhea. Whipworm eggs can survive in the environment for years. To get rid of them and to prevent infection, keep the dog's environment clean by following the measures described for roundworms on page 446.

Tapeworms can be diagnosed by examining stool samples, though they are more often discovered when segments of them, which look like wiggling grains of moist rice or dry sesame seeds, appear on a dog's bedding, anal area, or feces. (Whole tapeworms may reach up to two feet in length.) A dog can get tapeworms by eating infected insects, such as fleas, or mammals, such as rats, mice, and rabbits, as well as from raw fish, beef, or pork. Tapeworms can cause weight loss, occasional diarrhea, or be asymptomatic.

Deworming medication effectively kills them. To prevent infection, keep flea infestation under control, keep your dog away from rodents, and refrain from feeding your dog raw meat or fish.

Coccidia are single-celled parasites that are spread through the feces of infected animals. In some cases they cause bloody diarrhea, but often they are harmless, especially in adult dogs. Coccidia can be diagnosed through examination of a stool sample under a microscope. When treatment is needed, sulfa drugs are effective against them. To prevent coccidia infection, keep the dog's environment clean by following the measures described for roundworms on page 446.

Giardia, microscopic parasites spread by the feces of infected animals, are capable of infecting all animals. Infection can cause mild diarrhea, especially in puppies, or may cause no disease at all. Diagnosis is made by examining a fresh stool sample or, if necessary, through more sophisticated laboratory tests. Giardia are treated with antiprotozoal medication. To prevent infection, do not allow your dog to drink water from sources that may contain giardia cysts, such as creeks, ponds, and streams. Giardia infections can be transmitted from dogs to humans, so owners of infected dogs should wash their hands thoroughly after handling or cleaning up after their dogs.

Respiratory Problems

Signs of trouble in the respiratory tract are quite varied. For example, coldlike symptoms, such as sneezing and/or nasal discharge, are common signs of disease in the nasal passages; gagging may be associated with disease in the nasal part of the pharynx; and coughing and/or labored breathing characterize disorders of the larynx, trachea (windpipe), and lungs. Foreign objects, bacterial and fungal infections, allergies, and cancer cause disease in the upper respiratory tract (the nasal cavity and the nasal part of the pharynx). The lower respiratory tract (the trachea, bronchial tubes, and lungs) of dogs is most commonly affected by viral and bacterial infections. Parasitic and fungal infections, allergies, and tracheal collapse can also cause disease in the airways or lungs.

Coughing can signal a minor problem or a serious one. If a dog's cough is accompanied by fever, labored breathing, appetite or weight loss, low energy, blueness in the gums or tongue, or a history of heart murmur, heart disease, or a malignant tumor, see a veterinarian. Heartworms (page 450), tracheal collapse (described next), heart failure (page 449), metastasis (spread) of a malignant tumor, or chronic bronchitis (discussed at right) can all cause a dog to cough. A harsh, dry, unproductive cough may indicate tracheobronchitis (page 427).

Tracheal collapse, a narrowing of the trachea (windpipe) due to a loss in rigidity, is primarily seen in older toy and small-breed dogs such as Pomeranians and Yorkshire terriers. Signs include a cough (often like the sound of a honking goose), especially after excitement or stress; fatigue induced by exercise; labored, noisy breathing; and gagging. In severe cases there may be a bluish discoloration to the gums and skin because of a lack of oxygen, and the dog may faint. Treatment includes keeping the dog away from airborne allergens and irritants, such as cigarette smoke;

minimizing stress, excitement, and exposure to extreme cold or to heat and humidity; using a harness instead of a collar when walking the dog; reducing food intake (if the dog is overweight); using expectorant drugs and a humidifier or vaporizer to help clear airway secretions; and vaccinating the dog to prevent respiratory infections. The vet may also prescribe antibiotics in cases of bacterial airway infection, short-term use of steroids to reduce airway inflammation, and medication to dilate the airways. Severe cases may require tracheal surgery.

Chronic bronchitis is a continuous inflammation of the bronchial tubes primarily seen in small adult dogs. The condition may worsen, especially if left untreated, and cause heart enlargement and failure. The cause is unknown in most cases, however, a viral or bacterial infection may be to blame. Environmental pollutants, such as cigarette smoke, and allergens, such as pollen and dust mites, may contribute to the condition. Signs include a chronic cough, gagging, and occasional shortness of breath with exercise. Congestive heart failure must be ruled out, since the signs can be similar. The condition may worsen, and the dog may turn blue (cyanotic) and faint if he exercises or becomes excited or stressed. Fever, lethargy, and loss of appetite suggest that a respiratory infection or pneumonia has developed. Treatment of chronic bronchitis may include weight reduction; use of a harness instead of a collar when the dog is walked; reducing exposure to cigarette smoke, house sprays, house dust, and chemicals; use of a humidifier or a vaporizer; use of an air purifier; bronchodilators; antibiotics; and anti-inflammatory drugs.

Heart and Blood Problems

A diseased heart does not pump blood efficiently, depriving the body of life-giving oxygen and nutrients and/or allowing fluid to "back up" in various parts of the body. Signs of oxygen deprivation are weakness, perhaps most noticeable after exercise; panting or rapid open-mouth breathing; bluish gums and tongue; fainting, which may look like a seizure; and fluid in or around the lungs. Almost any form of heart disease can cause sudden death.

Heart failure occurs when the heart cannot pump efficiently and meet the body's need for oxygen. It can be caused by diseases involving the heart valves, heart muscle, or lining around the heart; congenital defects in the heart; abnormal heart rhythms (arrhythmias); heartworms; or drug toxicity. Signs include coughing, weakness during exertion, shortness of breath, a swollen abdomen, fainting, and blueness of the gums and tongue. Without treatment the dog will die. Treatment involves administering medications that strengthen the contractions of the heart and decrease the heart's workload by dilating blood vessels; removing any fluid buildup in the lungs or abdomen with diuretics or surgical drainage; and, when appropriate, administering antiarrhythmic drugs. Until these treatments begin to work the dog may also be given oxygen through a face mask or in an oxygen cage. Low-sodium diets and exercise restriction may also be recommended.

The most common congenital heart defects in dogs are ***patent ductus arteriosus*** (PDA), ***pulmonic stenosis***, and ***subaortic stenosis.*** PDA, the most common heart defect in puppies, is seen most often in poodles, German shepherds, collies, Pomeranians, cocker spaniels, and Shetland sheepdogs. Pulmonic stenosis occurs most often in beagles, bulldogs, Chihuahuas, Old English sheepdogs, fox terriers, schnauzers, and Samoyeds. Subaortic stenosis is usually seen in large breeds such as German shorthaired pointers, German shepherds, boxers, Newfoundlands, rottweilers, and golden retrievers. Although young dogs may not show any clinical signs of these conditions, a veterinarian may hear a murmur when listening to the dog's chest with a stethoscope. Tests such as an ECG or ultrasound examination of the heart can identify its cause.

Identification of congenital heart defects is important because correction is usually necessary to prevent gradual weakening of the heart (heart failure). As puppies with uncorrected PDAs get older, their lungs begin to become congested; they also begin to tire easily and experience shortness of breath and a deep cough. Puppies with pulmonic stenosis may develop fluid in the abdomen. Puppies with subaortic stenosis may have fainting spells and may die suddenly. Puppies with uncorrected congenital heart defects generally have short life expectancies (ranging from three to six months for those with subaortic stenosis, to three to four years for those with PDAs).

PDAs and pulmonic stenosis can usually be corrected surgically. When surgery is considered too risky or is unsuccessful, exercise restriction and medications to control heart failure may prolong life. Occasionally, pulmonic stenosis is so mild that no correction is needed and a normal life span can be expected. Only a full cardiac evaluation can determine the severity of the defect.

Cardiomyopathy is an enlargement of the heart caused by thickening (hypertrophic cardiomyopathy) or dilation (dilated cardiomyopathy) of the heart muscle. The causes are unknown. Dilated cardiomyopathy most often affects Doberman pinschers, boxers, and Saint Bernards. Hypertrophic cardiomyopathy is most common in large-breed dogs, such as German shepherds. Symptoms of cardiomyopathy, which may not be evident in the early stages of the disease, include coughing, weakness during exertion, shortness of breath, a swollen abdomen, fainting, and a blue tinge to the gums and tongue. Heart failure can often be controlled for a time with diuretics and medication, though death is usually inevitable.

Cardiac arrhythmias are heartbeat abnormalities—rapidity, slowness, weakness, or irregularity—that can make the heart pump inefficiently. Arrhythmias can be hereditary (especially in miniature schnauzers), but they are also caused by infection; certain medications; degeneration of the heart muscle; tumors, trauma; congenital heart disease; chronic heart failure (progressive weakening of the heart); electrolyte disorders (such as low or high potassium levels); lack of oxygen due to a respiratory disease; and endocrine disorders, such as hypothyroidism and Addison's disease (page 452).

Some arrhythmias affect many dogs but do not cause warning signs or disturb cardiac function. If the arrhythmia affects cardiac function, weakness, lethargy, fainting, difficulty breathing, seizures, shock, or sudden death may occur. The medication prescribed depends upon the type and degree of heart rhythm disturbance. If the cause of a slow heart rate cannot be identified, a cardiac pacemaker may be surgically implanted. Medications that influence cardiac rate and rhythm may be required.

Hypertension, or high blood pressure, is usually a result of an underlying disease, most commonly kidney disease, although heart disease or endocrine disorders including diabetes and Cushing's syndrome (page 451) can also cause it. Some cases do not produce signs but are detected when the veterinarian measures the dog's blood pressure; others may involve kidney or cardiac failure or hemorrhaging, with signs including confusion, seizures, walking in circles, sudden blindness, vomiting, and weight loss. Treatment may involve diuretics, restricted sodium intake, and blood-pressure-lowering medication.

Heartworms are slender white worms (four to twelve inches long) that cause obstruction of blood flow, resulting in lung disease and liver and heart failure. Female mosquitoes inject the baby heartworms into the skin of the dog. The larvae migrate through the body until they reach the right heart chamber and pulmonary artery, where they grow and mature into adult worms.

Signs of heartworm disease are directly related to the number of adult heartworms present and include weight loss despite a good appetite, coughing, labored breathing (especially during exercise), fatigue, and fainting. Consequences of nontreatment vary from nothing (if only a few heartworms are present) to congestive heart failure and death. Medications are usually given to kill the adult worms; treatment requires hospitalization since complications may arise as the worms are killed. Daily or monthly preventives are recommended for all dogs in areas where heartworms are prevalent. Even dogs that remain indoors most of the time are at risk, since female mosquitoes are very small and can enter the house through cracks around windows or doors.

Endocrine System Problems

The endocrine system is composed of tissues that secrete hormones. Some of the most important organs in the endocrine system are the thyroid glands, the parathyroid glands, the pancreas, the adrenal glands, the pituitary gland, and the ovaries and testes.

Diabetes mellitus occurs when a dog's pancreas doesn't produce insulin or, less commonly, when a dog's tissues are unable to use insulin, which the cells need to absorb glucose, their source of energy. The causes are uncertain, but some dogs, particularly females of all breeds, as well as male and female Samoyeds and dachshunds, may be genetically predisposed to the condition. Obese dogs are also at risk. Infection or the presence of another disease, such as Cushing's syndrome (discussed at right) or growth-hormone deficiency, may also cause diabetes. Common signs are increased appetite and water intake coupled with increased urination and continual weight loss. Cataracts causing vision loss can develop. Without treatment, the result is ketoacidosis, a life-threatening condition in which the blood is dangerously acidified; signs include dehydration, weakness, and vomiting.

Dogs that suffer from diabetes can lead long lives if they are given daily insulin injections, monitored carefully (water intake, urination, and body weight), and placed on high-fiber diets. Spaying female dogs is also recommended since female sex hormones affect blood sugar, especially during heat.

Cushing's syndrome affects the adrenal glands (bean-size glands adjacent to each kidney), which produce a number of hormones necessary for life. There are three causes of Cushing's syndrome: a pituitary tumor that releases a hormone that stimulates the adrenal glands; a tumor of the adrenal glands; and excessive administration of steroids meant to treat other diseases, such as skin disease or arthritis. Signs of Cushing's syndrome include dramatically increased water intake (possibly three to four times normal consumption), increased urination, abdominal enlargement, thin skin, and gradually worsening generalized weakness. Pituitary tumors causing Cushing's syndrome are usually quite small and can be treated with

Many breeds have a high incidence of hypothyroidism, including golden retrievers, Doberman pinschers, dachshunds (above), and cocker spaniels.

medication. However, pituitary tumors large enough to cause neurological signs (such as lethargy, blindness, circling, or clumsiness) are rarely treatable. If an adrenal tumor is detected or strongly suspected, medication or surgical removal of the affected adrenal gland is recommended; cure is much more likely if the tumor is benign rather than malignant.

Hypothyroidism occurs when a dog's body underproduces thyroid hormones, causing a generalized slowdown of the dog's metabolism. The most common cause of hypothyroidism is atrophy or immune-mediated destruction of the thyroid gland, although the reason for the destruction is poorly understood. Signs usually develop during middle age and may include a dull, dry coat; laziness; mental dullness; symmetrical hair loss on the neck, back, chest, legs, and tail; weight gain; and a tendency to seek warm places. Hypothyroidism can also cause chronic skin infections. To treat, daily thyroid hormone medication must be administered throughout the dog's life (without treatment, the dog could develop cardiac complications) and periodic thyroid tests must be carried out to make sure the dog is getting the correct dosage. Signs usually go away within two months after treatment begins.

Addison's disease occurs when the outer layer (cortex) of the adrenal glands shrinks or is destroyed, causing a shortage of steroid secretions that influence the function of many organs in the body. The condition is most common in middle-aged female dogs. The exact cause of this damage to the adrenal cortex is unknown.

Addison's disease is called the great pretender because it can cause signs associated with other illnesses, such as gastrointestinal, neuromuscular, heart, and kidney disease, and can therefore be difficult to diagnose. The most common signs of Addison's disease are vomiting, diarrhea, weakness, and depression. A veterinarian will also look for a slow heart rate, abnormal kidney function, dehydration, and high potassium and low sodium levels. Addison's disease may be intermittent, with signs coming and going, or acute, with a sudden onset of illness quickly progressing to collapse. Lack of treatment can lead to coma and death.

A veterinarian will treat Addison's disease with intravenous fluids and steroids. Most dogs need steroids for the rest of their lives, usually administered by daily pills or monthly injections. The vet may also recommend keeping the dog out of stressful situations, such as boarding kennels.

Hypoglycemia is a condition in which a dog's blood-sugar level is abnormally low. The most common causes of hypoglycemia are an excess of insulin given to a diabetic dog; a pancreatic tumor that lowers blood sugar; and malnourishment, especially in young toy puppies that have a lot of worms. The most common signs of hypoglycemia—weakness, collapse, and seizures—occur after eating, exercise, excitement, or fasting, and require immediate veterinary attention. A veterinarian who suspects hypoglycemia is likely to give the dog a sugary solution such as corn syrup or orange juice in order to alleviate symptoms within a few minutes. In addition, anticonvulsant medication and intravenous fluids containing dextrose and steroids may be necessary. Without treatment, a hypoglycemic dog may suffer permanent brain damage or death.

Urinary Tract Problems

The urinary tract is composed of two kidneys (that filter blood and eliminate waste products into the urine), the ureters (tubes that carry urine from the kidneys into the bladder), the bladder (an organ that stores urine), and the urethra (a tube from the bladder through which urine exits the body). Congenital abnormalities, inflammation, infection, cancer, and deterioration can affect the various components of the urinary tract.

Kidney failure occurs when a dog's kidneys lose their ability to excrete metabolic wastes and regulate fluids and electrolytes. When both kidneys lose seventy percent or more of that ability, the consequences are severe. Kidney failure can be acute (rapid) or chronic (taking place over a period of time). Acute cases are most commonly caused by toxins such as antifreeze, lead, zinc, and mercury or an adverse reaction to particular antibiotics or anti-inflammatory drugs, such as ibuprofen; other causes are infectious agents, such as bacteria, and compromised blood flow, which is caused by severe dehydration, prolonged anesthesia, or shock. The most common signs of acute kidney failure are the sudden onset of vomiting, diarrhea, and lethargy. Medical treatment usually involves intravenous fluids and diuretics, and may also include dialysis. Rapid, intensive medical treatment of this condition is critical.

Chronic kidney failure can be caused by congenital problems, infections, immune diseases such as lupus, tumors, or toxins, though in many cases, it is impossible to determine the cause. Many breeds are prone to this disorder, including cocker spaniels, Doberman pinschers, and standard poodles. The most common signs of chronic kidney failure are an increase in a dog's water intake and urination. The veterinarian must identify the underlying cause in order to treat properly. Treatments include medications to rectify electrolyte abnormalities caused by kidney disease; medications to stimulate red blood cell production if the dog is anemic (which is common in dogs suffering from kidney failure); a special diet that restricts protein, sodium, and phosphorus; and fluid therapy if the dog is dehydrated. Dogs suffering from this condition must have constant access to fresh water and should be kept out of stressful environments.

Bladder stones are formations of minerals caused by bacterial urinary tract infections or foods containing high levels of proteins and minerals. Some dogs (especially dalmatians) have an inherited inability to metabolize certain proteins and consequently form bladder stones. The most common signs of bladder stones are blood in the urine, apparent straining to urinate, and urinary accidents in the house, especially in males. If the bladder stones are accompanied by an infection, the kidneys can be affected. The stones can also block urine outflow and cause uremia, a toxic buildup—and death (see urethral obstruction, page 454). Veterinarians frequently recommend surgery to remove the stones. Sometimes, however, a tube called a cystoscope can be passed up the urethra to view and remove a stone, or a special diet that dissolves the stones in the bladder may be prescribed. If a bladder infection is present, antibiotics will also be required. To prevent a recurrence of the problem, a prescription diet may be recommended.

Urinary incontinence, or loss of bladder control, occurs when the bladder muscle, the nerves connected to it, and the urethra are not properly coordinated. The most common cause of incontinence is a hormonal disorder that usually occurs in dogs over eight years of age. Other causes are spinal degeneration, most frequently seen in German shepherds; spinal trauma; a protruding spinal disc; prostate disorders in males; and birth defects, such as a malpositioned ureter, in which the tube from the kidneys doesn't enter the bladder in its normal location. The most common signs of incontinence are dripping of urine and resulting skin irritation. Without treatment, some types of urinary incontinence may come and go, while others may worsen, leading to bladder or kidney infections.

Cystitis, most commonly seen in female dogs, is an infection of the bladder, usually caused by bacteria. Signs are bloody urine, straining to urinate, and possibly urinary accidents in a previously house-trained dog. Cystitis is treated with antibiotics.

Prostate disease can result from several conditions that affect the prostate gland: benign prostatic enlargement, infection of the prostate, and cancer of the prostate. The most common, benign prostatic enlargement, occurs in unneutered middle-aged and older male dogs. Often it comes without warning. However, symptomatic dogs usually have difficulty defecating, along with blood dripping from the end of the penis. Castration usually resolves the problem.

Infection of the prostate (prostatitis), caused by bacteria, is much less common than benign prostatic enlargement. Signs include the frequent need to urinate, inappropriate urination in the otherwise house-trained dog, blood in the urine, and painful defecation evidenced by grunting or crying. Fever, lethargy, loss of appetite, vomiting, and diarrhea may also occur. The veterinarian will culture the urine to detect the bacteria causing the infection and treat with an appropriate antibiotic. After two to three weeks of antibiotic therapy, castration is recommended to prevent future infection. Without treatment, bacterial prostatitis can lead to the formation of abscesses in the prostate. These abscesses can rupture into the abdominal cavity and cause illness and death.

Prostatic cancer is rare but can occur in aged males regardless of whether they have been castrated or not. The most common sign is straining to urinate. Unfortunately, most dogs with prostatic cancer, which has usually spread to the lymph nodes, spine, or lungs by the time it is detected, are not treatable. The dog may be in pain. Euthanasia is usually recommended.

Urethral obstruction/rupture occurs when the urethra, a thin tube through which dogs pass urine and sperm, becomes blocked by "stones," mineralized masses originating in the bladder; by tumors of the urethra; or by diseases of the prostate (discussed at left). Female dogs rarely suffer this problem, since their urethras are shorter and wider. The urethra can also rupture as a result of physical trauma. The most common signs of urethral obstruction or rupture are straining to urinate, bloody urine, and urinary incontinence. A complete obstruction or rupture causes kidney failure and blood poisoning or toxemia.

Both urethral obstruction and rupture require surgery. A small urethral tear (not as serious as a complete rupture) can usually be treated by placing a catheter in the urethra for seven to ten days until it is healed. Antibiotics may be prescribed and a special diet that dissolves stones recommended to prevent recurrence of these problems. Urethral tumors are very rare and treatment is seldom successful.

Nervous System Problems

The delicate structure of the nervous system—the brain, the spinal cord, and the sensory and motor nerves that carry messages between the spinal cord or brain and the rest of the body—is prone to disease from many different sources. Even though the brain and spinal cord are well protected from trauma by bony armor, they can be seriously injured by automobiles, falls, bites, and other traumatic episodes. Because the tissues of the brain and spinal cord have a limited ability to regenerate, the consequences of disease and injury can be profound. The signs of nervous system disorders vary depending on the cause and the location, but seizures, behavior problems, weakness, and paralysis are among the most common.

Seizures, also called convulsions or fits, are brought on by temporary disturbances of the electrical activity in the brain. Seizures may last for seconds, minutes, or hours. They can be caused by infectious diseases such as canine distemper and rabies; kidney and liver disease; metabolic disorders such as low blood sugar and low blood calcium; toxins such as lead; brain trauma such as a blow to the head; and brain tumors, especially in boxers and Boston terriers. Epilepsy usually begins between the ages of six months and three years. Seizures may occur at regular intervals, for example, weeks or months apart. Between seizures, epileptic dogs behave normally.

Some epileptic dogs have preseizures that can last from seconds to hours. They are characterized by twitching, staring, lip licking, restlessness or nervousness, salivating, hiding, pacing, and clinging to a human companion as if anticipating something. A dog having a seizure, which begins immediately after the preseizure

Poodles, beagles, Irish setters, German shepherds, Belgian Tervurens, cocker spaniels, Saint Bernards, golden retrievers (above), and Labrador retrievers have an inherited tendency toward epilepsy, but all breeds, including mixes, can be afflicted by it.

ends and typically lasts one to two minutes, will usually fall on her side, make running motions with her legs, whine or bark, salivate, and lose control of bowel and bladder function. For instructions on how to care for a dog experiencing a seizure, see page 469. Any dog that has a seizure that lasts five or more minutes requires immediate veterinary treatment; veterinary treatment is also necessary if the dog has a shorter seizure, but it does not have to be immediate. After the seizure, the dog may be unresponsive, seem confused, appear blind, salivate heavily, and pace back and forth.

The long-term outlook for dogs in which seizures are secondary to an underlying cause depends on the severity and treatability of that cause. For example, if the cause is rabies, the outlook is grim, as rabies is invariably fatal; if the cause is low blood sugar in a diabetic dog given too much insulin, the outcome is potentially much better. Dogs with epilepsy may lead relatively normal lives depending on the frequency and severity of their seizures and on how well the seizures can be controlled with anticonvulsant medications.

Intervertebral disc protrusion causes dogs to experience neck and back pain. Intervertebral discs (jellylike material located between the bones in the neck and back) act as shock absorbers for the spinal cord. When the disc material protrudes into the space occupied by the spinal cord or the nerves coming from the cord, affected animals are reluctant to move, will frequently hold their heads rigidly (maneuvering their bodies to see rather than turning their heads), and may dislike being touched around the head and neck. One foreleg may be held up, an indication that the nerves to that leg are being pinched by the disc. A disc protrusion in the back can produce pain, weakness, or paralysis of the back legs (often in combination with a reluctance to move or a "sawhorse stance"—standing rigidly with back arched) and loss of bowel and urine control. If the pressure on the spinal cord is severe and prolonged, the involved spinal cord dies and paralysis is permanent. In general, irreversible damage is indicated by the combination of acute paralysis with a total lack of feeling in the limbs. Beagles, Pekingese, dachshunds, French bulldogs, miniature poodles, and cocker spaniels suffer disc protrusions more often than other breeds.

Disc protrusions in the neck and back are often treated with high doses of anti-inflammatory drugs. Strict confinement in a crate for several weeks is always required. Afterward physical therapy may help recovery. In dogs with severe pain or paralysis, surgery to remove the disc and decrease further injury is required. Early treatment may avert paralysis.

Radial nerve paralysis inhibits movement and support of the front legs. Injury to the nerve is usually caused by bruising or fractures of the upper bone in the leg (humerus). With radial nerve paralysis, the dog may be unable to support weight on the leg because the elbow can't be extended, or may be able to support some weight but will drag the paw when walking. If the nerve has been severed by the injury, the condition will worsen and the limb will have to be amputated. (Fortunately, most three-legged dogs can continue to walk unassisted.) If the nerve is bruised, the veterinarian may administer steroids to decrease inflammation. Physical therapy may help after recovery from the initial injury. In many cases only the passage of time (about one to six months) will determine how much function will return to the leg. During that time the paw needs to be bandaged or covered with a sock to prevent abrasions to the top of the paw.

Reproductive System Problems

False pregnancy is brought on by a high hormone level typical of actual pregnancy. Six to eight weeks after heat (estrus), a female dog enters diestrus, an approximately two-month period when her uterus prepares for developing fetuses and eventual delivery. Near the "delivery" date, the dog may become restless, her appetite may decrease, and she may even have uterine contractions, produce milk in her enlarged mammary glands, and carry slippers, socks, or other puppy-like soft objects to her "nest." Although false pregnancy is not a serious condition, some owners become concerned with their dog's overprotective attitude toward her "pups." In such situations steroid medications can be given orally to diminish the signs associated with false pregnancy. Otherwise, these signs usually go away without treatment within seven to twenty-one days after the "delivery date." If the dog will not be breeding, she should be spayed to prevent the almost certain recurrence of false pregnancy after her next heat.

Pyometra, a potentially life-threatening bacterial infection of the uterus, is most common in middle-aged and older unneutered female dogs. The condition usually occurs four to eight weeks after heat (estrus) as the uterus prepares itself for possible pregnancy. The signs of pyometra may include vaginal discharge of pus, fever, abdominal enlargement, lethargy, weight loss, decreased appetite, and increased water intake, urination, and, occasionally, bleeding from the vagina. A dog exhibiting these signs should be examined by a veterinarian immediately. A closed cervix, which prevents pus from draining out of the uterus, can hasten septicemia, a life-threatening infection in which the bacteria spread through the circulatory system, causing peritonitis (an inflammation of the lining of the abdominal area) and multiple organ failure; vomiting and diarrhea are both signs of peritonitis. All dogs with pyometra should be neutered without delay. Some valuable breeding animals that are not severely ill have been treated with antibiotics and prostaglandins (hormones that cause the uterus to contract and expel the infected contents) instead of surgery. However, this nonsurgical option is not always successful and increases the risk of uterine rupture, peritonitis, and septicemia.

Mastitis is an infection of the mammary glands that occurs after heat, whelping, or false pregnancy. The glands become red, hot, hard, and painful, and the dog suffers fever and loss of appetite. She may lose interest in nursing her puppies, which then become restless and weak. Most veterinarians successfully treat the infection with antibiotics. A veterinarian may recommend taking the puppies away from the mother so that she can't nurse them, as the antibiotics or the infected milk may be toxic. The veterinarian will advise hand feeding puppies under three weeks of age; older puppies are weaned. If untreated, mastitis may worsen or lead to a systemic infection.

Home Nursing

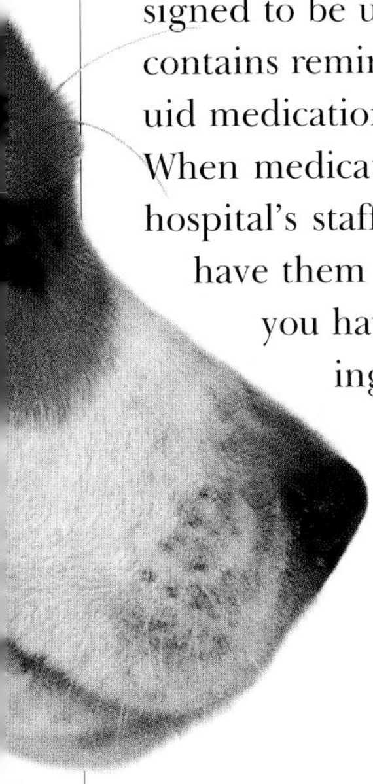

Ill or elderly dogs sometimes need to be nursed at home. This chapter, designed to be used in combination with instructions from your veterinarian, contains reminders on how to administer eyedrops, eye ointment, pills, liquid medication, eardrops, and injections, and take your dog's temperature. When medication is prescribed, ask your veterinarian or a member of the hospital's staff to show you exactly how to give it to your dog. If possible, have them observe you administering the medication, just to make sure you have it right. If you have problems medicating your dog or taking his temperature, ask your veterinarian for assistance; the techniques described here work in most situations, but sometimes other approaches work better.

Responsibly carrying out your veterinarian's directions will result in a swifter return to good health.

Medicating Your Dog

Regardless of the procedure you need to perform, make sure your dog is as relaxed as possible, and find a comfortable position for both of you. With few exceptions, the less restraint the better. Sometimes placing your dog on the floor next to you works well; in other cases it's better for the dog to be on a table or for you to stand over the dog, facing in the same direction, with one leg on each side of his body. Trial and error will show what's best. If possible, have someone assist you. Your partner can gently hold, soothe, and distract the dog while you are doing whatever needs to be done. Smoothness and speed are your best allies; if you are struggling with your dog, take a break and try again later.

Injections

Draw the medicine into the syringe, then hold the syringe with the needle pointed upward. Flick it a few times so any bubbles rise to the top, then push the plunger to expel any air. Injections are easiest to give in the loose skin anywhere along the back, avoiding the spine. Lift a "tent" of skin and part the hair at the base of the tent (it is not necessary to clean the surface with alcohol, but avoid any visibly dirty areas). Push the needle into the skin where the hair is parted, and gently pull back on the plunger. If blood comes back into the syringe, change needles and try another site, because you may have hit a blood vessel. If air comes in, you've pushed the needle in one side and out the other. If no air or blood comes back, push the plunger to administer the medication.

Pills

Giving a dog a pill can be accomplished in several ways. By far the easiest is to hide the pill in a bit of food. If this cannot be done, place yourself on the floor directly in front of a medium- to large-size dog; sit a small dog on your lap or on a raised surface. Open the dog's mouth either by grasping the bottom jaw and drawing downward or by pulling up on the upper jaw. Place the pill as far back on the tongue as possible, then close the mouth, tilt up the chin and stroke the throat to aid in swallowing. Watch your dog to be certain the pill was swallowed.

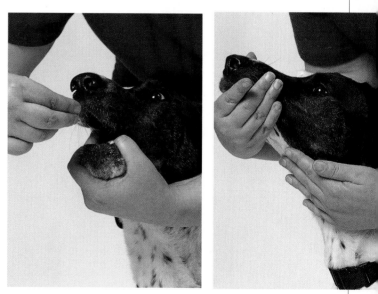

Expect some resistance when you give your dog a pill. Gently open the mouth by pulling down on the lower jaw, place the pill toward the back of the tongue, and hold the muzzle closed until you feel your dog swallow.

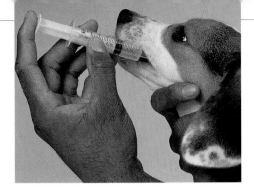

Squirt the medicine slowly, giving your dog a chance to swallow.

Liquid Medication

Fill the dropper with medication and place your dog in a sit-stay. Tilt his head back at a 45-degree angle, pull back the lip fold, and place the dropper containing medication in the pouch between the cheek and gums and squirt slowly.

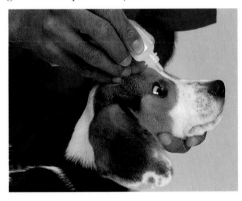

Be careful not to touch the dog's eye with the dropper.

Eyedrops

Place the dog in a sit-stay. With one hand on your dog's chin, lift his head and gently pull down the lower eyelid with your thumb. Hold the bottle between the thumb and forefinger of your other hand and hold the upper eyelid open with the heel of your hand. Squeeze one or two drops out of the bottle onto the surface of the eye. Apply drops onto the white of the eye, as this is more comfortable for the dog.

Eye Ointment

Hold the dog in a sit-stay. Place a strip of ointment (amount specified by your veterinarian) directly on the white of the eye or in the pocket between the eyelid and the eye. Do not poke the eye with the container.

Eardrops or Ointment

Place the dog in a sit-stay. Lift the earflap so that you can see into the ear canal. Squeeze drops or ointment into the ear opening, making certain that the medicine goes down the canal. Gently massage the base of the ear to distribute the medicine; you will hear a squishing sound as it distributes. It is normal for your dog to shake his head after you've administered eardrops.

Taking Your Dog's Temperature

Do not assume your dog has a fever if his nose is warm or dry. Use a standard glass rectal thermometer; shake it down to 96°F (35°C) or below. Lubricate the tip with petroleum jelly or mineral oil before inserting it.

Place the dog in a stand-stay. If possible, have a partner hold him still. If you are alone, turn the dog so his rear is facing the same direction you are facing. Hold him firmly against your side, with your arm over his body. Gently insert the thermometer and leave it in place for three minutes, holding it and the tail so that the thermometer won't slide out and break. If your dog struggles, remove the thermometer immediately. Normal temperature should be about 100.5° to 103°F (around 38°C). A temperature of 104°F (39.6°C) is considered a fever.

Emergency cases such as broken limbs are
best handled by professionals.

First Aid

When an emergency occurs, reason does not always prevail. Panic, fear, and confusion can hinder your ability to think clearly and act appropriately, so it is very important to have an emergency plan. If your dog has suffered a traumatic injury—been struck by a car or mauled by another dog, for instance—the first priority is to protect yourself. A dog that is hurt and frightened can seriously injure a person who is simply trying to help.

Your next priority should be to transport a seriously injured or ill dog to a veterinarian immediately. If possible, have someone call the veterinarian to warn the vet of the incoming emergency case. Although there are ways that you can help your dog on the spot if immediate transport is not available, don't lose precious time—first aid delivered at the scene is rarely as effective as seeking immediate professional help.

Know your veterinarian's office hours and emergency procedures. Some veterinarians work with a team of doctors, one of whom is always on call and will meet you at the office. Others are associated with emergency care facilities that are open when the veterinarian's office is closed. If your veterinarian works with a separate emergency care facility, make sure you know the phone number, address, and how to get there. Post the name and phone number of the veterinarian and, if applicable, emergency facility in the same place in your home that you post other vital numbers, such as those of the fire and police departments.

It's a good idea to practice techniques for measuring heartbeat and other vital signs on a well dog so that you can cope more easily in an emergency.

Handling an Injured Dog

An injured dog must be handled very carefully to avoid worsening the dog's pain or the seriousness of the injury and because the dog may bite out of fear or pain.

Approach the dog quietly and slowly, calling his name. (If you don't know the injured dog, it is wisest to call a veterinarian or animal control specialist, listed under "animal shelter" in most phone books. This is especially important in areas with a high incidence of rabies.)

Kneel down to the dog's level, speaking to him very calmly, and extend a closed hand, palm down. Keep your face at a distance from the dog's mouth, and avoid direct eye contact.

If the dog doesn't exhibit any aggression, pet him with a closed hand. If the dog shows aggression, do not proceed; call an emergency number.

If the dog is capable of running away, attach a leash to prevent this from happening (if there is no leash available, improvise with a rope, cloth, or a belt).

If the dog shows aggression but is breathing normally, is not vomiting, and has no facial injuries, consider applying a muzzle (described next). If you are

---

Home First Aid Kit for Dogs

- Your veterinarian's office phone number and after-hours emergency number
- ASPCA National Animal Poison Control Center number (888-426-4435)
- Clean, heavy towels or thick blankets to protect yourself from injury, and to protect the dog from further injury
- Sterile nonstick bandaging material (such as Telfa pads) to place directly on an open wound
- Absorbent cotton or gauze pads to place over nonstick pad
- Roll of gauze bandaging material to wrap around nonstick or gauze pad or to fashion a muzzle
- One-inch adhesive medical (not masking) tape to hold bandages in place
- Scissors with rounded tips
- Cotton-tipped swabs
- Rubbing alcohol
- Antiseptic solution, such as povidone iodine (Betadine), to clean wounds
- Eyewash for flushing eyes
- Styptic pencil or powder to stop toenails from bleeding if cut too short
- Syrup of ipecac or 3 percent hydrogen peroxide to induce vomiting. Never induce vomiting without first consulting your veterinarian or poison control center (see What to Do If Your Dog Is Poisoned, page 471, and Household Poisons, page 476)
- A syringe obtained from your veterinarian to administer liquid by mouth (a turkey baster can be substituted for larger dogs)
- Pair of thick gloves to protect yourself
- Flashlight or penlight
- Strip of cloth for making a tourniquet
- A pencil to tighten a tourniquet
- Antibiotic ointment
- Tweezers to remove thorns
- Rectal thermometer for taking your dog's temperature (page 461)
- Current photograph of your dog to put on posters in case your dog gets lost
- Copy of your dog's medical record

---

concerned that you will not be able to apply a muzzle without getting hurt, call for help.

Find or improvise a makeshift stretcher, such as a plank of wood, blanket, coat, air mattress, or even a window screen. Change the dog's position as little as possible as you transfer him to the stretcher. First place the stretcher along the dog's back. If you have assistance, support the dog's head, back, and pelvis and gently lift him onto the stretcher. If you are alone, grasp the skin over the neck and lower back and drag the dog onto the stretcher. If you suspect neck or back injuries, it is important not to twist the spine or the neck. Cover the dog with a blanket to keep him warm and drive to the veterinarian's office or other emergency care facility, keeping the dog as still as possible.

How to Apply a Muzzle

If an injured dog shows aggression—even a friendly dog may bite if scared or in pain—you should apply a muzzle as a precaution. Do not muzzle a dog that is having trouble breathing, is vomiting, or has facial injuries.

Using a length of gauze, a piece of rope, a necktie, or a cloth belt, form a loop from under the chin around the dog's mouth and tie it securely over the nose. Bring the ends of whatever you are using back under the jaw and tie again. Pass the ends behind the ears and tie them behind the head. If you are having difficulty applying a muzzle to a short-nosed dog, wrap a coat or blanket over the dog's head to avoid getting bitten (take care not to smother him).

If a muzzled dog tries to vomit, *remove the muzzle immediately*.

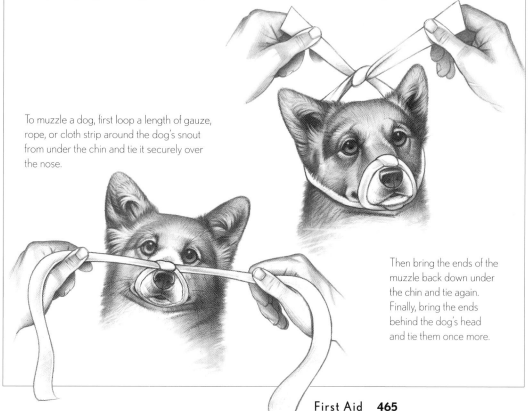

To muzzle a dog, first loop a length of gauze, rope, or cloth strip around the dog's snout from under the chin and tie it securely over the nose.

Then bring the ends of the muzzle back down under the chin and tie again. Finally, bring the ends behind the dog's head and tie them once more.

Lifesaving ABCs

If your dog has been seriously injured and does not respond to you when you speak to her or stroke her head, she may be unconscious. If she is breathing, transport her to a veterinarian as quickly as possible. If she is not breathing, the next steps you take—the ABCs—may spell out the difference between life and death. Your dog can die or suffer brain damage if her brain is deprived of oxygen, which happens if the heart stops beating or if breathing stops for more than four minutes. Perform the ABCs described below as someone else prepares for immediate transport to a veterinarian; you can also perform these steps during transport if another person is driving. If you are alone, shout or call someone to assist you, then perform the steps below.

If a dog is not breathing despite a clear airway (see A. Check the Airway, above), perform artificial respiration. Rest the dog on her belly or side, extend her head and neck, wrap your hands around her muzzle to keep the jaws closed, put your mouth tightly up against your hands, and blow into the dog's nostrils once every three seconds for fifteen minutes or until the dog resumes breathing.

A. Check the Airway

Extend the dog's head and neck, open the mouth, pull the tongue forward, and, using a flashlight, look as far back into the throat as possible. Clean away any debris, blood, or mucus from the mouth, using a cloth if necessary, and check for foreign objects at the back of the throat that might be obstructing breathing. If a foreign object is present, remove it (see What to Do If Your Dog Is Choking on page 470). If you have rubber or latex gloves, put them on before placing your hand in a strange dog's mouth. Make certain the dog is unconscious before putting your hands in her mouth to avoid being bitten.

B. Check for Breathing

If the dog has not resumed breathing once you've removed any obstructions at the back of the throat, place her on her belly or side and perform artificial respiration. (Now is a good time to feel for a heartbeat as well; see "C," next, and follow the instructions.) Extend the dog's head and neck, being careful to support the head to prevent twisting in case of neck injury. Place both hands around the dog's muzzle to hold the jaws closed, and then put your mouth in an airtight seal against your hands and blow into the dog's nostrils. No air should leak out from between your mouth and the dog's nose, and the dog's chest should expand. Blow into the dog's nostrils once every three seconds for fifteen minutes, or until the dog breathes on her own.

C. Check Circulation (Heartbeat)

Place your palm over the dog's left chest wall. You should feel a heartbeat. (You can also check for a pulse by gently placing your index and/or middle fingertips on the dog's upper inner thigh.) If you don't feel a heartbeat, you'll need to perform cardiac massage while also giving the dog artificial respiration. Together these two procedures are called cardiopulmonary resuscitation, or CPR.

Place the dog on her side. Put the heel of your hand in the same position used for checking the heartbeat, and cover it with the palm of your other hand. Compress the chest firmly and quickly three times (at the rate of one or two compressions a second). Ideally, one person should provide artificial respiration while another massages the heart. If you're alone, after three chest compressions, blow into the dog's nostrils one time quickly so that the chest expands, then compress the chest three times, and so on. Continue chest massage until you detect a heartbeat and artificial respiration until the dog begins to breathe. If heartbeat and breathing have not resumed within fifteen minutes, the dog cannot be revived.

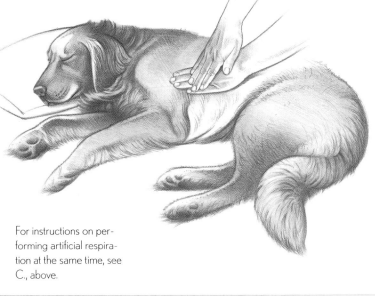

Feel for a dog's heartbeat by placing your palm over the dog's left chest wall. If there is no heartbeat, perform cardiac massage while also giving the dog artificial respiration. To massage the heart, place the dog on her side, put the heel of your hand in the same position used for checking the heartbeat, and cover it with the palm of your other hand. Compress the chest firmly three times at the rate of one or two compressions per second.

For instructions on performing artificial respiration at the same time, see C., above.

How to Stop Bleeding from a Wound

To stop bleeding, firmly press a clean cloth directly on the wound (if possible, put a nonstick pad on the wound first) and apply pressure for five minutes. Do not remove the blood-soaked pad from the wound or you may disturb the clot; instead, place another pad over the old one.

Consider applying a tourniquet to a limb only as a last resort when all other efforts at stopping the bleeding have failed. Leaving a tourniquet on too long or applying it too tightly can cause irreversible tissue damage—and perhaps result in the loss of the limb.

To apply a tourniquet, form a loop by loosely tying a piece of cloth, a handkerchief, or a cloth belt about one inch above the wound but not over a fracture or joint. Place a strong stick in the loop and twist the stick until the blood stops flowing. Loosen the tourniquet every five minutes to see if the bleeding has stopped and to allow blood to flow back to the limb.

Bandaging a Wounded Limb

Bandages can be applied at home to stop bleeding, to keep wounds clean, to support an injured area, and to deter a dog from scratching or excessively licking a wound until the dog can be taken to your veterinarian.

First, clean away any dirt in the wound with warm tap water or antiseptic solution. Carefully dry the area with a towel. Apply a small amount of antibiotic ointment (such as Neosporin) to the wound. Wrap the cleaned wound firmly with a nonstick pad, gauze bandages, or a clean cloth. Securely (but not too tightly) wrap adhesive tape around the covering in overlapping bands.

To prevent excessive swelling, the bandage must include all of the extremity. For example, if the wound is located on the ankle, apply a bandage from the ankle to the bottom of the paw.

After cleaning and drying a wound on a limb, cover the wound with a clean nonstick bandage or pad and wrap it with adhesive tape in overlapping bands.

How to Tell If Your Dog Is in Shock

When a dog is in a severe accident, the amount of fluid circulating in the blood vessels may be decreased (possibly due to bleeding or to a redistribution of the fluid). As a result, the heart and blood vessels are unable to deliver nutrients and oxygen to vital organs such as the brain or heart and the dog may go into shock. Other causes of shock include heatstroke (see page 471), severe infection, and heart failure.

If the dog is in shock, cover him with a blanket or coat to keep him warm and transport him to the veterinary hospital immediately. Lift the dog very slowly; a fast lift or rotation can be fatal.

Signs of Shock

- Pale or muddy (brown) gums
- Gums that do not turn a normal pink color from white within 2 seconds of being pressed by your finger
- A weak and rapid pulse
- Rapid breathing (over 40 breaths per minute)
- A low rectal temperature (below 100°F/37°C), with the skin and legs cool to the touch
- Difficulty standing
- Loss of consciousness
- In end stages, decrease in heart and respiratory rate (see page 467 for instructions)

How to Handle a Broken Limb

If a limb is obviously fractured, do not try to splint it. You will only cause the dog a lot of pain and further damage to the soft tissues around the fracture. If the fracture is accompanied by an open wound, gently cleanse the area with warm tap water and remove as much hair and debris from the wound as possible; dry the area with a clean towel, then apply a small amount of antibiotic ointment. Carefully cover the wound with a sterile nonstick pad and wrap lightly. Get the dog to a veterinarian as soon as possible.

Signs of a possible fracture include a crooked limb, pain and/or swelling of the limb, a piece of bone protruding through the skin, and reluctance to bear weight on the limb.

What to Do If Your Dog Has a Seizure

Seizures, also called convulsions or fits, are caused by electrical malfunctions in the brain. They have a multitude of causes, among them infection, low blood sugar or low calcium, poisoning (such as from lead or pesticides), or epilepsy. A dog that is having a seizure may collapse, twitch and jerk his legs, become rigid or unconscious, vocalize, salivate, and urinate and/or defecate.

If your dog is having a seizure, stay calm—watching a seizure can be a frightening experience. Move away any objects that could injure your dog during the seizure. If necessary, carefully push him away from any edge he might fall from (use a broom or even your foot). *Do not place anything in the dog's mouth to prevent him from biting his tongue*—this is a sure way to get your hand bitten and is not necessary. Seek immediate veterinary attention, especially if the seizure lasts more than a few minutes or if seizures follow one after the other.

What to Do If Your Dog Is Choking

You must act quickly to save a choking dog. Open the dog's mouth and try to see the object in the back of the throat; remove it if possible. Be careful, because a choking dog will be panic-stricken and may try to bite you. If you are not able to remove the object, the next step is to suspend the dog upside down from her hindlegs (if the dog is a manageable size) and to pat the dog firmly on her back just behind the shoulder blades to dislodge the object. If that does not work or if the dog is too large to lift, compress the dog's chest briskly by wrapping your hands and arms around the abdomen just behind the breast bone or on the sides of the chest. Repeat until whatever the dog is choking on is released.

What to Do If Your Dog Has Bloat

Bloat is a life-threatening condition in which air and fluid accumulate in the stomach and cause it to distend and, sometimes, to twist on itself. This twisting, called torsion, blocks blood flow to the heart and causes shock, tissue damage, and heart failure.

The cause of bloat is not known. It is usually seen in large, deep-chested dogs such as Great Danes, Saint Bernards, Irish setters, retrievers, shepherds, and bloodhounds. Dogs with bloat vainly attempt to vomit, salivate profusely, become very restless, and breathe heavily.

Transport a dog with bloat gently—and immediately—to a veterinary hospital, preferably one that has twenty-four-hour service with an intensive care unit. Curing this condition frequently requires sophisticated critical-care services. A stomach tube is passed down the throat into the stomach to release the trapped gas and fluid. If the tube cannot be passed, surgery must be performed to relieve the torsion and fluids and medications must be given to control shock.

Reviving a Drowning Dog

To reduce the risk of drowning, try not to let your dog swim for too long (until he is exhausted) or walk on a body of water that is not completely frozen. If your dog does need to be rescued, reach for him with your hand and try to pull him in. If you need to swim out to meet the dog, take a float with you. Grab the dog by the tail or the back of the neck and swim to shore.

There is no need to resuscitate the dog if he is conscious. If he is unconscious, before performing CPR (see page 467), water must be removed from the airways. First, remove any debris from his mouth. Then, if he is a small dog, hold him by his hindlegs to let the water drain out. Place a large dog on his side and lift the hindlegs as high as possible to help drainage. Press down on the chest and belly to expel water from the lungs and stomach. If the dog is still not breathing, check for a heartbeat (see page 467) and proceed with CPR.

What to Do If
Your Dog Has Heatstroke

Heatstroke, a condition marked by extremely high body temperature, can occur when a dog is in a very hot environment, perhaps without access to water and/or a cool spot (such as in a hot parked car), and is unable to regulate her body temperature by panting. Shock, organ failure, a swelling of the brain, and death are possible consequences. Dogs with short noses (such as boxers and Pekingese) and old or overweight dogs are most vulnerable to heatstroke.

To treat heatstroke, try one or a combination of the following techniques until body temperature comes down and the signs (see box at right) abate:

- Put the dog in a cold-water bath or shower.
- Apply ice to the head and between the rear thighs.
- Move the dog to an air-conditioned room or to a room with a fan.
- When your dog responds, give her ice cubes or a small amount of water.
- Monitor your dog's temperature when treating for heatstroke. Overly aggressive treatment can result in hypothermia (excessively low temperature). Stop cooling methods when the dog's temperature reaches 103°F (39°C) (normal temperature is about 100.5 to 103°F or around 38°C).

See a veterinarian as soon as possible, even after the dog responds. Additional treatment, such as intravenous fluids, may be needed to prevent permanent organ damage.

Signs of Heatstroke

- Rectal temperature over 106°F (41°C)
- Excessive panting
- Fast-pounding pulse
- Vomiting
- Seizurelike tremors
- Weakness
- Collapse

Removing a Fishhook
from Your Dog's Lip

Try to keep your dog away from areas where careless fishermen may have left debris. If your dog gets a hook embedded in his skin, first put a muzzle (page 465) on him. If the barb is embedded, push it through the skin until it protrudes and cut the barb off with pliers, then pull the back portion of the hook out. Better yet, if your dog gets a fishhook stuck in his lip, take him to a veterinarian who can use sedation to remove the fishhook with less trauma to the dog and with less danger to you.

What to Do If
Your Dog Is Poisoned

If you suspect that your dog has ingested something poisonous, contact your veterinarian immediately. Signs of poisoning are extremely variable depending upon the poison ingested but may include vomiting, diarrhea, drooling, bleeding, difficulty breathing, seizures, and coma, and can be fatal. If possible, give the veterinarian or poison control center the following information: the full name of the product

Preventing Poisoning

Hundreds of household products are potentially poisonous to animals—everything from household cleansers to car-, lawn-, and garden-care products to human medication to some houseplants. Even chocolate is poisonous to dogs. As a precaution, keep all potentially poisonous products out of the reach of your dog, do not leave open containers unattended, and make sure that containers are tightly sealed and properly labeled.

Dogs are most likely to ingest household detergents and disinfectants by licking the substance off their fur or feet during grooming. Make sure that any surface that has been cleaned and/or disinfected is completely dry before a dog is allowed back on it. *Never use a detergent or disinfectant with pine oil or phenol on the list of ingredients around dogs.* One of the safest, most effective, and most inexpensive disinfectants is a 1:32 dilution of household chlorine bleach in water (half a cup of bleach per gallon of water). Mix a fresh batch of solution prior to each use, and do not mix it with any ammonia-containing products.

If your dog gets a toxic or irritating substance on his fur, rinse him with lukewarm water for 10 to 15 minutes.

If you have your lawn commercially treated with fertilizer, keep your dog indoors during application of the product, and for 24 hours afterward; water the lawn before allowing the dog to walk on it; and discourage the dog from eating the treated grass.

Make sure any flea product you apply is designed for use on dogs. Do not apply a flea product to a sick or debilitated dog without first checking with your veterinarian. Follow the label instructions scrupulously; resist the urge to over-apply the product or to use several products at once. Do not apply a flea product unless you can monitor the dog closely for at least several hours after administration, as dogs will usually exhibit a problem within hours after the product has been applied.

Dogs can be poisoned by eating poisoned rodents or insects; use rodenticides and insecticides with caution, if at all.

ingested; the ingredients and their concentrations; the amount ingested and whether the product had been diluted; and the route of exposure (for example, did the dog eat it, drink it, lick it off her fur).

If your dog requires examination by a veterinarian, be sure to take along the container that held the toxic substance. If you don't know what kind of poison your dog has ingested, bring some of the dog's vomitus.

If you think your dog may have ingested something poisonous and you cannot reach your veterinarian, call the ASPCA National Animal Poison Control Center at 888-426-4435, 800-548-2423 (a per-case fee is charged to your credit card at these numbers), or 900-680-0000 (a per-minute fee is billed to your phone) before taking action. Use the chart on page 476 as a last resort.

When and How to Induce Vomiting

Although in some cases inducing vomiting can help to rid the dog of the poison, in others it can worsen the situation, so always speak to a veterinarian or poison control center before taking action. If more than several hours have elapsed since the poison was consumed, inducing vomiting is generally of no benefit.

- Never induce vomiting if the dog is unconscious, as the vomitus may run down into the lungs or obstruct the airway.
- Never induce vomiting if the dog has swallowed a corrosive substance, such as toilet-bowl cleaner, lye, or dishwasher detergent, as it will damage tissue coming up just as it did going down.
- Never induce vomiting if the dog has consumed a petroleum distillate, such as gasoline, kerosene, or paint thinner, because the consistency of the product may allow it to run backwards into the lungs and cause severe damage.
- Never induce vomiting if the dog has consumed a plant from the arum family, which includes philodendrons, dieffenbachia, and pothos.

Vomiting can be induced by giving one tablespoon of a mixture of equal parts hydrogen peroxide (3 percent strength) and water. Or, place one tablespoon of dry mustard in a cup of water and pour a teaspoon to a tablespoon at a time (depending on the size of the dog) into the back of the mouth or give the dog one teaspoon (small dog) to three teaspoons (medium to large dog) syrup of ipecac. Repeat if no vomiting occurs within five minutes. If after two doses no vomiting has occurred, you can try a third time with the dry mustard or hydrogen peroxide mixtures (not the syrup of ipecac).

If products to induce vomiting are not available and the dog is conscious, dilute the poison by giving milk (preferably) or water by mouth, and take the dog to the veterinarian.

Bites and Stings

Venomous insects, snakes, and toads account for a smaller percentage of dog poisonings than household products, but it is important to know what to do, just in case.

Yellow Jacket

Stinging Insects

Stinging insects (such as bees, yellow jackets, wasps, and hornets) inject a painful toxin into the skin. Pain and swelling at the site of the sting, the most common outcome, is rarely life threatening, but severe swelling on the face or mouth may impede, or even obstruct, breathing. Some dogs develop severe generalized reactions causing rapid breathing, rapid heart rate, and loss of balance regardless of where they were stung.

If your dog is stung, remove the stinger (if it is still there) by gently scraping it off with a stiff object such as a credit card or a thumbnail. (It's not a good idea to use tweezers or your two fingers because you may squeeze the venom sac attached to the stinger and release more toxin into the dog's skin.) Apply a cold pack to the site for ten to fifteen minutes. To be on the safe side, watch your dog closely for several hours afterward.

Call a veterinarian if the dog's face or mouth has been stung. Antihistamines and cortisone-like drugs prescribed by a veterinarian may help reduce swelling. Rarely, intravenous fluids, oxygen, or even an emergency tracheotomy are required.

Snakebites

If your dog is bitten by a nonpoisonous snake, clean the wound with an antiseptic solution and call a veterinarian for advice. If your dog is bitten by a coral snake or pit viper (rattlesnakes, copperheads, and cottonmouths are in the pit viper family), *do not attempt any first aid at home.* Keep the dog still and take him to a veterinarian as quickly as possible. Treatment must be aggressive, and usually involves IV fluids and antivenin if it's available (and if the snake is identified). Survival depends to a great extent on the size of the dog (bigger is better), the location of the bite (on the tongue or body is worse than on a limb), and the amount of venom injected into the wound.

The first sign of a bite by a snake in the pit viper family is swelling and redness that begins at the bite wound and progresses to surrounding areas. Within a few hours, excessive bleeding, lethargy, rapid breathing, a rapid and irregular heartbeat, and/or death may occur. Over

the course of a few days after the bite, a host of other serious disorders may develop. Coral snake bites cause little pain or swelling at the bite wound. Instead, paralysis sets in, which leads to death if the muscles needed for breathing are affected.

Toad Poisoning

The Colorado River Toad (*Bufo alvarius*), which is found only in the Colorado Sonoran Desert, and the Cane Toad (*Bufo marinus*), which lives along the Gulf Coast from Texas to Florida as well as in central Florida and the Caribbean, contain poisonous glands in their skin. Dogs that pick up these toads in their mouths may become poisoned. Depending on the amount of toxin that gets in the mouth, poisoned dogs will salivate profusely, develop cardiac disturbances and pulmonary edema, and collapse, and could possibly die—all within fifteen minutes. Rinsing the mouth with water for five to ten minutes helps wash away the poison. Poisoned dogs should be taken to a veterinarian immediately.

Cane Toad

Poisonous Plants

Almost any plant can adversely affect a dog if enough is ingested. Certain plants contain substances that will cause poisoning in a dog. Toxins may be present in only certain parts of the plant or only during certain seasons or growth stages.

The signs of plant poisoning vary depending upon the plant ingested and may include excessive drooling, vomiting, diarrhea, heart irregularities, and coma, and may be fatal. Bear in mind that it is common for dogs to vomit after chewing on any plant, poisonous or not.

If you suspect that your dog has eaten a poisonous plant, contact your veterinarian or a poison control center immediately. The ASPCA National Animal Poison Control Center number is 888-426-4435, 800-548-2423 (a per-case fee is charged to your credit card), or 900-680-0000 (a per-minute fee is billed to your phone). Learn the names of the plants in your house and yard—preferably both the common (English) and scientific (Latin) names—so that you can give this information to the veterinarian or to poison control if necessary (keep the labels from plants you buy).

Hundreds of plants are potentially poisonous to dogs. Following is a brief list of some of the more common ones.

Amaryllis family
Hippeastrum species (e.g., amaryllis)
Narcissus species (e.g., daffodil)

Arum family
Alocasia antiquorum (Elephant's Ear)
Caladium species (e.g., Angel's Wings)
Dieffenbachia species (e.g., Dumb Cane)
Epipremnum aureum (Pothos)
Philodendron species (e.g., Sweetheart Plant)

Begonia family
Begonia semperflorens-cultorum (Wax Begonia)
Begonia tuberhybrida (Tuberous Begonia)

Bellflower family
Lobelia species (e.g., Lobelia)

Buttercup family
Aconitum species (e.g., Monkshood)
Delphinium species (e.g., Larkspur)

Carrot family
Cicuta maculata (Water Hemlock)
Conium maculatum (Poison Hemlock)

Daphne family
Daphne species (e.g., Rose Daphne)

Dogbane family
Nerium oleander (Rosebay)

Ginseng family
Hedera species (e.g., English Ivy)
Schefflera actinophylla (Umbrella Plant)

Heath family
Kalmia species (e.g., laurels)
Rhododendron species (e.g., rhododendrons, azaleas)

Holly family
Ilex species (e.g., American Holly)

Horse Chestnut family
Aesculus hippocastanum (Horse Chestnut)

Lily family
Asparagus densiflorus (Asparagus Fern)
Convallaria majalis (Lily-of-the-Valley)
Lilium lancifolium (Tiger Lily)
Lilium longiflorum (Easter Lily)

Mistletoe family
Phoradendron serotinum (Mistletoe)

Nightshade family
Datura stramonium (Jimson Weed)
Solanum americanum (Common Nightshade)

Pea family
Abrus precatorius (Rosary Pea)

Snapdragon family
Digitalis purpurea (Foxglove)

Spurge family
Euphorbia pulcherrima (Poinsettia)
Codiaeum variegatum (Croton)
Ricinus communis (Castor Bean)

Poinsettia

Yew family
Taxus canadensis (Canada Yew)
Taxus cuspidata (Japanese Yew)

Household Poisons

If you suspect your dog has ingested a poisonous product, consult a veterinarian immediately. This chart is meant to alert you to possible signs of poisoning and to inform you of potential veterinary treatment.

Poison	Signs	Treatment
Insecticides such as flea and/or tick sprays and shampoos, especially those containing the chemical permethin, and roach and/or ant sprays	Muscle tremors, excessive drooling, vomiting, diarrhea, lack of coordination, breathing difficulty, convulsions. Potentially fatal.	Vet may recommend bathing dog in body-temperature water and pet shampoo (not a flea shampoo!) before bringing him in. Make sure dog does not become chilled. Vomiting may help if insecticide is ingested.
Household cleansers, detergents, disinfectants	Oral lesions, vomiting, diarrhea, lethargy, collapse, and coma. Potentially fatal.	Do not induce vomiting. Veterinary treatment involves fluid therapy and medication to soothe the stomach.

Poison	Signs	Treatment
Rodent poisons such as warfarin, brodifacoum, and other anticoagulants	Weakness, pale gums, external bleeding (from the nose, mouth, or wounds), gastrointestinal or urinary bleeding, breathing difficulty. Signs may take several days to appear. Potentially fatal.	Vomiting may help if induced within a few hours of ingestion. Treatment and antidotes administered by vet are often successful if given quickly enough.
Antifreeze	Lack of coordination followed 8 or so hours later by extreme listlessness, vomiting, kidney pain or swelling, seizures, and coma. Potentially fatal; 1 tablespoon of standard 50:50 antifreeze mixture can kill a medium-size dog.	Vomiting may help if induced within a few hours of ingestion. Once signs are evident, vomiting is of no benefit. Dog must receive appropriate treatment (including an antidote of ethanol) by veterinarian within hours of exposure to have any chance of survival. Antizol-Vet is a new treatment for antifreeze poisoning in dogs.
Nonsteroidal anti-inflammatory drugs (NSAIDs) such as Advil and Motrin	Low dose: lack of coordination, vomiting, and abdominal pain due to gastric ulcers. High dose: kidney failure or sudden death due to respiratory and heart failure.	Vomiting may help if induced within 2 or 3 hours of ingestion. Prompt treatment at a veterinary hospital is often successful.
Chocolate	Small quantity: vomiting, diarrhea, excitation, or weakness; usually not fatal. Large quantity: seizure and/or heart disturbances. One ounce of baking chocolate, 4 ounces of sweet cocoa, or 10 ounces of milk chocolate can kill a 10-pound dog.	Poisoned dogs are likely to have vomited already. If not, vomiting may help if induced within 2 or 3 hours of ingestion. Treatment to control dehydration, seizures, and heart disturbances may be necessary.

The Beginning and End of Life:

Times for Special Care

Much of this book is devoted to the everyday needs of growing puppies and adult dogs. Because there are other important times in your dog's life, it is important to also consider special-care situations: mating and birth, and the senior years. It is the ASPCA's founding purpose to safeguard the health and well-being of animals. To help further that purpose, pet owners should leave breeding to qualified, reputable professionals. Choose a pet conscientiously, and remain wholeheartedly committed to meeting that pet's needs throughout her entire life.

Mating and birth are discussed here only to present a complete overview of canine life and health, not as encouragement to breed your dog. If your dog does become pregnant—or if you adopt a pregnant dog from a shelter—consult immediately with your veterinarian (and, if possible, with qualified breeders) and educate yourself on the subject by reading the books listed in the Recommended Reading appendix and any other literature that your veterinarian recommends.

In their senior years, dogs require extra attention from owners, so the end of this chapter outlines specific advice for attending to your pet's comfort as she grows older.

Whelping a litter puts physical demands on a female dog.

Mating, Pregnancy, and Birth

If you are interested in breeding your dog, first seriously consider all of the reasons why you should not do it; a list of reasons is given below. The two most compelling reasons are that millions of unwanted dogs are euthanized every year and that neutering your dog has significant behavioral and medical benefits (see page 482 for a detailed explanation of these benefits). If after considering all of this information you still want to breed your dog, educate yourself about all aspects of the process—including the medical facts and the financial and time commitments required—and accept the responsibilities of caring for the parents and the puppies. All dogs that are not going to be bred should be neutered to prevent accidental pregnancies and unwanted puppies.

Finding a Suitable Mate

If you are going to breed your dog, it is extremely important to select a healthy and even-tempered mate. Begin by consulting with reputable breeders, your veterinarian, or a local breed club. Before breeding, both the mother and father should be examined by a veterinarian, vaccinations should be updated (page 423), and the dogs should be checked and treated, if necessary, for internal and external parasites (pages 439 and 446) and brucellosis, a bacterial disorder that can cause infertility and orchitis (testicular swelling and infection) and can be transmitted during breeding (many dogs that appear healthy can be carriers). Both dogs should also be screened (by reviewing the family tree and running tests) for hereditary problems. Only good-tempered, healthy dogs that have tested negative for any breed-related disorders are suitable for breeding.

Setting a Date

The age at which dogs reach puberty (the onset of sexual maturity) varies greatly, from six to eighteen months depending on the breed. Generally, the smaller breeds reach sexual maturity earlier than the larger breeds. In order to rule out hereditary disorders such as epilepsy and

---

Reasons Not to Breed Your Dog

- Millions of unwanted dogs are euthanized every year.
- Neutering your dog has significant health and behavioral benefits (see page 482).
- It is hard work that requires a great deal of energy and attention.
- It is expensive. Few breeders ever break even financially, much less make a profit. Be aware of the financial burdens you'll be undertaking.
- It is a long-term commitment, and your responsibilities literally multiply with each litter.
- It requires a rigorous education. To be a good breeder, you must understand canine genetics, infectious diseases, and, of course, reproduction.
- Although most healthy dogs do not experience complications during pregnancy and delivery, you are still putting your dog's life at unnecessary risk when you allow her to breed.

A female dog should not be bred until she is at least two years old, when she is old enough for any hereditary disorders to be diagnosed.

progressive retinal atrophy (PRA), it is important to wait to breed dogs until they are at least two years old. For female dogs, it is best to wait at least twelve to eighteen months between litters.

In order to schedule a date to mate two dogs, you must understand the female reproductive cycle, which consists of several phases: proestrus, estrus, metestrus (also known as diestrus), and anestrus. See pages 328–329 for anatomical illustrations of the male and female canine reproductive systems.

Proestrus occurs just before estrus. (The term "heat" refers to both proestrus and estrus.) During proestrus the vulva, or lips of the female's vaginal opening, swell and a bloody discharge is excreted. At this stage, the female teases the male, standing still for inspection of her rear end but running away or menacing him if he attempts to mount.

Estrus begins between nine and fifteen days after the bloody discharge and the swelling of the vulva are first seen and usually lasts five to nine days. During this time, ovulation (the release of an unfertilized egg) occurs. Although the exact date of ovulation cannot be determined without special tests, the female is likely to become pregnant if she is bred on the ninth, eleventh, or thirteenth day after proestrus begins. To determine when a female is ovulating, a veterinarian can measure her plasma progesterone levels or examine under a microscope a smear of cells taken from the vagina (this is called vaginal cytology). During estrus, the bloody discharge stops and the female will present herself to the male with her rear end up, tail to the side, and the vulva twitching up and down (called "winking").

Metestrus is the two-month period after estrus when the uterus is prepared for the fetus. The hormone progesterone is secreted by the ovaries and is responsible for the uterine and mammary gland changes during this period. (Hormonal changes occur regardless of whether the female is pregnant.)

In the final phase of the cycle, *anestrus*, the ovaries rest from egg production for two or three months. This period begins with delivery (whelping) and ends with proestrus. It lasts about eleven weeks.

Mating

Ideally, the dogs should meet once, at the breeding site, before they mate so they can get to know each other and the environment. Most males seem to perform more reliably in familiar surroundings, so breeding is usually best done at the male's home (either inside in a room with a door that can be closed or outside in a fenced area). This is because males are more likely to dominate the female on their own territory; a female will not mate with a submissive male. An experienced male will mount from the rear, holding the female's waist with his front legs so that she can't sit down. After a few pelvic thrusts, his penis enters her vagina, he ejaculates, and he stops thrusting. The swollen bulb of the penis and the muscles in the vaginal area cause a delay in separation called a copulatory tie, which helps ensure fertilization. The male will usually swing one leg over the female so that they are facing in opposite directions. When the swelling subsides, the male will walk away. The entire mating routine usually lasts ten to sixty minutes from the time that the male mounts. The more experienced the male, the more likely pregnancy will occur. (If more than one male is present, as is typically the case with strays, several males may mate with the female, in which case littermates may have different fathers.)

Mating is most successful if it takes place on the male's territory.

Pregnancy

An experienced veterinarian can usually diagnose pregnancy by gently feeling the dog's abdomen twenty to thirty days after mating. (Owners should not try to determine if a dog is pregnant by probing her abdomen, as doing so could harm the fetuses.) If necessary, ultrasounds or X rays can confirm the condition and provide further information about the size, number, and health of the fetuses.

If your dog is pregnant, your vet will test her for heartworms and intestinal parasites and may recommend blood tests to ensure that she has not picked up anything since she was mated. Your veterinarian will also discuss diet, exercise, and a schedule for future appointments.

About five weeks after conception, the dog's appetite will increase and she will gain weight. By the end of pregnancy, most dogs have gained about 35 percent of their original weight. After thirty-five days, the abdomen and mammary glands will start to swell. Gestation usually lasts approximately sixty-three to sixty-five days.

There is usually no need to change the type of food a dog eats or provide vitamin or mineral supplements when she is pregnant as long as her diet is nutritionally complete, though the quantity of food should be increased. A general rule of thumb is to increase the daily ration by about 5 percent each week (many dogs will not show an increased appetite until the fifth week). During the last few weeks of pregnancy (when the increasing size of the uterus leaves less room in the stomach and intestines), the total daily ration should be divided into three or four small meals.

Regular exercise will keep the pregnant dog from gaining too much weight and will make the delivery of the puppies easier. Strenuous exercise should be restricted starting three days before the expected delivery date.

Most pregnant dogs gain about 35 percent of their original weight by the time they deliver their pups, about nine weeks after conception.

Whelping Box A pregnant dog needs a safe, clean whelping box in which to deliver her puppies and in which to care for them during the first few weeks of their lives. A couple of weeks before the due date, place the box in a quiet, warm, draft-free area of the home that is familiar to the dog (not an area she's usually not allowed in). The box must be large enough for the mother to stretch out in so that she can nurse comfortably. Line the box with towels or sheets that extend all the way to the edges (so that the puppies cannot get stuck underneath the lining and suffocate) and that can easily be removed to be cleaned regularly. The sides of the box should be high enough to keep the puppies inside, but low enough to allow the mother to get in and out. The inside walls of the box should have a ledge three to six inches above the floor of the box that projects about four inches so that a pup cannot be crushed against the wall by the mother. The temperature in at least half of the box needs to be maintained at 85°F (29°C) at all times starting one to two weeks prior to the whelping date (in case of early delivery) and for the first two weeks after delivery; puppies are not able to regulate their body temperature effectively and can die if they get chilled. Place a 250-watt infrared (heat) bulb above the box so that half of the area is heated and the mother can find a comfortably warm spot for herself and her pups (and can also get away from the heat if she wants to). Attach a thermometer to the side of the box to monitor the temperature.

Delivery

Beginning one week before the due date, you should take your dog's temperature two to three times daily. A few days before delivery (whelping), milky fluid may seep from her nipples.

When delivery time is near (within twenty-four hours), the dog will pace, pant,

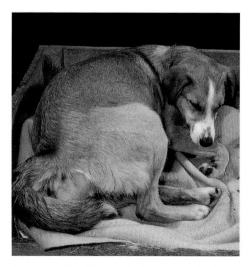

Mom rests after delivering the first puppy in her litter.

and lose her appetite, and her temperature will drop from 102°F (39°C) to 99° or 100°F (37°C). Milk may appear at her nipples and a straw-colored fluid may seep from the vulva.

Once labor (straining and intermittent contractions) has begun, the first puppy should begin to emerge within three hours. The amniotic sac that surrounds each puppy will break upon delivery or the mother will chew it open so that the puppy can breathe on its own. The mother will then stimulate the puppy by licking it and will chew off the umbilical cord. A few minutes after delivering each puppy, the mother will deliver a placenta, which she may or may not eat. Each subsequent puppy is usually born within one to two hours of the preceding one, although the mother may rest, and have no contractions, for up to six hours between puppies. Some mother dogs will begin nursing pups while delivering the rest of the litter.

Your Role During Delivery The dog owner's role during delivery is to observe closely and intervene as little as possible. Healthy dogs rarely experience any problems during delivery, and an owner's best intentions to help usually only complicate matters.

One exception is a situation in which the mother does not chew open the amniotic sac and sever the umbilical cord. If this happens, open the sac yourself and, with your finger, remove the mucus from the puppy's mouth. Then, with a piece of thread dipped in alcohol, tie off the umbilical cord about an inch from the puppy's abdomen and cut the cord on the mother's side with scissors that have been dipped in alcohol. Finally, rub the puppy with a clean, soft towel to stimulate circulation and respiration and place the puppy back in the whelping box.

When to Call the Vet During Delivery If you are concerned about how the mother dog's labor is progressing—or if you

Mom opens the amniotic sac, severs the umbilical cord, and cleans the pup.

Most moms nurse their pups, supplying them with all their nutritional needs, for approximately the first month.

observe any of the following conditions—call your veterinarian:

- if no puppies are born within twenty-four hours of the rectal temperature drop (to 99° or 100°F/37°C)
- if the first puppy isn't born within three hours of active labor (intermittent contractions)
- if subsequent puppies are not delivered within one to two hours of active labor (intermittent contractions)
- if a puppy doesn't appear within fifteen minutes of constant straining
- if labor seems to have stopped before the expected number of puppies have been delivered
- if the mother doesn't deliver a placenta for each pup; a retained placenta can cause infection
- if a puppy is protruding from the vulva for more than several minutes despite strong contractions

When to Call the Vet After Delivery Even if delivery has seemed uneventful, problems can develop after birthing appears to be complete. Contact your veterinarian immediately if any of the following complications arise:

- if the mother seems nervous, staggers, trembles, has a fever, convulses, strains to urinate, seems weak, or loses her appetite
- if the mother has a foul-smelling reddish or puslike vaginal discharge
- if the mother has a painful, hot, hard, swollen (red or purple) breast
- if the mother ignores the pups
- if any pup is not nursing, doesn't gain weight, has diarrhea, or appears weak
- if any pup has difficulty breathing or cries constantly
- if any pup has pale gums or swollen eyes or eye discharge

A golden retriever puppy at one week, three weeks, five weeks, and seven weeks of age

If one puppy is ill, the mother and the entire litter will need to be examined by your veterinarian.

Postnatal Care

After delivery, as during, most mothers need very little help from their owners. Assuming the delivery went smoothly, your job is simply to see to it that she is fed properly, make sure she is producing milk, and, if necessary, clean her by wiping her down with a moist cloth or giving her a bath with a mild shampoo (be sure to rinse her well so the pups don't ingest soap residue when nursing). In terms of feeding, a general rule is to offer the mother an additional one hundred calories per pound of puppy (weigh the puppies on an ounce or gram scale). By the end of the nursing period (at about five to six weeks), she may be eating three times as much as she was eating before the pregnancy. A well-balanced commercial dog food should meet her nutritional requirements, but if she seems to need something extra, try supplementing her diet with high-protein foods such as dairy products and cooked eggs. As always, she should have access to fresh drinking water at all times.

In terms of taking care of the pups, all you need to do is make sure they are nursing and keep the environment clean, quiet, and subdued, especially if this is the mother's first litter. Too much noise and activity may decrease milk production or divert her attention away from her pups and can even make her behave aggressively toward them.

Puppies will nurse every one to two hours during the first week. They should gain 5 to 10 percent of their birth weight each day, usually at least doubling their weight during the first two weeks of life. Check their weight daily on an ounce or gram scale and call the vet if any of them is not growing. In the rare event that the mother does not produce enough milk, her hungry pups will constantly cry and fail to stay at the nipple. Unless they are hand-fed (contact your vet for instructions on how to do this), or allowed to nurse from another lactating dog, they will not survive.

After each feeding, the mother will meticulously groom each puppy, paying particular attention to the face and anal region. Puppies lack the ability to urinate and defecate on their own until they are two to three weeks of age. To stimulate these essential functions, the mother licks the anal area, then ingests the urine and feces as it passes. However unsavory this may seem to humans, it is absolutely necessary to help keep the nest area clean.

The puppies' eyes and ears usually begin to open between ten days and two weeks after birth. By about two weeks, the puppies are crawling, and by three weeks they are walking and playing with each other.

For the first two weeks only one or two people should be handling the pups and only when necessary, such as when weighing them or cleaning the whelping box. In order for pups to be properly socialized with humans, starting at week three and continuing until they are placed in new homes, they should be handled regularly by a diverse group of people.

Weaning Puppies

Mother's milk alone supplies all the nutritional needs for healthy puppies for about a month, at which time the puppies need supplemental food. When the puppies reach three weeks of age, make a gruel by mixing a small amount of warm water with a specially designed "puppy food" or growth formula, and place it in a shallow dish. Allow the puppies ready access to their food several times daily. At first they will walk and run through the dish and basically make a mess of themselves, but with time the puppies will begin to eat this semisolid mixture, and by five weeks they should consume it readily. At about six weeks of age puppies are able to chew dry food, so there is no longer any need to moisten the diet.

Puppies usually can be weaned from their mother by seven to eight weeks. The following method works best to help prevent the mother's mammary glands from becoming engorged. On the day the puppies are to be weaned, take the mother away from her puppies; let the puppies eat their food as usual, but don't allow them to nurse, and don't give the mother any food. That evening, don't feed the puppies or the mother, but allow the puppies to nurse again so the mammary glands will be drained. The next day, keep the mother and her puppies completely separated from each other. If they are more than eight weeks of age, the puppies can be adopted out as soon as desired. (Some breeders prefer to wait until the puppies are at least four months old in order to assess their fitness for showing.) Feed the puppies their regular food as usual, but feed the mother only half the amount of food she was consuming before she was bred. On the third day—and subsequent days—she can be fed the entire amount she was eating before becoming pregnant.

After their first month of life, puppies need food to supplement their mother's milk.

Older Years

With proper care, most dogs live full and happy lives. The giant breeds, like the Great Dane and Irish wolfhound, are "old" at eight years of age while toy breeds reach their senior years later—at about twelve. Sadly, no beloved dog ever seems to live long enough. The next few pages provide guidance for taking care of your aging dog, including how to prepare yourself for the death of a canine companion, when to consider euthanasia, and what this humane act entails.

A dog in her senior years may need special care.

Creating a Comfort Zone

As dogs age, like people, they often develop aches and pains and muscle weakness. Speak to your veterinarian about things you can do to minimize discomfort and consider making some of the following accommodations.

Special Bedding Old dogs appreciate soft, cushioned bedding. A piece of egg-crate foam with a cotton covering works well if your dog has joint pain or stiffness. Place the cushioning in your dog's favorite sleeping spot.

Temperate Environment Old dogs do not regulate their body temperature as well as young dogs and should be kept indoors in a warm, dry area when not outside exercising or playing. Osteoarthritis, common in old dogs, is exacerbated by cold and dampness. Similarly, older dogs are prone to heatstroke and need to be protected from hot or humid conditions.

Massage

Gentle rubdowns may ease your old dog's joint stiffness and pain, and will also provide you and your dog with mutually beneficial time together. Work gently and slowly. With the dog on his belly, run your hands down his back, on both sides of the spine, toward the tail. Turn the dog onto one side and run your hands down his legs, gently rubbing the joints and flexing and extending them. Massage each toe. Turn the dog onto his other side and repeat. Massage his head and around the eyes.

Special Bowls The aches, pains, bone changes, and muscle weakness of old age can make it difficult for your dog to eat and drink from bowls placed on the floor. To make your dog more comfortable, purchase elevated food and water bowls or build your own stand. The stand should be at about the height of the dog's shoulder and the bowls should fit securely in cut-out holes or should be heavy enough not to slide off the surface.

Mobility Aids Old dogs may have difficulty walking on slippery surfaces, such as wood and vinyl flooring. To make getting around easier, place pieces of carpeting in areas your dog frequents. If your dog has trouble with steps leading to the entrance to your home, you may wish to build a ramp for her. If your dog has a favorite chair or is allowed to sleep on your bed, make sure she has a way to get up into it. To help an old dog get up or walk, position a large towel like a sling under the body in front of the back legs and lift gently.

Special Diet The diet and feeding routine of an old dog needs to be adapted to accommodate the slowing down and decreasing efficiency of all of his systems. Fewer calories are needed because your old friend is less active and his metabolic rate is slower. Small, frequent feedings rather than one or two large meals will make digestion easier. Constipation is a common problem among older dogs; it is often easily remedied but sometimes indicates a more serious problem. Speak to your veterinarian about your dog's dietary needs, which may be met with a specially formulated prescription diet, especially if your dog suffers from heart, liver, or kidney disease, or other medical problems.

Special Dental Care Some old dogs develop severe gingivitis (gum inflammation), tartar buildup, and periodontal disease. Your veterinarian may recommend teeth cleaning or periodontal work, which may require anesthesia. Before administering anesthesia the veterinarian will evaluate your dog's readiness (the condition of his heart, lungs, liver, kidneys, and blood) with all or some of the following procedures: a physical exam, blood tests (often called a CBC and Chem-Screen), urinalysis, electrocardiogram, and chest X rays. If your dog has a heart murmur or severe dental disease, you may be instructed to give him antibiotics for a week before and a week after the procedures to minimize the risk of infection. Fluids may be given intravenously or under the skin during the dental procedures. After the dental work, regular home care (page 382) will help retard further tooth and gum deterioration and should improve your dog's health, appetite, and well-being.

Routine Exercise Unless restricted by a medical condition, try to give your older dog regular exercise, taking into consideration her physical condition and interests. Walking, jogging, swimming, and hiking as well as indoor games are all fine for an old dog in generally good health. However, if your dog sits down, pants heavily, resists exercise, or is sore or lame afterward or the next day, contact your veterinarian and lessen the intensity of the exercise program.

Exercise keeps dogs—and people—youthful.

Extra Grooming and Bathing Old dogs often need more brushing, combing, and bathing because they are less active than young dogs. Dry skin and a lusterless coat can be a normal part of aging, or they can be signs of a serious medical condition. Once you and your veterinarian have ruled out an underlying medical condition, speak to him about moisturizing shampoos and conditioners. He may also recommend that you add fatty acids or other supplements to the diet.

More Frequent Nail Trimming Older dogs usually don't exercise on hard surfaces or as vigorously as younger dogs. This means that their nails grow longer and faster and must be trimmed more frequently. For instructions on how to trim your dog's nails, see page 377.

Common Medical Concerns with Older Dogs

Throughout a dog's life it is important to maintain a schedule of annual well-pet visits with your veterinarian. It is even more crucial when a dog ages and medical problems become more common.

In addition to examining your dog and running any necessary tests, your veterinarian should spend time talking to you about your older dog's daily life and any changes you may have noticed. Following are some common concerns. Additional information about many of them appears in Common Canine Health Problems, starting on page 425.

Hearing loss is common among old dogs. Sometimes what seems to be hearing loss is actually caused by an ear infection or buildup of wax or debris in the ear, both of which can be easily treated. The veterinarian may use an otoscope, a medical instrument with magnification and a light source, to examine the eardrum and the external ear canal.

Deteriorating eyesight may be caused by "dry eye" (keratitis sicca), diminished tear production that causes inflammation and deterioration of the cornea; glaucoma; or cataracts. All of these conditions can be treated effectively if diagnosed early; however, a veterinarian may not advise treatment for cataracts if the dog's vision is not severely compromised. Your vet may recommend a consultation with a veterinary ophthalmologist before treating any of these conditions.

Joint pain and muscle weakness that result in difficulty getting up are quite common in geriatric canines. Your veterinarian will determine, by physical exam, ultrasound, and/or X rays or other tests, the nature of the problem. If it is osteoarthritis, a combination of medication, physical therapy, and a specialized exercise program will most likely be recommended. Sometimes muscle weakness or trouble getting up can be signs of intervertebral disk disease, hypothyroidism, Cushing's syndrome, heart disease, or abdominal tumors. Older German shepherds develop a degeneration of the spinal cord called giant axonal neuropathy that causes weakness of the hindlegs.

Bad odors can be caused by dental or kidney disease, ear infections, or abscessed tumors.

Growths, no matter how small or seemingly insignificant, should always be examined by the vet, who will decide if a biopsy is necessary. Check your old dog for growths during your regular grooming routine (page 372).

Behavioral changes may be related to medical problems, such as kidney, heart, or liver disease. Chronic pain; diminished senses of hearing, sight, or smell; hypothyroidism; or brain disorders, such as tumors or Alzheimer's-like syndrome, may all affect your dog's behavior. For example, a deaf or partially deaf dog may bite if startled. A dog with a hypothyroid condition may appear too lazy to respond to stimuli.

Coughing in older dogs is commonly caused by tracheal collapse, chronic bronchitis, and heart failure. Call your veterinarian at the first sign of coughing.

Loss of balance exhibited along with a head tilt and rapid eye movements probably indicates "old dog" vestibular syndrome, which is a disruption of the balancing mechanism in the inner ear and is usually curable with medication in a few weeks. Loss of balance may also be caused by a tumor or infection.

Urinary accidents can be caused by various illnesses that afflict older dogs: bladder or sphincter malfunction, bladder inflammation or infection, kidney disease, Cushing's syndrome, and diabetes. Your doctor will recommend appropriate tests (such as blood tests, urinalysis, ultrasound, and/or cystoscopy) and treatments.

Bloody discharge from the penis or straining to urinate may indicate that the prostate gland is enlarged because of age, infection, or a tumor. Your veterinarian will perform a rectal exam and may recommend X rays, a urinalysis, blood tests, and possibly an ultrasound and biopsy.

Brownish red discharge from the vagina may indicate an infected uterus (pyometra). Treatment is usually an emergency ovariohysterectomy (removal of the uterus and ovaries).

Old age may slow a dog down, but frequent visits to the vet will keep him going for years.

Increased or decreased appetite, increased water intake, increased urination, vomiting, or diarrhea may be signs of illness (as with a younger dog). Your veterinarian will be more effective if you contact her when you first notice any of these signs.

Cancer is more common in older dogs than younger dogs. Warning signs include sores that don't heal; bleeding or discharge from the mouth, nose, urinary tract, vagina, or rectum; abnormal swellings; bad odor (the source of the odor—death of tissue—depends on where the cancer is located); difficulty eating and/or swallowing; difficulty urinating or defecating; loss of appetite; loss of energy; weight loss; vomiting; persistent lameness; lumps in the mammary glands (breasts); and change in the size or shape of a testicle. Cancer is most successfully treated when diagnosed early.

Euthanasia

If an illness or injury is terminal and there is no hope for a cure, then euthanasia (literally "good death") is often suggested as a means of sparing a dog needless suffering. The procedure usually involves an injection that causes the dog to slip away peacefully and painlessly within a matter of seconds.

For many, the choice of whether to euthanize their dog is even more difficult than dealing with the loss itself. To come to a decision regarding euthanasia, you might ask your veterinarian some of the following questions:

- Can you tell me if my dog is suffering?
- What kinds of treatments are available? What might they accomplish? How much will they cost?
- Can I expect a cure, alleviation of pain, or prolongation of life?
- What kind of care will I need to provide?

Even though your veterinarian will answer as many of your questions as possible, ultimately the decision rests with you. You might ask yourself:

- Is my dog comfortable and happy? With treatment, will she ever be comfortable and happy?
- How much longer can I reasonably expect her to live?
- Will the quality of my dog's life improve or worsen?

If you decide to have your dog euthanized, discuss with your veterinarian whether you or other family members should be present. Most veterinarians will allow the family to participate; some will perform the procedure at your home so that the dog can die in the peace of her own environment. Ask your veterinarian to explain in advance the details of the procedure. You will also need to decide how the remains should be handled, either by burial or cremation.

Coping with Loss

The loss of a beloved dog is never easy. Guilt, regret, anger, uncertainty, terrible sadness, and/or feelings of emptiness may accompany the loss. But remember that it is important to allow yourself time to grieve. It is impossible to predict how long it will take before you start to feel better. Do not hesitate to seek professional help if you begin to feel seriously depressed or if you just need someone to talk to.

Most veterinarians can suggest professionals trained in grief counseling. Additionally, an organization called the Delta Society makes available a national directory of pet-loss counselors, publications that deal with pet-loss, and contacts for pet-loss support groups nationwide (see Resources appendix). Pet-loss telephone hotlines, available from the ASPCA and many veterinary colleges (see Important Telephone Numbers appendix), can also lend support.

When to Adopt Again

A new dog will not replace your deceased pet in your affections or your heart but can help ease the pain of the loss. The right time to adopt again is a very personal decision. Some people choose to bring home a new dog right away; others need months to mourn. Do whatever feels right to you and your family. A new dog will bring laughter and companionship into your home. When you are ready, there is a dog waiting to share his life with you.

Glossary of Dog-Related Terms

Belton In English setters, a coat pattern of white hairs mixed with colored hairs.

Benched show A show that allows participating dogs to be viewed on assigned benches when not competing.

Blaze A white patch or stripe down the center of a dog's face, usually extending from forehead to nose.

Breed standards Standardized descriptions defining a breed's ideal characteristics. Used as guidelines by breeders and by dog show judges.

Brindle A coat pattern that features streaks or flecks of darker and lighter colors, creating loosely formed stripes. Common in many breeds and mixes.

Button ears Ears with flaps that fold forward so that their tips lie close to the skull and cover the ear openings. Characteristic among certain breeds such as pugs and Manchester terriers.

Cropping The practice of surgically removing portions of a dog's ears to make them stand erect. Illegal in some countries.

Crossbreed The offspring of two different breeds of purebred dog.

Culotte Long hair that grows on a dog's thighs.

Dewclaw A digit, sometimes called the fifth claw, located high on the inner side of a dog's front and hind paws.

Dewlap Loose, pendulous skin that hangs under a dog's neck. Characteristic among certain breeds such as mastiffs and bloodhounds.

Docking The practice of surgically removing part of a dog's tail. Customary according to American breed standards for most spaniels and terriers. Illegal in some countries.

Double coat A weather-resistant coat that has both a soft, insulating undercoat and a coarse, protective outercoat. Characteristic among certain breeds such as Newfoundlands and Great Pyrenees.

Estrous The female reproductive cycle.

Estrus The phase of the female reproductive cycle when the dog is fertile (commonly called "heat").

Euthanasia The use of deliberate medical means, usually lethal injection, to cause death. Used to avoid suffering in sick and aging pets, and to limit populations of dogs in shelters.

Feathering Fringes of hair on a dog's ears, tail, legs, and body. Characteristic among retrievers and spaniels.

Grizzle A fine mixture of gray or red hairs with white hairs. Common in various terriers.

Harlequin A coat pattern of white with black or gray patches.

Heat *See* Estrus.

Heatstroke A condition induced by prolonged exposure to heat that causes extremely high body temperature and dehydration. Can result in collapse, shock, and, in some cases, death.

Lure coursing An organized sport in which sight hounds chase an artificial lure.

Marking Canine method of attracting a mate or staking out territory by urinating to deposit scent. *See also* Pheromones.

Mastiff A type of dog characterized by a massive, muscular body and a powerful head and jaw.

Merle A coat pattern characterized by blotches of dark hair against a background of lighter hair.

Mixed breed A dog with one or both parents of mixed ancestry (nonpurebred). *See also* Purebred.

Molossian An ancient breed of massive and powerful guard and war dog, forebear of today's mastiff.

Neuter To render incapable of breeding by surgically removing reproductive organs —the testes in males, the ovaries and uterus in females ("spaying").

Nictitating membrane A thin protective membrane located at the inner corner of the eye, beneath the lower eyelid. Also called the "third eyelid."

Obedience training The process by which a dog is taught to follow commands and behave obediently.

Outercoat A dog's protective coat of coarse primary hairs. Also called the "topcoat."

Particolor A coat pattern featuring white with patches of color.

Pedigree The record of a dog's ancestry. In purebred dogs, a certificate of unmixed breeding.

Pet clip A simple grooming style for dogs that do not compete in shows. *See also* Show coat.

Pheromones Hormone-like chemical substances (found

in a dog's urine) with associated odors that trigger social and sexual responses in dogs. *See also* Marking.

Pile A dense undercoat of soft, fine fur.

Plume A spray of soft, feathery hair on a dog's tail.

Prick ears Erect, pointed ears.

Primary hairs Strong, coarse hairs, also called "guard hairs," that make up a dog's protective outercoat.

Purebred A dog of unmixed ancestry—that is, with both parents of the same breed. *See also* Mixed breed.

Quarantine A period of isolation imposed on animals brought to or from foreign countries in order to prevent the spread of disease or pests.

Roan A coat pattern in which the base color (often red) is mixed with white hairs and looks lightened or mottled.

Rose ears Small, creased ears that fold back to reveal the ear opening.

Secondary hairs The soft, fine hairs that surround the primary hairs and make up a dog's dense, insulating undercoat.

Service dog A dog specially trained to assist a person that is physically or mentally challenged.

Show coat An elaborate style of grooming a show dog's coat in accordance with its particular breed standard. *See also* Pet clip.

Socialization The process of acclimating a puppy to the company of humans and other animals.

Spay *See* Neuter.

Spitz-type dog A dog with features characteristic of the Northern breed category, such as prick ears, a double coat, a bushy tail, and a powerful body.

Third eyelid *See* Nictitating membrane.

Ticking A coat pattern characterized by specks of black or another color against a lighter background.

Topcoat *See* Outercoat.

Undercoat The underlying layer of soft, smooth secondary hair that insulates a dog's coat.

Vocalization A dog's method of communicating through vocal sounds such as barking, growling, howling, and whining.

Whelping Giving birth.

Wirehaired A coat in which an abundance of coarse primary hairs gives it a "wiry" look and texture.

Important Telephone Numbers

Veterinarian _____

Animal emergency clinic _____

Boarding facility _____

Pet sitter _____

ASPCA Companion Animal Services Behavior Helpline
212-876-7700 ext. HELP (4357) Free general behavior and care information.

ASPCA National Animal Poison Control Center
888-426-4435 Consultation fee charged, payable by major credit card.

800-548-2423 Consultation fee charged, payable by major credit card.

900-680-0000 Consultation fee charged to your phone number.

AKC Companion Animal Recovery Service
800-252-7894 This 24-hour pet recovery service maintains a worldwide database for recording identification numbers for owners of pets with permanent identification, i.e., a microchip or tattoo. Contact this service to report a lost or found animal with permanent identification.

National Association of Professional Pet Sitters (NAPPS)
800-296-PETS Pet sitter referral hotline. http://www.petsitters.org

National Dog Registry
800-NDR-DOGS Maintains a registry of dogs with permanent i.d. for the identification and return of lost pets.

Pet Loss Support Hotlines (grief counseling)
800-404-7387 PetFriends, Inc. Returns long-distance calls collect. Free for southern New Jersey and the Philadelphia area.

602-995-5885 The Companion Animal Association of Arizona. Provides 24-hour grief counseling, support groups, and referrals. No fee.

530-752-4200 Staffed by University of California-Davis veterinary students. No fee.

630-603-3994 Staffed by the Chicago Veterinary Medical Association. No fee.

607-253-3932 Staffed by Cornell University veterinary students. No fee.

888-478-7574 Staffed by Iowa State University veterinary students. No fee.

517-432-2696 Staffed by Michigan State University veterinary students. No fee.

614-292-1823 Staffed by Ohio State University veterinary students. No fee.

508-839-7966 Staffed by Tufts University veterinary students. No fee.

540-231-8038 Staffed by Virginia-Maryland Regional College of Veterinary Medicine students. No fee.

212-876-7700 ext. 4355 Staffed by ASPCA Counseling Services. No fee.

Spay USA
800-248-SPAY This free service will help you locate a low-cost spaying and neutering facility in your area.

Breed Organizations and Kennel Clubs

Each major kennel club has its own roster of recognized breeds and its own breed standards. Their common objectives are maintaining the purity of the breeds they classify, registering pedigrees, licensing shows, and providing relevant information to the public. Contact the following organizations for information on finding reputable breeders, showing your dog, obtaining brochures on canine health and obedience, or subscribing to their respective publications.

The American Kennel Club (AKC)
5580 Centerview Drive
Suite 200
Raleigh, NC 27606-3390
Tel: 919-233-9767
http://www.akc.org
E-mail: info@akc.org

American Mixed Breed Obedience Registry (AMBOR)
10236 Topanga Boulevard
Suite 205
Chatsworth, CA 91311
Tel: 818-887-3300

http://www.amborusa.org
E-mail: ambor@amborusa.org

The Canadian Kennel Club
89 Skyway Avenue
Suite 100
Etobicoke
Ontario M9W 6R4
Canada
Tel: 416-675-5511
http://www.ckc.ca
E-mail: information@ckc.ca

The Kennel Club
1-5 Clarges Street
Piccadilly
London W1Y 8AB
Great Britain
Tel: +44 171 629 5828
http://www.the-kennel-club.org.uk

The United Kennel Club (UKC)
100 East Kilgore Road
Kalamazoo, MI 49002-5584
Tel: 616-343-9020
http://www.ukcdogs.com

Organized Sports and Showing

Information about competing in either organized group sports or dog shows can be readily obtained by contacting breed and kennel clubs as well as the specific organizations listed below.

American Herding Breed Association
c/o Lisa Allen
277 Central Avenue
Seekonk, MA 02771
Tel: 508-761-4078
http://www.glassportal.com/herding/ahba.htm
E-mail: pecans@ix.netcom.com

The American Kennel Club
See above
Information on dog shows, the Canine Good Citizen Program, and other activities

American Sighthound Field Association
c/o Jack Helder
2975 Zimmer Road
Williamston, MI 48895
Tel: 517-655-1173
http://www.asfa.org
E-mail: helder@paceandpartners.com

Disc Dog Quarterly
54 South Oak Avenue
Pasadena, CA 91107
Tel: 626-793-3985
http://www.ddqjournal.com
E-mail: news@ddqjournal.com

International Federation of Sleddog Sports (IFSS)
c/o Maureen Nicholls
Secretary General
Prospect House
Charlton, Kilmersdon
Bath BA3 5TN
Great Britain
Tel: +44 176 143 6599
http://www.worldsport.com/worldsport/sports/sleddog
E-mail: secretary.ifss@ukonline.co.uk

International Sheep Dog Society
Mr. A. Philip Hendry, CBE
Chesham House
47 Bromham Road
Bedford MK40 2AA
Great Britain
http://www.glassportal.com/
herding/herding.htm

Newfoundland Club of America
P.O. Box 2614
Cheyenne, WY 82003
http://www.geocities.com/
~newfdogclub

North American Flyball Association (NAFA), Inc.
1400 W. Devon Avenue, #512
Chicago, IL 60660
http://www.flyball.org
E-mail: flyball@flyball.org

North American Skijoring and Ski Pulk Association
(NASSPA)
P.O. Box 240573
Anchorage, AK 99524
http://www.ptialaska.net/
~skijor
E-mail: brockra@alaska.net

Portuguese Water Dog Club of America
c/o Sandy Overton
Tel: 360-675-9539
http://www.pwdca.org

The United Kennel Club
See above
Information on dog shows

United States Dog Agility Association (USDAA)
P.O. Box 850995
Richardson, TX 75085-0955
Tel: 972-231-9700
http://www.usdaa.com
E-mail: info@usdaa.com

Recommended Reading

Breeding a Litter: The Complete Book of Prenatal and Postnatal Care
Beth J. Finder Harris
Howell Book House, 1993

The Dog Care Book
Sheldon L. Gerstenfeld, V.M.D.
Addison-Wesley Publishing Co., 1989

A Dog Is Listening: The Way Some of Our Closest Friends View Us
Roger A. Caras
Fireside, 1993

The Dog's Mind: Understanding Your Dog's Behavior
Bruce Fogle, D.V.M.
Howell Book House, 1992

The Domestic Dog
Edited by James Serpell and Priscilla Barrett
Cambridge University Press, 1996

The Encyclopedia of the Dog
Bruce Fogle, D.V.M.
DK Publishing, 1995

How to Teach a New Dog Old Tricks, 2nd edition
Ian Dunbar, Ph.D., M.R.C.V.S.
James & Kenneth, 1998

The Intelligence of Dogs: A Guide to the Thoughts, Emotions, and Inner Lives of Our Canine Companions
Stanley Coren
Bantam Books, 1995

The Loss of a Pet: New Revised and Expanded Edition
Wallace Sife, Ph.D.
Howell Book House, 1998

Medical & Genetic Aspects of Purebred Dogs, 2nd edition
Edited by Ross D. Clark and Joan R. Stainer
Cortlandt Group, 1994

Pet Emergency First Aid: Dogs (video)
Apogee Entertainment, 1998

Pet Loss: A Thoughtful Guide for Adults & Children
Herbert A. Nieburg, Ph.D., and Arlene Fischer
HarperCollins, 1996

Show Me! A Dog Showing Primer
D. Carolyn Coile
Barrons Educational Series, 1997

The Toolbox for Remodeling Your Problem Dog
Terry Ryan
Howell Book House, 1998

UC Davis Book of Dogs
Edited by Mordecai Siegal
HarperCollins, 1995

Resources

AKC Gazette
260 Madison Avenue
New York, NY 10010
Tel: 212-696-8390
http://www.akc.org/text/
gazet.htm
E-mail: info@akc.org

The American Animal Hospital Association's "Your Link for Healthy Pets"
Provides behavior, nutrition, and health information.
Tel: 800-883-6301
http://www.healthypet.com
E-mail: aaha@aol.com

The American Veterinary Medical Association's "Web Page on Animal Health"
Provides information on canine health, buying a dog, safety issues, and pet loss.
Tel: 800-248-2862
http://www.avma.org/care4pets

The Association of Pet Dog Trainers
Referrals for affiliated dog trainers in the U.S.
P.O. Box 385
Davis, CA 95617
Tel: 800-PET-DOGS
http://www.apdt.com
E-mail: apdtbod@aol.com

The Delta Society
Publishes a directory of pet loss support groups and counselors in the U.S. Also publishes a listing of trainers and programs for service dogs through its National Service Dog Center and offers a certification program for animal-assisted therapy through Pet Partners.
289 Perimeter Road East
Renton, WA 98055-1329
Tel: 425-226-7357
http://www.deltasociety.org
E-mail: deltasociety@cis.compuserve.com

Dog Fancy Magazine
P.O. Box 6050
Mission Viejo, CA 92690
Tel: 949-855-8822
http://www.dogfancy.com
E-mail: dogfancy@fancypubs.com

Dog World Magazine
500 N. Dearborn, Suite 1100
Chicago, IL 60610
Tel: 312-396-0600
http://www.dogworldmag.com
E-mail: info@dogworldmag.com

Dogs for the Disabled
Trains and places service dogs.
c/o D.H. Dannheisser
P.O. Box 25628
Greenville, SC 29616
Tel: 864-322-9879
E-mail: dhmsd@juno.com

Greyhound Pets of America
Tel: 800-366-1472

The Humane Society of the United States
Promotes animal welfare, offers adoption services and health care for unwanted animals, and maintains a pet health care Web site.
National Headquarters
2100 L Street NW
Washington, DC 20037
Tel: 202-452-1100
http://www.hsus.org

National Greyhound Adoption Network
Tel: 800-446-8637

National Greyhound Adoption Program
8301 Torresdale Avenue
Philadelphia, PA 19136
Tel: 800-348-2517
http://www.ngap.org
E-mail: ngap@ix.netcom.com

NetVet Veterinary Resources and the Electronic Zoo
http://www.avma.org/netvet

Project BREED (Breed Rescue Efforts and Education)
Publishes a directory of breed rescue groups and services.
P.O. Box 15888
Chevy Chase, MD 20825
Tel: 202-244-0065
E-mail: lmlevin@erols.com

The Seeing Eye Inc.
Trains and places seeing-eye dogs.
P.O. Box 375
Morristown, NJ 07963-0375
Tel: 973-539-4425
http://www.seeingeye.org
E-mail: semaster@seeingeye.org

The American Society for the Prevention of Cruelty to Animals

Since 1866, the American Society for the Prevention of Cruelty to Animals has been committed to alleviating pain, fear, and suffering in all animals. Founded by Henry Bergh, the ASPCA is the oldest humane organization in America and one of the largest nonprofit animal welfare groups in the world, with offices in New York, California, Illinois, and Washington, D.C. The ASPCA encourages respect for all life and offers a variety of hands-on programs designed to improve the condition of animals.

Adoptions and Animal Placement Finds suitable homes for animals that have been relinquished by their owners, rescued, or abused. The Society's policy is to spay or neuter all animals available for adoption in order to control pet overpopulation.

Bergh Memorial Animal Hospital Offers complete medical, surgical, radiographic, clinical laboratory, and biopsy services for all domestic pets. The goal is to provide excellent veterinary care at the most reasonable cost possible.

Companion Animal Services Provides training and behavior information about cats and dogs. The department offers obedience classes, operates animal behavior and counseling help lines, and provides literature and interviews on responsible pet ownership.

Consumer Products Develops positive commercial and promotional projects that help fund and create awareness for animal welfare programs.

Government Affairs Promotes and defends laws that protect the health and well-being of animals. A legislative alert program informs the public about issues affecting animals and how to contact their representatives to take appropriate action.

Humane Education Extend the Web, the ASPCA's humane education program, helps educators incorporate humane themes into the classroom through the distribution of materials, workshops, and educational forums. It is currently active in more than 6,000 schools.

Humane Law Enforcement Special ASPCA agents and investigators respond to more than 4,000 cases each year. Along with rescuing hundreds of abused and neglected animals, they have been responsible for crackdowns on dogfighting and cockfighting.

National Animal Poison Control Center NAPCC is the only poison control center for animals in North America. Through a 24-hour emergency telephone hotline, veterinary toxicologists provide rapid expert advice about chemicals, products, or plants toxic to animals.

National Shelter Outreach Fosters a network of communication among humane societies to address the needs of animal shelters and the local communities. The ASPCA is dedicated to promoting excellence in local shelters and assisting in the development of programs for the protection of animals at the grass-roots level.

ASPCA national headquarters are located at 424 East 92nd Street, New York, NY 10128. To learn more about these and the many other valuable programs the ASPCA provides, or how to become a member of the ASPCA, call 212-876-7700.

Please visit us on the Web at http://www.aspca.org.

Acknowledgments

Many people and their dogs have contributed to this book, especially all my patients and their caretakers. For much help and information over the years I thank Louise Alcott, Wendy Eckerd, Margie Rutbell, Richard Tomlinson, and the library staff at the following institutions: the University of Pennsylvania Veterinary School, the American Kennel Club, the United Kennel Club, and the Pennsylvania Federation of Dog Clubs. I am deeply grateful to my wife, Traudi, and my son, Tyler, for their inspiration, encouragement, and patience.

Jacque Lynn Schultz played a vital role in the creation of this book. As director of special projects for the ASPCA's animal sciences division and as director of its dog training center and greyhound rescue fund, she gave generously of her expertise and wisdom to help make this guide both informative and accessible.

I extend special thanks to series editor Miriam Harris, who tirelessly guided this project to fruition. I am also grateful to project editor Melanie Falick for her invaluable help.

I thank Andrew Stewart and the staff of Chanticleer Press for producing such an outstanding book. Editor-in-chief Amy Hughes provided essential guidance and encouragement. Managing editor George Scott's sound judgment, moral support, and unfailing good humor were invaluable. Ann ffolliott, Mike Jackson, Lisa Leventer, Anne O'Connor, Micaela Porta, Mary Sufudy, and John Tarkov lent their considerable editorial expertise to reviewing, revising, and refining the text. Assistant editor Elizabeth Wright provided boundless editorial support. Sarah Burns, Virginia Beck, associate editor Michelle Bredeson, Karla Eoff, and Kate Jacobs offered additional assistance with copyediting and proofreading. Janet Mazefsky created the index.

With photo director Zan Carter's guidance and support, photo editor Ruth Jeyaveeran sifted through thousands of photographs in her search for the engaging images that contribute so much to the guide. Photo research assistance came from Robin Raffer, Robin Sand, and Julie Tesser. Permissions manager Alyssa Sachar facilitated the acquisition of photographs and ensured the accuracy of all credits. For the photographs illustrating care and training, photographer Mary Bloom worked with models Terry Bhola and Linda James. Thanks also to Valerie Angeli, Alison Boak and Alan Weinstein, Beth Douglas Fidoten, Jane Kopelman, and Steve Zawistowski for allowing their dogs to be photographed for this guide.

Art director Drew Stevens led a team of talented designers—Kirsten Berger, Brian Boyce, Anthony Liptak, Vincent Mejia, Virginia Pope, and Bernadette Vibar—in the process of creating a guide that is both beautiful and useful. Holly Kowitt designed the icons for the breeds section. Illustrators John Yesko and Todd Zalewski created the anatomy and first aid drawings, respectively.

Director of production Alicia Mills and production manager Philip Pfeifer saw the book through the complex production and printing processes. Interns Megan Lombardo, Sarah Schleuning, and Morgan Topman assisted them.

Contributing greatly to the information on canine health care were veterinary consultants Lila Miller, D.V.M., senior director of animal sciences at the ASPCA, and Christine Ann Bellezza, D.V.M., staff veterinarian at Cornell University's College of Veterinary Medicine. Dr. Howard E. Evans and John W. Hermanson of Cornell University provided valuable advice on the anatomy illustrations. Stephen L. Zawistowski, Ph.D., ASPCA senior vice president and science advisor, reviewed the entire manuscript. Many thanks to Roger Caras, president emeritus of the ASPCA, for the Foreword and for his work on behalf of animals everywhere.

Thanks also to Jay Schaefer, Laura Lovett, and Judith Dunham at Chronicle Books for their insightful contributions to the content and design of this volume.

Picture Credits

The credits are listed by page number, left to right, top to bottom.

Front cover: (three puppies) Mary Bloom, (two puppies) Jane Burton/Bruce Coleman, Inc., (group of dogs) Ron Kimball. **Spine:** (dog) Ron Kimball, (two puppies) Mary Bloom. **Back cover:** (group of dogs) Ron Kimball, (two puppies) Jane Burton/Bruce Coleman, Inc. **Front flap:** (puppy) Mary Bloom, (four puppies) John Daniels/Bruce Coleman, Inc. **Back flap:** (author) Tyler A.I. Gerstenfeld, (two puppies) Jane Burton/Bruce Coleman, Inc. **Half-title page:** Jane Burton/Bruce Coleman, Inc. **Title page:** Jane Burton/Bruce Coleman, Inc. **Copyright page:** Jane Burton/Bruce Coleman, Inc. **Table of contents (7):** Ashbey Photography. **Foreword (8):** Tetsu Yamazaki. **10:** Jane Burton/Bruce Coleman, Inc. **12:** Bonnie Nance. **14a:** Renee Lynn/Photo Researchers, Inc. **14b:** Ken Dufault/The Picture Cube. **15, 16a:** Ron Kimball. **16b:** Margaret Miller/Photo Researchers, Inc. **18:** Dale C. Spartas. **19:** Pet Profiles-Isabelle Francais. **20:** John Daniels/Bruce Coleman, Inc. **21:** Paulette Braun. **22–23:** Ron Kimball. **24:** Jeanne White/Photo Researchers, Inc. **25:** Ron Kimball. **26–27:** Norvia Behling. **26a:** Ron Kimball. **28** Pet Profiles-Isabelle Francais. **30:** Bonnie Nance. **31:** Harry Hartman/Bruce Coleman, Inc. **32:** Norvia Behling. **33:** Richard Hutchings/Photo Researchers, Inc. **34:** Mary Bloom. **35:** Jean-Michel Labat/Jacana/Photo Researchers, Inc. **36:** Bonnie Nance. **37:** Norvia Behling. **38:** Bob Schwartz/Excalibur. **39:** Tetsu Yamazaki. **40–41:** Jane Burton/Bruce Coleman, Inc. **42:** Bonnie Nance. **43:** Norvia Behling. **44:** Bonnie Nance. **45:** Kent & Donna Dannen. **46:** Ron Kimball. **47:** Grace Davies/Omni-Photo. **48:** Tim Davis/Photo Researchers, Inc. **49:**
Bonnie Nance. **50:** Jane Burton/Bruce Coleman, Inc. **51:** William H. Mullins/Photo Researchers, Inc. **52:** Mary Bloom. **53:** Norvia Behling. **54:** Dale C. Spartas. **55:** Jane Burton/Bruce Coleman, Inc. **56:** Ron Kimball. **57a:** Pet Profiles-Isabelle Francais. **57b:** Paola Visintini/Excalibur. **58a:** Pet Profiles-Isabelle Francais. **58b:** David Falconer/Bruce Coleman, Inc. **59:** Bonnie Nance. **60–61:** Pet Profiles-Isabelle Francais. **62:** Alexandra B. Trub. **63:** Norvia Behling. **64:** Mary Bloom. **65:** Alexandra B. Trub. **66–71:** Norvia Behling. **72:** Dennie Cody/FPG International, LLC. **73:** Mary Bloom. **74:** Dale C. Spartas. **76:** Tetsu Yamazaki. **78:** Paola Visintini/Excalibur. **79a:** Norvia Behling. **79b:** Jane Burton/Bruce Coleman, Inc. **80:** Ron Kimball. **82:** Tim Davis/Photo Researchers, Inc. **83:** Kent & Donna Dannen. **84:** Ron Kimball. **86:** Norvia Behling. **87:** Ashbey Photography. **88–89:** Tetsu Yamazaki. **88a:** Larry & Judy Reynolds. **88b:** Tetsu Yamazaki. **88c:** Cheryl A. Ertelt. **89a:** Tara Darling. **89b:** Isabelle Francais/Landmark Stock Exchange. **90:** Stephen Simpson/FPG International, LLC. **91a:** Marc Henrie, ASC NUJ. **91b:** Pet Profiles-Isabelle Francais. **91c:** Kent & Donna Dannen. **91d:** Ashbey Photography. **91e:** Pet Profiles-Isabelle Francais. **91f, g:** Ashbey Photography. **92a, b:** John Daniels/Bruce Coleman, Inc. **92c:** Tetsu Yamazaki. **92d:** Pet Profiles-Isabelle Francais. **92e:** John Daniels/Bruce Coleman, Inc. **92f:** Tetsu Yamazaki. **92g:** Ashbey Photography. **92h, i:** John Daniels/Bruce Coleman, Inc. **92j:** Tetsu Yamazaki. **93a:** Larry Allan. **93b, c & d:** Ashbey Photography. **93e:** John Daniels/Bruce Coleman, Inc. **93f:** Tetsu Yamazaki. **93g:** Ashbey Photography. **93h:** John Daniels/Bruce Coleman, Inc. **93i:** Tetsu Yamazaki. **93j:** Porterfield/
Chickering/Photo Researchers, Inc. **93k:** Mary Bloom. **94a:** Tetsu Yamazaki. **94b:** Marc Henrie, ASC NUJ. **95a, b:** Pet Profiles-Isabelle Francais. **96:** John Daniels/Bruce Coleman, Inc. **97a:** Ashbey Photography. **97b:** Paulette Braun. **98a:** Pet Profiles-Isabelle Francais. **98b:** Superstock. **99a:** Kent & Donna Dannen. **99b:** Ashbey Photography. **100a:** Jacana/Photo Researchers, Inc. **100b:** Ashbey Photography. **101a:** John Daniels/Bruce Coleman, Inc. **101b:** Larry Allen. **102a, b:** John Daniels/Bruce Coleman, Inc. **103a, b:** Tetsu Yamazaki. **104a:** Jacana/Photo Researchers, Inc. **104b:** Pet Profiles-Isabelle Francais. **105a:** John Daniels/Bruce Coleman, Inc. **105b:** Ashbey Photography. **106a:** Isabelle Francais/Landmark Stock Exchange. **106b:** Tetsu Yamazaki. **107a, b:** Ashbey Photography. **108a:** John Daniels/Bruce Coleman, Inc. **108b:** Pet Profiles-Isabelle Francais. **109a:** E. A. Baumbach/OKAPIA/Photo Researchers, Inc. **109b, 110a:** John Daniels/Bruce Coleman, Inc. **110b:** Tetsu Yamazaki. **111a:** Larry Allan. **111b:** Pet Profiles-Isabelle Francais. **112a & b, 113a:** Ashbey Photography. **113b:** Isabelle Francais/Landmark Stock Exchange. **114a:** Ashbey Photography. **114b:** Larry Allan. **115a:** Tara Darling. **115b:** John Daniels/Bruce Coleman, Inc. **116a:** Paulette Braun. **116b:** Tetsu Yamazaki. **117a:** Ashbey Photography. **117b:** Chris Luneski. **118a:** Ashbey Photography. **118b:** Ron Kimball. **119a:** Ashbey Photography. **119b:** John Daniels/Bruce Coleman, Inc. **120a:** Kent & Donna Dannen. **120b, 121a:** Tetsu Yamazaki. **121b:** Hans Reinhard/OKAPIA/Photo Researchers, Inc. **122a:** Phillip Roullard. **122b:** Close Encounters of the Furry Kind. **123a:** Ron Kimball. **123b:** Porterfield/Chickering/Photo Researchers, Inc. **123c:** Ron Kimball. **124a:** Larry

Allan. **124b:** Norvia Behling. **125a:** Close Encounters of the Furry Kind. **125b:** Mary Bloom. **125c:** Pet Profiles-Isabelle Francais. **126:** Ron Kimball. **127a:** John Daniels/Bruce Coleman, Inc. **127b:** Kent & Donna Dannen. **127c:** Ashbey Photography. **128a:** John Daniels/Bruce Coleman, Inc. **128b:** Ashbey Photography. **128c:** Pet Profiles-Isabelle Francais. **128d:** John Daniels/Bruce Coleman, Inc. **128e:** Norvia Behling. **128f:** Tetsu Yamazaki. **128g, h:** Pet Profiles-Isabelle Francais. **129a, b:** Isabelle Francais/Landmark Stock Exchange. **129c:** Pet Profiles-Isabelle Francais. **129d:** Larry & Judy Reynolds. **129e:** Ron Kimball. **129f:** Tetsu Yamazaki. **129g:** Tara Darling. **129h:** Pet Profiles-Isabelle Francais. **129i:** Stephen Ingram. **130a:** John Daniels/Bruce Coleman, Inc. **130b:** Tetsu Yamazaki. **131a, b:** Scott McKiernan/Zuma. **132a:** Betty Derig/Photo Researchers, Inc. **132b, 133a:** Ashbey Photography. **133b:** John Daniels/Bruce Coleman, Inc. **134a:** Ashbey Photography. **134b:** John Daniels/Bruce Coleman, Inc. **135a:** Bob Schwartz/Excalibur. **135b:** Pet Profiles-Isabelle Francais. **136a:** John Daniels/Bruce Coleman, Inc. **136b:** Scott McKiernan/Zuma. **137a:** Norvia Behling. **137b:** Isabelle Francais/Landmark Stock Exchange. **138a:** Tetsu Yamazaki. **138b:** Kent & Donna Dannen. **139a:** Pet Profiles-Isabelle Francais. **139b:** Tetsu Yamazaki. **140a:** Close Encounters of the Furry Kind. **140b:** Pet Profiles-Isabelle Francais. **141a:** Isabelle Francais/Landmark Stock Exchange. **141b:** Toni Tucker. **142a:** Isabelle Francais/Landmark Stock Exchange. **142b:** K. G. Vock/OKAPIA/Photo Researchers, Inc. **143a:** John Daniels/Bruce Coleman, Inc. **143b:** Pet Profiles-Isabelle Francais. **144a:** Larry Allan. **144b, 145a:** Tetsu Yamazaki. **145b:** Larry & Judy Reynolds. **146a:** Tetsu Yamazaki. **146b:** Ron Kimball. **147a:** Tetsu Yamazaki. **147b:** Kent & Donna Dannen. **148a:** Tara Darling. **148b:** Alan & Sandy Carey. **149a:** Pet Profiles-Isabelle Francais. **149b:** Kent & Donna

Dannen. **150a:** Ron Kimball. **150b:** Mary Bloom. **151a:** Kent & Donna Dannen. **151b:** Stephen Ingram. **151c:** Norvia Behling. **152:** Jim Yuskavitch. **153a:** Ashbey Photography. **153b, c:** Pet Profiles-Isabelle Francais. **153d, 154a:** Ashbey Photography. **154b:** Pet Profiles-Isabelle Francais. **154c:** Ashbey Photography. **154d:** John Daniels/Bruce Coleman, Inc. **154e:** Tetsu Yamazaki. **154f:** John Daniels/Bruce Coleman, Inc. **154g:** Faith A. Uridel. **155a:** John Daniels/Bruce Coleman, Inc. **155b:** Tetsu Yamazaki. **155c:** John Daniels/Bruce Coleman, Inc. **155d:** Mary Bloom. **155e:** John Daniels/Bruce Coleman, Inc. **155f:** Pet Profiles-Isabelle Francais. **155g:** H. Reinhard/Bruce Coleman, Inc. **155h:** Pet Profiles-Isabelle Francais. **155i:** Kent & Donna Dannen. **156a:** Isabelle Francais/Landmark Stock Exchange. **156b:** Ashbey Photography. **157a:** Bill Bachmann/Photo Researchers, Inc. **157b:** Pet Profiles-Isabelle Francais. **158a:** Kent & Donna Dannen. **158b:** Pet Profiles-Isabelle Francais. **159a:** Ashbey Photography. **159b:** Christian Grzimek/OKAPIA/Photo Researchers, Inc. **160a:** Ashbey Photography. **160b:** Isabelle Francais/Landmark Stock Exchange. **161a:** Marc Henrie, ASC NUJ. **161b:** Pet Profiles-Isabelle Francais. **162a:** Kent & Donna Dannen. **162b:** Ashbey Photography. **163a:** John Daniels/Bruce Coleman, Inc. **163b:** Pet Profiles-Isabelle Francais. **164a:** Jacana/Photo Researchers, Inc. **164b:** Tetsu Yamazaki. **165a:** Ashbey Photography. **165b:** Kent & Donna Dannen. **166a:** Jim Yuskavitch. **166b:** John Daniels/Bruce Coleman, Inc. **167a:** Larry & Judy Reynolds. **167b:** Kent & Donna Dannen. **168a:** Faith A. Uridel. **168b:** Paola Visintini/Excalibur. **169a:** John Daniels/Bruce Coleman, Inc. **169b:** Kent & Donna Dannen. **170a:** Norvia Behling. **170b, 171a:** Tetsu Yamazaki. **171b:** Tara Darling. **172a:** Larry & Judy Reynolds. **172b:** John Daniels/Bruce Coleman, Inc.

173a: Jean-Michel Labat/Jacana/Photo Researchers, Inc. **173b:** Kent & Donna Dannen. **174a:** Mary Bloom. **174b:** Close Encounters of the Furry Kind. **175a:** Frederick Sears. **175b:** Mary Bloom. **175c:** Grace Davies. **176a:** Kent & Donna Dannen. **176b:** John Daniels/Bruce Coleman, Inc. **177a, b:** Pet Profiles-Isabelle Francais. **178a:** John Daniels/Bruce Coleman, Inc. **178b:** H. Reinhard/Bruce Coleman, Inc. **179a:** Alan & Sandy Carey. **179b:** Pet Profiles-Isabelle Francais. **180a:** Kent & Donna Dannen. **180b:** Close Encounters of the Furry Kind. **181a:** Norvia Behling. **181b:** Kent & Donna Dannen. **181c:** Norvia Behling. **182:** George Holton/Photo Researchers, Inc. **183a:** John Daniels/Bruce Coleman, Inc. **183b:** Pet Profiles-Isabelle Francais. **183c:** Ashbey Photography. **183d:** Isabelle Francais/Landmark Stock Exchange. **183e:** Ashbey Photography. **183f:** John Daniels/Bruce Coleman, Inc. **184a:** Pet Profiles-Isabelle Francais. **184b, c:** Kent & Donna Dannen. **184d:** Tara Darling. **184e:** John Daniels/Bruce Coleman, Inc. **184f:** Ashbey Photography. **184g:** Pet Profiles-Isabelle Francais. **184h:** Ron Kimball. **185a:** John Daniels/Bruce Coleman, Inc. **185b:** Kent & Donna Dannen. **186a:** Ashbey Photography. **186b:** Pet Profiles-Isabelle Francais. **187a:** Kent & Donna Dannen. **187b:** Ashbey Photography. **188a, b:** Isabelle Francais/Landmark Stock Exchange. **189a:** Ron Kimball. **189b:** G. Trouillet/Jacana/Photo Researchers, Inc. **190a:** John Daniels/Bruce Coleman, Inc. **190b, 191a:** Kent & Donna Dannen. **191b:** Pet Profiles-Isabelle Francais. **192a, b:** Kent & Donna Dannen. **193a:** Alan J. Carey/Photo Researchers, Inc. **193b:** Kent & Donna Dannen. **194a:** Tara Darling. **194b:** Paulette Braun. **195a:** Alan & Sandy Carey. **195b:** John Daniels/Bruce Coleman, Inc. **196a:** Norvia Behling. **196b:** Ashbey Photography. **197a:** Pet Profiles-Isabelle Francais. **197b:** Isabelle Francais/Landmark Stock Exchange. **198a:** Ron Kimball. **198b:** Cheryl A.

Ertelt. **199a, b:** Norvia Behling. **199c:** Kent & Donna Dannen. **200:** Tara Darling. **201a, b:** Ashbey Photography. **201c:** Tara Darling. **201d:** Marc Henrie, ASC NUJ. **201e:** Tara Darling. **202a:** Kent & Donna Dannen. **202b:** Tetsu Yamazaki. **202c:** Pet Profiles-Isabelle Francais. **202d:** Tetsu Yamazaki. **202e:** Tara Darling. **202f:** Grace Davies. **203a:** Tara Darling. **203b, 204a:** Ashbey Photography. **204b:** Larry & Judy Reynolds. **205a:** Toni Tucker. **205b:** Tara Darling. **206a:** Ashbey Photography. **206b:** Marc Henrie, ASC NUJ. **207a:** Kent & Donna Dannen. **207b:** John Daniels/Bruce Coleman, Inc. **208a, b:** Tara Darling. **209a:** Larry & Judy Reynolds. **209b:** Kent & Donna Dannen. **210a:** Tetsu Yamazaki. **210b:** Susan McCartney/Photo Researchers, Inc. **211a:** Kent & Donna Dannen. **211b:** Pet Profiles-Isabelle Francais. **212a:** Robert Noonan/Photo Researchers, Inc. **212b:** Tetsu Yamazaki. **213a:** Pet Profiles-Isabelle Francais. **213b:** Tara Darling. **214a, b:** John Kaprielian/Photo Researchers, Inc. **215a:** Pet Profiles-Isabelle Francais. **215b, c:** Grace Davies. **216:** Ashbey Photography. **217a:** Isabelle Francais/Landmark Stock Exchange. **217b, c:** Kent & Donna Dannen. **218a:** Pet Profiles-Isabelle Francais. **218b:** Ashbey Photography. **218c:** Kent & Donna Dannen. **218d:** Tetsu Yamazaki. **218e:** Kent & Donna Dannen. **219a:** Ashbey Photography. **219b, c:** Kent & Donna Dannen. **219d:** John Daniels/Bruce Coleman, Inc. **220a:** Kent & Donna Dannen. **220b:** Isabelle Francais/Landmark Stock Exchange. **221a & b, 222a:** Kent & Donna Dannen. **222b:** Ron Kimball. **223a:** Pet Profiles-Isabelle Francais. **223b:** Jeanne White/Photo Researchers, Inc. **224a:** Ashbey Photography. **224b:** Larry & Judy Reynolds. **225a:** Kent & Donna Dannen. **225b:** Isabelle Francais/Landmark Stock Exchange. **226a:** Tetsu Yamazaki. **226b, 227a:** Kent & Donna Dannen. **227b:** Jeanne White/Photo Researchers, Inc. **228:** Ashbey Photography. **229a, b:** Kent & Donna Dannen.

230a: Tetsu Yamazaki. **230b** Kent & Donna Dannen. **231a, b:** John Daniels/Bruce Coleman, Inc. **232:** Dale C. Spartas. **233a, b:** Ashbey Photography. **233c:** Isabelle Francais/Landmark Stock Exchange. **233d:** Tara Darling. **233e:** Ashbey Photography. **233f:** Isabelle Francais/Landmark Stock Exchange. **233g:** Ashbey Photography. **233h:** Kent & Donna Dannen. **234a:** Ashbey Photography. **234c:** Norvia Behling. **234d:** Ashbey Photography. **234e:** Tetsu Yamazaki. **234f:** Kent & Donna Dannen. **234g:** Ashbey Photography. **234h:** Tara Darling. **234i:** John Daniels/Bruce Coleman, Inc. **234j:** Ron Kimball. **235a:** Kent & Donna Dannen. **235b:** Ron Kimball. **235c:** Kent & Donna Dannen. **235d, e:** Ashbey Photography. **235f:** John Daniels/Bruce Coleman, Inc. **235g, h:** Ashbey Photography. **235i:** Isabelle Francais/Landmark Stock Exchange. **235j:** Ashbey Photography. **236a:** Alan & Sandy Carey/Photo Researchers, Inc. **236b, 237a:** Ashbey Photography. **237b:** Larry & Judy Reynolds. **238a:** Dale C. Spartas. **238b:** Isabelle Francais/Landmark Stock Exchange. **239a:** Tara Darling. **239b:** Larry & Judy Reynolds. **240a:** Ashbey Photography. **240b:** Kent & Donna Dannen. **241a:** Isabelle Francais/Landmark Stock Exchange. **241b:** Jane Burton/Bruce Coleman, Inc. **242a:** Ashbey Photography. **242b:** Jacana/Photo Researchers, Inc. **243a:** Larry & Judy Reynolds. **243b:** Kent & Donna Dannen. **244a:** Ashbey Photography. **244b:** John Daniels/Bruce Coleman, Inc. **245a:** Ashbey Photography. **245b:** John Daniels/Bruce Coleman, Inc. **246a:** Norvia Behling. **246b:** Dale C. Spartas. **247a:** John L. Ebeling/Unicorn Stock Photos. **247b:** Mary Bloom. **247c:** Kent & Donna Dannen. **248a:** Ashbey Photography. **248b:** Jeanne White/Photo Researchers, Inc. **249a:** J. C. Carton/Bruce Coleman, Inc. **249b:** Tetsu Yamazaki. **250a, b:** Kent & Donna Dannen. **251a:** Jean-Michel Labat/Jacana/Photo Researchers, Inc. **251b:** Ashbey Photography.

252a: Tara Darling. **252b:** Larry & Judy Reynolds. **253a:** John Daniels/Bruce Coleman, Inc. **253b:** Larry & Judy Reynolds. **254a:** Kent & Donna Dannen. **254b:** Ron Kimball. **255a & b, 256a:** Alan & Sandy Carey. **256b:** Kent & Donna Dannen. **257a:** Faith A. Uridel. **257b:** Kent & Donna Dannen **258a:** Ron Kimball **258b:** Scott McKiernan/Zuma. **259a:** Renee Lynn/Photo Researchers, Inc. **259b:** Ron Kimball. **259c:** Dale C. Spartas. **260a:** Dale C. Spartas. **260b:** Kent & Donna Dannen. **261a:** Dale C. Spartas. **261b, 262a & b:** Ashbey Photography. **263a:** John Daniels/Bruce Coleman, Inc. **263b:** Isabelle Francais/Landmark Stock Exchange. **264a:** Dale C. Spartas. **264b, 265a:** Ashbey Photography. **265b:** Norvia Behling. **266a, b:** Isabelle Francais/Landmark Stock Exchange. **267a:** Kent & Donna Dannen. **267b:** Ashbey Photography. **268:** Lothar Lenz/OKAPIA/Photo Researchers, Inc. **269a:** Ashbey Photography. **269b:** Pet Profiles-Isabelle Francais. **269c:** Tetsu Yamazaki. **270a:** John Daniels/Bruce Coleman, Inc. **270b:** Tara Darling. **270c, d, e & f:** Ashbey Photography. **270g:** John Daniels/Bruce Coleman, Inc. **270h:** Tara Darling. **271a:** Paulette Braun. **271b:** Tetsu Yamazaki. **271c:** Pet Profiles-Isabelle Francais. **271d:** Tetsu Yamazaki. **271e:** Kent & Donna Dannen. **271f:** Mary Bloom. **271g:** John Daniels/Bruce Coleman, Inc. **271h:** Ashbey Photography. **271i:** Tetsu Yamazaki. **272a:** Tim Davis/Photo Researchers, Inc. **272b:** John Daniels/Bruce Coleman, Inc. **272c, d:** Tetsu Yamazaki. **272e, f:** Pet Profiles-Isabelle Francais. **272g:** Close Encounters of the Furry Kind. **272h:** Ashbey Photography. **272i:** Kent & Donna Dannen. **272j:** Ron Kimball. **273a:** Isabelle Francais/Landmark Stock Exchange. **273b:** Ashbey Photography. **274a:** Larry Allan. **274b:** Pet Profiles-Isabelle Francais. **275a:** Tara Darling. **275b:** Tetsu Yamazaki. **276a:** Norvia Behling. **276b:** John Daniels/

Bruce Coleman, Inc. **277a:** Ashbey Photography. **277b:** Kent & Donna Dannen. **278a:** Tara Darling. **278b:** Scott McKiernan/Zuma. **279a:** Kent & Donna Dannen. **279b:** John Daniels/Bruce Coleman, Inc. **280a & b, 281a:** Ashbey Photography. **281b:** Kent & Donna Dannen. **282a & b, 283a:** Ashbey Photography. **283b:** John Daniels/Bruce Coleman, Inc. **284a:** Isabelle Francais/Landmark Stock Exchange. **284b:** Tara Darling. **285:** Paulette Braun. **286a:** Kent & Donna Dannen. **286b:** Tetsu Yamazaki. **287a:** Pet Profiles-Isabelle Francais. **287b, 288a & b:** Tetsu Yamazaki. **289a:** Isabelle Francais/Landmark Stock Exchange. **289b:** Kent & Donna Dannen. **290a:** Paul Murphy/Unicorn Stock Photos. **290b:** Pet Profiles-Isabelle Francais. **291a, b:** Norvia Behling. **291c:** Mary Bloom. **292a:** Isabelle Francais/Landmark Stock Exchange. **292b:** John Daniels/Bruce Coleman, Inc. **293a, b:** Ashbey Photography. **294a:** Kent & Donna Dannen. **294b:** Tetsu Yamazaki. **295a:** Tim Davis/Photo Researchers, Inc. **295b:** Alan & Sandy Carey. **296a:** John Daniels/Bruce Coleman, Inc. **296b, 297a:** Kent & Donna Dannen. **297b:** Tetsu Yamazaki. **298a:** John Daniels/Bruce Coleman, Inc. **298b:** Tetsu Yamazaki. **299a & b, 300a:** Pet Profiles-Isabelle Francais. **300b:** John Daniels/Bruce Coleman, Inc. **301:** Close Encounters of the Furry Kind. **302a, b:** Ashbey Photography. **303a:** Jane Burton/Bruce Coleman, Inc. **303b:** Kent & Donna Dannen. **304a & b, 305a & b:** Ron Kimball. **305c:** Norvia Behling. **306:** Kim Taylor/Bruce Coleman, Inc. **308–309:** Erich Lessing/Art Resource, NY. **310:** Jeff Lepore/Photo Researchers, Inc. **312:** Giraudon/Art Resource, NY. **313a & b, 314:** Art Resource, NY. **315a, b:** Giraudon/Art Resource, NY. **316:** Palazzo Ducale, Mantua, Italy/Superstock. **317:** Fine Art Photographic Gallery, London/Art Resource, NY. **318:** Culver Pictures, Inc. **319:** Alan & Sandy Carey/Photo Researchers, Inc. **320–321:** Cheryl A. Ertelt. **322:** Toni Tucker.

323a: Kent & Donna Dannen. **323b:** Larry & Judy Reynolds. **324a:** Tara Darling. **324b:** Kent & Donna Dannen. **331a, b:** Mary Bloom. **331c, d:** John Elk III. **332a:** Pet Profiles-Isabelle Francais. **332b:** Tetsu Yamazaki. **333a:** Pet Profiles-Isabelle Francais. **333b:** Larry Allan. **335a:** Jacana/Photo Researchers, Inc. **335b:** Paola Visintini/Excalibur. **337:** Mark Newman/Bruce Coleman, Inc. **338a:** John Daniels/Bruce Coleman, Inc. **338b:** Tetsu Yamazaki. **338c:** Pet Profiles-Isabelle Francais. **338d:** John Daniels/Bruce Coleman, Inc. **339a:** Kent & Donna Dannen. **339b, 340–341:** Jane Burton/Bruce Coleman, Inc. **342a:** Renee Lynn/Photo Researchers, Inc. **342b:** Toni Tucker. **343:** Ashbey Photography. **344:** Ron Kimball. **345, 346a:** Larry & Judy Reynolds. **346b:** Jane Burton/Bruce Coleman, Inc. **347:** David Falconer/Bruce Coleman, Inc. **348a:** Paola Visintini/Excalibur. **348b:** John Daniels/Bruce Coleman, Inc. **349:** Ron Kimball. **350, 351:** Jane Burton/Bruce Coleman, Inc. **352:** Arthur Tilley/FPG International, LLC. **354–357:** Jane Burton/Bruce Coleman, Inc. **357a:** Scott McKiernan/Zuma. **358–359:** Pet Profiles-Isabelle Francais. **360–361:** William H. Mullins/Photo Researchers, Inc. **362–363:** Pet Profiles-Isabelle Francais. **364:** Dale C. Spartas. **365a:** Paola Visintini/Excalibur. **365b:** Kent & Donna Dannen. **366–367:** Dale C. Spartas. **366a:** Jay Vergenz/The Picture Cube. **367a:** Alan & Sandy Carey. **368–369:** Kent & Donna Dannen. **369a:** Cheryl A. Ertelt. **370:** Peter Miller/Photo Researchers, Inc. **371:** Norvia Behling. **372:** Jim Cummins/FPG International, LLC. **373:** Mary Bloom. **374–375:** John Daniels/Bruce Coleman, Inc. **374a:** Ashbey Photography. **374b, 375a:** Tetsu Yamazaki. **375b:** J. L. Klein & M. L. Hubert/OKAPIA/Photo Researchers, Inc. **377:** Pet Profiles-Isabelle Francais. **378, 379:** Mary Bloom. **380:** Pet Profiles-Isabelle Francais. **381a, b:** Mary Bloom. **382:** Norvia Behling. **382–383:** Paulette Braun.

385: Larry & Judy Reynolds. **386–387, 386a, 387a & b, 388–389, 388a, 389a & b, 390–391, 390a, b & c, 391a & b, 392–393, 394:** Mary Bloom. **395:** Scott McKiernan/Zuma. **396:** Bonnie Nance. **397:** Alan & Sandy Carey/Photo Researchers, Inc. **398:** Renee Lynn/Photo Researchers, Inc. **399:** Bonnie Nance. **400:** J. C. Carton/Bruce Coleman, Inc. **402:** Jane Burton/Bruce Coleman, Inc. **403:** Mary Bloom. **404:** Ashbey Photography. **405:** Varin-Visage/Jacana/Photo Researchers, Inc. **406:** Pet Profiles-Isabelle Francais. **407:** Norvia Behling. **408:** Jane Burton/Bruce Coleman, Inc. **411:** Superstock. **413:** Mary Bloom. **414–415:** Jane Burton/Bruce Coleman, Inc. **416–417:** Ron Kimball. **418:** Glen Korengold/Zuma. **421a, b:** Norvia Behling. **424–425:** Jane Burton/Bruce Coleman, Inc. **428:** Norvia Behling. **433:** Toni Tucker. **439:** Alfred Pasieka/Science Photo Library/Photo Researchers, Inc. **442a & b:** John & Maria Kaprielian/Photo Researchers, Inc. **445:** Larry & Judy Reynolds. **451:** Ashbey Photography. **455:** Ron Kimball. **458–459, 460a & b, 461a & b:** Mary Bloom. **462–463:** Norvia Behling. **473:** Phillip Roullard. **474:** Suzanne L. & Joseph T. Collins/Photo Researchers, Inc. **476:** Alan & Linda Detrick/Photo Researchers, Inc. **478–479:** Jane Burton/Bruce Coleman, Inc. **481:** John Daniels/Bruce Coleman, Inc. **482:** Michael Habicht. **483:** Jane Burton/Bruce Coleman, Inc. **484a:** Kent & Donna Dannen. **484b, 485a & b:** Jane Burton/Bruce Coleman, Inc. **486, 486–487, 487a & b:** John Daniels/Bruce Coleman, Inc. **488, 489:** Jane Burton/Bruce Coleman, Inc. **490:** Dale C. Spartas. **492–493:** Kent & Donna Dannen.

Anatomy illustrations (322–33, 325, 326–27, 328, 329, 330, 333, 334, 336): John Yesko. **First aid illustrations (379, 465, 466, 467, 468):** Todd Zalewski. **Icons (26–28, 85–303):** Holly Kowitt.

Index

Dog breed names are in **boldface**, as are the page numbers of each breed's entry in the Reference Guide to Dog Breeds.

Heartworms, 450–451
"Heat." *See* Estrus
Heatstroke, 471, 494
Herding dogs, 152. *See also specific breed*
Herding mixes, 180–81
Herding trials, 368
Hereditary diseases, screening for, 40–41
Hernias, 441
Hiking, 365
Hip dysplasia, 442
Hookworms, 447
Hot spots, 438
Household poisons, 476–77
House soiling, 398
House training, 68–71
Howling, 347
Hypertension, 450
Hypoglycemia, 452
Hypothyroidism, 452

I

Ibizan hound, 230
Identification, 59
    travel and, 408
Infectious canine hepatitis (ICH), 426–27
Injections, 460
Insect bites and stings, 473–74
Insecticides, first aid, 476
Intervertebral disc protusion, 456
Irish setter, 250
Irish terrier, 278
Irish water spaniel, 243
Irish wolfhound, 226
Italian greyhound, 221

J

Jack Russell terrier, 19, 24, 44, 86, **295**
Japanese Chin, 94
Japanese spaniel. *See* **Japanese Chin**
Jumping up, 399

K

Keeshond, 20, **195**
Kennel cough, 427
Kennels, 412–13
Keratoconjunctivitis sicca, 433
Kerry blue terrier, 17, 20, **279**
Kidney failure, 453
Komondor, 133
Kuvasz, 134

L

Labrador retriever, 256
Laekenois, 164
Lakeland terrier, 280
Lameness, 441
Leashes, 58–59
    introducing puppy to, 68
Legg-Perthes disease, 443
Leptospirosis, 429–30
Lhasa apso, 95
Lice, 440
Licensing, 59–60
Lick granuloma, 438
Liquid medication, 461
Lost dog, 60
Lungs, described, 325
Lure coursing, 370, 494
Lyme disease, 429, 439, 440
Lymphoma, 432

M

Malinois, 164
Maltese, 105
Manchester terrier, 24, **296**
Marking, 348, 494
Massage, 489
Mast cell tumors, 431
Mastiff, 126, **141**
Mastitis, 457
Mating, 329, 480–82
Medicating dog, 460–61
Miniature bull terrier, 288
Miniature pinscher, 111
Miniature schnauzer, 297
Mixed breeds. *See also specific mixed breed*
    adopting, 25, 32–34
    ancestry of, 34

defined, 495
evaluating, 82
showing, 34
Molossians, 126, 495
Mounting behavior, 349
Mouth
    examining at home, 417
    health problems, 444
Mouthing, in puppies, 401–02
Muscles, described, 322–23
Musculoskeletal system
    described, 322–23
    health problems, 441–43
    illustrated, 322–23
Muzzle, applying, 465
    illustrated, 465

N

Nail trimming, 377–79
    illustrated, 379
    older dogs, 491
Neapolitan mastiff, 142
Nervous system
    described, 323
    health problems, 455–57
Neutering
    defined, 495
    described, 329
    importance of, 75, 482
Newfoundland, 20, **147**
Norfolk terrier, 17, 20, 27, **298**
Northern breed mixes, 198
Northern breeds, 182–99. *See also specific breed*
Norwegian elkhound, 186
Norwich terrier, 299
Nose
    described, 333–35
    examining at home, 417
    illustrated, 334

O

Obedience training, 385–86, 495
    adult dogs, 77
Old English sheepdog, 176
Older dogs, 489–93
    bathing, 491

Prepared and produced by Chanticleer Press, Inc.

Founder: Paul Steiner
Publisher: Andrew Stewart

Staff for this book
Editor-in-Chief: Amy K. Hughes
Senior Editor: Miriam Harris
Managing Editor: George Scott
Project Editor: Melanie Falick
Contributing Editors: Ann ffolliott, Mike Jackson, Lisa Leventer,
Anne O'Connor, Micaela Porta, Mary Sufudy, John Tarkov
Associate Editor: Michelle Bredeson
Assistant Editor: Elizabeth Wright
Editorial Assistant: Kate Jacobs
Art Director: Drew Stevens
Designers: Kirsten Berger, Brian Boyce,
Anthony Liptak, Vincent Mejia, Bernadette Vibar
Photo Director: Zan Carter
Photo Editor: Ruth Jeyaveeran
Associate Photo Editor: Jennifer McClanaghan
Assistant Photo Editor: Meg Kuhta
Permissions Manager: Alyssa Sachar
Photo Assistant: Leslie Fink
Director of Production: Alicia Mills
Production Manager: Philip Pfeifer
Production Interns: Megan Lombardo, Sarah Schleuning, Morgan Topman

Illustrations by Todd Zalewski (first aid),
Holly Kowitt (icons), John Yesko (anatomy)

Book design by Virginia Pope

All editorial inquiries should be addressed to

Chanticleer Press
665 Broadway, Suite 1001
New York, NY 10012

Copies of this book are available from

Chronicle Books
85 Second Street
San Francisco, CA 94105
800-722-6657
www.chroniclebooks.com